LIVING ABROAD
COSTA RICA

ERIN VAN RHEENEN

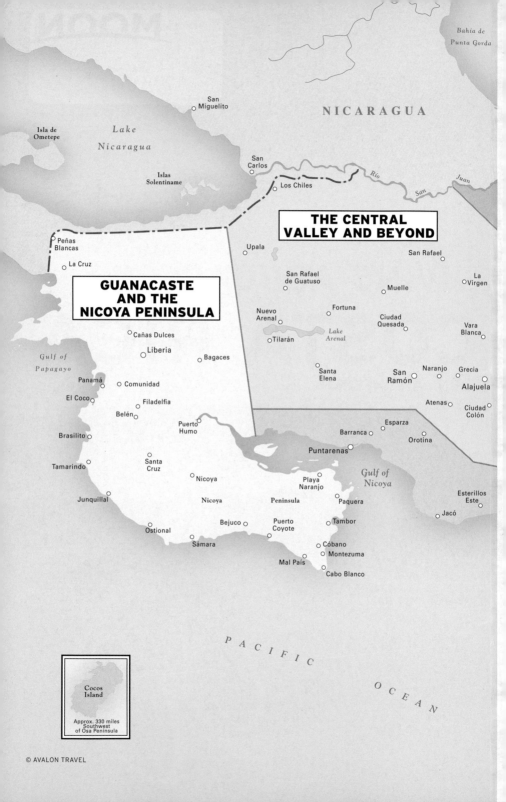

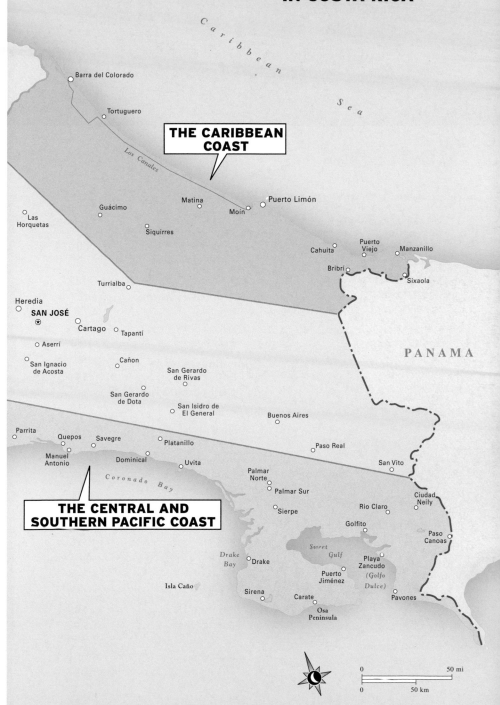

PRIME LIVING LOCATIONS IN COSTA RICA

Caribbean Sea

Barra del Colorado

Tortuguero

THE CARIBBEAN COAST

Los Canales

Las Horquetas

Guácimo

Matina

Moín

Puerto Limón

Siquirres

Cahuita

Puerto Viejo

Manzanillo

Bribrí

Sixaola

Turrialba

Heredia

SAN JOSÉ

Cartago

Tapantí

PANAMA

Aserrí

San Ignacio de Acosta

Cañon

San Gerardo de Rivas

San Gerardo de Dota

San Isidro de El General

Buenos Aires

Parrita

Quepos

Savegre

Platanillo

Paso Real

San Vito

Manuel Antonio

Dominical

Uvita

Coronado Bay

Palmar Norte

Palmar Sur

Ciudad Neily

THE CENTRAL AND SOUTHERN PACIFIC COAST

Sierpe

Río Claro

Golfito

Paso Canoas

Drake Bay

Drake

Sweet Gulf

Playa Zancudo

(Golfo Dulce)

Isla Caño

Sirena

Puerto Jiménez

Carate

Pavones

Osa Peninsula

0		50 mi
0		50 km

Contents

Y ou wake to the roar of howler monkeys and the smell of locally grown coffee. Mug in hand, you pad barefoot out onto your front porch, breathing in air supercharged with green. You gaze out over... waves breaking on the beach, or a steep-sided volcano across the valley, or scarlet macaws like flying rainbows winging toward the rainforest canopy.

There are dozens of Costa Ricas, and all are alive with more than their fair share of the world's biodiversity. Most people who visit or settle here come—at least in part—for the flora, the fauna, and the land itself.

But the country is also justly famous for being one of the most stable, peaceful, and just downright enjoyable places in Latin America.

The so-called Switzerland of Central America has made the right choices, eliminating its army and creating a thriving nation with enviable national parks, high education levels, and excellent health care. It provides a model of green development for other countries and is high on the World Happiness Index, which ranks nations on quality of life rather than gross domestic product.

Yet this is still a wild place, especially outside the heavily populated Central Valley. Where else can the country's own environment minister get lost in a famous national park (Corcovado)?

And despite facile comparisons to retirement havens like Florida, Costa Rica will never be a pink-hued place to nap away your golden years.

There's a bit of an outlaw quality here. "Totally straight people and outright criminals won't last here," a long-term expat tells me. And while he may be joking, I think he's hit on something. Costa Rica is not for the

faint of heart or for those who insist on imposing an old order on a new experience.

But if you're ready to take this country on its own terms—to trade your hazy dream for a riotously green reality—then it looks like you're overdue for a nice long visit.

Beyond all the rational reasons for relocating to Costa Rica, I've spoken with a surprising number of expatriates who speak of being "called" here. These are often average North Americans—which is to say they are logical, restless, and driven. It's just that they've chosen to pay attention to the signals we all get but usually ignore: to slow down, open up, and find a place where life is relaxed enough to let them jump on board.

If a voice is telling you to go to Costa Rica, why not listen? However crazily you come to making the choice to go, it may be the sanest choice you ever make.

Clockwise from top left: great green macaw, sunset on the Nicoya Peninsula, beach town abundance on the Caribbean Coast, basilisk lizard, front porch in Puerto Viejo.

What I Love About Costa Rica

- Talking politics with taxi and Uber drivers.

- Learning Costa Rican slang, like *chunche*, *tuanis*, and *mae* (thingy, cool, and dude).

- Waiters and shop girls calling me *mi amor* (my love) or *mi reina* (my queen).

- In small towns, women carrying umbrellas against the tropical sun.

- It's okay if you have a day—or a week—where you don't get much done.

- Erupting volcanoes, bubbling hot springs, and the occasional earthquake all remind you that the earth is still a work in progress.

- You'll never catch this country declaring war; it has no army.

WELCOME TO COSTA RICA

INTRODUCTION

At an outdoor café in San José, the capital of Costa Rica, a tourist is talking about his travel plans. "I want to get out of the city," he says. "See the rest of the island."

A few hours north, in the town of La Fortuna, another visitor walks into a tour agency within sight of perfectly conical Arenal Volcano. "What I need to know," she says, "is when they turn the volcano on."

For all its popularity, Costa Rica draws many people who have a somewhat distorted view of the country. You probably already know that despite lucking out with a disproportionate amount of coastline for such a small nation, Costa Rica is not an island. And if

you've picked up this book, chances are you want to know more.

Much of what you've heard is true. Costa Rica is the most stable and peaceful nation in Central America. It abolished its army in 1949; when Lyndon Johnson visited in 1968, the Costa Ricans had to borrow a cannon from Panama so they could give him the customary 21-gun salute. The country's national health care system covers almost all of its citizens, and the quality of care at private clinics is so good that medical tourists flock here for treatment they can't afford back home. A world model for green development, it protects 25

percent of its territory in parks and aims for total carbon neutrality by 2021.

In 2010, this country of 4.5 million inhabitants chose its first female president. Shortly after Laura Chinchilla was elected, she asked, "Who gets to decide if a country is developing or developed?" Who indeed? For Costa Rica is more "developed"—in ecological efforts, pacifism, medical care for all, and gender equity in politics—than many supposedly more-developed countries.

Still, many parts of Costa Rica have a Wild West feel. If you're off the beaten track—a place just down the road from the overrun—you'll be amazed by how untamed this country still is. One of the country's headiest charms is its biodiversity. Accounting for just 0.03 percent of the earth's landmass, Costa Rica is said to host nearly 5 percent of the planet's plant and animal species.

The nation is no utopia, of course, and is by no means undiscovered. But even in the hot spots filling up with international expatriates, know that your life here will be radically unlike the one back home. To say that the pace is slower and the language and culture very different only scratches the surface of the new worlds you'll encounter.

You'll need to be prepared, and this book will show you the nitty-gritty of life in Costa Rica: working, shopping, banking, buying or building a house, dealing with immigration, and arranging for the best health care. It describes the different parts of the country, from the dry northern Pacific coast to the luxuriant Zona Sur. You'll read the many case studies of people like you who've made the move and are happy to be here. And, of course, you'll come and visit. When you step off the plane into the balmy Costa Rican air, you'll start to know in your skin and bones whether or not this is the place for you. Do your research, soak up the atmosphere, then make your own decision. The independent attitude you'll need to thrive here can start right now, as you move through myths and misconceptions and into the heart of the real Costa Rica.

The Lay of the Land

Talk about centrally located. Picture the bent elbow of land that connects North and South America: Costa Rica rests in the crook of that arm, at the northern edge of where North America funnels down into a narrow isthmus separating the Pacific and the Caribbean.

The country lies at the hub of two continents and at the crux of two geographic plates: the Cocos and the Caribbean. In millennia past, the isthmus served as a land bridge, allowing flora and fauna to come up from the south and trickle down from the north. The resulting diversity of plant and animal life is staggering.

Imagine 1,400 species of orchids and more than 100 kinds of bats, and you get a taste of the huge feast spread on this small table of a country.

At 50,000 square kilometers (19,305 square miles), Costa Rica is the second-smallest country in Central America after El Salvador. Its Caribbean coastline is a mere 160 kilometers (99 miles) long, while the Pacific coast, with more bays and peninsulas, measures 480 kilometers (298 miles) from the Nicaraguan border to Panama. At its widest—280 kilometers (174 miles)—Costa Rica is still a narrow country that can be traversed in a few hours.

Costa Rica Fast Facts

- **Total population:** 4,814,144
- **Religions:** Roman Catholic 76.3 percent, Evangelical 13.7 percent, Jehovah's Witnesses 1.3 percent, other Protestant 0.7 percent, other 4.8 percent, none 3.2 percent
- **Median age:** 30.4 years (median age in the U.S. is 37.8; in Canada it's 41.8)
- **Literacy:** 97.8 percent
- **Official language:** Spanish
- **Form of government:** Democratic republic
- **President:** Luis Guillermo Solis, elected in May 2014 for a four-year term
- **Date of independence from Spain:** September 15, 1821
- **Military:** Costa Rica abolished its military in 1949.
- **Bordering Countries:** Nicaragua to the north, Panama to the south

- **Area:** 51,100 square kilometers/19,730 square miles (slightly smaller than West Virginia)
- **Highest point:** Cerro Chirripó, 3,810 meters (12,500 feet)
- **Natural hazards:** Occasional earthquakes, hurricanes along Atlantic coast; occasional flooding of lowlands and landslides during rainy season; active volcanoes
- **Volcanoes:** Costa Rica has many active volcanoes. Poás (elev. 2,708 meters/8,885 feet), and Turrialba (elev. 3,340 meters/10,958 feet) were especially active in 2017, with blasts reaching up to 3 km in altitude, and ash falling on nearby towns and cities. Arenal (elev. 1,670 meters/5,479 feet) experienced major eruptions in 1968 and 2010. When Irazú (elev. 3,432 meters/11,260 feet) erupts, it can spew ash over San José.
- **National symbol:** The clay-colored robin, known as the Yigüirro

The country doesn't feel so small when you're clanking along a rutted back road at 15 kilometers per hour (9 mph), wondering when you'll hit the next gas station, but it feels very intimate in terms of people. Sometimes the whole country feels like a small town. When I first arrived in San José, I met a North American named Jay who worked as a builder in the northern province of Guanacaste. He said he'd be happy to talk to me about his profession and his adopted country. When later I traveled to Guanacaste, I had, of course, left Jay's number in my San José apartment. But when I looked up a friend of a San Francisco friend, it turned out he was working construction, and his boss was . . . Jay. Guanacaste, let me add, is not a small town. At around 10,000 square kilometers (3,860 square miles), it's Costa Rica's second-largest province, with a population of about 350,000.

This wasn't an isolated case. The Italian woman I bummed a cigarette from in a San José café? A month later I walked into a yoga class in the Pacific beach town of Nosara, and there she was. Even in the capital city I would often run into friends and acquaintances. And if you live in a small town (most of Costa Rica seems to be made up of small towns), you'll see people you know about seven times a day. "After a while," one local admits, "you just smile and nod. How many times can you ask after someone's kids, their mate, or their health?" But the fact that people do ask after your family and your health, and that they do smile and nod, makes Costa Rica a very friendly place indeed.

COUNTRY DIVISIONS

Costa Rica is divided into seven provinces: San José, Heredia, Alajuela, Cartago, Puntarenas, Guanacaste, and Limón. In

Country Divisions

Lake Nicaragua

NICARAGUA

Liberia

GUANACASTE

ALAJUELA

Río San Juan

Caribbean Sea

Puntarenas

HEREDIA

PUNTARENAS

Alajuela

Heredia

LIMÓN

SAN JOSÉ

Cartago

CARTAGO

Río Pacuare

Puerto Limón

SAN JOSÉ

PACIFIC

OCEAN

PUNTARENAS

0   50 mi

0   50 km

PANAMÁ

© AVALON TRAVEL

every province except Guanacaste, the province and its capital share the same name (Guanacaste's provincial capital is Liberia). San José, with nearly two million inhabitants, is by far the most populous province, while Puntarenas, which accounts for most of the country's Pacific coastline, is the largest. The provinces of San José, Cartago, Heredia, and Alajuela fan out from the Central Valley; the latter two stretch north all the way to the Nicaraguan border.

Each province is divided into counties, of which the country has 81. Counties are divided into districts; there are 449 districts in Costa Rica.

Locals also divide the country into zones, which have less precise boundaries. There's the Zona Norte (Northern Zone), composed of the northern parts of Heredia and Alajuela, along with some of inland Guanacaste. From misty mountain towns to fiery Arenal Volcano to Caño Negro's flocks of roseate spoonbills and snowy egrets, the Zona Norte is nothing if not varied.

The Zona Sur (Southern Zone) is best known for spectacular Corcovado

National Park, Costa Rica's Amazon, which takes up much of the Osa Peninsula. But the zone also includes inland marvels like Cerro Chirripó, at 3,819 meters (12,530 feet) the highest peak in the country, as well as cool and verdant towns like San Vito, not far from the Panamanian border. The large and placid Golfo Dulce (Sweet Gulf) is part of the Zona Sur, as are the fabled beaches along that gulf's eastern edge: Playa Zancudo and Pavones are the best known of the seemingly endless number.

The Zona Caribe (Caribbean Zone) is almost, but not quite, synonymous with Limón Province—the zone is mainly the Caribbean coast, while the province extends inland into mountain ranges like the mighty Talamanca. Many tourists know of the sea turtle migrations at Tortuguero National Park, some have heard of the famed Salsa Brava wave at Puerto Viejo, but only a select few have visited the indigenous reserves and the vast unexplored wilds inland from Costa Rica's lesser-known coast.

The Central Valley, sometimes called the Meseta Central or Central Mesa, is the heart of the country. Measuring about 80 by 40 kilometers (50 by 25 miles), the area is ringed by a series of steep-sloped volcanoes, some of them still active. The capital city, San José, lies at the center of the Central Valley, and at 1,150 meters (3,772 feet) elevation, it enjoys year-round temperatures between 21°C and 26°C (70-80°F).

WEATHER

Great weather is one of the country's big draws. Those who've had it up to their wool turtlenecks with cold and snow find relief in Costa Rica's tropical sun and balmy breezes. The northern province of Guanacaste in particular is a sun-worshipper's dream, with hardly a drop of rain falling between December and May. The

Just How Hot Is It?

If you're among that minority of world citizens who think 32° means you'd better bundle up, it's time to learn about Celsius. In Costa Rica, 32° weather means you'd better break out your bathing suit – it's almost 90° Fahrenheit. To convert from Celsius to Fahrenheit, multiply by 1.8, and then add 32. To convert from Fahrenheit to Celsius, subtract 32, and then divide by 1.8.

Below are the average temperatures in major Costa Rican cities on a day in late March:

- **Alahuela:** 25°C (77°F)
- **Golfito:** 29°C (84°F)
- **Liberia:** 29°C (84°F)
- **Limón:** 26°C (79°F)
- **Puntarenas:** 28°C (82°F)
- **Quepos:** 29°C (84°F)
- **San José:** 23°C (73°F)

green season brings more rain, but even then showers are usually confined to afternoon and evening hours, with mornings as glorious as ever.

But if you've never been a beach person, don't worry. Even those who prefer cooler climes will thrive here. Temperature in Costa Rica is less a function of season than altitude, and you can fine-tune your weather by going up or down a few hundred meters. If you like an occasional bite in the air, just look for an emerald-green lot on the side of one of the inactive volcanoes, where the sun shines brightly at midday but dawn and dusk bring cooling mists. At higher elevations you'll see pine trees alongside vine-draped tropical hardwoods.

The variety of climates means that the natural world is one of the most varied you'll ever see. Of course it helps that Costa Rica has set aside a quarter of its territory in parks and reserves, where rare animals still roam freely. Jaguars, tapirs, sloths, and monkeys call this country's rainforests home, as do a stunning variety of birds, including 50 species of hummingbirds, various toucans, parrots, macaws, and the elusive resplendent quetzal, with the male's iridescent green tail feathers more than three times the length of his body.

EARTHQUAKES AND VOLCANOES

Costa Rica is the child of a volatile but enduring relationship between sections of the earth's crust that want to have—or rather want to *go*—their own way. The Caribbean and Coco Plates come together just off Costa Rica's coast, and the resulting clash produces pent-up geological energy that finds release in earthquakes and volcanic eruptions. Of the country's many volcanoes, at least five are still active. Truck-size hot rocks tumbling down Arenal Volcano's perfect cone and Turrialba Volcano's mile-high plumes of ash are impressive reminders that the earth's surface is still very much a work in progress.

Earthquakes have also played their part in teaching Ticos to respect the "fire down below." The colonial capital of Cartago was destroyed by quakes in 1841 and again in 1910. In 1991 a magnitude 7.5 earthquake rocked the Caribbean and South-Central zones, destroying the San José-Limón railroad and countless roads and bridges. In 2012, a 7.6 quake was centered off the Nicoya Peninsula. Gentler quakes are commonplace.

Volcanic peaks help make up the country's four major mountain ranges. In the north, the Cordillera de Guanacaste rises up in a series of peaks that includes Rincón de la Vieja, 1,895 meters (6,217 feet) high and the centerpiece of a national park of the same name. The Cordillera de Tilarán is dominated by Arenal Volcano, one of the most active in the world. Hemming in the Central Valley to the east is the Cordillera Central, which includes Poás, Irazú, Barva, and Turrialba Volcanoes. To the south of the valley surges the Cordillera Talamanca.

A GREEN REPUBLIC

The varied terrain makes for an amazing number of microclimates, each with its own complicated ecosystem. Incredibly, less than 20 percent of this biodiversity has been scientifically identified, making it all the more important to preserve the land until scientists can catch up with nature. Who knows if a cure for Alzheimer's or a solution to world hunger lies in the depths of the disappearing rainforest? The National Institute of Biodiversity (INBio), a joint public-private venture, is working hard to find out.

Costa Rica is devoted to protecting its own environment—more than 25 percent of the nation's territory is set aside in parks and reserves. Still, there are serious challenges. The country doesn't have the money or human resources to fully enforce environmental laws or patrol preserves. Poachers and lumber companies continue to chip away at the land ringing the protected areas, even making forays into national parks when they think they can get away with it. Another problem has been the government's inability to pay landowners for the territories expropriated for national parks. Sometimes these uncompensated landowners return to their land and continue farming, mining, or logging it.

Still, with all its problems, Costa Rica is teeming with life, and the country knows that it's this life that draws tourists. And since tourism is a huge business, there's yet another incentive to pass—and enforce—laws that protect the environment.

It's not only the land that boasts so many species; Costa Rica has 10 times as much protected territory underwater as it does on land and is working hard to protect everything from giant sea turtles to shark populations, recently threatened by the practice of "finning"—removing fins for the Asian markets in which they are a delicacy, while leaving the rest of the mutilated shark to a watery grave.

On a happier note, the Tourism Institute has created a Bandera Azul (Blue Flag) program to recognize beach towns that commit to cleaning up their act. Program assessors not only look at whether there's trash on the beach, but also judge waste disposal, security issues, and environmental education efforts. More and more beaches, on both the Pacific and Caribbean coasts, are working to be green enough to fly the blue flag.

Local newspapers are filled with accounts of struggles to balance industries like fishing, mining, large-scale agriculture, and oil exploration with protection of the land. Some call Costa Rica hypocritical for billing itself a green republic while still allowing some exploitation of its natural resources, but it seems inevitable that there will be conflict and compromise along the road to balancing all the

country's needs. Those who lament the sometimes slow progress and backsliding often take matters into their own hands, joining forces with national and international conservation organizations or even buying up land so developers won't be able to get their hands on it.

NATIONAL PARKS

The strength and importance of the National Conservation Area System (SINAC) is all the more impressive when you realize it began very recently—in the 1970s. And Costa Rica's 26 national parks are just the tip of the iceberg; there are also more than 100 reserves and refuges that seek to protect varied habitats and ecosystems for both present and future generations.

One of the most popular parks is Manuel Antonio on the central Pacific coast, with its beaches bordered by wildlife-rich rainforest and its location only a few hours from San José. Also popular and even closer to the capital are Braulio Carrillo, a teeming, dripping forest that you can see via aerial tram if you'd rather not get your shoes muddy; and stunning Irazú Volcano, from which on a clear day you can see both coastlines.

entrance to Tortuguero National Park

A little more effort is required to get to two other popular parks: the Caribbean coast's Tortuguero, with its canals, crocodiles, turtles, manatees, and teeming bird population; and Corcovado, on the lushly wild Osa Peninsula, where tapirs and jaguars roam.

Significantly more effort is required to reach Isla de Cocos, 532 kilometers (331 miles) off the country's Pacific shore. Protected as a park in 1978 and declared a UNESCO World Heritage Site in 1997, this uninhabited island is a favorite of scuba divers who come for the rays, dolphins, and hammerhead sharks. Isla de Cano, just off Drake's Bay on the Osa Peninsula, is another island reserve known for its undersea life. Isla San Lucas, near Puntarenas, is Costa Rica's version of Alcatraz, where the ruins of an old penitentiary sit on a wildlife-rich isle.

After you've visited the big guns of the system, it's a pleasure to start exploring the lesser-known and less-visited reserves, where you might not see anyone else on the path for hours or even days.

BIODIVERSITY

You may know that tiny Costa Rica is a giant in terms of all the animals and plants you can see here, but have you thought about why the country supports so many different kinds of life? First, it has a neotropical climate: a warm, humid, predictable environment with an almost constant food supply. Second, it has a great variety of habitats or ecozones—from high cloud forest to lowland swamp—that support different kinds of plants and animals. Third, the country is part of a land bridge that millions of years ago connected the North and South American continents, allowing animals and plants from the south to come up and those from the north to trickle down. They met in Costa Rica (and neighboring Panama), and, lucky for us nature lovers,

they decided to stay. And if you're a nature lover, the flora and fauna may factor into your decision to stay as well.

GETTING AROUND

Costa Rica is small enough that you can snorkel the Caribbean in the morning and surf the Pacific in the afternoon. And if you choose to fly instead of drive, puddle jumpers will speed you to places that used to require a full day (or two) of journeying. A 40-minute flight from San José puts you in Golfito (an eight-hour drive) for a day of sportfishing, and then you can hop back up for a gourmet dinner in San José.

Those on a budget will appreciate the extensive network of buses that can take you anywhere in the country for no more than US$20. Buses run often, they run on time, and most are as comfortable as the Greyhounds you've ridden back home.

Renting a car is another option. A four-wheel drive will be your best bet so you won't be denied if a highway suddenly peters out into rutted track. It's exhilarating not to have to stop for anything—not even a river—to get where you want to go. For those accustomed to glassy-smooth interstate highways, Costa Rica's roads will come as a shock, but soon enough you'll be four-wheeling with the best of them. Getting back on an easy track even starts to be somewhat of a disappointment, like eating a hot dog after you've been chewing on a char-grilled steak.

Getting to Costa Rica is easy. You don't need a visa—just a valid passport. Airfares from the United States and Canada are US$500-1,000, depending on your departure city. At the airport you can get a stamp on your passport saying you have up to 90 days in the country. And if you have no interest in San José, international flights now speed you to Liberia, only half an hour from some of the best beaches in Guanacaste.

A small plane approaches the Tortuguero airport.

Social Climate

"Stay a week and you think you know a country," goes the old adage. "Stay a year and you know you never will." When you first arrive in Costa Rica, you may be struck by how similar it is to the United States, especially in and around the capital city of San José. You'll see the same fast-food franchises, like McDonald's and KFC; the same stores, from Foot Locker to Office Max; and the same products in U.S.-style supermarkets, even Häagen-Dazs ice cream and Celestial Seasonings teas. Food labels are almost always in Spanish and English, and at ATMs you can opt for instructions in English.

When there's a problem here, people dial 911, just like in the States. On TV, many programs and even commercials are in English. In U.S.-style multiplex theaters in U.S.-style malls, you'll see trailers for the latest Hollywood movies as you munch on overpriced hot dogs and popcorn. And just like back home, you can drink the water—probably one of the most profound differences between Costa Rica and its Latin American neighbors. Somehow that small fact looms large and is one of the many reasons North Americans feel comfortable here.

Stay a little longer and you start to notice the differences. "The idea that we're all the same is a myth," says one expat. "Sure, there may be superficial commonalities, but deep down, Costa Rican culture is very, very different from U.S. culture." This is doubly true for towns outside of the populous Central Valley.

STANDARD OF LIVING
Newcomers to Costa Rica are often surprised that the country doesn't have that Third World shantytown look that they were expecting of a Central American banana republic. Indeed, Costa Rica is a relatively well-off nation that takes care of its own much better than many more

developed countries. Everyone here has access to decent health care and education, which makes for infant mortality rates comparable to those of Canada and the United States, and literacy rates that rival those of Europe. People look healthy, and even those with little money take care to dress in clean, new-looking clothes. If you see people with holes in their jeans, they're almost certainly tourists affecting a down-and-out look while no doubt having more money in their pockets than the smartly dressed locals.

Life here is not cheap, but it can be less expensive than living in the United States or Canada, depending on your lifestyle. A single person can live modestly on as little as US$1,200 a month, and a couple can live frugally but not without a few frills for perhaps US$2,000-3,000 a month. Travel within this small but wondrously varied country could be one of those frills, since buses are a bargain, and there are plenty of reasonably priced beachfront or mountaintop hotels.

Real estate is affordable, much more so if you stay away from the hottest markets like well-known beach towns or upscale suburbs of San José. Labor here is cheap, so building a house won't cost as much as it would up north. Some areas have overestimated the appetite for condos, bad news for developers but good news for those looking for better prices.

POLITICAL AND ECONOMIC STABILITY

Costa Rica enjoys one of the most stable democratic governments in all of Latin America and an economy that has long attracted foreign investors. In 1983 President Luis Alberto Monge described the country's stance as one of "permanent, active, and unarmed neutrality." Ticos believe this "active" peace can only be sustained through social justice and economic development.

To help foster development, the government here offers incentives to foreign businesses, including tax breaks and exemptions from some export tariffs. Big and small companies come to Costa Rica because of the solid telecommunications network, an educated workforce, and a high standard of living.

Multinational corporations with branches in Costa Rica include Intel, Hewlett-Packard, Colgate-Palmolive, Monsanto, and Pfizer. All the baseballs used in the U.S. Major Leagues are sewn by hand in one small Costa Rican town called Turrialba.

It's easy for a foreigner to start a business here—you can do it even if you only have a tourist visa. Many expats work successfully in the burgeoning tourist sector, starting restaurants, hotels, and tour companies. Many say that although there are, of course, regulations to learn about and follow, in general there exist fewer constraints on businesses here than in their home countries.

UNIVERSAL HEALTH CARE AND PRIVATE CLINICS

Too many Americans live with insufficient medical insurance. There are efforts to improve the situation, but it will be a long time before people in the United States have the same level of care—in terms of the percentage of the population with access to medical care—as the residents of Costa Rica have enjoyed for decades. Costa Rica has made a commitment to provide health care to all of its residents, and even visitors can take advantage of the high-quality, low-cost care. For a small monthly fee (usually under US$70 and sometimes considerably less), residents become part of the public system that includes everything from drugs to dentistry as well as care in public clinics and hospitals. It used to

The Mystery of the Spheres

ancient stone spheres in Palmar Sur

In the southern Pacific region of Costa Rica, perfectly spherical sculptures made of granite, andesite, and sedimentary stone have been found. Some you can hold in your hand; others weigh up to 900 kilograms (1 ton) and are 2.4 meters (8 feet) in diameter. These *bolas* (spheres) are found nowhere else, and it has long been a mystery how these apparently ceremonial objects—found along riverbeds and in cemeteries—were transported up to 30 kilometers (nearly 19 miles) from the source of the stone to where those remaining now stand like sentinels to a lost world. How the ancients made them so perfectly round has also long been debated.

Theories abound and are all over the map. Erich von Däniken, in his *Chariots of the Gods,* proposes that they came from extraterrestrials; others have speculated that the spheres were shaped and polished at the base of thundering waterfalls, tumbling like ball bearings until smooth and perfectly round. Many experts believe they were formed by heating and cooling the stone—causing it to slough off layers—then chipping and finally polishing the stone through abrasion.

Whatever their origin, the *bolas* have become a symbol of Costa Rica and can be seen in parks, museums, and wealthy homes. Some can still be visited at their original sites, in places like Caño Island off the Osa Peninsula.

be that foreigners who are legal residents could choose whether or not to be part of the system; now they are obligated to become part of it, even if they plan to use private insurance for their medical bills. If you're not a legal resident, you can sign on with the INS, the state insurance provider—this route lets you choose your own doctor. International policies like Blue Cross Blue Shield are accepted at the excellent private hospitals and clinics. If you have no insurance and don't want to join up with the public system, you can pay out-of-pocket and still spend one-third less than you would in the United States.

If you're cringing when thinking about Third World hospitals with poor hygiene and badly trained staff, think again. The University of Costa Rica has one of the most respected medical schools in all of Central America and the Caribbean, and many doctors do further study in Europe, Canada, or the

What's a Tico?

Costa Ricans love nicknames; they even have one that covers the entire population of their country. They call themselves Ticos after the local habit of adding the diminutive to as many words as possible. While other Spanish speakers are likely to add *it* to make a word like *chico* (small) even smaller (*chiquito*), Costa Ricans would say *chiquitico*. *Ya voy en un minutico* is Tico for "I'll be there in a tiny little minute." Of course, another Tico habit is lateness, so that tiny little minute may be closer to a big fat hour.

Costa Ricans call themselves "Ticos."

United States. Hospitals often have up-to-date equipment, and the three major private clinics have international accreditation through Joint Commission International (JCI). Confidence in the system is expressed by the number of people who come to Costa Rica just to have surgery, whether a face-lift or a triple bypass.

AWARD-WINNING FRIENDLINESS

It has long been agreed that Costa Ricans are very friendly, but a few years ago science confirmed that impression. A study published in *American Scientist* revealed that, of 23 cities worldwide, San José ranked number two in Latin America in terms of friendliness (Rio de Janeiro came in first). The six-year study measured "simple acts of kindness," ranging from whether passersby returned a dropped pen to whether a blind man got help crossing a street. The Costa Rican capital received consistently high marks in every category.

Robert Levine, the head of the study, commented that the cities with the friendliest inhabitants were ones where the pace of life was slower, and where the culture emphasized the value of social harmony.

And outside of the urban areas, where life is slower, people are even friendlier. In small towns, everyone greets everyone else on the street, and citizens pitch in when their neighbors need help. Need to get to a bigger town? Start walking and you'll almost certainly get offered a ride. Need someone to look after your kids? Small-town folks routinely and casually trade child-care duties. If your car gets stuck in the mud, before you know it you'll have half a dozen people there to help you push it out. And the more generous you are, the more it comes back to you. Social scientists would call it reciprocity. Whatever you call it, it makes Costa Rica a very nice place to live.

Moving Abroad Makes You More Creative

Several studies in the past few years have found that living abroad stimulates creative thinking, whether as expressed in fiction or painting or entrepreneurship.

Scientific American reported on the link between living abroad and creativity, and a paper titled *Cultural Borders and Mental Barriers: The Relationship Between Living Abroad and Creativity* cites many cases in which artists have done their best work while abroad.

GO ABROAD, YOUNG (AND OLD) ARTIST!

According to a paper that cites five separate studies, "living abroad is often seen as a necessary experience for aspiring artists." Some creative individuals, the study continues, produce their best-known masterworks during or following a stint abroad. Think about Vladimir Nabokov and his novel *Lolita*, or Ernest Hemingway and his *The Sun Also Rises*. In fact, all four winners of the Nobel Prize in literature who are from Ireland (Yeats, Shaw, Beckett, and Heaney) spent significant portions of their lives abroad. In addition to writers, many famous painters, (e.g., Gauguin and Picasso) and composers (e.g., Handel, Prokofiev, Stravinsky, and Schoenberg) created many of their most admired works while living in foreign countries.

THREE WAYS LIVING ABROAD STIMULATES CREATIVITY

According to the paper:

- Living abroad gives you access to a greater number of novel ideas and concepts, which then act as inputs for the creative process.

- Living abroad allows people to approach problems from different perspectives. For example, in some cultures (e.g., China), leaving food on one's plate is an implicit sign of appreciation, implying that the host has provided enough to eat. In other countries (e.g., the United States) the same behavior may often be taken as an insult, a condemnation of the quality of the meal.

- Experiences in foreign cultures can increase the psychological readiness to accept and recruit ideas from unfamiliar sources, thus facilitating the processes of unconscious idea recombination and conceptual expansion.

And while I agree with all of that, the ponderous language of the study makes me want to blurt out, "Yeah, and living abroad is also good *fun!*"

WHY PEOPLE COME TO COSTA RICA

More and more North Americans are looking for a place to start a new life—whether it's for retirement, a career change, or plying one's current profession in a new market. Millions are choosing to live abroad, with many drawn to the physical beauty and lower prices of places like Costa Rica.

Many North American workers have been "made redundant" by ongoing corporate efforts to reduce operating costs. Other workers retain jobs that they feel are sucking the life out of them, and they dream of a time when they can get back in touch with themselves and with simple pleasures. Many fantasize about a place where the living is cheaper and the pace more humane. Parents of young children may long for an environment where kids can be immersed in another language and culture, one that emphasizes basic human values over relentless accomplishment and acquisition.

And for those approaching retirement age (or already there), places like Costa Rica are looking better and better. Persons over age 65 make up one of the fastest-growing segments of the U.S. population,

guaria morada: Costa Rica's national flower

and many hit retirement with modest pensions and little savings. For those on a budget, Costa Rica is a place to live well for less.

Of course, Costa Rica is no paradise, and in fact it may be a victim of its own popularity. Tourism has mushroomed into an industry sometimes at odds with environmental protection. The influx of foreign visitors and residents can strain basic infrastructure in this country of just under 5 million people. "We weren't ready for all of you," laughs Anabelle Furtado, a Costa Rica native who worked for the Association of Residents of Costa Rica (ARCR). Economic hard times have meant cuts in previously flush social services, and locals complain that foreigners, with their easy spending habits, drive up prices on everything from pineapples to a four-bedroom house. And as in most other countries, crime and other social ills are on the rise.

Still, the benefits outweigh the problems. Costa Rica has an appealing combination of the exotic and the familiar. It's a far-off land less than three hours by air from Miami, an international destination with a decidedly local feel, a sophisticated place where life is still fueled by basic human warmth.

HISTORY, GOVERNMENT, AND ECONOMY

For nearly a century, Costa Rica has been an island of stability in an often turbulent sea. Although the country has much in common with its Central American neighbors, the differences are perhaps even more striking. Costa Rica has an enviable political and economic climate, a high standard of living, and a commitment to peace underlined by the abolition of its army.

Travel farther back in time and we see a pre-Columbian crossroads, where cultures from the south and the north met and merged. Fast-forward a few centuries and we find ourselves in one of the poorest backwaters of the opulent and cruel Spanish colonial empire—a territory that, ironically, became the most prosperous of Central American nations.

One of modern-day Costa Rica's big drawing points is its political stability. Since 1948 power has changed hands peacefully and democratically. Ticos elect a new president every four years, just as in the United States, and Costa Rica has a similar system of checks and balances composed of the executive, judicial, and legislative branches of government. The economy is steady and strong enough to attract a host

of multinational corporations—from Abbott Labs to Intel. This stability and the fact that Costa Rica works in ways familiar to North Americans make it an attractive place for expats to live and do business.

History

Tens of thousands of years ago early settlers in what is now Costa Rica hunted mastodon and giant sloth, tracking their prey through dripping tropical forests. Between 8000 and 4000 BC, these nomadic bands learned to domesticate plants, and around the first century, they made the transition to farming. Sedentary life brought on a more complex social hierarchy and division of labor. Instead of making tools only for hunting, like stone spearheads and knives, people began creating farming implements and vessels to cook and store their food.

Located on an isthmus between two great continents, Costa Rica was a meeting place for cultures from the south and the north. From South America came yucca, sweet potatoes, coca leaves for chewing, and Andean gold-working techniques. Native Americans from the southern forests and Caribbean coast of Costa Rica traded with the peoples of Panama, Colombia, and Ecuador. Other parts of the country—especially the Gran Nicoya, located in what is now Guanacaste—were more influenced by Mesoamerican cultures to the north. From Mesoamerica came corn, beans, jade, hieroglyphic books, the practice of filing teeth to points, and certain pottery styles still in use today.

There were cultural and linguistic differences among the many indigenous groups, but the groups also had a lot in common. Most were matrilineal, and some—including the Chibchas and the Diquís—are said to have been matriarchal. Religious beliefs pivoted on the conviction that not only animals and plants were alive but that even natural phenomena like rivers and stones were animate and possessed their own spirits. Funeral rites implied a belief in an afterlife—ritual objects and even slaves were buried with the bodies of powerful women and men.

People congregated in large and small settlements, and the village was, according to Molina and Palmer in *The History of Costa Rica,* "the axis of everyday life, which was taken up by agriculture, crafts, commerce, and war." Ethnic groups and villages banded together to form *cacigazcos* (chiefdoms), and *cacigazcos* sometimes unified into larger political and military alliances called *señoríos.*

In the northwestern part of what's now Costa Rica, the *cacigazcos* of the Gran Nicoya, influenced by Maya, Aztec, and Olmec cultures, practiced human sacrifice and cannibalism. Three times a year, on dates coinciding with the corn harvest, the nobility dressed in their finery, drank *chicha* (corn liquor), and presided over the ritual murder of five or six preselected women and men. These chosen few had their hearts cut out, their heads chopped off, and their bodies rolled down the side of the temple—to later be eaten as the most sacred of food.

War was widespread and was waged for a variety of reasons: to expand or defend territory, to gain access to trade routes, to take prisoners for slave labor, or, in the case of women of childbearing age, to serve as breeders. In some areas, like the Diquís region in southern Costa Rica, both men and women went into battle together.

REMNANTS OF THE PAST

The National Museum estimates that in Costa Rica today, there are at least 2,000 archaeological sites, most of which are still buried in deep forest or under mounds of earth. The region that was the Gran Nicoya, now in Guanacaste, has the most sites, but the most accessible and fully excavated site is Guayabo, now a national monument. Located on the southern flank of Turrialba Volcano in the Central Valley, Guayabo shows us the remains of a settlement at its height between 1000 BC and AD 1400, when an estimated 10,000 people lived in its conical structures and walked its cobblestoned streets. An aqueduct system built more than 2,000 years ago still functions today.

Other sites take more effort to find and visit. Until Costa Rica can devote time and expertise to more excavations, locals will probably continue to stumble upon old stone roads and pre-Columbian artifacts half-buried in cattle pastures or strewn along centuries-old rainforest paths.

One type of relic that is *puro Tico* (purely Costa Rican) is the *bola,* stone spheres found mostly in the southern part of the country near the Valley of Diquís. Researchers still can't say for sure how they were made or what their function was, but some of these strangely moving sculptures measure more than two meters across and weigh several tons. There are a few at the National Museum, which may whet your appetite to see others in their original context, like the ones on Caño Island off the Osa Peninsula. Since the spheres are found nowhere else in the world, they have become a symbol for Costa Rica, and you'll see the *bola* motif worked into the architecture of government buildings and upscale homes.

At Guayabo National Monument, one can still see the circular stone foundations of pre-Columbian wooden huts built in the 1300 or 1400s.

INDIGENOUS CULTURE TODAY

For years it was thought that as few as 30,000 people were living in Costa Rica when the Spaniards arrived. This figure supported the myth that the country has little indigenous heritage, but more recent scholarship puts the number at between 400,000 and 500,000.

The half-million people here when Columbus landed in 1502 were reduced to 120,000 by 1569 and whittled down to 10,000 by 1611 mostly due to infectious diseases brought by the Spaniards. The 2011 census counted 104,143 indigenous persons (in a nation of 4.3 million), but one of the few books on indigenous Costa Rican culture by indigenous authors, *Taking Care of Sibö's Gifts,* by Paula Palmer, Juanita Sánchez, and Gloria Mayorga, says that fewer than

Ethnic Makeup of Costa Rica

- **White or mestizo:** 83.6 percent
- **Mulatto:** 7 percent
- **Indigenous:** 2.4 percent
- **Black:** 1 percent
- **Chinese:** 0.2 percent
- **Other:** 0.84 percent
- **None of the above:** 2.8 percent
- **Undeclared:** 2.2 percent

Figures are from the 2011 census. For matters of race, those interviewed self-identify, telling the census worker into which racial or ethnic category they think they fall. Consequently, different people may have different definitions of terms. In general "mestizo" is a term used in Latin America to denote someone of mixed European and indigenous heritage, while "mulatto" is a term for someone of mixed European and African heritage.

25,000 people here "retain a cultural identity as indigenous people." Whatever the true figure, native peoples make up only about 1 percent of the national population. Many live on 1 of 22 reserves, which collectively make up about 6 percent of national territory.

Quite a decline, to be sure. But some aspects of indigenous culture have survived since the arrival of Europeans, and other features are being revived. The largest ethnic groups are the Cabécar and the Bribrí, concentrated on the Caribbean coast and in the Talamanca mountains. Both groups actively work to maintain and revive their language and customs, as well as adapt tourism to their own needs, allowing a few visitors onto their reserves for cultural and natural history tours. When I took a tour of the Kekoldi Reserve (within which Cabécares and Bribrí live), a native guide walked us through mud and heavy brush to a spectacular waterfall deep within the reserve, stopping along the way to point out trees and vines traditionally used for medicinal purposes.

In the 1970s, legislatures passed the *Ley Indígena* (Indigenous Law), establishing autonomous governing structures within the existing indigenous reserves. During the same period, CONAI (the National Commission for Indian Affairs)

was established, but indigenous people felt it did not represent them and so created their own organization in 1981, the Pablo Preserve Indigenous Association. Members of both organizations work to forge alliances among various indigenous groups within Costa Rica and to reach out to similar groups throughout the Americas. They also try to maintain the reserves, which are threatened on all sides by mining and lumber companies, hydroelectric projects, tourism, and nonindigenous peasants who want land to farm. The government still holds deed to all reserves and has been known to cut deals with outside companies at the expense of indigenous land and autonomy.

Besides trying to revive their customs, indigenous groups are also looking to their economic future. In 1995, for example, the Cabécares and Bribrí created their own bank, the Banco Indígena de Talamanca, which they say is "neither a private nor state bank. It is a bank of and for Indians."

In Costa Rica today there are at least eight indigenous cultures: the Bribrí of the southern Caribbean coast; the Cabécar of the Talamanca mountains; the Guaymí, who live along the Panamanian border; the Térraba and Boruca of southern Costa Rica; the Malecu of northern Alajuela

Province; the Huetar, who live near Ciudad Colón and Puriscal in the Central Valley; and the Chorotega of Guanacaste and the Nicoya Peninsula.

AFRO-COSTA RICANS IN HISTORY

A small number of people of African descent were brought to Costa Rica as slaves shortly after the Spanish conquest of the territory, but it wasn't until around 1870 that the black community in Costa Rica began to grow by leaps and bounds. At that time a large number of Jamaicans and smaller numbers of other Caribbean islanders were hired to build the Atlantic railroad, which has since fallen into disuse.

Migrations continued into the 20th century and included Jamaican Marcus Garvey, who arrived in 1910 and worked briefly on the United Fruit Company's banana plantations in Limón. Garvey would later found the Black Star Line and become an international icon in the movement for Black Nationalism and self-reliance (known in the 1920s as the "back to Africa" movement).

The Black Star Line was an all-black steamship company that transported cargo and passengers between Costa Rica, Jamaica, Panama, Haiti, Cuba, and the United States. The Costa Rican headquarters was in Puerto Limón, and the Black Star Line building there did double duty as Costa Rica's branch of Garvey's Universal Negro Improvement Association (UNIA).

Garvey's stay on Costa Rican soil was short but memorable. It was while working on Limón plantations that he was reinforced in his belief that black people were victims of prejudice on a worldwide scale. Garvey encouraged workers to form unions and start newspapers, to make public the struggles of workers in general and black workers in particular. Within a year of his arrival, Garvey was expelled from Costa Rica. Some accounts say it was for harassing the British Consul, while others maintain it was his activism that got him ousted.

Until it burned down in 2016, the Black Star Line building was one of Limón's most important cultural centers, the venue for events culminating in Black Culture Day every August 31.

Puerto Limón is the city with the largest Afro-Costa Rican population, estimated to be about 35-40 percent. In the

pre-Columbian bowl

White People Are Leaf-Cutter Ants

In the book *Taking Care of Sibö's Gifts,* coauthor Gloria Mayorga, of the Kekoldi Indigenous Reserve on Costa Rica's Caribbean coast, writes of the mythic origin of white people:

> The origin of white people is the King of Leaf-Cutter Ants. Just look at the leaf-cutter ants, how they all work together cleaning and clearing the land around their nests. Where the leaf-cutter ants live, all the vegetation is gone because they cut every last leaf and take them back to their big nests. That's how the white man is. He works very hard, but he destroys nature. He chops down all the trees to make his cities, and where he lives all the vegetation is gone. There is nothing there. The white man cuts down everything that is green, and where he lives there are no trees, no rivers, no animals. He destroys everything in his path.

province of Limón, the figure is around 15 percent, while nationwide the black population is officially given at about 1 percent.

Chinese-Costa Ricans in History

The first Chinese in Costa Rica came from Guangzhou (historically known as Canton) to the Pacific Coast port of Puntarenas. A Chinese colony began to form in the area. In fact, the city of Puntarenas was so widely known among those looking to emigrate from China that many mistook the city's name for that of the entire country.

Twice—in 1862 and again in 1896—the Costa Rican government prohibited immigration of "Orientals," claiming "that race is hurtful to the progress of the Republic." The laws were quickly repealed when cheap labor was needed, as in 1873 when 600 Chinese were allowed to immigrate and then were paid one-fifth of the going wage to help build the Atlantic railroad.

Nowadays, China has become an important trading partner and a source of funding for new infrastructure (also see *Looking to the East: Free Trade with China* on page 42). Besides giving or loaning money for a new national stadium and

an expansion of the state oil refinery, in 2011 China contributed US$1 million to create a Chinatown in the capital city of San José. The new neighborhood, near the pedestrian-only Paseo de los Estudiantes, was built on an existing cluster of Chinese restaurants and markets, along with the Chinese Cultural Center and a branch of Cathay Bank.

The two best-known Chinese-Costa Ricans are NASA astronaut Franklin Chang-Diaz and Harry Shum Jr. of the television show *Glee.*

THE COLONIAL ERA

On his fourth and final trip to the New World, Cristóbal Colón (Christopher Columbus, to English speakers) landed in September 1502 at what is now Puerto Limón on Costa Rica's Caribbean coast. His four ships had been damaged by storms, and his crew of 135—one-third of whom were young men between the ages of 13 and 18—badly needed a break.

The indigenous people of the area welcomed the new arrivals, swimming out to the ships with gifts of finely woven cloth and pendants made of *tumbago,* an alloy of copper and gold. These necklaces, among other finds, convinced arriving Europeans that the area was rich in mineral deposits, and later the region was named Costa Rica, or Rich Coast.

In fact, Costa Rica turned out to be one of Spain's poorest colonies, and this lack of wealth made it a backwater of the empire for the next several hundred years. Thick forests, impassable mountains, and raging rivers didn't help matters. Settlers had a rough time of it, and they often lived like the "savages" they had come to conquer, dressing in clothing made of pounded bark, employing native farming methods, and using cacao beans as money when paper bills and metal coins ran out.

Early Settlements

Sixty years after Columbus's arrival, Juan de Cavallón founded what was to become the first permanent settlement in Costa Rica. It was named Garcimuñoz in 1561 and was located in what is now the Río Oro de Santa Ana region of the Central Valley. Towns had been founded earlier on both coasts, but most didn't last long as settlers battled harsh conditions, lack of supplies, infighting among the townspeople, and attacks from pirates and what were then called *indios bravos* (wild Indians). Garcimuñoz was moved and renamed several times until it ended as Cartago, which would become the colonial capital.

In *The Ticos,* coauthors Mavis, Richard, and Karen Biesanz characterize Spanish Costa Rica as "the Cinderella of Spanish colonies, [which was] taxed, scolded, ignored, and kept miserably poor. An isolated and neglected province of the captaincy general of Guatemala, it was unable to raise enough revenue to pay its own administrative expenses. Its clergy was subordinate to the bishop of León in Nicaragua, who rarely visited."

In addition, the colonial practice of *encomienda,* in which European invaders were granted land that didn't belong

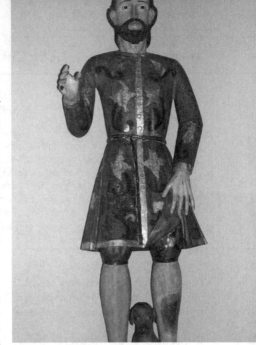

a wooden saint from Costa Rica's colonial period

to them and allowed to extract labor or tribute from the true owners (indigenous people), never really took hold in Costa Rica, in part because the indigenous people either died from disease, headed for the hills, or offered up armed resistance to the idea that they should become slaves on their own land.

So instead of the vast *encomiendas* found elsewhere in Central America, in Costa Rica small family-owned farms were more the norm, and even governors were said to work their own land. This was less true in Guanacaste, where enormous cattle ranches were worked by not only indigenous people but also by black slaves. Guanacaste was part of the richer colony of Nicaragua until just after both countries declared independence from Spain, when it chose to ally itself with poor but peaceful Costa Rica over wealthy but war-torn Nicaragua.

William Walker and Juan Santamaría

An egomaniacal mercenary from Nashville, Tennessee, ended up playing an unexpectedly large role in the formation of Costa Rican national identity. The man's name was William Walker, and he dreamed of ruling over a Central American empire that would be a fresh source of slaves for the United States.

As crazy as the idea sounds, Walker had an army and the backing of several U.S. industrialists, and he had some success, first taking Nicaragua and then invading Costa Rica. The year was 1856, not far into the first decades of a fledgling nation in which people still felt more identified with their city or region than their country. Cutting across these regional identities, President Juan Rafael Mora called together a ragtag army to drive Walker's forces from the northern province of Guanacaste.

The Costa Rican army, some of them armed with little more than farming tools, chased Walker into Nicaragua, where, at the town of Rivas, a young soldier named Juan Santamaría set fire to Walker's barracks before collapsing under a hail of bullets. Costa Rica thus reclaimed its territory and also got its first national hero. Santamaría now has his own holiday, celebrated most fervently in his hometown of Alajuela.

Santamaría's nickname was El Erizo ("The Hedgehog"), for his thick hair that stood straight up. These days, El Erizo lives on in an airport named after him: the Juan Santamaría International Airport in Alajuela, outside the capitol city of San José.

Many historians believe that Costa Rica's poverty during the colonial era actually helped to lay the foundation for a democratic nation of equals, where all struggled just to survive and where class differences were not as pronounced as elsewhere.

INDEPENDENCE AND EARLY NATIONHOOD

When, in September 1821, the captaincy general of Guatemala declared independence from Spain, Costa Rica didn't receive word until a month later. The news sparked confusion in a land that was less a nation than a loose collection of rival city-states. Some Costa Ricans wanted to become part of the powerful Mexican Empire, while others wanted to help create a federation of newly free Central American states. Still others suggested that Costa Rica become part of Colombia, which then included present-day Panama and was ruled by the "Great Liberator," Simón Bolívar.

The four most powerful Costa Rican cities—San José, Cartago, Alajuela, and Heredia—all had different plans for newly liberated Costa Rica, and they backed up their ideas with guns. A side issue was which of the cities should be the capital. For a while the honor was rotated among the cities, and then a battle decided the issue in San José's favor.

Those who wanted Costa Rica to become a state in the Central American Federation won out, but a few decades later in 1848, when it was obvious the experiment had failed, the country became its own republic.

The first head of state after independence was Juan Mora Fernándes, who founded the country's first newspaper, expanded public education, and established a judicial system. Braulio Carrillo, remembered as a heavy-handed dictator who nonetheless fostered national unity, ruled from 1835 to 1842; he presided over Costa Rica's withdrawal from the federation of Central American states and its emergence as an independent country.

Carrillo is also known for planting the seeds of the nation's coffee economy—he offered free land to those who would reap and sow the glossy-leafed crop.

The 1880s brought a succession of liberal governments that made far-reaching and lasting changes, most involving the separation of church and state. Presidents during this period secularized schools, making primary and secondary education free and obligatory; shut down the church-run University of Santo Tomás; and expelled the Jesuits and one Catholic bishop. They also allowed for civil marriage and divorce, secularized the cemeteries, and abolished the death penalty.

A PIVOTAL DECADE

During the volatile 1940s, two larger-than-life political figures fought each other for power, war was declared on Nazi Germany, and Costa Rica suffered through its own 40-day civil war. The constitution drafted after that battle (in 1949) provided the basis for what was seen at the time as a new nation.

The decade began with the election of Rafael Ángel Calderón Guardia, who gave workers' rights a huge boost with reforms such as a guaranteed minimum wage, unemployment compensation, and paid vacations. Calderón's administration was responsible for the Labor Code of 1943, a lengthy series of constitutional amendments that is still in effect today.

During Calderón's tenure the country declared war on Nazi Germany just one day before the United States did the same. Germans in Costa Rica lost their property and were sent to internment camps, many located in the United States.

When Calderón lost the 1948 elections, his government cried fraud; the resulting conflict erupted into a battle that killed 2,000 people, most of them civilians. José María ("Don Pepe") Figueres Ferrer and his National Liberation Party emerged victorious, and Don Pepe became head of the Founding Junta of the Second Republic of Costa Rica, pushing through reforms such as nationalizing banks and insurance companies, abolishing the army, and finally giving blacks and women full citizenship, including the right to vote.

THE MODERN ERA

Don Pepe's National Liberation Party (*Partido de Liberación Nacional,* or PLN) ruled Costa Rica from the late 1940s to the late 1970s, consolidating the reforms of its early days and building an even larger bureaucracy to promote social justice through a welfare state. A growing middle class began to undercut the power of the traditional elite, such as coffee barons, even as the government worked to attract foreign capital to help industrialize the country.

In the late 1970s and the early 1980s, the bill for big government came due concurrent with a time of worldwide economic crisis. In 1981, Costa Rica was forced to suspend debt payment to its creditors and had to ask for help from lenders like the World Bank and the International Monetary Fund (IMF). Costa Rica got its loans, but at a price: The country had to promise to cut government spending and begin to privatize its economy.

This puzzle—of how to maintain the best parts of the welfare state while still cutting costs and moving toward privatization—is still being pieced together today.

Government

The Costa Rican constitution of 1949 guarantees a host of rights for residents and foreigners alike. These rights include freedom of speech, press, and assembly, all of which are exercised on a daily basis and underline Costa Rica's enviable place among its neighbors. Unlike many other Latin American nations, Costa Rica has no standing army, no guerrillas, and no political prisoners. For more than half a century, power has changed hands peacefully.

The voting age is 18, and the country is a democratic republic that elects a new president every four years. Although the presidency is a powerful position, the constitution guards against concentration of power in any one of the three branches of government: executive, legislative, and judicial.

EXECUTIVE BRANCH

The president coordinates government programs, commands the police, and directs national and international policy. He or she exerts considerable power through ties to all manner of ministries but must also answer to the party that sponsored his or her candidacy, to labor unions, and to public opinion. There also are two vice presidents and a 15-member cabinet that includes one of the vice presidents.

Since 1969 presidents had been limited to one four-year term, but in 2003 the Costa Rican high court brought the law back in line with the 1949 constitution, which states that ex-presidents may run for reelection after they have been out of office for two presidential terms (eight years). Many former presidents had been waiting for just such a development, and in 2006 Nobel Peace Prize winner Óscar Arias Sánchez, president from 1986 to 1990, was elected once again. In 2010 Arias's former vice president, Laura Chinchilla, was elected president. She was Costa Rica's first female president and Latin America's fifth in the last two decades. In 2014, Luis Guillermo Solís Rivera was elected president. Solís, the son of an educator and a shoemaker, come from a family with Chinese and Afro-Caribbean roots, who came to Costa Rica from Jamaica in the early 1900s. Like many Latin American politicians, part of his education took place in the United States: he earned a master's in Latin American Studies from Tulane University in New Orleans, and was a Fulbright Scholar at the University of Michigan.

LEGISLATURE

Fifty-seven elected *diputados* (deputies) serve four-year terms in the *Asamblea Legislativa* (Legislative Assembly); they can seek reelection after a term spent out of office. The legislature makes, amends, and repeals laws, and imposes taxes. It also has some say on budget issues, including foreign loans negotiated by the president, which it must ratify by a two-thirds majority. Deputies may run for reelection after sitting out one four-year term.

JUDICIAL SYSTEM

"Costa Rica has the best judicial system in the region," says Dr. Arturo Condo, professor and dean of INCAE, a business school with campuses in Costa Rica and Nicaragua. "A trial here doesn't depend on bribing the judge or what political party you belong to."

The legislature chooses the Supreme Court's 22 magistrates, who serve for eight years and then, usually, renew their

Old Plane Speaks of Covert Ops Past

An old plane sits grounded atop a lush hillside on Costa Rica's Pacific coast. The battered Fairchild C-123, built in 1954 and now part of a popular open-air bar, is the perfect place to nurse a cold *cerveza*, watch the sunset, and remember a bizarre chapter in history: the Iran-Contra Affair, which from this Central American vantage point would more accurately be called the Contra-Iran Affair, with the illegal arms sale to Iran a minor chapter in the 1980s-era U.S. covert funding of armed guerillas (the Contras) bent on bringing down Nicaragua's Sandinista government.

Part of the Hotel Costa Verde in Manuel Antonio, the Avion Bar is the perfect place for ruminating on that 1980s arms-for-hostages (and while we're at it let's fund some paramilitaries) scandal because the plane itself played a starring role in the fiasco.

The plane was dubbed Ollie's Folly for its connection to Oliver North, chief architect of a covert operation—lodged firmly in the heart of the Reagan administration—that funded and provided military assistance to the Contras.

Although the U.S. government supported the Contras in the early 1980s, Congress cut off all funding in late 1984, afraid that Nicaragua would become the next Vietnam and alarmed by reports that the CIA had secretly mined Nicaraguan harbors.

WHO NEEDS CONGRESS WHEN YOU'VE GOT OLLIE NORTH?
Despite signing into law the bill cutting off all funds to the Contra's paramilitary operations, Reagan ordered his staff to find a way to help the Contras keep "body and soul together," in his words. Reagan and his staff—especially those in the National Security Council (NSC)—secretly raised US$34 million for the Contras from other countries, with an additional US$2.7 million from private contributors, and, later, funds from the illegal arms sale to Iran. This money was funneled into a private company called the Enterprise and put under the direction of Lieutenant Colonel Oliver North.

The Enterprise had its own operatives, Swiss bank accounts, airfields, and airplanes, including two Fairchild C-123s, one of which now holds up the roof of the Avion Bar.

term. The Supreme Court in turn appoints judges for civil and penal courts. The Supreme Court itself oversees electoral issues, from the functioning of political parties to the counting of votes. Ticos, more and more cynical about politicians, still tend to hold the Supreme Court in high regard.

BIG GOVERNMENT

There's no denying that Costa Rica has opted for big government. It's estimated that 90 percent of public expenditures go to paying the salaries of public employees. Besides the three branches of government, autonomous institutions like ICE, the state electricity company, exert influence over national policy and everyday life. Along with ICE (pronounced EE-say),

the Caja (Social Security) and RECOPE, the state oil agency, are important players on this field.

Government not only controls most utilities and a large part of health care, it also has monopolies or majority interests in liquor production, insurance, banking, and tourism. Both Ticos and foreign residents complain of the inefficiency of the bureaucracy. Often an agency's budget goes almost entirely to salaries and operating expenses rather than to the purpose—say, alleviating poverty—for which the agency was created.

Sometimes it's all but impossible to know which institution does what, and people who enter the system (to obtain residency, for example) can be shunted from one office to the next. The authors

For 16 months in the mid-1980s, the Enterprise provided covert aid to the Contras—aid that the U.S. Congress had specifically prohibited. When U.S. and world press caught wind of the operation and reported on it, Reagan, National Security Adviser Robert McFarlane, and other administration officials repeatedly assured the public (and Congress) that nothing illegal or untoward was going on.

THE GAME IS UP

On October 5, 1986, evidence to the contrary fell to Earth over southern Nicaragua. A plane carrying supplies to the Contras was shot down; the two pilots were killed, but Eugene Hasenfus, a former Marine from Wisconsin who'd been hired by the CIA, parachuted to safety, only to be captured by Nicaraguan government forces. Hasenfus's capture was instrumental in uncovering the U.S. covert operation providing money and military help to the Contras. The plane shot down that October day was the sister plane to the one now reincarnated as a hilltop bar in Costa Rica.

The owner of the Hotel Costa Verde was intrigued by the plane's history and bought it in 2000 for US$3,000. He had the plane moved, at great expense and trouble, to its current perch close to Manuel Antonio, Costa Rica's most popular national park. The Costa Verde has a taste for giving old modes of transport new life—they also transformed a 1965 Boeing 727 into a high-end ocean-view suite. And they operate what must be one of the few places in Costa Rica where you can get a Hebrew National kosher hot dog. It's called The Wagon, and it's housed in an old train car.

But let's return to the 1980s for a minute. What happened in Nicaragua back then didn't stay in Nicaragua. Ollie North had a secret airstrip built in Costa Rica to support his covert ops in Nicaragua, then got himself barred from Costa Rica for life for that and for his alleged part in drug smuggling to fund the Contra effort.

of *The Ticos* acknowledge that "the public sector includes such a bewildering maze of agencies that it is often difficult to know who is responsible for making what decisions—and who actually does make them. And therefore, it is easier to understand why some decisions are slow to be made and why many others are made only symbolically, if at all."

POLITICAL PARTIES AND ELECTIONS

Voting is mandatory in Costa Rica, but that doesn't stop people from staying home on Election Day. More than 30% of Ticos stayed home for the 2006, 2010, and 2014 general elections.

The 2014 election was the first general election in which Ticos living outside of Costa Rica were eligible to vote through the nearest consulate *The Tico Times* wrote that of the 10,264 Ticos living abroad and registered to vote, New York has the most registered Tico expats, at 2,382, followed by Los Angeles, with 1,347.

The Basics

In Costa Rica, third, fourth, and even fiftieth parties seem to have a good shot at being part of the governing structure of this country of four million. Including the local parties that field candidates for local city councils (municipalities), there are about 50 political parties here.

There are 463 electoral districts in seven regions (which correspond to the seven provinces). Though the president is elected through a national popular vote,

Costa Rican Presidents Schooled in the US

The last six presidents of Costa Rica have all headed north to the United States for university or graduate studies. Many other Costa Rican presidents further back in history also have close educational ties to the United States.

- **Luis Guillermo Solís** (President from 2014-2108): master's degree in Latin American Studies at Tulane University in New Orleans; Fulbright scholar at the University of Michigan
- **Laura Chinchilla** (2010-2014): master's degree in public policy from Georgetown University.
- **Óscar Arias Sánchez** (1986-1990; 2006-2010): enrolled in Boston University to study medicine, then returned home to get a law degree; has more than 50 honorary doctorates, including degrees from Harvard, Princeton, Dartmouth and Washington University in St. Louis.
- **Abel Pacheco de la Espriella** (2002-2006): Earned an MD in Mexico, then did his specialization in psychiatry at Louisiana State University.
- **Miguel Ángel Rodríguez Echeverría** (1998-2002): earned both an MA and PhD in economics from the University of California, Berkeley.
- **José María Figueres Olsen** (1994-1998): majored in Engineering at the United States Military Academy (West Point); master's in public administration from Harvard's John F. Kennedy School of Government. Figueres' mother was Karen Olsen Beck, an American social worker.

the 57 seats in the National Assembly are elected by proportional representation; seats are allocated to districts by population.

Why Proportional Representation Matters

Proportional representation in Costa Rica means that instead of voting for individual *diputados* (deputies) to represent them in the National Assembly, people vote for a party list. The assembly seats are allocated to the parties according to what percentage of the vote each party wins. If a party wins enough of the vote to garner two seats, it will send the first two candidates on its list to the assembly.

Historically, the two largest and most powerful parties have been the National Liberation Party (*Partido de Liberación Nacional,* or PLN) and the Social Christian Unity Party (*Partido de Social Cristiana,* or PUSC). The PLN was founded in 1951 by "Don Pepe" Figueres,

who in 1948 dissolved Costa Rica's army, expanded social welfare programs, gave women the vote, and nationalized banks. A coalition of parties opposing the PLN had been around for a long time and became the powerful PUSC in the 1980s. But PUSC lost a great deal of its luster in 2006 when two former presidents of Costa Rica, both PUSC members, were implicated in corruption scandals.

Political winds shift often, and in 2010, while the PLN did very well (the outgoing and incoming presidents belong to the PLN), the once-mighty PUSC was bested by both the Citizens' Action Party (*Partido Acción Ciudadana,* or PAC) and the Libertarian Movement Party (*Partido Movimiento Libertario,* or PML). Luis Guillermo Solís of the Citizen's Action Party became president in 2014.

Political Diversity and Gender and Racial Equality

There are many powerful "third" (and

fourth, and fifth . . .) parties in Costa Rican politics, and proportional representation appears to allow for a greater political diversity, especially in the powerful National Assembly, which is roughly equivalent to the U.S. House of Representatives. The 2010 elections in Costa Rica saw the country's National Assembly peopled with politicians from seven parties, and many more parties received votes but not enough to earn them a seat. In this system people don't think they're "wasting" their vote on nondominant parties, because nondominant parties have a better chance of winning seats.

While the National Assembly can boast of a diversity of political parties, it doesn't have much to be proud of in terms of racial diversity. Not one of the deputies elected for the 2010-2014 term was Afro-Costa Rican, and none were of indigenous heritage. There was a first in the 2006 election, however: Epsy Campbell, a black woman, was the vice presidential candidate for the Citizens' Action Party (PAC). In the early stages of the 2010 election, it looked as if Campbell, the granddaughter of Jamaican immigrants, would be a contender for the presidency, but PAC fielded Otton Solís instead. Afro-Costa Ricans make up about 2 percent of the total population of Costa Rica, while indigenous peoples make up a little less.

Women have fared better, mostly because of a 1996 electoral reform requiring that political parties have at least 40 percent women on their election roster (though the women tend to be relegated to the bottom of the list, which means that they don't always win seats in the assembly even if their party wins). In the 2010 election, 36.8 percent of the seats in the Costa Rican National Assembly went to women; in that same year, only 16.8 percent of legislators in the U.S. Congress were women. Also in 2010, Costa Rica elected its first woman president, Laura Chinchilla. Interesting that a so-called *machista* society like Costa Rica has so much more female participation in politics than a nation that boasts of equal opportunity for all.

It's these seeming anomalies that get me thinking about the assumptions I've made about the world. And for that reason alone—that the experience opens your mind to other ways of doing things—I believe that living abroad makes you a better international citizen. If and when you go back to your home country, you may find yourself a lot more political and informed (even about your own country) than you were when you left.

Economy

COFFEE, BANANAS, AND BEEF CATTLE

Costa Rica will forever be associated in the world's imagination with both the *grano de oro* (golden grain, aka the coffee bean), which wakes up half the world every morning, and the yellow fruit that became synonymous with Central American backwaters (banana republics). Historically the country's primary exports have been agricultural, principally coffee—so well suited to the rich volcanic soil and mild climate of the Central Valley—and bananas, which thrive in the wet coastal lowlands. Of the two crops, coffee is perhaps more tied up with the national identity, but bananas are more lucrative. Pineapples are another important crop, as are melons, ornamental plants, and oil from African palm nuts.

Though farming is still important, the country's economy is now much more diversified. Cattle ranching began in the early colonial period, and in the 1960s many Ticos invested in beef cattle. By 1975, there were almost as many cows as people in Costa Rica. These "locusts with hooves" have not been kind to the environment or the economy. Demand for beef waned in the 1980s—fast-food chains up north were ordering less as North Americans became more health conscious. Forest converted to pasture causes drought in many regions (like Guanacaste), and ranching puts people out of work—it takes fewer people to work a herd then to work fields planted in crops.

NEW INDUSTRY

In 2015 agriculture made up 6 percent of the country's gross domestic product (GDP), industry had 20 percent, and services, which include tourism, made up almost 75 percent.

Starting in the 1990s, electronic components, medical equipment, and pharmaceuticals (among many others) became important exports. At least 29 major multinational companies operate in Costa Rica, including Intel, Abbot Labs, Bristol-Myers Squibb, Johnson & Johnson, Colgate-Palmolive, Monsanto, Pfizer, Panasonic, and Rawlings, whose Turrialba plant makes all the baseballs used in the U.S. Major Leagues.

Tech giant Hewlett-Packard, with two facilities in Heredia and one in Escazú, employs thousands of people in Costa Rica; many of them provide phone support in English to callers from the United States and Canada. When in late 2010 HP announced its US$1 billion plan to expand offshore outsourcing services, Costa Rica was named one of the company's six new global delivery hubs. HP officials went on record as saying Costa Rica was chosen for "the increasing amount of client demand in the Americas for time-zone-approximate support," "cultural affinity with local and national governments," and "the availability of skilled resources and the cost footprint, not just in immediate terms but as you look at labor-rate inflation and real estate expenses going forward."

Intel, another tech giant, began to build assembly plants here in 1997. The big

Costa Rica's economy is too diversified to qualify the country as a "banana republic," but bananas are still an important crop.

daddy of foreign investors, Intel has three sprawling plants in Costa Rica, which churn out one-third of its worldwide production of computer chips and provide more than 3,500 jobs. In 2005, Intel opened a new financial services center in San José. For better or worse, more and more North America-based companies are outsourcing jobs to the "Switzerland of Central America."

TOURISM A MAJOR DRIVER OF THE ECONOMY

Tourism, the "industry without smoke-stacks," exploded in the 1990s, with the number of foreign visitors rising from 376,000 in 1989 to more than one million in 2000, then shooting up to a record 2.66 million in 2015. That means that the equivalent of more than half the population of the entire country of Costa Rica visited the country. About 40% come from the United States, and each of them stays an average of 11 days and spends $1,340. Many Europeans visit as well, with a marked increase of Brits coming in 2015 due to new direct British Airways flights. Chinese tourists make up a relatively small of the total but tourism from China increased 29% from 2014 to 2015.

Costa Rica remains the most-visited Central American country by far, with tourism its number-one source of income.

U.S. INFLUENCE

The United States is Costa Rica's most important trading partner, buying up about 33 percent of its exports in recent years. In 2015, China bought about 6 percent of Costa Rica's exports, while Mexico, Nicaragua, Guatemala and Holland each bought around 4% of the total.

Of the goods that it imports, Costa Rica buys about 45 percent from the United States, while China buys about 10% and Mexico 7%. Add to that the

fact that U.S. companies account for well over half of foreign investment in Costa Rica, and you'll see why the United States plays a disproportionately large role in the Costa Rican economy. Almost every day, the local press reports on the ins and outs of this crucial relationship, like when CEOs of U.S.-based companies with branches in Costa Rica threaten to take their business elsewhere unless the government agrees to give them more tax breaks. Articles on the state of the U.S. economy also appear daily, since activity up north can have a dramatic effect on countries like Costa Rica that are so closely tied to the world's biggest economic engine.

THE PRICE OF A LOAN

The United States exerts its influence in other ways as well. In the 1960s and 1970s, Costa Rica borrowed large sums of money—mostly to improve infrastructure and social services—from international lending institutions, many of them based in the United States. When the country had trouble repaying the loans, the lenders—United States Agency for International Development (USAID), the International Monetary Fund (IMF), the World Bank, and the Inter-American Development Bank—offered up easier repayment terms in exchange for what in essence became their greater control of the Costa Rican economy. Other developing countries were in similar positions, and similar deals were struck around the world, as the lending institutions saw their "opportunity to convert the world's many state-managed and protectionist economies into free-market systems," as coauthors Mavis, Richard, and Biesanz explain in *The Ticos*.

In 1985 Costa Rica signed the first of many structural adjustment pacts (PAEs) with these lenders. The PAEs require increased imports, reduced external tariffs, and the privatization of some state

The Jungle Train

More than 140 years ago, an ambitious engineering project began that would transform a tiny Central American backwater into a prosperous nation with thriving international trade. The project was a railroad from the inland capital of San José to the Caribbean coast port of Limón. It spanned the previously all-but-impassable route that meant goods shipped from Costa Rica to Europe departed the Pacific Coast and went the long way around, past the tip of South America. The railroad was to change all that, and the men brought in to build it would alter the ethnic mix of this country's Caribbean coastline.

The first chapters of the railroad story are dominated by coffee and then bananas. Using beans imported from Jamaica in 1808, Costa Rica became the first Central American country to grow coffee. By 1830 the highland Central Valley, with its rich volcanic soil and mild climate, had become a major coffee-producing region. Europe was growing fonder of this natural stimulant, and Costa Rica's prize crop fueled many a coffeehouse debate in London, Paris, and Prague.

But the route from highland farm to European cup was long and tortuous. Beans were transported by mule (and later, when the roads were widened, by oxcart) to the Pacific coast port of Puntarenas. Boats to Europe sailed around the southernmost tip of South America, and then made their way across the Atlantic.

Why not send boats from the Caribbean side of the country, canceling the need for the long detour around Cape Horn? Because the route from the Central Valley to Costa Rica's humid and sparsely settled eastern coast was all but impassable. Primitive tracks crossed raging rivers, skidded down mountainsides, and meandered through vast swamplands. Firmer ground became a stew of mud during the rainy season.

Merchants and officials talked incessantly of ways to improve that eastern route. But it wasn't until 1871 that the Costa Rican government set in motion a project unprecedented in scope and magnitude—a railroad from San José to the Caribbean coast port of Limón. President Tomás Guardia Gutérare awarded the contract to American Henry Meiggs. Meiggs was known as a visionary scoundrel who left many creditors in the wake of his big ideas. But he'd built about 320 kilometers (200 miles) of railroad in Chile and about 1,125 kilometers (700 miles) in Peru, and he was a great orator, party-thrower, and wooer of government officials.

Workers were imported to do the backbreaking labor. The first wave included 400 Chinese, 600 Jamaicans, and 500 from the Cape Verde Islands off the western coast of Africa. Subsequent waves included Italians, Hondurans, Nicaraguans, and many more workers from Jamaica and other Caribbean nations like Barbados. Nearly two decades of work on the railroad claimed the lives of more than 4,000 workers. Many succumbed to yellow fever, dysentery, and malaria.

agencies. That last requirement was especially onerous to Costa Rica, whose national identity was largely based on its strong state-run agencies.

GOVERNMENT MONOPOLIES AND FREE TRADE

Modern-day Costa Rica is considered moderately open to international trade and foreign investment. More than 200 multinational corporations do business here. First-time North American visitors may be surprised to see so many familiar names, from Taco Bell to Hertz to Best Western. The rules regulating foreign businesses are for the most part the same as those that govern Tico-owned enterprises, though businesses that operate in the special zones around the airport get a lot of perks Tico businesses do not.

In 2010, Costa Rica became party to the Central American Free Trade Agreement (CAFTA, this region's NAFTA), known

Partway into the job, Meiggs bowed out and turned the reins over to his nephew, Minor Keith, who'd been managing the workers' commissary near Limón. Money was running out—for months the workers hadn't been paid. Keith offered to arrange funding for the railroad's completion if the Costa Rican government would grant him a 99-year lease on the railroad and deed him a whopping 323,750 hectares (800,000 acres) of land along the rail route. Keith planted his new land with banana trees, hoping the crop, as yet unexploited in Costa Rica, would provide much-needed revenue to complete the railroad.

It was an extraordinarily smart move. Bananas flourished and exports increased by leaps and bounds, going from 100,000 stems in 1883 to 1 million stems in 1890. The banana trade attracted U.S. co-investors like the United Fruit Company (known as La Yunai in Latin America), which would come to wield such enormous influence over the so-called banana republics of Latin America.

On December 7, 1890, nineteen years after work began, the 164-kilometer (102-mile) Costa Rican Railroad was inaugurated. On a bridge high above the Burrís River, tracks from the Central Valley met up with tracks from Limón, finally creating a seamless conduit for products on their way from San José to markets abroad. The trip to Europe no longer required sailing around the tip of South America and was thus shortened by three months. International trade flourished.

By 1900, bananas rivaled coffee in economic importance. The Caribbean workers who'd come to build the railroad now worked on banana plantations, and the influx of Afro-Caribbeans (mostly from Jamaica) changed the face of Costa Rica's eastern coast. Today, the port city of Limón has the highest percentage of Afro-Costa Ricans (around 40 percent); nationwide, black citizens make up 2-5 percent of the general population. On Costa Rica's eastern coast, spicy Jamaican food wins out over the traditional and rather bland *casado*, and patois-inflected English is more common than Spanish.

As the Caribbean coast became less isolated and roads improved, the railroad wasn't as important as a means of getting products to port. And with the opening of the Panama Canal in 1914, goods shipped from the Pacific coast no longer had to make their way around the tip of South America.

In the early and middle part of the 20th century, the Atlantic railroad gradually became more of a passenger train. For several years before it shut down for good in 1991 due to earthquake damage, the railroad became known as the Jungle Train, an eight-hour ride that cost US$2 for coach passage and about US$50 for first class. In the late 1970s, Paul Theroux took the train and wrote about it in *The Old Patagonia Express*, a travel classic that traces his journey by rail from Massachusetts to Tierra del Fuego. He calls the route "the most scenic in Central America."

WELCOME TO COSTA RICA
HISTORY, GOVERNMENT, AND ECONOMY

as TLC (*Tratado de Libre Comercio*) in Spanish. The treaty, whose signatories are the United States, Costa Rica, El Salvador, Guatemala, Honduras, Nicaragua, and the Dominican Republic, obliged Costa Rica to open up some of its government-controlled sectors, namely telecommunications and insurance.

Not everyone in Costa Rica is happy about CAFTA. Though the pact was signed in 2004, it was three years before the treaty was put to a national referendum. The issue sparked protests, and fierce debate continues as to whether the treaty is good for the country and for the average Costa Rican.

Foreign businesses welcome the opportunity to invest in previously off-limit sectors, and some Ticos and expats think the increased competition brings better services and lower prices, especially in cell-phone technology and Internet access.

CAFTA proponents say it allows Central America to "speak with one voice," to band together to negotiate better trade opportunities with North American markets. Others say that Costa Rica cannot compete with the United States on this so-called level playing field and will come out the loser in any battle. "It's like a fight between a wild tiger and a tied-up mule," said one critic of the agreement.

Looking to the East: Free Trade with China

Another high-profile and controversial free trade agreement was signed with China in 2010. Trade talks with the Asian giant began in 2007, when Costa Rica became the first nation in Central America to end longstanding diplomatic ties with Taiwan (China and Taiwan don't recognize each other diplomatically, and neither will deal with countries that recognize the other).

Poor Taiwan had invested quite a bit in Costa Rica, including funding the Friendship Bridge (*Puente de la Amistad* in Spanish), which connects the mainland to the Nicoya Peninsula. The bridge, which opened in 2003, was a gift in exchange for fishing rights in Costa Rican waters. The bridge still stands but the friendship has been quite strained since Costa Rica dumped its former pal in favor of the New World economic powerhouse. Locals renamed the Taiwanese-built bridge *Puente de la Apuñalada* (Backstab Bridge).

Under the new deal, 99.6 percent of Costa Rican goods qualify for duty-free access to the Chinese market. Agricultural exporters are the primary beneficiaries, although Chinese negotiators would not allow sugar to be added to the list of tariff-free products. What does China get? Tariffs removed on 58 percent of Chinese goods entering Costa Rica.

China didn't build Costa Rica a new bridge, but it did rebuild the country's national stadium. In 2009 and 2010, workers imported from China labored night and day, erecting a US$100 million stadium in San José with room for 35,000 fans under its retractable roof. China is also pouring nearly US$1 billion into revamping the state-run oil refinery near the adjacent Caribbean ports of Limón and Moín, and millions more into upgrading port facilities and the highway (32) that runs from San José to Limón. It looks like little Costa Rica will play an important role in fueling China's ongoing industrial boom. (See also *Chinese-Costa Ricans in History* on page 29.)

GAMBLING AND SPORTS BOOKS

Gambling is legal in Costa Rica, and it's big business. You can play the tables at the casinos, but the real money is online and over the phone. Call centers are one of the fastest growing sectors of the Costa Rican economy. Row upon row of workers sit at their computer terminals, speaking into telephone headsets, taking calls from all over the world and arranging bets in dozens of languages. Callers from the United States are (or were) some of these call centers' best customers.

Prior to 2006, online gambling occupied a legal gray area in the United States. To avoid run-ins with federal prosecutors, sites were set up offshore in places like Costa Rica. But in September of 2006, the U.S. Congress passed the Unlawful Internet Gambling Enforcement Act, and it became a crime for businesses anywhere in the world to take payment for Internet gambling from U.S. players.

It took a while for the fallout to hit Costa Rica, but in 2011, the U.S. government shut down three major online betting sites operating in Costa Rica: PokerStars, Full Tilt Poker, and Absolute Poker. Besides shutting down the sites, 75 bank accounts were seized and 11 people indicted on charges of illegal Internet gambling, bank fraud, and money laundering. The day became known as Black Friday within online poker circles.

There have been other shutdowns, such as in early 2012, when U.S. authorities seized the gambling website Bodog, which had been operating at least in part from Costa Rica. Four Canadians were indicted on charges of illegal sports betting. The site responded by changing its name and registering its business in Latvia.

No doubt online betting will continue to thrive, but Costa Rica may no longer be the websites' location of choice. Even for those Costa Rica-based sports books that have not been bothered by U.S. officials, the environment is not as attractive as it once was. In June 2012 the Costa Rican assembly approved a 10 percent tax on casinos and betting call centers—not onerous but a lot more than they had to pay previously, which was a big fat zilch.

STABILITY

On balance, Costa Rica is still a good place to live and do business. It has one of the more stable economies in all of Latin America, a fact that draws many foreign companies here, further anchoring the economy. Top foreign investors include Intel, Dole Fruit, Chiquita, Abbott Laboratories, Baxter Healthcare, Hanes Underwear, Scott Paper, PriceSmart, Payless Shoes, McDonald's, and Bechtel.

Compared to its neighbors, Costa Rica has a fairly high per capita gross domestic product (GDP), a figure often used to measure a country's standard of living. In 2015 Costa Rica's per capita GDP was US$15,500, while Nicaragua's was US$5,000 and Honduras clocked in at US$4,900. At US$21,800, Panama has the highest per capita GDP in Central America. For comparison to wealthier, more developed countries, the U.S. per capita GDP for the same year (2015) was US$55,800 while Canada's was US$45,600, and the United Kingdom was $41,200.

Sure, there are problems. The country is battling a large foreign debt, trying to impose IMF-mandated austerity measures while continuing to provide the social services its people have come to expect. Free education and health care are priorities for Costa Rica, and they don't come cheap. But for the moment, at least, Costa Rica is still erring on the side of maintaining a high level of social services while offering incentives to foreign businesses so that they might come here and provide jobs for Ticos.

PEOPLE AND CULTURE

A former colony of Spain, Costa Rica bears the mark of that country's culture, language, and religion. Indigenous peoples present in Costa Rica before the coming of the Spaniards have also added their culture to the mix, as have successive waves of immigrants, from Jamaicans and Chinese to the more recent influx of North Americans and Europeans.

Although the Tico national identity is as hard to pin down as any other, one current that runs through the culture is the belief that Costa Rica is unique. Ticos define themselves against their neighbors in ways that range from the "whiteness" of their racial makeup to the pacifism that does indeed distinguish this country from others in the region. Since 1948 Costa Rican leaders have come to power not through violence or fraud but via more or less honest elections. Ticos are proud of this democratic heritage. They're also justifiably proud of the fact that more than 25 percent of their national territory has been set aside as parks and reserves, and that the country has a world-renowned commitment to preserving its natural heritage.

Ethnicity and Class

WHO IS *PURA TICA?*

As recently as the early 1990s, a Costa Rican president (Rafael Calderón, on a visit to Spain) was claiming publicly that there had been no indigenous people in his country when Columbus arrived. Of course there had been—perhaps as many as 500,000—but only lately have Ticos begun to assimilate that truth into their national consciousness. And until very recently, tourist literature mentioned the overwhelmingly "European" blood of the country's inhabitants as one more plus for prospective visitors.

Whiteness has been, and still is, to some extent, a national preoccupation. This is not so different from some other nations in the Americas, where indigenous and African influences are not much celebrated, and where darker-skinned peoples tend to be overly represented in the

Boruca man

lower socioeconomic strata. But because there's a kernel of truth in the Tico myth of whiteness—Costa Ricans do tend to be lighter-skinned than, say, Nicaraguans or Mexicans—the country seems slower than most to embrace the mixture of ethnicities present in even the lightest-skinned citizen.

In 1995, utilizing five decades' worth of research, University of Costa Rica (UCR) geneticists Ramiro Barantes and Bernal Morera declared that almost all Costa Ricans are mestizos (people of mixed racial heritage) with varying combinations of the general population's gene pool: 40-60 percent white, 15-35 indigenous, and 10-20 percent black. The census tells a different story (see the sidebar on page 27 of the *History, Government, and Economy* chapter), in part because people interviewed by census workers self-report their ethnicity and because "race" here, as elsewhere, is often less a matter of ancestry than of culture. A Guanacasteco with a fair share of African blood, for instance, may or may not think of himself as black, depending on his cultural affiliations. And though there is pride among minority ethnicities, there are also plenty of incentives to assimilate into the mainstream.

After all, the word *indio* (Indian) here is still usually an insult, and many "white" Ticos think blacks aren't "real" Costa Ricans. During the 19th century, the elite boasted of their pure European stock and slandered their rivals with racial epithets. Presidential portraits often showed the men as being lighter-skinned than they actually were. And when, in the 1930s, the United Fruit Company moved its banana plantations from the Caribbean to the Pacific coast, President

Ricardo Jiménez forbade the transfer of "colored" employees, saying the move would "upset racial balance" and cause "civil commotion" in Costa Rica. The decree was repealed in 1949. In recent decades, the influx of an estimated one to two million Nicaraguan immigrants has rekindled Tico resentment against darker-skinned outsiders. Ask any taxi driver why violent crime is on the rise in Costa Rica, and he will have an easy answer: It's the Nicaraguans, so accustomed (goes the prejudice) to bloodshed. Colombian immigrants are often viewed similarly.

Chinese, Jews, and members of other immigrant groups are often not considered *pura Tica,* even if their families have been here for generations. Despite the fact that the country is populated almost entirely by mestizos, to this day the nation is dominated by a handful of families who trace their ancestry back to the Spanish *hidalgos* (aristocrats) who arrived during the colonial period. No matter that many of the Spaniards were poor and had to work their own land, or that because most settlers were men they coupled with non-Spaniards, setting into motion the genetic mixing of Spanish, indigenous, and African blood that has made Ticos who they are. But even today, the perception of European blood seems stronger in Costa Rica than the mestizo reality. (Also see *Indigenous Culture Today* on page 26, *Afro-Costa Ricans in History* on page 28, and *Chinese-Costa Ricans in History* on page 29.)

Still, Costa Rica has done much to combat racism. The 1949 constitution declared that anyone born in Costa Rica has the full rights of citizenship, which means that blacks, women, and members of other marginalized groups finally had the right to vote. In 1992, President Calderón (the same man who had claimed his country had no indigenous people) signed the United Nations Treaty on Indigenous Populations and Tribes, which puts indigenous sovereignty above national law and guarantees indigenous people bilingual education and health care. Academics study indigenous language and culture, and encourage "average Ticos" to value their indigenous heritage rather than separate themselves from it by calling it pre-Columbian culture. And while past tourism campaigns showcased the country's

Anyone who doubts that Costa Rica has shantytowns need only take a ride on one of the recently reintroduced urban trains.

whiteness, now you'll often see indigenous and black people pictured in ads.

COSTA RICA'S MIDDLE CLASS

While racial and ethnic biases may be on the wane, economic inequities seem to be on the rise. One of Costa Rica's claims to fame has been its large middle class, the group thought to stabilize a country economically and politically. Historically, Costa Rica was a poor Spanish colony, less a society of land barons and peons than surrounding states. When coffee began dominating the national economy in the 1880s, the tradition of small independent landowners persisted in a core of small coffee growers that made up a significant middle class. And although economic frustrations led to the 1948 civil war, for three decades after the war, far more Ticos climbed up the class ladder than slid down it.

Beginning in 1979, worldwide recession and a sharp devaluation of the colón had a chilling effect on the economy. Between 1980 and 1983, the number of poor families doubled, and buying power was so severely reduced that even nominally middle-class families began to feel poor. The latest world economic crisis hit Costa Rica hard as well.

The increasing availability of credit and the pressures of consumerism don't help matters. An influx of relatively well-off foreign residents has also driven up prices, especially in real estate, making it harder for Ticos to buy property.

Still, a newcomer to Costa Rica who has traveled in other Central American countries will see far less evidence of dire poverty here than elsewhere.

Customs and Etiquette

More than one observer has noted the similarities between Asian and Latin American cultures: Both emphasize social harmony and saving face. To North Americans, who often value honesty above harmony, the Costa Rican method of preserving accord and personal honor can sometimes look a lot like lying. Ticos don't much like our version of honesty, however, thinking it clumsy and rude.

What you see here is not what you get. Ticos are known as icebergs because often only a fraction of their true selves is visible; it's easy to crash into the 95 percent hidden beneath the surface. The smiling exterior of a Tico acquaintance might conceal many things. Attempts to set things straight—to speak perhaps uncomfortable truths for the good of the relationship—don't find much favor in this culture.

Things do get communicated, but to the uninitiated, the language might as well be code. In the rare instances I manage—with the help of locals—to gain insight into problematic situations, I hear comments like, "I thought you knew," or "But wasn't it obvious?"

No, it wasn't obvious. When you're new to a culture, what's obvious to natives is not obvious to you. One consolation is that you're expanding your awareness of your own assumptions as well as opening your eyes to the fact that there are dozens of ways in this world to solve the same problem. Keen observation, good will, and a boundless sense of the absurd will serve you well as you adapt to your new environment. The process brings unexpected gifts of self-knowledge as you discover which parts of yourself you're willing and able to change, and which are more bedrock aspects of your character. If all else fails, remember the old saying: What doesn't kill you makes you stronger.

PERSONAL SPACE

You're on a crowded bus, and you've been lucky enough to get a seat. In the press of bodies, the señorita in the aisle has her ample behind smashed up against your shoulder, the kid in the seat behind you is playing with your hair, and a man leans over, a few inches from your face, to open the window. No one says *"perdón"*; no one even glances your way to acknowledge that they are—by North American standards, at least—making serious incursions into your personal space.

Whether you think this normal, charmingly different, or downright rude will depend on your culture and upbringing. It's one of my pet peeves, in part because my response to it is so very physical. I can explain away other cultural differences, but this one makes me feel like a dog with her hackles up. A local told me to think of it as a sort of compliment—a collective hug, welcoming me to the extended family.

This reduced margin can also be seen in the way Ticos drive. Costa Ricans pull out into traffic that would give North Americans pause, pass even if a truck is bearing down from the other direction, and cut off cars so closely you're amazed that there aren't even more accidents.

EARLY (AND NOISY) RISERS

Most Ticos are up before six in the morning, and they aren't tiptoeing around, trying not to wake the gringos who sleep till eight. Señoras bang pots, kids squeal, and the buses that pick up schoolchildren honk at every door. Construction crews hammer away, leaf blowers are turned on high, and even the birds get up early to contribute to the racket.

If you can't fight them (and you can't), you may as well join them. You will be much, much happier if you adjust to Tico hours, which means getting up with the sun and going to bed as early as 9pm. Out in the country there's little to do at night, and even in cities things are usually quiet by midnight. After the adjustment period you may even find that you really like being up for the sunrise.

Love, Marriage, and Family

WOMEN AND MEN

Officially speaking, women and men in Costa Rica enjoy absolute equality. The 1949 constitution says as much, and a 1966 constitutional amendment prohibits discrimination based on sex, race, or religion. The 1974 family code stipulates that husbands and wives share equal rights and responsibilities, and that a woman can do everything from inherit property to form a corporation on her own. There are laws on the books against sexual harassment and gender discrimination. The

far-ranging 1990 *Ley sobre la Igualdad Real de la Mujer* (Law for Women's True Equality) was intended to help close the gap between women's legal rights and their "true" lives. It provided for a host of reforms, including that schools were supposed to modify materials that promote sexist stereotypes, such as books that state "Mother kneads the dough while Father reads the paper."

Laura Chinchilla's reign as President (2010-2014) was a real boost to the morale of all Ticas, showing just how far a (well-connected) woman can rise in a male-dominated society.

Traditions Die Hard

Sound like a feminist utopia? Not exactly. Traditions die hard, and Costa Rica is still a *machista* society, where little girls are taught to serve their brothers at the dinner table. In hiring, men are more likely to get high-level positions. The Institute of Social Studies in Population (IDESPO) reported recently that Costa Rican men earn, on average, 40 percent more than women, with the majority of female workers employed in low-paying agricultural, domestic, and manufacturing positions. Add to that high rates of teen pregnancy, single motherhood, and domestic violence, and you'll see that Ticas have a lot to contend with.

On the other hand, there are more women than men currently enrolled in most of the country's universities, though it is still common for women to give up their studies or careers once they marry.

Marriage and Kids

Most Ticos are married by the age of 25, although those who are studying for advanced degrees tend to wait longer. Increasingly, both husband and wife work, and often a nanny or female relative spends more time with the children than their parents do. In 2013, the fertility rate dropped to a historic low of 1.76 children per woman, the fifth consecutive year below the replacement rate of 2.1 children per woman. The *Wall Street Journal* even took note, reporting that declining fertility rates "aren't just a problem for wealthy countries anymore."

Although Costa Rica is a Roman Catholic country, outside-of-marriage births are common. The law deals with this trend by insisting that both parents, whether they are married to each other or not, are responsible for their children.

But when a deadbeat dad skips town, there are no official resources to track him down.

A study in the early 2000s showed that a majority of women in active sexual relationships used contraceptives, at least some of the time. Abortion is illegal in Costa Rica (except when the mother's life is at stake), though it is available in private clinics for those with money, and in back alleys for those without.

I've heard from several Tico sources that the single most important piece of advice a father can give his son is, "*Hijo,* you can't expect to sleep with every woman in the world. But you've got to at least try!" Sure, it's a joke, but like many jokes it has a large grain of truth in it. Men here are expected, to a certain extent, to proposition every eligible woman they meet, and there's still a strong double standard when it comes to fidelity. A man who strays expects to be forgiven by his long-suffering partner; a woman had better not expect the same indulgence.

THE FAMILY

In Costa Rican society, it's all in the family, with the law backing up generations of tradition. Slights of honor against family members—even long-dead ones—are punishable by law. A person who murders a relative may get a longer jail sentence than one who kills a stranger. Adults are legally responsible not only for their spouses and children, but also for other family members in need, such as a sibling with disabilities.

Relatives who live outside the city may come to live with urban relations in order to find better work or attend school. Children are more likely to play with their siblings or cousins than with "outsiders." Many adults count their siblings among their best friends and spend most of their social time with family members. Families go into business together, and

What's in a Name?

Let's say your new friend introduces herself as María José Mora Pacheco de Vargas. Before you roll your eyes in exasperation and wonder why anyone would need five names, let's dissect her monikers and see what we can find out.

- **María** – first name
- **José** – second name; like a middle name (middle names can go against gender)
- **Mora** – first surname; comes from María's father
- **Pacheco** – second surname; comes from María's mother
- **de Vargas** – married name; comes from María's husband

Confused yet? OK, let's take a step back. First of all, like other Latin Americans, Costa Ricans trace descent through both their mother and father. The father's last name is the child's *primer apellido* (first surname); the mother's last name is the child's *segundo apellido,* or second surname.

María's father's name is Wilbur Álvaro Mora Espinoza; his first surname becomes his daughter's first surname (as for the "Wilbur," English names are popular in Costa Rica). María's mother's name is Soledad Berta Pacheco Molina; her first surname becomes

government officials hand out prime jobs to family members.

What does this mean to the newcomer? Many North Americans leave home at an early age, perhaps settling far from their family of origin. They create a new sort of family out of good friends and community. That happens much less in Costa Rica, where people tend to stay put and are more insular and clannish.

It can be hard to break into these clans, and although Ticos are known as polite and welcoming, the welcome often stops at the front door—literally. Especially in the country, visitors are not often asked to come inside, although you may be invited to sit on the front porch and have a lemonade. Long-term expats joke that if you're lucky enough to have a Tico invite you to his house, he won't tell you how to get there. Ticos may also be wary of people who they think will be here today and gone tomorrow.

It's not impossible to make Costa Rican friends, but it takes time and effort. Start by being as polite as you know

how, and try not to take offense if your friendly overtures are not reciprocated as you would like. If you have children, you're one step ahead—you'll have a door into Tico families with kids the same age as yours. If you work with locals, that's another way in. And remember, there are plenty of other foreign residents who are in the same boat and more than happy to commiserate about it. Enduring friendships have been based on less.

EXPAT SOCIAL LIFE AND ROMANCE

The unspoken motto in many of this country's far-flung, sometimes incestuous expat communities seems to be "all's fair in love and real estate." The subject of conversation is most often the selling of land or the switching of romantic allegiances. On the real estate side, most people who've been down here for a while get into that game on some level—from becoming developers to feeding clients to a local real estate agent and getting a small cut of the deal.

María's second surname. María's husband's name is Victor Hernán Vargas Salas; his first surname is sometimes appended to María's parade of names, preceded by "de" (of) to denote that she is married to him. But for most purposes, including legal documents and medical files, María will not use the "de Vargas."

If she wants to be quick, María may write her name María J. Mora P., spelling out the most important names (first name, first surname), while abbreviating the less important names (second name, second surname). If she works with North Americans, she might call herself María Mora, knowing that nonnatives sometimes get confused by the Costa Rican carnival of names. Poor gringos, she might be thinking, with so few names.

If you meet someone with two identical *apellidos*, like Julio Ricardo García García, either both Julio's parents had the same *primer apellido*, or his father is unknown, and they repeated his mother's surname twice on the birth certificate.

For official records, which are set up to require two surnames, clerks may try to solve the inconvenience of a one-surname foreigner by repeating her surname twice. Thus I became Erin Kathleen Van Rheenen Van Rheenen for Social Security purposes. My documents are sometimes filed under *V*, sometimes under *R*, and often not filed at all because no one can figure out why the gringa has not two surnames but four.

On the love side, couples who move here together sometimes thrive but just as often the big life change puts all sorts of new stresses on the relationship. People adjust differently—maybe one partner loves the place immediately, and the other takes a while to warm up to it or never does. A move to a totally new culture also shows you things about your partner that you may never have known—that she treats employees rudely, for example (maybe you never had any employees before, so it didn't come up), or that he can't go a day without complaining that there's nothing to do here.

Some couples who arrive together split up and then start looking for a new partner. Some stick to the expat world, reasoning that relationships are hard enough without additional language and cultural barriers. Others, noting that their ex spoke English perfectly but that they never understood what she or he was saying, conclude that communication is about more than language. These folks expand their field of vision and might take up with a local or an expat from another country.

THE LURE OF THE TICA

There's a contingent of North American and European men, often quite advanced in years, who come to Costa Rica expressly to meet and sometimes marry a Tica (Costa Rican woman), often half or a third their age. Some will tell you Ticas are unencumbered with feminist notions, don't care about a man's age or attractiveness, and that they "spoil their men rotten" without asking for anything in return. If that sounds plausible to you, you're in for a few surprises. Those who know a variety of Ticas and have observed Tica-gringo relationships know the situation is significantly more complex. As with other aspects of Costa Rica, you should be suspicious of extravagant claims that the rules that apply everywhere else are somehow suspended in Costa Rica.

And if you marry a Costa Rican, you marry his or her extended family. You

The Art of the *Piropo*

Attractive women get plenty of attention on the street in Costa Rica, some of it rather crude. If your roadside Romeo offers up a reptilian *psst!* or a porcine grunt, you'll do well to walk on with your head held high.

But some of the curbside tributes are quite flowery and creative, as when a (usually older) gentleman says something like, *Si la belleza fuera delito, yo te hubiera dado cadena perpetua* (If beauty were a crime, you'd get life in prison).

Such a comment is a *piropo* (pee-ROH-poh). The tradition of these elaborate and often suggestive compliments can be traced back to medieval Spain. Originally part of a ritualized courtship, *piropos* also demonstrate that Spanish is a more florid and baroque language than get-to-the-point American English. Modern *piropos* range from PG to X-rated fare; here's a sampling of a few of the tamer ones.

- *Bendita sea la madre que te pario.* (Bless the mother who gave birth to you.)
- *Tantas curvas, y yo sin frenos!* (So many curves, and me with no brakes!)
- *Quisiera nadar en tus ojos hasta ahogarme.* (I want to swim in your eyes until I drown.)

might get long-lost cousins showing up so you can *darle la mano* (give them a hand).

FOR WOMEN ONLY

Women seeking adventure will most likely find it, as Tico men are often on the lookout for new conquests. Those hoping for something more lasting may find that Costa Rican men can be less egalitarian and faithful than North American women are accustomed to. Many of the single expat women I meet go out with fellow expats, not necessarily from their own country.

Some women, especially middle-aged and older, complain of a dearth of eligible men here. Expat Margie Davis wrote:

Even though I love my life in Costa Rica, there's one big gaping hole—I have no one to date. I am attractive with a petite body, yet I can't find a suitable man to ask me out. When I moved down here I left a 17-year marriage, and getting into another relationship was the last thing on my mind. But now that I've been here and gotten on with my life, I want to date again. I've had three dates in 13 months. I am not alone in this situation. My single gringa and Tica women friends in their 40s, 50s, and 60s have the same lament.

I'd have to agree with Margie, at least in part. Wherever I go in this country, when I speak with single women expats, the conversation usually rolls around to "do you know any eligible men around here?"

A SMALL POND

There's a rueful saying around here that many of the expats who arrive in Costa Rica are either "wanted or unwanted." (For the "wanted" part of that equation, think of the posters on U.S. Post Office walls.) Expat communities (even in the well-populated Central Valley, but especially outside of it) are small, so there's not a lot to choose from.

Just as when you're traveling you end up hanging out with people you might not be able to tolerate at home, when you are part of a small expat community, you might end up dating or being friends with people who back home wouldn't have been your cup of tea. This isn't necessarily a bad thing—one of the great things about living in Costa Rica is that you'll probably make friends with all sorts of people from many different countries. In the end I think it's a positive thing to be compelled to let more (and different) people into your heart.

Those looking for same-sex partners will find an even smaller dating pool. But many a great love is based on exceptions to all sorts of rules, so never say never.

LGBTQ

San José is known as a gay-friendly city. There are many openly gay bars in town, lots of gay-friendly restaurants and guesthouses, and in 2003 the city organized its first gay pride festival. One speaker at the festival joyfully proclaimed that Costa Rica had come out of the closet, but it's clear that most gay Ticos still live a fairly closeted life, especially if they are in positions of power. Guides to gay Costa Rica stress that the country is a fairly tolerant place as long as you're not openly affectionate in public. Gay men, by the way, are far more visible than gay women, and there is a big transvestite community, with cross-dressing sex workers much in evidence along some downtown streets.

"Being gay in Costa Rica is really a nonissue," counters Scott Pralinsky, who came to Costa Rica in early 2004. "Most people here, both Ticos and expats, are very discreet about their sexuality. But we [he and his boyfriend] certainly don't hide anything and have never run into any kind of friction. I feel more comfortable in Costa Rica being myself than in most places I've lived in the U.S."

Around the country, there are pockets of openly gay culture; Manuel Antonio (near Quepos, on the Pacific coast) is one of the best known. In general, though, outside of the Central Valley, more traditional mores hold sway, and gay individuals should be as aware as they'd be in the less-tolerant areas of their own countries.

Legally speaking, homosexual activity is not a crime between consenting adults (over age 18). There have also been court rulings prohibiting police raids and harassment at gay locales.

For a list of gay organizations in Costa Rica, see page 335 in the *Resources* section.

Religion

CATHOLICISM

Costa Rica is a visibly Roman Catholic country, and the great majority of Ticos call themselves Catholic. Churches are everywhere, and shrines to the Virgin can be seen in parks, public buildings, and even taxicabs. Most Ticos are baptized and married in the church, and everyday speech is full of religious phrases. Ask a Tica how she is, and most likely she'll reply, *"muy bien, gracias a Dios"* ("very well, thank God"). A fair number of people cross themselves when passing a church or beginning a journey. Religious festivals are often national holidays: The

country all but shuts down during Easter week, and on August 2, hundreds of thousands of Ticos make the pilgrimage to the Cartago cathedral that houses the Virgin of the Angels, Costa Rica's patron saint (see the sidebar on page 267 in *The Central Valley and Beyond* chapter).

One of 48 countries worldwide that claims a state religion, Costa Rica has its relationship to the Roman Catholic Church written into its constitution, which stipulates that the church is "the religion of the state," and that the country must provide "contributions for its maintenance."

church in San Gerardo de Rivas

There have been many attempts by the national assembly to edit this out of the constitution and to fully separate church and state in Costa Rica. But Óscar Arias, president from 2006 to 2010, opposed such a move, and recent President Laura Chinchilla noted her opposition as well.

Although Catholicism has been the state religion since 1871, Costa Ricans are not necessarily devout. Catholic influence here seems more cultural than religious, with people observing the outward rituals but lukewarm to the Catholic precepts that don't fit with their individual philosophy. Premarital and extramarital sexual activity is common, out-of-wedlock births are on the rise, and contraception is promoted by the government and embraced by the people (but abortion is still illegal).

This lukewarm faith is nothing new. In 1711, the bishop in charge of Costa Rica was so appalled by low church attendance and nonpayment of church fees that he ordered chapels built in every town and mandated that fees be paid before any marriage or funeral could be performed. His decree had little effect.

The country's first constitution specified Roman Catholicism as the state religion, but in 1853, a visiting German Catholic noted that Ticos "attend church more from hereditary custom than from individual impulse. . . . Above all, they do not want to give much money to the church." Although Ticos have historically been less than pious, neither have they been anticlerical, perhaps because the church was never powerful enough to thwart secular desires. Still, the church is the strongest nongovernmental organization, and Roman Catholicism remains the official religion.

OTHER FAITHS

Just over 10 percent of Costa Ricans identify themselves as Protestants, and most belong to one of the approximately 100 small evangelical sects active here. Most of the country's black population arrived in this country as Protestants and remain so today.

Denominations include Baptists, Methodists, Mormons, Seventh Day Adventists, and Jehovah's Witnesses. As elsewhere in Latin America, Protestant fundamentalism is on the rise, in part because converts feel a greater sense of community in their small sects than in the often-impersonal state-sanctioned Catholic Church. Many Protestants belong to missionary orders, and sometimes you'll see the faithful going door-to-door or performing concerts or plays in local parks. At my local park there are occasional Christian rap concerts, with Christ-centered lyrics and heavy bass booming through our quiet suburban streets.

Several synagogues in San José serve the city's Jewish community. Some Jews are new arrivals, many from Israel or North America; others are descended from families that came from Europe in the early 20th century. Many Jewish children attend the Weizman Institute in San José, a trilingual school with classes in English, Spanish, and Hebrew.

Many Ticos of Chinese descent have converted to Catholicism, though some still practice Buddhism or Confucianism. There is a small Quaker community, mostly living in the northern mountain town of Monteverde. As in the United States, many Ticos study yoga, Zen, or Asian martial arts, and they may shoehorn a bit of Eastern spirituality into their mostly Catholic or secular worldview.

Expats will have a wide choice of services to attend, some in English. The weekly *Tico Times* lists the various options. There is also plenty of New Age spirituality on offer, from indigenous-inspired rites to A Course in Miracles.

The Arts

For such a small country, Costa Rica gives a fair amount of support to its arts. The Ministry of Culture, Youth, and Sports sponsors music and dance performances in towns throughout the country, workshops for kids, and an annual international arts festival. The government subsidizes the House of the Artist, founded in 1951 and offering free painting and sculpture lessons—many Tico artists began their careers here. Musicians and dancers have the Conservatorio Castella, started in 1953, and the state-subsidized Editorial Costa Rica, founded in 1959, publishes local writers and sponsors yearly writing awards.

There is also the National Symphony Orchestra, until the early 1970s a small ensemble playing a few poorly attended concerts each year. President Pepe Figueres sparked the revitalization of the orchestra, asking "Why should we have tractors if we lack violins?" Now the orchestra is first-rate, featuring famous international soloists but still staying true to its roots, playing not only in the elegant National Theater but also in small-town plazas throughout the country. When musicians are hired (often from outside the country), they know they must not only play but also teach: The "second orchestra" is one of the few state-sponsored youth orchestras in the world.

The National Dance Company is also on the upswing, as are all sorts of theater groups, including expat troupes that perform works in English. During one typical week in San José, arts lovers might choose among flamenco dance, Tibetan music, a monologue about Nicaraguan immigrants, many broad comedies in Spanish, *You're a Good Man, Charlie Brown* put on by an expat theater group, and all sorts of popular music and dance concerts. Tickets are usually very reasonably priced.

WELCOME TO COSTA RICA
PEOPLE AND CULTURE

A Children's Museum and Its New Siblings

When first lady Gloria Bejarano de Calderón decided she wanted to build a hands-on children's museum in San José, Costa Rica, most people thought she was crazy. The year was 1990, and the government was so broke it had to borrow money to pay federal workers' salaries. It didn't help that Gloria Bejarano intended to build the new museum on the site of a notorious penitentiary that was now a burned-out ruin.

Seeing the place now, you'd never imagine the building's dark history. Painted a cheerful yellow, the turreted Museo de los Niños (Children's Museum) looks like a kid's dream of a storybook castle. Inside, 36 rooms offer up everything from an earthquake station (that simulates a 7.0 quake) to a Nightmare-Eating Dragon: visitors jot down their nightmare, put it in a box, and the formidable dragon, as tall as two men, gobbles it down.

Out back there's a real plane (kids can mess around in the cockpit), old train cars to play in, a fire truck, a kid-size banana plantation where kids can be part of the harvest, and much more. School groups and children with their parents and grandparents fill the place with happy clamor.

The museum is part of the Costa Rican Center for Science and Culture, which includes the National Gallery and the National Auditorium, where plays are produced and Miss Costa Rica is crowned each year. As of 2017, the complex now also houses a STEM (Science, Technology, Engineering, and Math) Educational Center, along with a small Penitentiary Museum, featuring some of the original cells, with their massive metal doors, along with oral histories from former inmates.

Back in 1990, the building didn't look like it could house much of anything except snakes and rats. "I remember the grass came up to my shoulders," says Gloria Bejarano's daughter, Gloria del Carmen, who, 26 years later, works with her mother at the Children's Museum. "There was no ceiling, and vines crawled up the walls. You opened the doors and bats flew out."

"The prison was shut down in part because of human rights abuses," says Gloria Bejarano. "It was overcrowded; there were riots. There's a story about the prisoners killing a snitch, then playing soccer with his heart. You know your Alcatraz? Alcatraz was a Hilton Hotel compared to this place.

"Elizabeth Odio, Minister of Justice at the time, closed this prison and many others. She's amazing. She's since been appointed a judge on the Inter-American Court of Human Rights."

They even brought in priests to bless the site. But it took more than blessings to make the project happen.

"I knew the government wasn't going to build it," says Gloria Bejarano, "so I created a private foundation. I had to be resourceful. Fire fighters helped clean the place, and prisoners from other facilities helped, too. I found a government program that paid minimum wage for certain kinds of temporary labor. The prisoners qualified, so they got paid. I'd approach private companies for donations; if they said no, I'd ask them to donate materi-

Private financing of the arts is also on the rise, with some of the larger multinational corporations supporting mostly music and theater, and *La Nación* sponsoring yearly writing awards.

LITERATURE

Despite the high literacy rate here, Costa Rica is not a country of readers. The scarcity of public libraries attests (and contributes) to this, and apart from newspaper journalists and advertising copywriters, Costa Rican writers might win prizes but are unlikely to make a living at their craft.

Even so, there are plenty of Tico authors who have made their mark on popular culture. All the works

als for the renovation." Even now, the museum has to be scrappy and resourceful. That nightmare-eating dragon I mentioned earlier? Salvaged from a parade float.

"It helped that my mom and dad were true partners," says Gloria del Carmen. "He [President Rafael Ángel Calderón, in office 1990-1994] had her back. It was harder to turn her down, knowing that the President supported her and the project."

"The most difficult part," says Gloria Bejarano, "was fighting the nay-sayers. We had to convince people that Costa Rica had the capacity to undertake a project like this – to transform a place of pain into a place of positivity and possibility."

"It helped that Costa Ricans have always valued education highly. They want their children to do better than they have." Little by little, she convinced people that a museum for kids could be both fun and educational, that play was an important part of learning, and that children learned best by doing.

Gloria del Carmen recently joined her mother in volunteering at the museum. She left behind a career as a photojournalist to raise her three kids and now works part-time as a creative consultant at the Center for Science and Culture. She's helping revamp the museum store and the on-site restaurant, as well as assisting with marketing and outreach efforts. "I've had the good fortune of traveling all over the world and seeing many, many museums. It helps to have that background as we imagine new directions for the Children's Museum, the new STEM center—we sent staff to various California museums and universities, getting ideas—and the new Penitentiary Museum.

The Penitentiary Museum is a way to recreate and remember a dark chapter in the country's history, to give voice to the inmates who did time there, and to educate young people about the consequences of their actions. Gloria Bejarano says she hopes kids currently in youth correctional facilities, as well as high school students, will come to the museum and "understand that they need to have goals in life."

"Maybe we'll close the door on them," Gloria del Carmen half-jokes, "so they can see what it feels like to be locked up."

Visitors can spend time in the cells and see the bunks, the graffiti, and the magazine photos pasted on the walls. Some of the cells have glittering swaths of what, on closer examination, are hundreds upon hundreds of silver origami shapes made from the paper in cigarette packages. "We actually hired people to make what the prisoners used to make," says Gloria del Carmen.

Gloria Bejarano says that at first she was reluctant to include information about the sexual lives of prisoners, including transvestism. "But Elizabeth Odio convinced me. She said, 'Are you going to tell a little story or are you going to get at the truth?'"

Whether it's getting at the truth of prison life or convincing people that a children's museum makes sense for Costa Rica, Gloria Bejarano doesn't shy away from a challenge. All who visit the Center for Science and Culture benefit from the dedication of her, her daughter, and the center's talented staff.

mentioned here have been translated into English unless otherwise noted.

Carmen Lyra is known for her 1920 collection of folkloric short tales, *Los cuentos de mi Tía Panchita (My Aunt Panchita's Stories),* still read today. Lyra was also an activist and is known for organizing a protest in 1919 that ended up burning down the headquarters of dictator Federico Tinoco's official newspaper.

Carmen Naranjo (1928-2012) was a writer, visual artist, activist, and stateswoman. She was the first woman appointed to a cabinet post (in the Ministry of Culture, Youth, and Sports, in 1974), was ambassador to Israel, and published dozens of novels, plays, essays, and books of poetry. Her best-known works are the novel *Diario de una multitude* (*Diary of a Crowd*, 1974), a book of short stories titled *Ondina* (1983), and *Mujer y cultura* (*Women and Culture*, 1989), essays that take on cultural myths relating to gender.

Carlos Luís Fallas (1909-1966) is known for *Mamita Yunai* (1941), a lively novel about banana workers and the role of United Fruit in Costa Rica in the early 20th century.

Quince Duncan, a descendant of English-speaking West Indian blacks, is known for his two novels, *Los cuatro espejos* (*The Four Mirrors*, 1973) and *La paz del pueblo* (*The People's Peace*, 1978). Eulalia Bernard also explores the black Costa Rican experience with her books of poetry, including *My Black King*, written in a medley of Spanish, Standard English, and Jamaican English.

Anacristina Rossi takes on the environmental destruction wrought by foreign investment and tourism in her novel *La loca de Gandoca* (*The Crazy Lady from Gandoca*, 1992). *El expediente* (not translated, 1989), by Linda Berrón, shows the comeuppance of a compulsive womanizer. Jaime Fernández Leandro writes of the life of petty bureaucrats in *Aquel fue un largo verano* (not translated, 1993).

Author José León Sánchez wrote several novels, the most famous being *La Isla de los Hombres Solos* (literally "The Island of Lonely Men," but available in English under the title *God Was Looking the Other Way*), a fascinating and fictionalized account of the author's incarceration on San Lucas Island, Costa Rica's notorious island prison.

Playwright Alberto Cañas has been enormously influential, both through works like *En agosoto hizo dos años* (*Two Years Ago in August*, 1966) and through his work as the secretary of the Ministry of Culture, Youth, and Sports, where he did much to bring the arts to a wider audience.

Jorge Debarvo, who died in 1967 at the tender age of 29, is one of Costa Rica's most famous poets. He gives his name to Jorge Debarvo Day, January 31, which is also known as National Poetry Day.

PAINTING AND SCULPTURE

The best-known Costa Rican artist is probably the sculptor Francisco Zúñiga (1912-1998), whom many people mistakenly believe to be Mexican because he lived much of his life in that country. Zúñiga left his homeland in anger after critics said that his *Maternity* sculpture, placed outside a San José hospital, looked more like a cow than a woman. As is often the case in the art world, the artist had to go into exile before his work began to be appreciated at home. Now Ticos claim Zúñiga as a native son, and his work can be seen in many public spaces.

Sculpture has a long tradition in Costa Rica, both in stone and, especially, in wood, as artists take advantage of the gorgeous tropical hardwoods their native land has to offer.

In painting, Tico artists looked to Europe for their inspiration until around 1920, when a homegrown movement called *costumbrista* was launched. Up north in Mexico something similar was happening, as artists like Diego Rivera, David Alfaro Siqueiros, and Frida Kahlo rejected European models and embraced their national roots. Here in Costa Rica, artists painted scenes from daily life—farmers in their fields and tile-roofed rural houses were favorite subjects. In the 1950s, Tico artists moved toward the abstract, rejecting as corny the *casitas* (little houses) favored by their predecessors. More recently, Costa Rican artists have followed the international trend of

The National Theater

ticket office at the National Theater

The **Teatro Nacional** (National Theater) is perhaps the most impressive building in San José, if not the entire country. This neoclassical arts complex hosts visiting artists–from the Moscow Ballet to Chinese acrobats–and is home to the National Symphonic Orchestra, who perform Thursday and Friday evenings and Sunday mornings during their regular season (March-November).

Built in the 1890s, the National Theater was financed by a coffee tax and used new-fangled construction methods meant to withstand earthquakes (previous theaters had been laid low by the country's frequent *terrremotos*).

Construction of the theater was motivated by shame: Costa Rica had been humiliated when, in 1890, a European opera company featuring prima donna Adelina Patti toured Central America but bypassed Costa Rica because the country had no suitable performance venue.

On October 21, 1897, the theater opened amid much fanfare, with an audience of the country's elite–coffee barons, military officers, and politicians–dressed to the nines. They hobnobbed in the foyer, puffed on cigars in the second-floor pink marbled Smoking Room, and quaffed champagne until well past midnight. Oh, and there was an opera: a company visiting from Paris performed Goethe's *Faust*.

The theater's interior is an appropriately sumptuous venue for the tale of a man selling his soul in exchange for worldly pleasure. Finely veined Italian marble glows in the late afternoon sun, 22-karat gilt drips from the walls, cherubim and gargoyles frolic, and soaring ceilings are embellished with frescoes and murals, such as the *Allegory of Coffee and Bananas* by Milanese artist Aleardo Villa, which used to be featured on the five colón bill.

The interior features Italian marble, Belgian ironwork, stone from Cartago, and semi-precious tropical hardwood from Costa Rica's forests. Entering the theater through the Plaza de Independencia, you'll pass statues of Beethoven and Spanish poet and playwright Calderón de la Barca.

The new theater was so much more lavish than its surroundings that in Europe, Costa Rica became known as a village clustered around a National Theater. Even now, the theater stands out like a prima donna among street buskers.

exploring new media, from film to performance art to holographic sculptures.

MUSEUMS AND THEATERS

Most of the country's museums are in San José. You've got the National Museum, in a pleasant colonial-style building with breezy tiled verandas and a good view of downtown. The museum's small but interesting collection of archaeological artifacts refutes the notion that this country has little pre-Columbian history. The Gold Museum houses a remarkable collection of pre-Columbian gold pieces, while the Jade Museum has the western hemisphere's largest collection of pre-Columbian jade sculptures.

For more modern fare, there's the Costa Rican Art Museum, located at the eastern end of Sabana Park, on the site of the country's first airport. The Museum of Art and Contemporary Design is at Calle (Street) 15 and Avenida (Avenue) 3. Great for both kids and adults, the Children's Museum is housed in a turreted castle of a complex that was once a prison and is now the Costa Rican Center for Science & Culture. When the museum opened in 1994, it was the first interactive museum in Central America. The brainchild of then-First Lady Gloria Bejarano Almada, the museum's 36 rooms offer up everything from an earthquake station (where you can experience what a 7.0 quake feels like) to terrariums with poison dart frogs to a facsimile of the "bridge" of Star Trek's Starship Enterprise. The Science & Culture complex recently added a Penitentiary Museum and a STEM (Science, Math, Engineering and Technology) Center.

There are many theaters in San José; the most architecturally interesting are the splendid National Theater in downtown San José and the nearby Melico Salazar. Both host music, theater, and dance performances, and the former has a lovely café in its lobby.

(For contact information of museums and theaters, see page 334 in the *Resources* section.)

MUSIC AND DANCE

From the heel-toe stomping of the Punto Guanacasteco (the national folk dance) to the rhythms of cumbia, soca, merengue, and even Tex-Mex, Ticos love to dance. *National Geographic* magazine has written: "To watch the viselike clutching of Ticos and Ticas dancing, whether at a San José discotheque or a crossroads cantina, is to marvel that the birthrate in this predominantly Roman Catholic nation is among Central America's lowest."

There are dozens of dance companies, most in the capital city, performing everything from ballet to tango. San José has a hot dance and music scene, but Ticos wanting to shake a leg or be moved to tears by a ballad will not be denied anywhere across the country. Whether it's a traditional love song in Guanacaste, calypso on the Caribbean coast, or reggaeton in the capital city, there's no shortage of music in Costa Rica.

In 1970, Costa Rica's National Symphony Orchestra burst on the scene, and now internationally known soloists and conductors often appear with the "home team" at the National Theater in downtown San José. In 1989 singers from two state universities came together to form the Sura Chamber Choir, the first professional choir in Central America.

CRAFTS

Tourists looking for crafts may be disappointed to find that many of the "souvenirs" in Costa Rica are made in Indonesia—beach towns in particular offer up a glut of batik sarongs and colorful bikinis from halfway across the world. You'll also see street vendors—often

Calypso legend Walter Ferguson and his son, Jose Peck, a nature guide

itinerant South Americans—selling hand-made jewelry and head shop paraphernalia. Costa Rica lacks the rich tradition of native crafts enjoyed by nearby countries whose African and indigenous arts have been preserved or absorbed into a hybrid of Old and New World forms. Still, small pockets of indigenous cultures—like the Cabécar and Bribrí on the Caribbean coast—continue to create the colorful wooden masks and other crafts that their ancestors fashioned centuries ago.

Increased tourist demand and a growing pride in the country's pre-Columbian heritage have led to the revival of some other traditions, and now you may see reproductions of pre-Columbian stone statues and pottery that resuscitate ancient techniques and designs. The towns of Guatíl and San Vicente on the Nicoya Peninsula have become the center of an exciting revival of Chorotega ceramics.

One craft that is *pura Tica* is the kaleidoscope-bright painting of wooden oxcarts, based in the Central Valley town of Sarchí. Even in the mid-20th century, oxcarts were still used daily to transport coffee and other crops. Farmers would decorate their carts in patterns resembling Tibetan mandalas or Pennsylvania Dutch motifs. You'll still see the occasional cart in use today, though mostly they've been taken out of circulation and put in people's front yards, as North Americans might have flamingos or garden gnomes. Miniature painted carts are now popular in tourist shops.

Costa Rican craftspeople also make full use of the tropical hardwoods found here. Some of the objects—from bowls to chairs to keychain figurines—are crudely carved by hopeful amateurs, while other items are true works of art. Beisanz Woodworks in Escazu (just outside of San José) is a great source for quality bowls and other items. Also see *San José Area Sights & Activities under Practicalities* on page 87.

FILM

From *The Blue Butterfly* to *Endless Summer 2,* films regularly take advantage of Costa Rica's stunning locations. The beaches and impressive waves are featured in many surf films, and sometimes

WELCOME TO COSTA RICA
PEOPLE AND CULTURE

the country's jungles even stand in for other worlds, as in Steven Spielberg's *Jurassic Park* or Mel Gibson's *Apocalypto,* set in ancient Mexico but filmed in part in Costa Rica.

Costa Rica's own film industry is beginning to emerge. The country has its own government-run film center (Centro Costarricense de Producción Cinematográfica), which offers courses, rents equipment, and awards prizes, although young filmmakers in the Costa Rican trenches say the Center's services are limited, and they've had to look elsewhere for training and funding.

Aspiring directors often look outside of their own country for both schooling and funding. When Hernán Jiménez ran out of money before completing what would be his award-winning film *El Regreso* (The Return, 2011), about a young man who returns to his native Costa Rica after living in New York, the Costa Rican-born director turned to Kickstarter.com, an online grassroots funding tool. Costa

Rican director Paz Fábrega garnered expertise and funding from five different countries (Costa Rica, France, Spain, the Netherlands, and Mexico) to create her film, *Agua Fria de Mar* (Cold Water of the Sea, 2010). The collaboration paid off; the film won at least 15 international awards.

An exciting new development is the Costa Rica International Film Festival, held annually in San José. Showcasing and awarding Costa Rican, Central American, and international independent films, its roster of yearly winners is a who's who of up-and-coming talent. Check the festival out on Facebook or visit its website: www.costaricacinefest.go.cr. Scores of films are screened in several downtown San José venues, and there are talks, panel discussions, and meetings aimed at film industry professionals. For movie lovers, it's a great opportunity to see an infinitely wider range of shorts, documentaries, and feature films than is usually on offer in Costa Rican theaters.

(Also see *Suggested Films* on page 368.)

Sports and Recreation

FÚTBOL

To understand sports in Costa Rica, you only need to know three words: *fútbol, fútbol,* and *fútbol.* You might know it as soccer, but this sport has a stranglehold on the nation, with little boys taught to play before they're potty trained, and almost half of all front-page newspaper photos pertaining to recent matches. In taxicabs you'll be treated to games broadcast at full volume, the familiar "go-o-oal!" eliciting cheers and the honking of horns from half the drivers on the road, the waving of banners, and, in some cases, drunken revelry and mayhem. The streets often empty out during important matches.

In fact, soccer seems to excite more

passion in Ticos than anything else, including love and politics. A columnist in *La Nación* called it "a functional alternative to the violence of more militaristic peoples."

Boys kick the ball around in the streets, fishermen play impromptu matches on the beach as they wait for the tide to turn, and bus drivers play a little game before their shifts. Towns and neighborhoods organize their own teams, and most villages have at least one scheduled weekly *mejenga* (match), not to mention countless pickup games.

It used to be that soccer was the province of young men, but now there are leagues for girls, women, and older men.

Ticos, in fact, are much more active than they were just a decade or two ago, and if you get up early enough (while it's still cool), you'll see men and women of all ages jogging at the nearby *polideportiva* (sports center) or walking briskly along city streets, dressed in sneakers and sweats.

OTHER COMPETITIVE SPORTS

Basketball, baseball, and volleyball all have their fans here, with baseball more popular where this county borders either Nicaragua or Panama, places where the people are much bigger baseball fans than are Costa Ricans.

The small **tennis** community in Costa Rica enjoys the annual *Copa del Cafe* (Coffee Bowl), a well-regarded international junior tennis tournament that began in 1965. The tournament usually takes place in February or March at the Costa Rica Country Club in the San José suburb of Escazú. Past winners include Bjorn Borg (1973), Madison Keys (2009), and Monica Puig (2010), who won an Olympic gold medal in 2016.

Golf is relatively new to Costa Rica (considering that the game dates back to the 1400s), but courses are multiplying as well-heeled tourists and foreign residents arrive wanting to wield their clubs. The first golf course in the country was created in 1944 at the Costa Rica Country Club in Escazú. Next came a course (in the 1970s) at the Cariari Club, outside of San José. Since tourists began to come to Costa Rica in droves in the 1990s, many other resorts and clubs have constructed their own courses, including courses at Valle del Sol outside of San José, Los Sueños near Jacó, Hacienda Pinilla near Tamarindo, and the relatively new, Arnold Palmer-designed course at the Four Seasons on the Papagayo Peninsula.

There's one **polo** field (at Los Reyes, a gated community near San José), and another at Ellerstina, north of Tamarindo and Playas del Coco in northern Guanacaste.

TOPES, CALBAGATAS, RODEOS, AND BULLFIGHTS

Costa Rica is horse country, and there are many traditions here celebrating the noble animal brought by the Spanish to the New World. *Topes* are horse parades, where you'll see riders showing off their

Costa Rica is horse country.

high-stepping mounts. *Calbagatas* (from the verb *cabalgar,* to ride) are cross-country treks on horseback, with stops along the way for food and drinks and amateur rodeo contests.

The biggest *tope* of the year occurs the day after Christmas, when the National Day of the Horseman kicks off the multi-day *Festejos Populares* (Popular Festivals) in and around San José. Horsemen and women come to the capital from all over the country, tricked out in their best hats and rhinestone-studded shirts, their mounts prancing down a six-kilometer (four-mile) stretch of Paseo Colon and Avenida Segunda. Crowds are huge, music blares, and TV cameras record the action.

Another part of these post-Christmas *Festejos Populares* are bullfights, called *Toros a la Tica* (bullfighting the Tico way). But don't worry, it's against the law in Costa Rica to kill bulls in a bull-fight. Instead, amateurs (who must take a Breathalyzer test) jump into the ring to tease and taunt the bulls. Many are rewarded with being chased around, trampled, and even gored. If you don't make it out to Zapote for this annual dose of *locura* (craziness), you can see replayed again and again on TV how the bulls best the bumbling "bullfighters."

In mid-January is another well-known celebration, this time in Palmares, located between Alajuela and San Ramón. Hundreds of thousands of people converge on this town for concerts, soccer matches, Costa Rican-style bullfighting, and a traditional horse parade. But most of all, people come to drink. One blog puts it succinctly: "If you like crowds, drunks, and public urination, then Palmares is for you."

Outside of the Central Valley, Guanacaste is known for its horsemen, and there are two big ranch-themed events in the province's capital, Liberia. In late February or early March the city explodes with its *Fiestas Civicas* (Civic Festivals), which include a cattle auction and horse parade. On July 25, the Annexation of Guanacaste Day offers another excuse for horse- and cow-related revelry.

For those seeking lower-key festivities, there are small-town rodeos and *topes* all over the country—a great way to catch a glimpse of the real Costa Rica, sans stadium-size crowds and TV cameras.

SURFING

Surfing is first-rate on both coasts, with especially potent waves at places like Puerto Viejo on the Caribbean and Pavones on the Pacific. As soon as you've met a few planes at the San José airport and seen how many travelers arrive lugging board bags, you'll realize that Costa Rica is an internationally known surf spot.

There's more surfing on the Pacific side, for the simple fact of geography: the Caribbean coastline is a mere 160 kilometers (99 miles) long, while the Pacific coast, with more bays and peninsulas, measures 480 kilometers (298 miles). The Caribbean waves are known for their fast, short rides, while the Pacific waves have more variety, including a "hallucinogenically long" left-breaking wave in Pavones, according to Allan Weisbecker, Costa Rica-based author of the surf epic *In Search of Captain Zero.*

Surf Seasons

Different parts of the country have different surf seasons (though surfers come year-round). The best season on the Nicoya Peninsula is November-March, which roughly corresponds to Costa Rica's high tourist season. On the Central and South Pacific Coast (from Jacó to Pavones), the season is said to be April-November, the rainy ("green") season; this can also be a good time to look for price reductions in lodging and other amenities.

The Caribbean coast is best around the same time as the beaches of the Nicoya Peninsula: December-March. Unlike the Pacific coast, the Caribbean side can have crystal clear aquamarine water, like a picture-postcard version of a tropical island.

FISHING

Fishing is also a huge draw, especially in Quepos; Golfito; in the canals and off the coast of North Caribbean towns like Tortuguero and Barra de Colorado; and out of northern Guanacaste beaches like Flamingo and Tamarindo. Head out into the Pacific for sailfish, wahoo, or the hard-fighting blue marlin. Inland you'll find *trucha* (trout), *machaca* (a kind of shad), and *mojarra* (a bluegill with teeth), among many others. The Caribbean side has excellent tarpon and snook action. Fishing lodges abound, and it's easy to find an experienced captain to take you out, like Eddie Brown in Tortuguero, who more than one person told me was "the best tarpon captain between Florida and Venezuela."

RAFTING, WINDSURFING, AND DIVING

White-water rafting devotees have dozens of put-ins to choose from, with the Reventazón River and the lovely Pacuare the most popular choices. Tour companies big and small offer trips that take rafters through Alpine-like territory at higher elevations and through steamy rainforests closer to sea level.

For river running I've had good luck with Desafio Adventure Company, Costa Rica Expeditions, Ríos Tropicales, and Exploraderes Outdoors, who combine a day on the Pacuare with transportation to and from San José, the Arenal area, or Puerto Viejo on the Caribbean coast; you can start at one location and end up at another.

Windsurfers can try Bahía Salinas, on the northernmost Pacific coast, or head inland to Lake Arenal, considered one of the best freshwater windsurfing spots in the world. Desafio Adventure Company in La Fortuna pioneered paddle-boarding in Lake Arenal; others have climbed on board, in lakes and at the beaches.

Scuba diving and snorkeling are good on both the Pacific and Caribbean coasts when big waves aren't churning things up, and excellent at places like Caño Island off the Osa Peninsula. Dive boats take the truly dedicated on 10-day excursions to Cocos Island, 500 kilometers (311 miles) off Costa Rica's Pacific coast and one of the world's best dive spots. There you'll share the water with huge populations of white-tipped and hammerhead sharks, manta rays, and whales.

HIKING, RUNNING, AND BIKING

For those in search of more land-bound pleasures, there's hiking, from the challenging ascent of Chirripó (at 3,819 meters/12,530 feet, the highest peak in the country) to strolls through easy but gorgeous territory like Manuel Antonio National Park.

It used to be rare to see recreational runners or bikers along Costa Rica's roads, but in the past few years those two sports have exploded in popularity. There are more running races, bike events, and triathlons every year. On just about every highway you'll see bicyclists sharing the road with family sedans, 4-by-4s and 16-wheelers, especially on weekends. Mountain biking is also on the rise, with demanding events like the famed *Ruta de los Conquistadores,* an arduous four-day race that runs from the Pacific coast over rain-soaked mountains and down to the Caribbean port city of Limón.

BIRD-WATCHING

Serious bird-watchers have to make a pilgrimage to Costa Rica at least once in their lives to check off some of the 50 species of hummingbirds here or to catch a glimpse of the resplendent quetzal with its meter-long (three-foot-long) iridescent green tail feathers.

If you're not a birder before you come to Costa Rica, you will be once you've seen the country's neotropical stunners, including the scarlet macaw, roseate spoonbill, and the keel-billed toucan.

The birds here are so over-the-top you can't help but smile at their look-at-me plumage, wondering just what evolution had in mind. Why the rainbow of colors, the array of cacophonous calls, and the peculiar features, like the toucan's comically oversize beak? All great obsessions start with questions, and birding is no exception. Even as you learn that the toucan's beak moderates the bird's body temperature and that a parrot's brilliant plumage may have evolved to resist bacteria, you soon begin to appreciate the subtler species, even Costa Rica's oddly mundane national bird, the clay-colored robin.

Costa Rica contains 893 bird species, considerably more than the number of species in all of the United States and Canada combined. Smaller than the U.S. state of West Virginia, little Costa Rica nevertheless possesses the greatest density of bird species of any continental American country.

The diversity can be explained in part by the wide array of habitats, from mangrove swamps along the Pacific coast to chilly peaks as high as 3,820 meters (12,533 feet).

WILDLIFE VIEWING

Speaking of diversity, the wildly varied and exotic animal life in Costa Rica is one of the country's big draws for both tourists and longer-term visitors. This country accounts for just 0.03 percent of Earth's landmass but hosts between 5 and 6 percent of the planet's plant and animal species.

Once you're here, these dry statistics explode into a multicolored profusion of life prowling the jungles, swimming the seas, and circling above in the bright-blue sky.

Monkeys, sloths, tapirs, and rarely seen jaguars call this country's forests home; crocodiles and dolphins and manatees ply the protected waters; and a stunning variety of birds perch in trees or soar overhead.

Many people move to Costa Rica at least in part to be within squawking and hooting distance of such inspiration.

PLANNING YOUR FACT-FINDING TRIP

The only way to know if Costa Rica is the place for you is to come here as many times as possible for as long as your life will allow. But there's always a first time, or the first time you visit with the possibility of living here lurking in the back of your tourist brain.

A trip in which you're window-shopping for a new life will be different from one in which you just want to see volcanoes erupt and hear monkeys howl. That doesn't mean you can't take in some of the best-loved sights and have a little fun—in fact, it would be a shame not to take full advantage of what Costa Rica has to offer,

even as you assess the country for its longer-term potential.

The trick will be to strike a balance between hurrying around and seeing every area, and staying long enough in each place to get a sense of more than the airport or bus station. In this chapter I've outlined several itineraries: a 10-day whirlwind tour to sample as many areas as possible; a two-week trip that has you narrow down your options to two areas; and suggestions to make the most of a month-long stay.

If you're trying to squeeze in both relocation research and the best of the tourist

National Holidays

Official holidays in Costa Rica are listed here, but these are just the beginning of the revelry. Ticos also celebrate with fairs, festivals, and carnivals, not to mention the *festejo* that each town has to honor its patron saint.

- **January 1:** New Year's Day
- **April 11:** Juan Santamaría Day
- **May 1:** International Day of the Worker
- **July 25:** Annexation of Guanacaste
- **August 2:** Virgin of the Angels Day (Costa Rica's patron saint)
- **August 12:** Mother's Day
- **September 15:** Independence Day

- **October 12:** Day of the Cultures (Columbus Day)
- **December 25:** Christmas

The week before **Easter Sunday** is an unofficial vacation time. Much of the country shuts down. On Thursday and Friday of this week, only essential services function; even many of the public bus routes cease operation.

Though not an official national holiday, **Carnaval** is a great introduction to the culture of the country's Caribbean coast. Held in the city of Limón every October, the all-day street party is still, for now, off the main tourist track.

circuit, remember not to overbook in the activities department. A day hanging out and talking to locals is at least as valuable for your purposes as one spent whizzing above the treetops on a zip line. Hotel and restaurant owners—often expats themselves—are excellent sources of information, and life is slow enough that you needn't worry about "wasting" people's time. Talk is what people do here instead of going to the movies, since in most parts of the country there are no cinemas.

And when you find the place that speaks to you—that murmurs *you could be happy here*—well, it's never too soon to book your next trip.

WHEN TO GO

Costa Rica's tourist high season runs from early December through the end of April. This is the country's dry season—or summer, if you like—though temperatures remain fairly constant year-round, with variations more a function of altitude than season. In the Central Valley, for instance, temperatures usually stay around 21-26°C (70-80°F) throughout the year, while beachside temperatures are most often in the high 20s Celsius (80s Fahrenheit). The difference between Costa Rica's "winter" and "summer" is rainfall. Most rain falls between May and November, with the fiercest storms often in September or October. November and May are good times to come—they are relatively untouristed months in which the rains are either just beginning or just tapering off.

There are regional variations, of course. In lowland Guanacaste and on the northern Nicoya Peninsula, the dry season is bone-dry—hardly a drop falls between December and April. On the Caribbean coast (a different world, climatically speaking), you may find rain at any time of the year, with somewhat drier times to be had in February, March, September, and October.

Rain here can feel like one of the Seven Wonders of the World, with *aguaceros* (downpours) no umbrella can stand up to. But even when the rains are at their heaviest, it's rare that they come down all day long. Each microclimate has its patterns, to which you'll quickly adjust. During the

Though many in the tourist trade speak English (and some speak German), learning a little Spanish will make your trip a lot more rewarding.

Central Valley's rainy season, for example, the mornings are glorious, the rain comes after lunch (just in time for siesta), and most often the evenings are clear again.

The winter, or wet season, has been dubbed the green season by tourism promoters, and it can be a great time to come to Costa Rica. Sometimes there are deals on airfare or hotels during that time, though most hoteliers I spoke with said that they really have two high seasons—December through April and again in June and July, the northern hemisphere's summer, when kids are out of school and families take their vacations.

Easter week and around Christmas and New Year are especially busy times, since this is often when both foreign and domestic tourists have time off their job or school. If you must travel during these times, book your hotel and rental car early and expect to pay premium rates. Some hotels almost double their rates during these holidays—check websites in advance.

I've traveled during each and every month, and I've never had a bad trip. One caution: If you're heading to remote areas, the rains may turn unpaved roads into impassable stews of mud and turn streams into raging rivers that no sane person would attempt to ford. In the more developed areas, however, the rain doesn't have to slow you down. One Oregonian who'd relocated to lush Lake Arenal put it this way as we sprinted for cover: "You're not made of sugar—you're not going to melt!"

Preparing for Your Trip

LEARN A LITTLE SPANISH

Of the many things you can do to enhance your trip to Costa Rica, the most important is to study Spanish, even if you learn just a few basic phrases. The country will open up to you in direct proportion to how open you are to it, and making an effort to communicate with locals shows basic respect. Learning a language well is a lifetime endeavor, but even small efforts will yield great rewards.

How to begin? A class—perhaps at a nearby university or community college—is a good investment, but don't stop there. Rent movies in Spanish, watch Spanish-language television, and listen to Spanish radio stations. At first it may all sound like gibberish, but without even realizing it you'll be absorbing the tone and rhythm of the language. In many parts of the United States, there are large communities of Spanish-speaking residents. Perhaps a recent arrival from Central America would like to meet regularly to practice English. You could converse half the time in Spanish, half in English, and you'd both be learning a great deal. Or look for children's books in Spanish—the basic vocabulary is about the right speed for beginners, and the illustrations will help fix the vocabulary in your mind. (For more language-learning tips, see page 147 in the *Language and Education* chapter. For a list of language schools in Costa Rica, see page 345 in the *Resources* section.)

STUDY MAPS

Some people are map lovers and others aren't, but even if you don't know true from magnetic north and your refolded maps look like origami swans, get a map of Costa Rica and put it on your wall. As you read about the country, try to find the places mentioned. Soon you'll know that Guanacaste is up north and Osa down south, and that the oft-mentioned town of Escazú is just west of San José. You'll know that the volcanoes closest to the capital are Poás and Irazú (not to be confused with Escazú!), and that the Caribbean coastline is much shorter and straighter than the Pacific coast.

CHECK YOUR DOCUMENTS

Citizens of the United States or Canada don't need visas to enter Costa Rica, but they do need a passport. The U.S. State Department says to enter Costa Rica your passport must be valid for at least 30 days from the date of entry, but as visitors are often given 90 days on their entry stamp (and you might end up staying longer than you planned), it's good to have a passport valid for at least three months after your arrival date. In theory, customs officials have the right to deny entry to travelers without onward tickets. In practice, this almost never happens.

WHAT TO TAKE

Besides your passport, plane ticket, and a variety of forms of money, pack as light as possible. You may be taking buses or flying in small planes with luggage restrictions. Even with a car, you'll be happier if you don't have to pack up four large suitcases every time you change hotels.

It's seldom truly cold here, so don't worry about heavy sweaters or jackets, though a lightweight fleece jacket and a light, breathable raincoat will come in handy. Take beachwear, of course (two or three swimsuits may seem excessive, but you'll be happy not to have to put on a wet suit). Remember that in bigger

Mañana Just Means "Not Today"

BY SANDRA SHAW HOMER

If you let it, living in another culture can strip you of the culture you were born to and show you who you really are. At first, you may feel as vulnerable as a baby, but by opening up and turning off negative judgements of what's different, you'll start adapting to it. Here are a few things Costa Rican culture has taught me:

· Learning a new language is opening the door to a whole new world—and Ticos are wonderfully helpful if they see you're trying.

· This country is not the fast lane; life has more to do with relating to others and an abiding sense of courtesy, both of which take time.

· Humility: Ticos want to be seen as getting along with others, so consensus rules over confrontation. No one's better than anyone else. Losing your temper or displaying impatience won't get you anywhere.

· It's considered rude to say no, so they don't—which doesn't necessarily mean they're saying yes. They just don't want to make you feel bad. At any store when you're asked if you want something more, don't say no—say *solamente* ("only").

· Every transaction has the potential to become a social encounter, even with total strangers. Greet people with a smile and say "have a nice day" when you part. When you start using polite language, you'll find that you're feeling more polite naturally.

· Waiting in line is a part of life; so is death (it's important to go to funerals).

· Hospitality: make a pot of coffee and expect a two-hour visit. That's the minimum considered polite.

· Life is a lot less stressful when you're patient.

· Help first, ask questions later. And, finally, never ignore a generous impulse.

Sandra Shaw Homer has lived in Costa Rica for 26 years. She explores these and other issues in her forthcoming memoir, Evelio's Garden.

towns beachwear will mark you as a clueless tourist. Take at least one lightweight, wrinkle-resistant nicer outfit for dinners out and to feel at home in bigger towns.

Even if you're not a beach lover, take gear to protect you from the sun:

· hat

· long-sleeved lightweight shirt

· sunglasses

· sunscreen

   Other items to consider:

· camera (a good way to document different landscapes, housing types, and even road quality in the areas you might move to)

· small notebook and pen (you'll be learning so much it'll be hard to remember it all without writing it down)

· insect repellent

· sturdy shoes if you plan to hike, though lightweight running shoes will be fine for most purposes

· sturdy flip-flops

· a travel alarm clock—few of the clocks you see will have the right time. Because most areas of Costa Rica have regular power outages, electric clocks (in hotels, banks, government offices, and on church towers) are almost always wrong. It won't matter until you try to make a flight on time.

- your own washcloth (or one of those thin bath gloves that dries faster than a washcloth) and soap, especially if you're staying in bare-bones hotels—but even some nicer lodging options won't necessarily provide washcloths.

- a clothesline and clothespins: things get wet here, and they take a while to dry.

- extra medication and your prescription so customs officers won't think you're transporting illegal drugs

- extra contact lenses or an extra pair of glasses

- flashlight and extra batteries

- Ziploc plastic bags of various sizes to protect your things from rain or humidity; once you've had a notebook full of hard-won information bleed into a one-tone watercolor, you'll always keep your notebook in plastic.

- duct tape: to fix a window screen or a snorkel, hold your backpack together, and even do emergency repair on your shoes

- all the cables you think you'll need for your computer—Ethernet, telephone line, etc. You can get them here, but it'll be easier if you have them to begin with.

Currency

Credit cards are widely accepted in Costa Rica, especially in tourist areas, though it's always a good idea to have cash on you as well. Debit cards allow you to get money out of ATMs (some let you choose either dollars or colones, the local currency). ATMs are abundant, especially in larger towns. You can also get an advance of cash from a credit card, of course. Before you go, make sure you have PINs for both your credit and debit cards so you can use both in ATMs.

I also like to bring some cash with me, maybe a few hundred dollars in 20s. If there's a problem with the banks or ATMs nearby, you won't be left high and dry. U.S. dollars are accepted in the more touristed areas, and you can usually pay for a taxi in San José with dollars.

And speaking of diversification, it's a good idea to keep your money in a variety of locations—pockets, purse, backpack, and suitcase—so if one stash gets lost or ripped off, you'll still have the others.

Arriving in Costa Rica

CUSTOMS AND IMMIGRATION

U.S. and Canadian citizens don't need visas to travel to Costa Rica, but they do need valid passports, and customs officials may ask to see on onward ticket (this has never happened to me or to anyone I know). Children traveling with one parent are required to provide official permission from the other parent. You won't always be asked for it, but it's essential that you have a notarized letter on hand in case they do ask.

Note that there is an extra fee to leave Costa Rica: US$29, payable in dollars, colones, or a combination of the two.

There's a special counter at the airport where you pay the exit tax, get a slip of paper, and then check in for your flight (they don't let you check in unless you have the proof of payment).

Going through customs is usually fast and painless. If you know you'll be here for a while, bringing possessions in as regular luggage is the fastest and easiest way, even if you have to pay for the extra weight. (For details on bringing children, pets, or possessions into the country, see the *Making the Move* chapter.)

TRANSPORTATION

Taxis are easy to come by, though they're not as cheap as they used to be. There's a taxi stand at the San José airport; you can even pay with dollars. A cab to the center of town will cost around US$30.

Uber arrived in Costa Rica in late 2016, much to the consternation of taxi drivers. It remains to be seen how far Uber will spread outside of the heavily populated Central Valley, or whether Ticos take to this ride-sharing app the way other countries have. (For more on Uber, see page 243.)

Tip: Consider *not* picking up your rental car at the airport (and don't have the car rental representative meet you there and then take you to the rental lot). You've just flown in, it may be dark, you're tired, and you may never have driven in Costa Rica before. This is not the time to start learning. Have your hotel pick you up from the airport (most do that for free or for a small fee). Then ask your car rental company if it'll deliver your rental car to your hotel; most will if the hotel isn't too far outside the main Central Valley area. That way you don't have to try to find your hotel in a country where few roads have names and drivers play fast and loose with traffic laws. It's fun to gradually learn the ins and outs of driving in this country of beautiful (if potholed)

back roads, but for your first few hours (or days) here, give yourself a break and let others do the driving.

If your trip includes a chunk of time in the Central Valley, I would advise *not* renting a car for that time—it's much easier to take taxis or to hire your own driver (your hotel can usually suggest a good person) for a very reasonable fee by the hour, day, or trip. You'll reduce your stress level by at least 73.5 percent if you don't have to drive around San José and its suburbs.

Later, rent that car. Renting here isn't cheap but can be an excellent investment, especially if you want to explore off the beaten track.

Buses are one of Costa Rica's great bargains, and they go just about everywhere. Small planes fly throughout the country and are a good bet if you have limited time. A one-way flight from San José to the Guanacaste beach town of Tamarindo, for instance, will typically cost US$80-150 (there are three classes of fares). You'll get there in 40 minutes, be treated to spectacular views, and save yourself a five- or six-hour road trip.

Although Costa Rica is a small country, getting where you need to go can take a while. All roads lead to San José, and often it's quicker to return to the capital and venture out again, rather than try to get from one outlying area to the next.

You'd think, for instance, that going from the southern Pacific coast to the southern Caribbean coast would be easy. In practice, it's all but impossible. There are no roads, and small planes don't usually make the trip. Your best bet is to return to San José, by air or overland, and then either fly or take the well-traveled highway from the capital to the Caribbean coast.

For more detailed information on transportation to and within Costa Rica, see the *Travel and Transportation* chapter.

Finding Your Way

Whether you're driving on a dirt road deep in the jungle or walking along a crowded city street, finding your way in Costa Rica can be a real challenge. Roads – even major highways – are often not signed at all, and even main streets will have no indication of what they're called. Most buildings have no numbers, and a mailing address (and directions to the place) may look like this

de la Farmacia San Francisco
100e, 200n, 75e
Casa izquierda, rosada, dos pisos
La Pacífica, San Francisco de Dos Ríos
San José, CR

Translation, please.

Your starting point is the pharmacy in the San Francisco section of the city of San José. From there you go 100 meters to the east, then 200 to the north, then 75 to the east. One hundred meters is a block, so these directions instruct you to go one block east, two blocks north, and three-quarters of a block east. *Casa izquierda, rosada, dos pesos* means "house on the left, pink, two floors." La Pacífica is a section of San Francisco de Dos Ríos, which in turn is a neighborhood in San José.

If you think that's confusing, consider that many "addresses" aren't even that specific. Some use landmarks that you probably won't know; some of the landmarks used to be there but aren't any more. Addresses and directions in Costa Rica are definitely geared toward long-term locals – who would know that "Coca Cola" means where the Coca Cola bottling plant used to be 20 years ago. Some addresses take as their reference point a

TIPPING AND TAXES

Most Ticos leave no tip. If service has been exceptional, you might want to leave another 5 percent, but it's not required or expected. There will also be a sales tax—13 percent—added to restaurant bills, making the final bill 23 percent more than you were expecting.

That 13 percent sales tax applies to all goods and services (including hotel rooms) except fees to independent professionals like doctors and lawyers. The sales tax on airline tickets is 5 percent.

Taxi drivers are usually not tipped, while bellboys, hotel maids, and tour guides are.

SAFETY PRECAUTIONS

Crime is on the rise, especially in the capital city of San José. Costa Rica still has less violent crime than the United States and is safer than most of its Central American neighbors, but visitors need to be alert. Petty theft is common, and tourists are easy targets. Keep your bags close, your money in deep pockets or tucked into a money belt, and your wits about you. Make photocopies of important documents—passport, plane tickets, drug prescriptions, address book—and keep the copies separate from the originals.

Another option is to scan or take digital photographs of all your travel documents (and any important prescriptions for medication), then email those files to a webmail address that you can access from Internet cafés. That way you'll always have online copies of crucial documents in case you lose your luggage.

If you're traveling by bus, try to make sure that your luggage stays in sight (all

The good news: There's a sign. The bad news: It's on the ground.

tree (God help you if it's been cut down) or the big house where the doctor killed himself. I'm not kidding.

But people here are friendly and anxious to help. Asking for directions may not come easily to some people, but you'll need to learn to do it, again and again, if you want to get where you're going in Costa Rica.

As a taxi driver once told me, *"Preguntando, llegamos a Roma."* ("Asking [for directions], we get to Rome.")

the more reason to travel light, with one or two small bags). If you're driving, don't leave anything in your car, and make sure you find a safe place to park it overnight.

Keep your doors locked while driving. (For more on safety, see page 172 in the *Health* chapter.)

Sample Itineraries

There are two basic approaches for your fact-finding trip: Either cast a wide net, seeing as much as possible, or settle in for the duration, soaking up daily life in one or perhaps two places.

The 10-day itinerary I've included here casts the net as wide as possible for the time allowed; the two-week tour encourages you to narrow down your focus to two areas, choosing from four; the month-long stay can be spent either all in one area (if you've chosen the area you'd like to live in) or on a more leisurely tour of the entire country.

You can find more about the areas listed here in the *Prime Living Locations* chapters. *¡Buen viaje!*

10 DAYS: A WHIRLWIND SAMPLER OF EXPAT HOT SPOTS

Ten days will fly by in Costa Rica, especially if you're trying to catch a glimpse of many different parts of the country. This itinerary won't leave much downtime, but it will give you a taste of both coasts, the Central Valley (where most expats live), and the country's most active volcano. This tour hits on many of the most popular tourist areas as well, so you can surf or snorkel in the Pacific and the Caribbean, visit much-loved Manuel Antonio National Park, and soak in the hot springs below Arenal Volcano.

The three big tourist guns this tour leaves out are the mountain town of Monteverde, known for its cloud forest preserve and its Quaker community; the Osa Peninsula, Costa Rica's answer to the Amazon and home to Corcovado National Park; and Tortuguero National Park on the northern Caribbean coast, with its crocodiles, sea turtles, and even manatees. You could substitute Monteverde for Arenal on this 10-day itinerary, but to do justice to the Osa or Tortuguero, you'd want at least three days for each. Neither Tortuguero nor the Osa qualifies as an expat hot spot, though some hardy souls have braved these remote areas and now make their homes there.

In terms of transportation, if you feel confident about driving in unfamiliar territory, rent a car in San José and drive to all of the places mentioned. This approach has the added benefit of allowing you to see the hidden-away towns and striking landscapes between the more well-known destinations.

But if the thought of driving Costa Rica's fabled roads makes you anxious, with a little planning you can piece together short flights, bus or minivan travel, and taxi rides. All of the places listed on this itinerary are popular enough that such services will be easy to arrange. (See the *Travel and Transportation* chapter for more detailed information on getting around the country.)

Days 1-2: San José and Environs

Fly into Juan Santamaría airport just outside the capital city. Stay in town the first night, exploring some of the city's better neighborhoods (like Los Yoses and San Pedro in the west, Rohrmoser and La Sabana to the north). Get a sense of city life by walking the downtown pedestrian mall (the Paseo Colón), have coffee at the café in the historic National Theater, and check out the nearby Gold Museum. For your second night, stay in a hotel outside of the city, to the west if the next day you'll explore the western suburbs (Escazú, Santa Ana, Ciudad Colón) or to the north if you want to get a sense of cities like Heredia and Alajuela or towns such as Sarchí and Grecia. Give yourself a break and don't try to see both the towns west of San José and the northern ones. Leave time for a leisurely lunch and gossiping with the taxi driver or waitress. Take time, too, to see what's for sale in the omnipresent supermarkets and malls. The Central Valley is where the whole country comes to shop.

Even if you have rented a car, this part of the trip might be more enjoyable if you leave your car parked in the hotel lot and hire a driver. It takes some time to figure out how to get around San José and its environs; you don't want to spend all your time getting lost or cursing the traffic. Ask at your hotel for a car and driver, or negotiate with a taxi driver to hire him or her for a few hours or the entire day.

Another option is to rent a car the day you want to leave the San José area, relying on taxis or hotel shuttles until then.

Day 3: Zona Norte

Drive, take a small plane, or ride a bus or minivan north to the town of La Fortuna. Nearby you'll find Lake Arenal, famous among windsurfers, and active Arenal Volcano, with a variety of hot springs

Hot Springs of the Arenal Area

Costa Rica is a land of seismic shenanigans, and the Arenal region, a few hours north of San José, is an excellent place to get in on the action. Hot springs burble up from cracks in the earth's crust, and very active Arenal Volcano is one of the most dramatic sights in the country. There are plenty of free hot springs scattered throughout the area, but they are often on private property or you will need a local to show you the way. Ask around when you get here. For a more manicured and luxurious experience, try a day pass at one of the following springs.

Tabacón Hot Springs (13 kilometers/8 miles west of La Fortuna, tel. 506/2256-1500, www.tabacon.com, daily 10am-10pm, best to make reservations, starting from US$85 per adult) is the best known and definitely the most expensive of the bunch. A naturally warm river winds its way through beautifully landscaped grounds and is guided into a series of pools and over a small falls, which will drum the tension right out of your shoulders and neck.

There's also a largish swimming pool (not hot) with a swim-up bar. Things can get pretty raucous at night and when the tour buses arrive. Up the hill from the hot pools and full-service spa in the Tabacón Resort Hotel; you can walk from one to the other. A stay at the (moderately expensive) hotel allows you free admission to the hot springs.

At **Baldi Hot Springs** (5 kilometers/3.1 miles west of La Fortuna on the road to Lake Arenal, 15 minutes east of Tabacón, tel. 506/2479-9917, www.baldicostarica.com, 10am-10pm, from US$34 per adult), two dozen hot pools are set amid landscaped grounds at the foot of Arenal Volcano. The water in the pools varies in temperature from slightly warm to piping hot. There are decks and platforms near most of the pools, some partially covered to protect from the rain.

Massage and other spa treatments (like volcanic mud wraps) are available. There's also a 32-room hotel and a restaurant, although the food (especially the buffet) doesn't get high marks from most visitors.

Kids will love the three water slides (the longest is 99 meters/325 feet). But watch out—you can get going really fast! Near the entryway and bar, the pounding techno music doesn't feel too relaxing, but farther up the hill the environment is more peaceful.

Ecotermales Fortuna (5 kilometers/3 miles west of La Fortuna, on the road to Lake Arenal, on the right side, across from Baldi Hot Springs, tel. 506/2479-8484, www.ecotermalesfortuna.cr, 10am-9pm, book ahead, from US$36 per adult) is quieter and smaller than Baldi and Tabacón. The spa limits the number of people it allows in; visitors book ahead of time for one of three daily time slots: 10am-1pm, 1pm-5pm, or 5pm-9pm.

Four different pools of water range 31-39°C (91-105°F); one of the pools has a cascading waterfall you can sit under for a natural back massage. There are also separate changing rooms for men and women, individual lockers, toilets, and showers. Next to the restaurant is a shaded area with hammocks.

Unlike Baldi and Tabacón Hot Springs, Ecotermales doesn't have a view of Arenal Volcano.

Titoku Hot Springs (close to both Baldi and Ecotermales, see above; 506/2479-7156, book ahead from US$30 per adult), is also on the smaller side, with eight pools, and a limit of 80 people allowed in at any given time. Like Ecotermales, you book for one of three time slots.

nearby. The trip from San José to La Fortuna winds through some lovely scenery, and the Arenal area itself is lushly gorgeous. There's an ever-growing community of expats clustered around the lake, people who appreciate the cooler weather and the low-key vibe.

Days 4-5: Northern Guanacaste Beaches

Drive or fly to Playas del Coco or Tamarindo. Playas del Coco will be of interest to visitors drawn to the convenience of the area (less than an hour from Liberia's international airport and on good roads) or who'd like to take a look at all the condos going in there. Visit nearby Playa Ocotal, less hectic than Coco and one of the nicest little coves around, and head north to Playa Hermosa, another expat hot spot.

Tamarindo will appeal to young partiers set or to those who want to surf or see giant seas turtles laying their eggs. Once a little fishing village, these days Tamarindo is growing so fast you can hear its bones creak.

Day 6: The Nicoya Peninsula

Drive or fly to either the Nosara-Playa Sámara area (halfway down the Nicoya Peninsula) or the Montezuma-Mal País area (at the southern tip of the peninsula). Both areas are less developed than northern Guanacaste beaches like Tamarindo or Playas del Coco, though these southerly areas are also experiencing their own smaller booms. Nosara has the Nosara Yoga Institute and good beaches for swimming and surfing; Sámara is a more typical low-key resort popular with Ticos, with a beach good for learning to surf.

Montezuma is a pretty little alternative-flavored town popular with backpackers but also providing services for more luxury-minded travelers. Mal País (and nearby Santa Teresa) is a surfer's haven, and its one-strip wonder of a town has seen a lot of growth lately.

Between Montezuma and Mal País is Cabo Blanco Reserve, worth a day's visit—walk through the forest for a few hours and arrive at a pristine white-sand beach, where you may be the only one there. Both areas have growing international expat communities.

Day 7: Central Pacific Coast

Drive or fly to the popular beach (and slightly seedy) town of Jacó or to Quepos and nearby Manuel Antonio National Park, the most-visited park in all of Costa Rica. In both areas you are in high tourism mode, which may be a bit of a shock after laid-back Montezuma and Mal País. If you drive, you'll need to take the car ferry from the tip of the Nicoya Peninsula (Paquera) to Puntarenas, then drive south on the coast road. Jacó comes first, and it's easy to feel overwhelmed there. Literally hundreds of condos are in the works, and the town is getting more and more rambunctious, with partying of all kinds on the rise. But it's good to see the place, if only for comparison. Check out the condo prices here, compare them to houses for sale in out-of-the-way towns, and marvel at the huge difference.

Quepos, an hour south, is slightly less overwhelming. It's the gateway to Manuel Antonio National Park. Although crowded in high season, the park is also beautiful. Tangled jungle spills down the hill to meet white-sand beaches, and the trees are full of monkeys and sloths.

Day 8: Dominical Area

If you stay one night in Jacó and another in the Quepos area, skip Dominical, which is another hour south of Quepos on the coast. The farther south you go, the less touristy it gets. Dominical has a long beach where the waves pound in—great for surfers, not so great for swimmers. Nearby Ojochal is a little French-Canadian-infused haven with stylish hotels and a few excellent restaurants.

Days 9-10: Southern Caribbean Coast

If you're driving, you'll take the road inland from Dominical, pass through San Isidro de El General, then head north toward San José (driving time would be 3-4 hours, depending on road conditions). From the San José area to the Caribbean coast is another 3-4-hour drive. If you fly, you'll fly from Jacó or Quepos to San José, then from San José to Limón; each flight is under an hour.

This coast has a very different feel from the Pacific coast. It's wetter and less developed, and real estate is cheaper. It also has more racial diversity than the rest of Costa Rica; most of the country's blacks and indigenous people live in the Zona Caribe.

Check out Cahuita and its lovely beachside national park, then surf, party, and take long flat bike rides in Puerto Viejo. Down the road from Puerto Viejo is Gandoca-Manzanillo National Wildlife Refuge, one of the less-visited jewels in the national park system. You can also visit indigenous reserves.

TWO-WEEK ITINERARY: DIGGING DEEP

If you have two weeks, you could do the 10-day itinerary at a slower pace, add another one or two destinations to that tour, or choose two areas and explore both of them fully. The following describes a week in the four areas of the country most popular with expats. Depending on your tastes, choose two and get ready for a more in-depth experience of Costa Rica living.

A Week in the Central Valley

There's a reason so many expats live in the Central Valley. For those who don't do well with heat and humidity, the area's year-round springlike climate is a real plus. It also has most of the country's infrastructure, including major shopping centers and malls, good private schools, respected private medical clinics, government offices, and every imaginable cultural activity, whether you want to stay within the English-speaking expat community or branch out into the larger Spanish-language world.

Puerto Viejo

Stay in only one or two hotels the whole week, so you can really settle in and not have to worry about moving every other day. Staying a bit outside of the center of San José will be more relaxing than being in the thick of things, but even if you're sure you don't want to live in San José, do spend some time here. Visit the bustling University of Costa Rica (UCR) in the neighborhood of San Pedro—there are often lectures or events open to the public, sometimes in English. Walk the Paseo Colón, the pedestrian mall, and explore the Mercado Central, with its little stalls offering up everything under the sun.

Have lunch or dinner at one of the many upscale restaurants in the suburb of Escazú to see that the food here goes way beyond *gallo pinto* (the national dish of rice and beans). Check your email at a local Internet café and see who else is doing the same.

Read the newspapers and websites. See what events are on offer the week you're there. Maybe you'll catch a concert at the National Theater, attend an English-language play put on by the Little Theater Group, check in with the local Democrats or Republicans Abroad chapter, or join in an ultimate Frisbee game.

Talk to a few different real estate agents and see what they have on offer. Ask them to take you around the areas you're most interested in. Take a half-day trip or two to outlying areas like San Ramón (with its growing expat community and its convenient location, midway between San José and the Pacific coast); Cartago to the east (one of the oldest cities in the country); or Atenas (on the road to the Pacific coast), which, according to *National Geographic* magazine, has the best climate in the world.

Visit one of the private clinics such as CIMA in Escazú or Clínica Bíblica in downtown San José, perhaps making an appointment for a tour or to ask about the insurance they accept or the prices of particular procedures. Both places have English-speaking staff available, especially if you arrange your visit ahead of time.

If you're in San José the last Thursday and Friday of any month except December, consider attending the relocation seminar given by the Association of Residents of Costa Rica (ARCR). It costs US$70 for the two days (US$50 if you are a member; membership is US$100 per year, half that if you are a legal resident of Costa Rica). If you keep in mind that many of the presenters—lawyers, real estate agents, and the like—want your business and have a vested interest in getting you to move to Costa Rica, you can extract a lot of usable information from the gentle hype. Even better, you'll meet some people who live here and lots more who are thinking of making the move.

If you aren't here at the right time of month or if you choose not to devote two full days to sitting inside a conference room, you could visit the ARCR office (near La Sabana Park in San José) and talk to the staff about what membership would provide you. I know many people who feel that the ARCR has helped them a great deal.

A Week in the Arenal Area

The Arenal area is a beautiful mountainous zone with mild weather, great for those who don't want to live at the beach or in the highway-laden bustle of the San José area. Arenal is high enough to avoid the worst of the heat, though the perennial green here comes at the price of lots of rain.

Your week in Arenal will be significantly more laid-back than your week in the Central Valley—there's a lot less to do here. For some, that will be hard; for others, it will be a dream come true. A two-day side trip to nearby Monteverde will give you a glimpse of another lush

outdoor restaurant overlooking Lake Arenal

mountain town, this one settled in the 1950s by draft-resisting Quakers from Alabama.

Expats are scattered all around the stunning artificial Lake Arenal (there's a town, or what's left of it, at the bottom of that body of water). Some expats base themselves in La Fortuna, the lively small town from which tourists take off for volcano hikes, trips to the swinging bridges in the jungle, horseback riding, or visits to nearby waterfalls. Others are secreted away in the folds of the hills surrounding the lake; some are in the towns of Nuevo Arenal and Tilarán.

Do advance research to discover some of the local community groups, and attend a meeting or two. There are groups looking after the area's ecology, groups that work to spay and neuter stray animals; and of course more purely social groups that meet for lunch or activities.

A Week in Guanacaste and the Nicoya Peninsula

The northern Pacific region of Guanacaste is one of the hottest expat areas in the country. Its beaches draw surfers, sport fishers, and divers. It is the driest and sunniest part of the country, with nary a drop falling between December and April. The Daniel Oduber International Airport in Liberia has begun to receive more and more international flights, and it's only about an hour from the coast (flying in to San José means a four- or five-hour drive to northern Guanacaste).

Start in the Playas del Coco area, where a string of beach communities—Playa Hermosa, Playa Panama, and Playa Ocotal—are no more than 30 minutes from Coco, which has the most amenities of the lot: banks, a post office, and many well-stocked supermarkets. You might want to drive an hour north to see the impressive and very isolated Four Seasons Resort on the Gulf of Papagayo.

Head south down the coast, stopping in at Playa Flamingo with its full-service marina and sportfishing and diving opportunities.

Spend a day or two in Tamarindo and see how a fishing village can mushroom into a well-equipped resort area while still having dubious roads. There is no shortage of real estate agents in the area to show you what's available.

Then breathe a sigh of relief and leave the mixed-blessing bustle behind, striking out into less congested areas.

Head south, either just meandering where the road takes you (this is more possible in the dry season) or settling for a few days in the Nosara-Playa Sámara area, midway down the peninsula, or at the tip of the Nicoya, in the Montezuma-Mal País-Santa Teresa area.

A Week on the Central and Southern Pacific Coast

If you start in Jacó and head south, ending up in the surf haven of Pavones or on the rainforested Osa Peninsula, you'll see the full range of Pacific coastal habitats, from hyper-developed to way out there. In general, land prices drop and amenities disappear the farther south you go.

In and around Jacó are hundreds of condos on offer and hundreds more in various stages of construction. A few miles north of Jacó lies the five-star Marriott Los Sueños resort, marina, and golf course, which is definitely worth visiting, if only for the feeling of being inside a luxurious bubble. Continuing in that vein, have a drink at the nearby and over-the-top Hotel Villas Caletas, where the prices are nearly as stunning as the view.

Come down to earth and sit in a café or ice cream parlor in downtown Jacó, watching the parade of surfers, backpackers, locals, and tourists throng the sidewalks of this burgeoning beach town.

In Quepos and along the road to Manuel Antonio National Park, take in the hotels and homes perched on the forested hills with views of the beaches below.

Drive south and check in at Dominical, sometimes called a "tropical Big Sur." See if you can spot any whales at Ballena Marine National Park (*ballena* means

"whale"). Stop for lunch or dinner at one of the excellent international restaurants near the French-Canadian stronghold of Ojochal. Set aside some time for surfing, visiting waterfalls, diving, birding, or kayaking—this area is gorgeous and not as heavily touristed as Jacó and Manuel Antonio.

Still farther south, you'll need to decide whether to head on to the Osa Peninsula, basing yourself in Puerto Jiménez, with its enviable position right on the Golfo Dulce, or head to the scrappy port city of Golfito and on to the end-of-the-road surf town of Pavones, with its legendary left-breaking wave. Either way you'll get a taste of this tropical wild west, great for those who want to really get away from it all. This part of the trip will be harder in the rainy season—ask about weather and road conditions. If you don't want to be denied between May and November, drive a powerful and high-clearance four-wheel-drive vehicle when you're traveling. But even the most impressive vehicle can't cross a raging river, so be prepared to be flexible about where you'd like to go.

On your way back to San José for your flight home, you can either retrace your steps along the coast or head inland at Dominical and pass through San Isidro de El General, an agrarian crossroads town with its fair share of amenities and a very different feel from the coast.

ONE MONTH: SEEING IT ALL

Ah, a month in Costa Rica. If you're considering a stay of a month or longer, you may already know where you think you'd like to live. If so, I encourage you to spend the entire trip in that one place. Only then will you start to get a sense of the town or city's day-to-day rhythms. And if you're going to be one month in one place, this may be the time to sign up for Spanish classes. Learning Spanish is the single most important thing you can do to prepare for a move to Costa Rica.

If you're still in shopping mode, however, this itinerary will give you a lot of information as you try to decide where in this beautiful country to make your new home. A car (it's best to rent a high-clearance four-wheel drive) will make most of this trip much, much easier, though the last part of the trip (on the Caribbean coast) could easily be done without one.

Days 1-5: San José and Environs

Visit the towns mentioned in the 10-day itinerary: Los Yoses and San Pedro in the west; Rohrmoser and La Sabana to the north; and the western suburbs of Escazú, Santa Ana, and Ciudad Colón. Travel farther north to get a sense of Heredia and Alajuela or Sarchí and Grecia. Dine in Escazú, read the papers, talk to real estate agents, and sample some of the other activities mentioned in *A Week in the Central Valley* on page 79.

Days 6-8: Zona Norte

Travel north to La Fortuna and explore Arenal Volcano, Lake Arenal, Nuevo Arenal, and Tilarán. Spend a day in lush Monteverde. (For more ideas, see the itinerary on page 80.)

If you like, spend more time in San José and Zona Norte.

Days 9-15: Guanacaste and the Nicoya Peninsula

Start north in the Playas del Coco area and drive down the coast to the southern tip (Mal País), exploring towns along the way. The unpredictable roads are best tackled during dry season (December-April). (To explore the area further, see the itinerary on page 81.)

Days 16-21: Central and Southern Pacific Coast

Take the car ferry from Paquera (on the southern Nicoya Peninsula) to Puntarenas, then head south to Jacó. Quepos and Manuel Antonio are an hour or so from Jacó. Dominical is another hour from Quepos.

Head south for the Osa Peninsula and beyond. Choose to visit a few but not all of the following: Drake Bay, Corcovado National Park, Puerto Jiménez, Golfito, Playa Zancudo, Pavones. (To explore the area further, see the itinerary on page 82.)

WELCOME TO COSTA RICA
PLANNING YOUR FACT-FINDING TRIP

small town bus station

Days 22-24: San Vito and San Isidro

On your way from the Pacific coast back up to the San José area (you need to go this way to get to the Caribbean coast, your next and last stop on this itinerary), pass through the southern inland valley and stop at San Vito, a mountain town with an Italian flavor, and San Isidro de El General, a bustling crossroads town that is *puro Tico.*

Days 25-29: Caribbean Coast

Take in Costa Rica's less-visited coast, starting up north in Tortuguero (no cars here—you must fly or take a boat), then heading south for Cahuita and Puerto Viejo for surfing, biking, partying, and lounging.

Day 30: Back to San José

As you return to the capital city for your flight home, how does it feel now that you've seen the rest of the country? Some will appreciate all the amenities San José has to offer even more; others will find the urban chaos even less tolerable now that they've seen the remote beauty of some of the rest of the country.

Whatever your response, you'll go home with a wild assortment of vivid impressions that you'll need a while to absorb. If you've taken photos and recorded important points in a notebook, it'll help you continue to sort through your experiences even after you're back at work and your Costa Rica trip seems like a dream

you can barely remember. Keep those memories alive, and come back soon.

ONE MONTH: SETTLING IN

Let's say you've been here before, and you're pretty sure you want to relocate to Dominical or Grecia or Puerto Viejo. A great way to decide for sure is to spend at least a month in your area of choice.

Wherever you go, take the time to see with a resident's eye. Is this neighborhood safe after dark? Are there schools nearby for your kids? Where would you shop for food if you lived in this remote beach town? What are three-bedroom houses going for up that hill with a killer view? Where is the nearest medical care?

Check in with real estate agents and ask them to show you around. Find out where the expats congregate and make a point of hanging out there. Ask them what it's like to live here. What do they miss most? What brought them here? Is life in Costa Rica what they had expected?

Do things you'd do if you lived here. Get a haircut. Attend a church service. Read the local paper. See if there's an English-language reading group or an AA meeting in town. Go shopping for fresh fruit and vegetables. Sit on the beach and try to name all the colors of the sunset.

This is also a good time to lay the groundwork for that new job or business. Look for people engaged in similar or complementary endeavors. Pick their brains; take in the lay of the land.

Practicalities

Popular hotels fill up fast, especially during the über-high seasons of Easter week and Christmas-New Year. Book early and expect to pay more during high season—sometimes a *lot* more. Also contact car rental places early to get good rates and the car of your choice.

When booking a hotel (especially if you're right there at the front desk), offering to pay cash can sometimes get you a discounted rate. Be aware too that some hotels will quote you the cash price and then charge extra when you pay with a credit card. Try to nail everything down ahead of time.

Many hotels do their repairs or expansions during the low season (May-November). This can be a less crowded and less pricey time to visit, but be aware it also may be noisier. If you don't want to wake up to hammering or power tools at 6am, ask the hotel if they will be under construction during your proposed visit.

In terms of food, I wouldn't count Costa Rican food among the world's tastiest cuisines, but the *casado*—a typical meal consisting of meat, rice, beans, and a small cabbage salad—may start to grow on you. And areas with a critical mass of expats often have excellent restaurants, as transplants from France, Italy, Israel, and other countries bring culinary traditions from their homelands into their new lives.

If you're looking for value, try a *soda*, which in Costa Rica is somewhere between a café and a full-fledged restaurant. *Sodas* usually serve economical Tico-style meals, including the omnipresent *casado*.

SAN JOSÉ AREA
Accommodations
Hotel Aranjuez (Calle 19 between Avenidas 11 and 13, tel. 506/2256-1825, U.S. toll-free tel. 877/898-8663, fax 506/2223-3528, www.hotelaranjuez. com, US$42-70 per night for a double room) is a popular budget to midrange option in Barrio Aranjuez. It's within walking distance of downtown San José. This labyrinthine hotel sprawls across five contiguous old houses in a quiet, historic, and somewhat run-down neighborhood. Some rooms can be cramped and dark, but others are quite nice (ask to see what's available), and all are clean and satisfactory given the low price. Amenities include voicemail in each room, Wi-Fi (and a few computer terminals if you don't have a laptop), a small locked parking area, and luggage storage if you want to travel light for the rest of your trip. Great common areas (you'll meet lots of fellow travelers if you so choose) include an open-air dining room set in lush gardens and offering an ample and varied buffet-style breakfast that's included in the nightly rate. Make reservations as early as possible—this place fills fast. The reservation process can be lengthy and frustrating at times, and some people complain that the front desk clerks aren't overly friendly, but then again they are extremely busy, as the hotel is almost always full. Across the street (in a modern five-story building) they have fully furnished apartments to rent by the month (US$580-1,400).

Across the street is **Kap's Place** (Calle 19 between Avenidas 11 and 13, tel. 506/2221-1161, www.kapsplace.com), a smaller, less lively version of Hotel Aranjuez, with slightly lower prices and free breakfast.

A good budget option closer to downtown is **Costa Rica Guesthouse** (Avenida 6, between Calles 21 & 25, tel. 506/2223-7034, www.costa-rica-guesthouse.com,

US$35-50), basic but clean, safe, and quiet; some rooms have views of downtown or the mountains. Breakfast is included, parking is free, and they'll send a shuttle to the airport for you (for a fee).

Nearby is **Costa Rica Backpackers** (Avenida 6, between Calles 21 & 25, 506/2221-6191, http://costaricabackpackers.com, from US$15), a hostel with cheap bunks and the opportunity to meet others exploring the country on a budget.

If you want to be on the west side of town, closer to the airport, try **Aparthotel La Sabana** (across from the large green expanse of La Sabana Park; Sabana Norte, from Rostipollos Restaurant head 150 meters north, 506/2220-2422, www.apartotel-lasabana.com, from US$95). It has a pool, nice grounds, and comfortable rooms. Breakfast is included.

If you're not coming into San José proper and just want a comfortable place convenient to the airport, there are the expected chain hotels like the Marriott, Double Tree, Holiday Inn Express, and the very closest to the airport on Highway 1/Airport Boulevard, Hampton Inn and Suites. In general the chain hotels here will be a little less expensive and a little less impressive than their sister properties in the United States.

If you'd prefer a place outside San José but not so close to the airport that you hear planes roaring overhead, consider **Casa Bella Rita** (www.casabellarita.com, tel. 506/2249-3722, cell 506/8980-1137, double rooms from US$135), an appealing bed-and-breakfast perched on the rim of a scenic canyon between Santa Ana and Ciudad Colón. Owners Javier and Alejandra (who took over from Steve and Rita in 2016) preside over six charming rooms of various sizes. I love the Canopy Room: it feels like an attic hideaway in some rich aunt's mansion, with sloped beamed ceilings and views of the nearby hills and canyon. With a pool, hammocks,

and breakfast made to order, this is a true "soft landing" into the Central Valley. If you drive (rather than take a taxi), there's secure parking.

Further afield but worth the trip is **Villa Blanca** (tel. 506/2461-0300, www.villablanca-costarica.com, from $US190) on the road from San Ramon to La Fortuna. A worthwhile side trip and splurge, this boutique hotel is set amid a huge swath of misty and beautiful cloud forest. Wander by yourself on the well-maintained paths or benefit from a professional guide's good eye on tours to see resplendent quetzals, apple-green frogs, or the fascinating nighttime denizens of the zone. The hotel even has its own scientific research station.

Food

Places that try to do too much usually get into trouble, but **Tin Jo** (Calle 11 between Avenidas 6 and 8, tel. 506/2221-7605, Mon.-Thurs. 11:30am-2:30pm and 6:00pm-10pm, Fri.-Sat. 11:30am-2:30pm and 6:00pm-11pm, Sun. noon-9pm), in front of Teatro Lucho Barahona in downtown San José, takes on a full range of Asian cuisines, from Japanese tempura to Indian curry, and is the delicious exception to the rule. Highlights include creative cocktails, vegetarian-friendly offerings, and real cloth napkins!

Inexpensive **Vishnu** (Avenida 1 between Calles 1 and 3, tel. 506/2223-4434, daily 7am-9pm) is a chain of eight vegetarian restaurants with locations all over San José; try the one on a few blocks east of the big downtown post office. Vishnu serves fruit plates, filling *platos del día* (soup, salad, entrée, and dessert) for about US$8, and good smoothies. At the front counter you can get good whole-grain bread and hefty slices of banana bread.

Another inexpensive healthy option is **Restaurante Shakti** (Avenida 8 between

The café in the lobby of the National Theater is a great place to get an iced cappuccino and a light lunch.

Calles 13 and 11, tel. 506/2222-4475, http://restauranteshakti.com, Mon.-Fri. 7:30am-7pm, Sat. 8am-6pm). Formerly a vegetarian place, this appealing, airy restaurant still offers salads and fresh fruit juices and whole-grain bread but has added fish and chicken dishes to the mix. Upstairs, you'll find **Hostel Shakti** (http://hostelshakti.com).

Step into **Esquina de Buenos Aires** (Calle 11 near Avenida 4, behind the Soledad Church, tel. 506/2223-1909 or 506/2257-9741, Mon.-Fri. 11:30am-3pm and 6pm-11pm; Sat.-Sun. noon-11pm), an artfully lit restaurant with white tablecloths, flickering candlelight, and tango on the sound system, and you'll wonder if you're still in Costa Rica. Indulge in an Argentine *parrilla* (mixed grill), pasta with smoked marlin, spinach and gorgonzola, or grilled shrimp (to name just a few of the many options). Sip an Argentine malbec, tempranillo, or syrah, a Chilean chardonnay, or an Italian pinot grigio. Cozy and stylish, it's great for dates and special occasions. Reservations are recommended.

Alma de Café (Avenida 2 at Calle 3, tel. 506/2010-1119, www.almadecafe. cr, Mon.-Sat. 9am-7pm) is a lovely high-ceilinged café tucked inside the architecturally stunning National Theater. Soak up the Old World charm while sipping espresso and enjoying salads, sandwiches, smoothies, and great desserts.

Sights and Activities

The **Pre-Columbian Gold Museum** (Avenida Central at Calle 5, tel. 506/2243-4202, www.museosdelbancocentral.org, open daily) is right in the center of the capital behind the **National Theater.** The museum has a 1,600-piece collection of pre-Columbian gold objects that date from 500 to 1500 AD, ranging from intricately worked breastplates to sacred objects used in shamanic rituals. It also has stone and ceramic objects on display, but for a glimpse of the green milky stone that was worth even more than gold, walk several blocks north to the **Jade Museum** (Avenida Central, between Calle 13 y 13 bis, tel. 506/2521-6610,

Mon.-Sun., 10am-5pm). On display are jade pendants and other forms of jewelry, as well as an exhibit showing jade used as a decorative inlay in teeth and another demonstrating how the hard translucent stone was worked.

The Children's Museum (Calle 4 at Avenida 9, on a hill above downtown San José; tel. 506/2258-4929, www.museocr.org) in a huge turreted building that used to house a prison, was Central America's first interactive museum and is a fun place for kids to run around and learn about everything from earthquakes to dragons (there's a great Nightmare-Eating Dragon display, where visitors jot down their nightmare, put it in a box, and rest assured that the formidable dragon, salvaged from a parade float, will have it for dinner). In late 2016, a small Penitentiary Museum opened in the same building (which also houses a gallery and the auditorium where the Miss Costa Rica pageant is held). Visit the original cells, with their massive doors, and see how the prisoners lived.

In Escazú, Biesanz Woodworks (tel. 506/2289-4337, www.biesanz.com, Mon.-Fri. 8am-5pm, Sat. Dec.-Apr., 9am-3pm) sells exquisite (and expensive) wooden bowls and boxes made of tropical hardwood. It's not easy to find; look on its website for directions.

ZONA NORTE
Accommodations
There are countless places to stay around Lake Arenal, from hostels in La Fortuna to lakeside *casitas* and volcano-view lodges. One of the more unusual options is Rancho Margot (tel. 506/8302-7318, www.ranchomargot.org, from US$139 for a double occupancy bungalow and from US$39 per person for a bed in the bunkhouse). The rancho is primarily a successful organic farm and ranch, with

students of sustainable agriculture coming for workshops and hands-on experience. Nonworking visitors are also well provided for. Practice yoga in the open-air pavilion alongside the rushing Caño Negro River, soak in a hot pool with views of the wooded slopes near Arenal Volcano, and taste the food that is grown and raised almost entirely on-site. A big highlight for me was a tour of the 380-acre farm and ranch (included in the price of lodging), where you learn just what goes into making the place self-sustaining. It's positively inspiring! They also have horseback riding, mountain biking, kayaking on the lake, and other activities. It's located about 30 minutes from La Fortuna, 4 kilometers (2.4 miles) past the village of El Castillo on the rutted road around the south side of the lake.

If you'd prefer a more luxurious and conveniently located spot where people don't wax eloquent about compost, try Hotel Silencio de Campo (tel. 506/2479-7055, www.hotelsilenciodelcampo.com, from US$195, tax and breakfast included), 5 kilometers (3.1 miles) west of the center of La Fortuna. This Costa Rican-owned hotel offers up 21 individual slant-roofed casitas with stunning views of active Arenal Volcano from their front porches. The casitas have tiled floors, hardwood paneling, beamed ceilings, and two queen beds. They are spotlessly clean, spacious, and appealing, and each has two large windows, a private bath, air-conditioning, a coffeemaker, cable TV, a small fridge, and a safe box. One of the casitas is handicapped accessible. The beautifully landscaped property also features two swimming pools, a restaurant, a thermal hot spring pool, and spa services. The staff gets consistently rave reviews for friendliness and helpfulness-they can help you book tours and tell you about the area.

Food

Gingerbread Restaurant (2 kilometers/1.3 miles south of Nuevo Arenal on the lake road, tel. 506/2694-0039, http://gingerbreadarenal.com, Tues.-Sat. 5pm-9pm, cash only, call or make reservations on website) has been called "arguably the best restaurant in northwestern Costa Rica (if not the entire country)." That's a lot to live up to, but when chef Eyal Ben-Manachem cooked for us, we kept grinning and shaking our heads in near disbelief that the food did indeed warrant such praise. Ben-Manachem came from Israel to Costa Rica in 2003, and it was this country's gain. He creates an inspired fusion of French, Mediterranean, and California cuisine using the freshest local ingredients, some of which come from Rancho Margot's organic farm. The menu changes nightly, but I loved the caprese salad and the beef medallions (perhaps the tenderest beef I've had in Costa Rica) and the bread pudding for dessert. The prices seem high for Costa Rica, but the portions are meant to be shared, and they did provide plenty for two hungry people. Ben-Manachem is somewhat notorious for his strong personality and his habit of telling people what they should order. "I don't like people," he admitted to me. "But I like feeding people." Let Ben-Manachem feed you. You won't be disappointed.

Sights and Activities

About 5 kilometers (3.1 miles) south of La Fortuna lies **La Fortuna Waterfall,** a stunning cascade that plummets into a steep ravine. You can walk or drive from town, and then (after paying a small entrance fee) make your way down a sometimes slippery trail to the falls. Use the handrail! The pool at the base of the falls is lovely, but it's best not to go for a dip in the churning waters; swimming is safer a little way down the river (follow the path). If you're going to walk all the way, it's best to start relatively early in the morning, thus avoiding the midday heat.

Want to kayak, river raft, or rappel down a waterfall? **Desafio Adventure** (behind the church in La Fortuna, tel. 506/2479-0020 or toll-free U.S./Canada tel. 855/818-0020, www.desafiocostarica.com) is the outfitter of choice. Run by Suresh, an Indian-American kayaking madman, and his lovely and able wife, Christine, Desafio hires excellent guides and treats them well. They are deeply involved in the community, and they have a stellar safety record. Best of all, their trips are seriously fun.

There are no paths in remote **Caño Negro,** a swampy reserve up near the Nicaraguan border, often visited as a day trip from La Fortuna. The park's 24,620 acres (9,969 hectares) of lowland forest, rivers, lakes, and marshes draw fishing enthusiasts, wildlife fanatics, and birders, along with millions of migrating birds.

The park is right in the middle of the flyway for birds migrating from both the north and the south. Birds arrive to spend the northern winter (December-April, Costa Rica's summer), including various species of ibis, wood storks, and herons, along with the bright-pink roseate spoonbill, snake-necked anhingas, and the country's largest colony of neotropical cormorants. It's also one of the few places to see the Nicaraguan grackle.

The bottle-green river also provides refuge for caimans, crocodiles, river turtles, and the Jesus Christ lizard, so called because the bright green reptile skitters over the surface as if it's walking on water. Spider, capuchin (white-faced), and howler monkeys cavort in the trees along the riverbank, and the lucky and sharp-eyed may glimpse an ocelot, cougar, tayra (small cat), or even the elusive jaguar.

enjoying the beach on the Nicoya Peninsula

Fishing is allowed in the reserve with a permit; anglers hook snook, *guapote,* alligator gars, drum fish, and tarpon.

GUANACASTE AND THE NICOYA PENINSULA
Accommodations

These accommodations are listed from north to south.

In Playas del Coco, check out **Rancho Armadillo** (tel. 506/2670-0108, www.ranchoarmadillo.com, from US$139 for a standard double room to US$204 for a four-bedroom bungalow), a laid-back boutique hotel on 25 landscaped acres (10 hectares) above the fray of the actual town. Staying at the Rancho is like visiting a friend, if you're lucky enough to have a friend with a really cool house in the tropics, fragrant ylang-ylang trees, visiting monkeys, wireless Internet, comfortable king-size beds, rainforest showers, and breakfasts that include homemade waffles and huge platters of fruit. On the road from Liberia to Playas del Coco, turn left 2 kilometers (1.3 miles) past the

turnoff to Playa Hermosa, at the pink condominiums.

In Playa Hermosa, there are plenty of condos, Airbnb homes, and midrange hotels to choose from. I like the relaxed, local vibe of **Hotel El Velero** (tel. 506/2672-1017, www.costaricahotel.net, from $US70-90), right on the beach. Its 22 rooms have AC, comfortably firm beds, TVs, safes, and good water pressure for the showers. There's a small pool but why bother when the ocean is just a few steps away? Meals are satisfactory at its mid-priced open-air restaurant, and sometimes freelance massage therapists set up their tables under the nearby trees on the beach.

Just south of Sámara (which is south of Nosara), I like the **Hideaway Hotel** (tel. 506/2656-1145, www.thehideawayplayas-amara.com, from US$79) with big-hotel amenities and comfort but small-hotel warmth and intimacy. The 12 rooms are clustered around a pool in lush and well-maintained grounds. It's a five-minute walk to the southern end of Playa Samara, and a short taxi ride (or long walk) to the town of Samara. The hotel is on the road from Samara to Carrillo, 150 meters (492 feet) from the ICE tower.

Food

These establishments are listed from north to south.

On the road between Liberia and the beaches (Playas del Coco, Playa Hermosa, Playa Potrero, Tamarindo) is an air-conditioned haven with good food, cocktails, and coffee drinks. **The Greenhouse** (Sugar Beach Road, tel. 506/2654-6150, www.thegreenhousecostarica.com) serves delicious salads, ceviche, and Asian-inspired main courses. It's a nice place to take a break if you're coming from or going to the Liberia airport.

Tucked away on a side street in Playas del Coco, **Villa Italia** (tel. 506/2670-0284, www.villaitaliacostarica.com, open 6-10pm, closed Sundays) serves excellent Italian food in an intimate setting. It's 300 meters (325 yards) west of the Ferreterria San Carlos; best to call ahead for directions.

An old open-air favorite right off the main traffic circle in Tamarindo and on the beach is **Nogui's Sunset Cafe** (tel. 506/2653-0029). Everyone else will be there; you'd better go too. Nogui's has good breakfasts as well as salads, sandwiches, and quiches for lunch, and you must go at sunset to have a drink and chat up the expat crowd. There's also a low-key bar, where you can watch the game. It's open all day, but call for the exact hours.

In Playa Sámara, head upstairs to stylish and lively **Bar Arriba** (main street of Sámara, tel. 506/2656-1052) for drinks, tapas, shrimp kabobs, and a great view of the main street of this little beach town. Twenty-something brothers Alan and Glenn Westman from Nebraska opened the place in July 2009, and it has been going strong ever since. There's a good selection of beer, wine, and spirits, plus Spanish-inspired salads and entrées. They're open from 5pm until "the last man standing." Glenn told me, "Older people might want to come before 8:30 or 9pm," after which it starts to get a little raucous and crowded. I didn't ask Glenn how old you had to be to qualify as "older," or remind him that even geezers like to party sometimes.

In Montezuma, I love **Cocolores** (tel. 506/2642-0348, 4:30-10pm, closed Mondays), behind the Hotel Pargo Feliz. The artfully prepared fish dishes often involve coconut milk. There is shaded outdoor seating a stone's throw from the beach, and stylish servers who sometimes need to be reminded of your order.

Sights and Activities

Cabo Blanco Nature Reserve near Montezuma is Costa Rica's oldest nature reserve. It was brought into being by two Scandinavian expats. It's about 11 kilometers (6.8 miles) from Montezuma; you can either walk (a long and rather dusty—or muddy—trek), drive, or find a taxi in Montezuma. There are two trails—one a 2-kilometer (1.3-mile) loop through primary forest, the other a 4-kilometer (2.5-mile) each way walk up and down through forest to the pristine and oft-deserted beach. Howler monkeys call from the trees, and brown pelicans glide on the updrafts.

THE CENTRAL AND SOUTHERN PACIFIC COAST
Accommodations

These accommodations are listed from north to south.

In Jaco, Canadian-run **Aparthotel Vista Pacífico** (tel. 506/2643-3261, www.vistapacifico.com, from US$72) has great views, great service, and good value. It's safe and clean, with a swimming pool, cable TV, kitchenettes, and two pet-friendly rooms. Note that it's on a hill above town—nice on the way down, not so fun on the trudge back up. Taxis are available. The owners also have beach houses for rent.

Coyaba Tropical Bed and Breakfast (tel. 506/2777-6279, www.coyabatropical.com, from US$105) is a small, recently renovated, gay-owned B&B near Manuel Antonio National Park that provides good value and a relaxed, homey atmosphere. Run by a male couple who promise "Canadian and Jamaican hospitality," the inn is also straight-friendly.

At **La Paloma Lodge** (tel. 506/2293-7502, www.lapalomalodge.com, moderate-expensive) in Drake Bay on the Osa Peninsula, you'll meet your fellow guests in an open-air dining room with long communal tables. Potted palms, ceiling fans, and cloth napkins make you think you're back in the British raj, but the stunning views of Drake Bay and beyond are *pura Tica*. Spacious bungalows, modestly furnished, dot the hillside and share the view; some are big enough to accommodate whole families. Bungalows 1 and 3 are especially nice. You'll arrive at this remote area of the Osa Peninsula by boat or light plane, and the lodge arranges all manner of tours—to Corcovado National Park and Caño Island, among others. The guides are excellent; ours knew just where to look for the giant sea turtles, manta rays, and sharks that scared us halfway out of our snorkels.

Another lodge down the hill, **Aguila de Osa** (tel. 506/2296-2190, www.aguiladeosa.com), with similar package deals and amenities, is also an excellent option.

Food

These restaurants are listed from north to south.

If you're tired of Costa Rican food, try **Lemon Zest** (tel. 506/2643-2591, http://lemonzestjaco.com, Mon.-Sat. 5pm-10pm) for excellent international cuisine on the main drag in Jacó. Chef Richard Lemon, who grew up in the Bahamas, aims to bring classic techniques and new flavor combinations to fresh local ingredients. House specialties include ahi tuna with pickled ginger teriyaki and sautéed spinach, Caribbean-style jerk pork chop with pineapple-chipotle sauce, and peanut butter ice cream pie.

It's a delectable surprise that the tiny town of Ojachal, 35 kilometers (21.7 miles) south of Dominical, has not one but two excellent French(ish) restaurants. I've had excellent meals at **Exotica** (tel. 506/2786-5050, 5-9pm Mon.-Sat.), 1 kilometer (0.6 mile) down the dirt road from the Ojachal turnoff. Robert Levesque from Sherbrooke, near Montreal, built the restaurant in 1998; he is the chef, while his wife, Lucy, makes the desserts. They have a good wine list and a wide selection of domestic and imported beer and liquors. Exotica offers everything from classics like beef bourguignon to innovative curries full of locally caught fish. Prices are moderate to expensive.

Another good option in Ojochal is **Citrus** (tel. 506/2786-5175, restocitrus@yahoo.ca, Tues.-Sat. 11am-10pm), which offers French classics like escargot and foie gras as well as Mediterranean-inspired dishes that make use of local fresh fish and produce.

THE CARIBBEAN COAST
Accommodations

Hotels are listed from north to south.

Even if you don't think you'd ever want to settle in a remote coastal hamlet with no roads or cars, you may want to visit the Tortuguero area, with its quiet canals, abundant wildlife, and nesting sea turtles.

There are at least a dozen lodges along the canals, some with room for hundreds of people, along with highly scheduled activities and lines at the cafeteria. Though these high-volume lodges can be a relative bargain, I much prefer the smaller, more exclusive lodging options like Tortuga Lodge and Manatus Lodge.

Tortuga Lodge & Gardens (tel. 506/2521-6099, www.tortugalodge.com, 3-day packages including food, lodging, transportation and tours start at US$598 per person), run by the venerable Costa Rica Expeditions, was one of the first lodges built in Tortuguero, has been continually upgraded, and is still one of the very nicest. It has wonderfully landscaped grounds and excellent food (complete with freshly baked bread) served in a spacious canal-side dining room. There's a fixed menu every day, drawing from fresh local ingredients. Charming rooms and suites have hardwood floors, screened windows, ceiling fans that really do keep the rooms cool, safes, quality beds and bed linens, good reading lamps, Wi-Fi, hammocks out on your deck, and thatched roofs. The staff is remarkably friendly and attentive, and the wildlife tours they arrange are led by experienced and pleasant guides. Those who must have air-conditioning or television will not be happy here, but everyone else will be ecstatic.

Manatus Lodge (tel. 506/4270-98197, www.manatuscostarica.com, three-day packages including food, lodging, transportation and tours start at US$475 pp in a quadruple room), is another small, well-run lodge with 12 separate luxurious cottages equipped with cable TV, air-conditioning, minibars, and even private outdoor sunbathing areas and showers (along with large indoor showers). Its alfresco dining room has an extensive menu, complete with a tempting selection of cocktails and wines by the glass.

In Tortuguero proper, near the Catholic Church, is **Casa Marbella B&B** (tel. 506/2833-0827 or 506/2709-8011, fax 506/2709-8094, safari@racsa.co.cr, starting around US$45). If you want to see Tortuguero the independent way, leaving behind lodges and package tours, try this in-town option run by Canadian-born biologist Daryl Loth and his Tica wife, Luz Denia Loth. These are modest but spotlessly clean and appealing accommodations right on the river and breakfast is included. I'm partial to Room 7, with a full-size and a single bed, a private bath, good cross-ventilation, and a view of the canal. Daryl used to give wildlife tours but now his colleague Roberto

lunch at Tortuga Lodge and Gardens in Tortuguero

comes highly recommended; he plies the waterways in a stable flat-bottomed boat equipped with a quiet, environmentally friendly four-stroke motor and a silent electric motor (less likely to scare away the wildlife). Turtle tours are also fascinating; nesting leatherbacks can be seen March-May, green turtles July-October.

About 1 kilometer (0.6 mile) north of Cahuita, **Playa Negra Guesthouse** (tel. 506/2755-0127, www.playanegra. cr, US$54-144) is an excellent choice. All rooms have fridges, coffeemakers, ceiling fans, and Wi-Fi. The colorful stand-alone cottages also have front porches (and some have kitchenettes). It's steps from the beach and a short walk to **Sobre las Olas** restaurant.

In Puerto Viejo, **Cabinas Tropical** (Avenida 67 between Calles 217 and 219, tel. 506/2750-0283, www.cabin-astropical.com, from US$45) is a clean and comfortable mid-range option, a 10-minute walk to the beach and everything in town but on a quiet back street. Of the 10 rooms, 8 are doubles, and 2 are bi-level rooms for three or four people. All rooms have private baths with abundant hot water and good showerheads, along with mini-fridges, fans, mosquito nets, satellite TV, quality mattresses, and a terrace with chairs and a hammock. A few rooms have air-conditioning. There's safe parking, and it's within a few blocks of where the bus leaves you if you arrive by public transit. The hotel is owned and operated by German-born Rolf Blancke, a biologist who writes about tropical flora and fauna. He gives tours of nearby wildlife reserves, accompanied by his Costa Rican wife, Juana, said to be a skilled "spotter" of animals and birds. They have also recently added a guided tropical fruit and spice tour on their private 5-acre (2-hectare) farm, where they grow more than 170 species of tropical fruits and spices.

Three blocks down the street from Cabinas Tropical is **Coco Loco Lodge** (Avenida 67 at Calle 311, tel. 506/2750-0281, www.cocolocolodge.com, US$50-100 depending on bungalow size and season) offers private and charming bungalows set on nicely landscaped grounds. No AC but good fans, comfortable beds, hardwood floors, thatched roofs, refrigerator, safe, and an utterly enjoyable shaded front porch equipped with hammock and table and chairs. Sabina from Austria runs this place, and she runs it well. Besides the bungalows, there are rooms above the main reception area that cost a little less than then the bungalows. Breakfast is available but not included in the room price.

Food

Restaurants are listed from north to south.

In the town of Tortuguero, there are many good juice bars, a few bakeries, and at least two very enjoyable restaurants. The **Budda Café** (main street near the ICE building, tel. 506/2709-8084, www. buddacafe.com, Mon.-Sun. noon-9pm, free Wi-Fi) has an enviable location right on the canal. It doesn't look like much from the (carless) street, but once inside you'll be charmed by the lush garden and the water views. Hang out, boat watch, or appreciate the sunset while savoring ITs Mediterranean-inspired pizzas, sandwiches, and pastas. Service is not unduly attentive; go with the desire to linger and you'll be fine.

Wild Ginger (tel. 506/2709-8240, www.wildgingercr.com, US$10-20) is a stylish open-air restaurant that serves delicious food drawing from both Caribbean and California cuisines. The owners are a young couple, he from Costa Rica and she from California, and they work hard to make this a welcoming, high-quality place. Feast on ginger chicken, mango bacon roulade,

Budda Café in Tortuguero

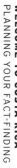

or a good old-fashioned cheeseburger smothered in guacamole. Top it off with a browned butter espresso brownie or a second or third fresh fruit daiquiri. It's located 150 meters (160 yards) north of the primary school in Tortuguero, along the beachfront path heading toward the Sea Turtle Conservancy museum and research station.

Sobre las Olas (tel. 506/2755-0109, Tues.-Sun. 2pm-10pm) in Cahuita is on the Playa Negra road (a short walk north of town). Right on the beach, this six-table wonder lets you dine alfresco on creative cuisine. There's lots of fresh fish, of course, but also treats like jerk chicken and pasta primavera, all for moderate prices.

One of the best things about the Zona Caribe is what they do with the country's ubiquitous rice and beans. On this island-inflected coast, they add coconut milk, and it makes all the difference. In Puerto Viejo, seek out a modest local place, like **Soda** or **Lidia's Place** (tucked into the back of town at Avenida 67 at Calle 217), often with just a few small tables and many local options. Order anything you want—shrimp, red snapper, jerk chicken—just make sure it comes with rice and beans (*not* the same as *gallo pinto*).

I like **Bread and Chocolate** (Calle 215 at Avenida 69, tel. 506/2750-0723) in Puerto Viejo, especially for breakfast, filter coffee, and handmade chocolate truffles made from local cacao. And everyone raves about Café Rico (Avenida 69 at Calle 217, tel. 506/2750- 0510), a long-standing favorite with a plant-filled open-air patio, a book exchange, and great food and coffee.

For a special dinner, try **La Casita Azul** (on the road from Puerto Viejo to Manzanillo, just past the Jaguar Rescue Center, tel. 506/8560-8186) for fresh and well-prepared seafood and a magical vibe. **El Refugio Grill** (on the road from Puerto Viejo to Manzanillo, near Punta Uva, 50 meters/164 feet south of Hotel Suerre, tel 506-2759 –9007) is a romantic, private place for delicious food, good wine, and caring service.

Sights and Activities

Activities are listed north to south.

In Tortuguero, be sure to take a **boat tour of the canals** and, if you've timed it right, **turtle nesting and hatching tours,** which happen at night on the beach. Pretty much every hotel and lodge you stay in will have guides it works with. Note that the premium lodges will charge you more for the same tours than the cheaper in-town lodging will—they take a bigger cut.

Avid fishermen and women will want to get in touch with **sport fishing captain Eddie Brown** in Tortuguero (tel. 506/8834-2221 or 506/8383-6097 or 506/8382-3350, http://captainediedorwn.com), who is considered one of the best tarpon fishermen and captains between Florida and Venezuela.

About an hour inland from Limón is **Veragua Rainforest Research & Adventure Park** (tel. 506/4000-0949, www.veraguarainforest.com, Tues.-Sat. 8am-3pm), where you can get your wildlife and adventure fix all in one 3,000-acre place. Scientists make use of the pristine rainforest and the well-equipped labs to do important work, including the discovery of new species. Day-trippers—often from cruise ships docked

in Limón—come for the zip line (canopy tour), the short aerial tram ride, and the snake, frog, insect, and butterfly exhibits that guarantee you up-close experiences with live fauna. An added bonus is that 95 percent of the facility is wheelchair accessible. It's also cooler here than on the oft-sweltering coast. When there are no cruise ships in port, you'll have the place pretty much to yourself—call for more information.

ATEC (Talamanca Association for Ecotourism and Conservation, tel. 506/2750-0398, www.ateccr.org) in Puerto Viejo is a grassroots group working to promote responsible tourism. Its Puerto Viejo office is a community center of sorts, offering Internet access, phone cards, photocopying, and tour information and booking. It offers everything from chocolate tours to dolphin watches to Caribbean cooking classes to visiting a women's art collective on the Bribrí reservation.

One of my favorite ATEC tours is a trip up the Sixaola River by motorized dugout to the remote Bribrí town of Yorkín, where visitors learn about the traditional indigenous skills of roof thatching, bow-and-arrow hunting, and roasting and grinding cacao beans to produce chocolate.

DAILY LIFE

MAKING THE MOVE

So you're all set. You've visited Costa Rica (preferably many times), done your homework, and you're still feeling the love. Your friends either think you're crazy or tell you to make sure your new house has a guest room. If you're making the move with family or friends, they are as ready as you are. And you've thought about what it will take—financially, logistically, and emotionally—to make the move of a lifetime. You're good to go.

But there are a few things to think about even before you get here.

First, consider what kind of residency status you'd like to have. Maybe you'll be content as a perpetual tourist, leaving Costa Rica every three months to maintain your legality. Or perhaps you'll want to plant your roots a little deeper, applying for *rentista, pensionado,* or *inversionista* status. This chapter gives detailed information about all the various options.

Those interested in permanent residency or citizenship will be in for a longer haul, and it should be noted that since 2010, marrying a Costa Rican citizen is no longer the short cut it once was (see page 106 for more information).

Next, think about what you want to bring with you and how best to do so. What might you be better off leaving behind? This chapter examines the relative merits of bringing your possessions into

Juan Santamaría International Airport, just outside of San José

the country as checked baggage on the plane, as air cargo, or by ship.

Even as your practical self is taking care of all these important details, keep on speaking terms with the adventurer inside, the part of you that came up with this crazy idea of moving to Costa Rica in the first place. You'll still need a heaping portion of audacity to get yourself across the threshold of your new life. As the proverb goes, you can't leap a 6-meter (20-foot) chasm in two 3-meter (10-foot) jumps.

Immigration and Visas

In March 2010, immigration regulations underwent an overhaul. The two biggest changes were that all legal foreign residents (in programs like the *pensionado* (retired) and *rentista* (nonretired) categories) must now sign up for medical insurance under the Costa Rican Social Security System (the CCSS, also known as the Caja), and that the two major categories of residency now require you to prove a larger monthly income than before.

But even these revised requirements are far from onerous. For health insurance, the Caja requires a monthly payment of 7-11 percent of your monthly income, with a dependent spouse covered

under that payment. The Caja offers very good medical care, probably the best in Central America, and just about everything is covered (see the *Health* chapter for more details).

The income requirements for *pensionado* (retired) and *rentista* (nonretired) residency categories are US$1,000 and US$2,500 a month, respectively. A married couple needs to show proof of only one monthly income; the other spouse can apply and be covered under his or her spouse's residency.

In 2012, further changes provided a few benefits to prospective residents. In the past, those people who wanted *rentista* status but were unable to prove a "permanent and stable" monthly investment income of US$2,500 had the option of putting down a lump sum equivalent to five years of US$2,500 per month, or US$150,000. Now, they only need to put down a lump sum of US$60,000.

Another positive change is that *inversionista* status used to require investment in an enterprise deemed of social benefit to Costa Rica, but now an investment in real estate will do the trick. The price tag has to be at least US$200,000, but now a prospective *inversionista* no longer has to prove they have a payroll account and employees. "That's a huge change," notes Roger Petersen, of Petersen & Philps law firm in Escazú.

BUREAUCRATIC HEADACHES

The *Tico Times* has called the agency that enforces immigration law "one of the country's most infamously inefficient bureaucracies" and noted that its policies subjected people to "astonishingly long lines and a mind-boggling lack of logic."

The agency in question is the Department of Immigration (Dirección General de Migración y Extranjería), which in turn is under the jurisdiction of the Ministry of Public Security and Police (Ministerio de Gobernación, Policía, y Seguridad Pública). There has been much effort in the past several years to streamline the application process, and there have been improvements. But there is still some confusion and frustration inherent in the process, not to mention a lot of waiting.

Even with the changes, immigration policy is anything but crystal clear, and enforcement (especially consistent enforcement) is even less so. Students of Costa Rican policy will find many contradictory statutes; it's often up to the individual official to play judge and jury, choosing which of the many laws he or she will enforce on any given day.

Lest you dismiss the situation as hopelessly Third World, remember that many U.S. agencies—the Internal Revenue Service (IRS) comes to mind—have been shown to operate in a similarly heavy-handed and arbitrary fashion. Big government means lots of laws; some are bound to contradict others. And then "public servants" around the world are often anything but, wielding their tiny swords with surprisingly lethal effect. When confronted with such officials, make nice. Count to 10, and then grit your teeth into a smile. For the moment, they have the power and you don't. Save your rage and dreams of revenge for later over a drink with friends. Then order another round.

APPLY FROM HOME OR WHILE IN COSTA RICA

In the past, Costa Rica's Department of Immigration required that residency applications be filed in your country of origin through the nearest Costa Rican Consulate. Now you also have the option of submitting your application directly to the Department of Immigration in San José. But even if you opt for the latter approach, you'll be interacting with the consular office in your home country to have your documents authenticated.

Filing from Costa Rica is more expensive: in addition to the US$50 application fee, you will be charged US$200 for a change of status fee, since you will be changing your status from that of tourist to the new category you are applying for. (Also see *The Application Process* on page 107. For lists of Costa Rican embassies and consulates in the United States and Canada, see page 330 in the *Resources* section.)

DUAL CITIZENSHIP

One more thing you should know is that if you gain any type of residency or even citizenship in Costa Rica, your U.S. or Canadian citizenship is not affected. And there's no problem on the Costa Rican end of things either. Since 1996 this country has recognized dual citizenship. The change in policy came about when Dr. Franklin Chang, a Costa Rica-born scientist and NASA astronaut, became a U.S. citizen and was consequently stripped of his Costa Rican citizenship. There was a public outcry—the country didn't want to lose such an illustrious Tico to the United States—and in response the policy was changed.

How does the United States look upon dual residency? The U.S. State Department website explains, "The U.S. Government recognizes that dual nationality exists but does not encourage it as a matter of policy because of the problems it may cause. Claims of other countries on dual-national U.S. citizens may conflict with U.S. law, and dual nationality may limit U.S. Government efforts to assist citizens abroad. The country where a dual national is located generally has a stronger claim to that person's allegiance."

Long story short: They don't like it, but it isn't illegal.

TOURIST VISAS

North Americans don't have to apply for visas to enter the country; a valid passport is all you'll need. Upon arrival you'll get a stamp on your passport authorizing a 90-day stay.

At the airport or the border you could be asked to prove that you have sufficient funds to support yourself for the time you intend to be here. They may also ask you to show a return or onward plane or bus ticket. In the past, this rarely happened. The country's new approach to immigration may or may not change that lack of enforcement.

You can renew your 90-day visa by going to another country for at least 72 hours. When you come back into Costa Rica, you'll get another 90 days on your visa. Doing this again and again, however, can get you in trouble. If you know you want to be in Costa Rica for a long time, it's better to go the legal route and get residency.

Reasons to Go Legit

There have always been shady ways to bypass official immigration requirements but still have the proper stamps and papers. They are, of course, indisputably illegal, not to mention that they're often not very effective. A guy knows a guy who can take care of it—and suddenly your money and passport are long gone.

Some expats brag about how their visa expired years ago and they never have any trouble. But if you have anything to lose in Costa Rica—a house, a business, a family—this gray-area existence is apt to make you a little bit anxious. And the fact that being a perpetual tourist is so much more difficult now makes legal residency look a lot more attractive.

Even if you don't have anything to lose in Costa Rica, there are reasons to apply for residency. "I'm not sure why I was so into getting those papers," says Peggy Windle, who took early retirement from her teaching job in Arizona and moved to Costa Rica. "I want to belong somewhere, I guess. To not be 100 percent vagabond."

Acronyms of Costa Rica

Like the rest of the world, Costa Rica is acronym crazy. Who can blame it? Would you rather tell a friend you've just come from the Equipo Básico de Atención Integral de Salud (your neighborhood public health clinic) or the EBAIS (eh-BICE)? Here's a quick key to some of the acronyms you'll be using frequently in Costa Rica.

- **AyA** (AH-ee-ah): Instituto Costarricense de Acueductos y Alcantarillados (Costa Rican Water and Sewer Institute), responsible for all water services in Costa Rica
- **CCSS, or the Caja:** Caja Costarricense de Seguro Social (Costa Rican Social Security System). In writing it's often CCSS, but in speech it's always the Caja (CAH-hah). This mammoth organization is in charge of the national health care system and some aspects of Social Security. EBAIS (neighborhood health clinics) are part of the Caja.
- **CONAVI** (co-NAH-bee): Consejo Nacional de Vialidad (National Roadway Council), part of MOPT, in charge of highway construction and maintenance
- **EBAIS** (eh-BICE): Equipos Básicos de Atención Integral de Salud (Basic Attention Integral Health Care Centers), or neighborhood health clinics. Part of the CCSS/the Caja.
- **ICE** (EE-say): Instituto Costarricense de Electricidad (Costa Rican Electricity Institute), responsible for electricity and phone service
- **INA** (EE-nah): Instituto Nacional de Aprendizaje (National Training Institute), provides vocational courses to adults

Types of Residency

There are countless types of residency, from refugee to diplomatic status, but for the purposes of the average North American or European, five of these will be of interest: *pensionado* (pensioner or retiree), *rentista* (loosely translated as "small investor" but often referred to simply as "non-retired"), *inversionista* (investor), permanent residency, and citizenship. Note that officials may do an international background search on people applying for residency.

PENSIONADO (RETIRED)

Most retired people opt for this category, which requires you to prove at least US$1,000 a month in pension income (and to prove that same income each time you renew your residency). The income can come from a public source, like the U.S. government, or a private source, like the brokerage house that administers your IRA account. You must document that you will be receiving at least US$12,000 a year and arrange to have the checks deposited to a Costa Rican account in colones, not dollars. For a married couple, the spouse with less (or no) retirement income is considered a dependent, and a dependent need show no proof of income—he or she rides free on the partner's US$1,000. Children under 18 (or a child between 18 and 25 enrolled in university) can also be claimed as dependents and receive the same immigration status as their parents.

The downside is that two people's incomes cannot be combined to make up the required US$1,000 a month, although

- **INS** (eens): Instituto Nacional de Seguros (National Insurance Institute), currently the only authorized dealer of insurance in Costa Rica, although implementation of CAFTA (yet another acronym, standing for the Central American Free Trade Agreement) will change this
- **MINAET** (mee-NIGH-et): Ministerio de Ambiente, Energía y Telecomunicaciones (Environment, Energy, and Telecommunications Ministry). Was MINAE, until the telecommunications part added the final *T* to the name.
- **MOPT** (mope): Ministerio de Obras Públicas y Transportes (Public Works and Transport Ministry), regulates public transportation as well as car and driver's licenses. Traffic police *(tránsitos)* are part of MOPT.
- **OIJ** (oh-ee-HO-ta): Organismo de Investigación Judicial (Judicial Investigation Police). The federal police, sometimes likened to the FBI.
- **RACSA** (ROCK-saw): Radiográfica Costarricense, part of ICE and in charge of providing Internet access
- **RITEVE** (ree-TAY-vay): Revisión Técnica Vehicular (Vehicular Technical Inspection)
- **UCR** (ooh-say-EH-ray): Universidad de Costa Rica (University of Costa Rica), located in the San José neighborhood of San Pedro
- **UNA** (OO-nah): Universidad Nacional (National University), located in Heredia, north of San José

the combined income sources of one person will do the trick. If the pensioner is a little short of the US$1,000 a month, the balance can be made up by depositing five years' worth of the difference in a Costa Rican bank.

You can't work as an employee, but you can own and receive income from a business.

RENTISTA (NON-RETIRED)

Those who have not yet reached retirement age but have managed to make investments that bring in regular income will want to consider the *rentista* option. You'll need to prove a monthly income of US$2,500 (usually a CD or annuity), guaranteed by a banking institution. Another option is to deposit US$60,000 (US$2,500 a month for two years) in a Costa Rican bank, which will authorize you to withdraw US$2,500 of your money each month. If, after two years of *rentista* status, you

apply for and receive permanent residency, you can withdraw all the money from the account.

Other details of the *rentista* visa are similar to those of a *pensionado:* You can own a business but not work as an employee; you may be in trouble if you spend more than two years outside of Costa Rica without returning; and dependents, whether spouse or child, enjoy the same immigration status as is awarded to the applicant.

INVERSIONISTA (INVESTOR)

Although you can legally own and operate any sort of business in Costa Rica even if you only have a tourist visa, an investment of at least US$200,000 in any business venture will qualify you for *inversionista* residency status. The amount is less if you invest in a sector the government deems a priority, like tourism, forestry, or low-income housing. How much less you need

Types of Residency at a Glance

PENSIONADO (RETIRED)

- **Requirements:** Requires proof of US$1,000 per month income from permanent pension source or retirement fund
- **Length of Stay:** Immigration reforms of 2012 stipulate that if a person with temporary residency (*pensionado, rentista,* or *inversionista*) stays out of Costa Rica for more than two years, they *may* lose their residency status.
- **Spouse/Dependents:** Can claim spouse and dependents under age 18
- **Employment:** Cannot work as an employee
- **Business Income:** Can own a company and receive income

RENTISTA (NON-RETIRED)

- **Requirements:** Requires proof of US$2,500 per month for at least two years (US$60,000), guaranteed by a banking institution.
- **Length of Stay:** The new immigration law (number 8764) stipulates that if a person with temporary residency (*pensionado, rentista,* or *inversionista*) stays out of Costa Rica for more than two years, they *may* lose their residency status.
- **Spouse/Dependents:** Can claim spouse and dependents under age 18 (with an increase in monthly income required of US$500 per child)
- **Employment:** Cannot work as an employee
- **Business Income:** Can own a company and receive income

INVERSIONISTA (INVESTOR)

- **Requirements:** US$200,000 in any business as of 2012, including an investment in real estate
- **Length of Stay:** The new immigration law (number 8764) stipulates that if a person with temporary residency (*pensionado, rentista,* or *inversionista*) stays out of Costa Rica for more than two years, they *may* lose their residency status.

to invest depends on how the government is prioritizing sectors at the time you apply for your residency.

For any investment, exercise extreme caution—many people who come to Costa Rica seem to leave their common sense at home. Perhaps lulled by the tropical climate and the friendliness of the people, they trust too easily and don't do their due diligence checking out every facet of the project before putting any money down. While living in the tropics is relatively easy, making a business profitable here is perhaps even more challenging than it would be at home.

LENGTH OF STAY REQUIREMENTS FOR *PENSIONADO, RENTISTA,* AND *INVERSIONISTA* RESIDENCY CATEGORIES

The old residency law (number 8487) said that people with temporary residence could lose their residency status if they were out of Costa Rica for more than six months of the year; even earlier regulations mentioned that you had to be in Costa Rica for four months every year, not necessarily all at once. But according to Roger Petersen, author of *The Legal Guide to Costa Rica,* the new law (number 8764), backed up by even newer changes in 2012, has a more generous provision,

- **Spouse/Dependents:** Cannot claim spouse and dependents under age 18; they must be processed separately
- **Employment:** Income allowed from the project
- **Business Income:** Can own a company and receive income

PERMANENTE (PERMANENT RESIDENCY)

- **Requirements:** First-degree relative status with a Costa Rican citizen through marriage to a citizen or by having a child in Costa Rica, *or* may apply after three years in another type of residency. Note that the immigration reforms of March 2010 provide for "closing the loophole" of marriages of convenience entered into solely for the purpose of obtaining residency.
- **Length of Stay:** The new immigration law (number 8764) stipulates that if a person with temporary residency (*pensionado, rentista,* or *inversionista*) stays out of Costa Rica for more than two years, they *may* lose their residency status.
- **Spouse/Dependents:** Cannot claim spouse or dependents under age 18; they must be processed separately
- **Employment:** Can work
- **Business Income:** Can own a company and receive income

REPRESENTANTE (COMPANY VISA)

- **Requirements:** Applicant must be a director of a company meeting certain requirements, such as employing a minimum number of local workers as established by the labor law, with financial statements certified by a public accountant.
- **Spouse/Dependents:** Cannot claim spouse or dependents under age 18; they must be processed separately
- **Employment:** Can earn an income from the company
- **Business Income:** Can own a company and receive income

saying that if someone with temporary residency (*pensionado, rentista,* or *inversionista*) stays out of Costa Rica for more than two years, they *may* lose their residency status, unless the absence is due to health, educational, or family-related reasons. I can't find anyone who's lost their residency status due to being out of Costa Rica for too long. If you know someone, please let me know.

RENEWING *RENTISTA* OR *PENSIONADO* STATUS

Expats who obtain *rentista* or *pensionado* status need to renew that status every two years. You'll have to prove that you've been receiving the money in Costa Rica

that you asserted you'd be receiving on a monthly basis. Roger Petersen, author of *The Legal Guide to Costa Rica,* writes that "the renewal process has greatly improved since the Department of Immigration created an alliance with Banco de Costa Rica, one of the largest banks in Costa Rica." Residents can renew their residency status at some of that bank's branch offices.

PERMANENTE (PERMANENT RESIDENCY)

After three years, *pensionados, rentistas,* and *inversionistas* can apply for permanent residency, which gives you most of the rights a Costa Rican citizen enjoys, save voting.

Applicants for permanent residency must demonstrate that they will make a positive contribution to the country. Benefits of permanent residency include being able to work (rather than just own a business, as is allowed under temporary residencies), reduced fares on air travel within Costa Rica, and much-reduced admission to national parks and reserves. Permanent residency also offers up the same sort of safeguards extended to citizens, such as protection against extradition (except in high-profile cases, like when drug lords or big-time financial scamsters try to hide out in the wilds of Costa Rica). As a permanent resident, you don't need to worry about remaining in the country for four months (to maintain *pensionado* or *rentista* status) or six months (to maintain *inversionista* status) out of each year. Your only obligation as a permanent resident is to visit Costa Rica at least once a year.

RESIDENCY BY CHILDBIRTH OR MARRIAGE

If a non-Costa Rican has a child in Costa Rica, that child is eligible for Costa Rica citizenship (parents simply fill out some forms). If you want to make sure the child will also be a citizen of your country of origin, you need to go to your embassy and fill out some other forms. And here's the convoluted kicker: If a child is a Costa Rican citizen, the mother and father (as direct relatives) qualify for foreign residency status.

Residency and citizenship via marriage has gotten a lot more difficult. It used to be that if a foreigner married a Costa Rican, he or she would be eligible for permanent residency and could get on the fast track to full citizenship. But because many people abused this possibility and entered into sham marriages to get residency, Costa Rica came up with a new system: The spouse of a Costa Rican citizen will be given temporary residency for a year, renewable in one-year periods. After three years of marriage, the spouse may apply for permanent residency. The path to citizen would then be the same as for any other foreign resident.

Note that the immigration reforms of March 2010 provide for "closing the loophole" of marriages of convenience entered into solely for the purpose of obtaining residency. Now immigration officials can aggressively investigate the legitimacy of a marriage.

COSTA RICAN CITIZENSHIP

There are many paths to citizenship (also known as naturalization), none of them short. The most common route is to begin by establishing temporary legal residency, securing *rentista, pensionado,* or *inversionista* status. After living here legally for seven years (five for citizens of Spain or other Latin American countries), you can apply for citizenship through the Office of Options and Naturalizations, a division of the Supreme Election Tribunal's Civil Registry (Calle 15 between Avenidas 1 and 3 in San José, tel. 506/2287-5477, www.tse.go.cr), the same agency that records birth, deaths, marriages, divorces, and election registrations, and issues the ID cards *(cédulas)* carried by all citizens. Citizenship exams are said to be rigorous.

If you're from the United States or Canada, you don't have to give up citizenship in your home country to get citizenship in Costa Rica. You can be a citizen of both your old and new countries.

OTHER TYPES OF RESIDENCY

Other types of temporary residency usually require a sponsor and may be the way to go for the following people:

- Anyone who renders special services to governmental, international, or educational institutions in Costa Rica

- Highly specialized technical or professional workers granted prior authority by the Ministry of Labor. Managers and executives of multinational corporations with branches in Costa Rica often fall into this category. The company that sponsors these workers must meet certain qualifications, such as having at least 50 million colones in real capital investment

and employing a labor force that is made up of at least 90 percent Costa Rican citizens. Companies that routinely sponsor their workers are likely to be already registered with the Department of Immigration.

- Students at public or private schools or universities recognized by the government

- Domestic servants

Sometimes the company that employs you, the institution you are rendering services to, or the school you attend will take care of the paperwork. Make sure that is the case and contact your Costa Rican consulate or embassy for the latest on these categories of temporary residency.

The Application Process

PAPERWORK FOR RESIDENCY

Different categories of residency have different requirements, but in general, you'll need the following:

- Birth certificate

- Marriage license if you're married (no divorce papers required)

- Proof of income. This is the most important part of your application. The more income, the better; the government wants to be sure you have enough money to support yourself while in Costa Rica.

If you're going for *pensionado* or *rentista* status, you'll need a letter from your financial institution saying that you will be receiving at least US$1,000 a month (for

pensionados) or US$2,500 a month (for *rentistas*). The financial institution must be an "internationally recognized entity," listed in Polk's International Banking Directory. If your income is from a brokerage or insurance company, you'll need to submit a copy of its annual report along with your residency application. The letter issued by your financial institution is supposed to say that your income is "permanent and irrevocable" for at least the next five years. Since it is the client who ultimately controls the investments, some financial institutions balk at using the phrase "permanent and irrevocable." The usual way around this is to have them add in their letter a line that states, "in the event the funds invested or on deposit are reduced in any manner, the bank shall notify the Costa Rican Tourism Institute," which, along with the Department of Immigration, has a say in residency issues.

For *inversionista* applications, you'll be submitting business rather than personal financial records. If you invest in an existing business, you'll need to provide balance sheets and profit-and-loss information along with your residency application. For a new business, especially if you're hoping your enterprise will qualify as "priority" and thus allow you to invest less than the usually required US$200,000, the forms and documents needed are beyond the scope of this book. A good accountant and a lawyer familiar with the Costa Rican business world will be your best resources. Starting a business in Costa Rica need not be bound up with a residency application. Many people start businesses with far less than US$50,000, and they do so while here on a 90-day tourist visa. This is perfectly legal.

- Copies of academic or professional degrees (if you plan to practice your profession in Costa Rica)

- Police certificate of good conduct for at least two years from the last place you've lived. The police certificate should be obtained last, as it is only good for six months and may expire while you wait for your other documentation to come through.

- Interpol background check. This is done in Costa Rica; you'll need to provide your fingerprints. The background check usually takes about a month.

- Authenticated copies of dependents' birth certificates (spouse and children) if they are to be included in the residency application. You'll also need police certificates of good conduct for dependents over age 18 you're including in your application.

- Photos—take at least 10 facing front and five side views. You'll need photos at almost every step of the process.

- Proof that you've registered with your embassy

- You may be asked to provide proof of a doctor's exam. There are laws on the books allowing Costa Rican officials to refuse entry into the country to people with AIDS, although I've never heard of that happening.

Note: All documents must be translated into Spanish by the office of the Costa Rican consulate, then submitted to and authenticated by the Costa Rican consular officer in the country where the documents are issued. Having your documents authenticated by a Costa Rican consulate is not the same as having them notarized. Documents that are not "public documents" must be certified by a notary public of the state where the documents were issued. Public documents (those issued by a governmental institution) do not need to be notarized.

Authorization means that the consulate makes sure the documents are valid and belong to you; the consulate will also make sure the notary who notarized your documents is fully certified. There is, of course, a fee for each document authorized (usually around US$40 per document).

WHAT HAPPENS NEXT

Once you submit your complete application to Costa Rica's Department of Immigration or to the nearest Costa Rican consulate in your home country, you'll get a receipt. This receipt is worth its weight in gold: It's proof that you have a pending residency application with the Department of Immigration. If, as often happens, they don't get to your application for a while, you are legal in the country while that application is still pending.

If your application is approved, the Department of Immigration issues a formal resolution indicating the date on which the application was approved. You or your legal representative goes to the Department of Immigration to retrieve the resolution. Next, you must register with the Costa Rican Social Security System (CCSS, also known as the Caja) for medical coverage. Then you request an appointment with the Department of Immigration so they can issue you a picture identification residency card. (For more on registering with the Caja for medical insurance, see page 158 in the *Health* chapter.)

GETTING HELP

The residency process can be lengthy and frustrating. In Costa Rica, you could hire a lawyer or go through the Association of Residents of Costa Rica (ARCR, www. arcr.net; also see page 335 in *Resources*), which has a good reputation and has helped many expats through the residency maze.

Moving with Children

Costa Ricans love children, and the society as a whole is more kid-friendly than the United States. Even unplanned children are cherished, and motherhood is still seen by many here as a woman's highest calling. Many family decisions—like where to live—are heavily influenced by what would be best for the children.

Ticos are indulgent parents, and kids are often given a lot of freedom, their misdeeds ignored. An interesting historical explanation of this phenomenon is offered up in *The Ticos:* "Until half a century ago, many children died very young, and parents let small children enjoy what might be a brief stay on earth. Infants and toddlers are still allowed much free rein."

If you move here with kids, you'll be in the majority—almost all Costa Rican couples have children—and you will have an edge in making friends with locals. An expat mother in San José told me that her social life consisted mostly of children's birthday parties, where the kids would go outside and play and the mothers would stay inside, gossip, and eat cake.

Schooling, of course, will be a concern if you're moving with kids. See the *Language and Education* chapter for information on education in Costa Rica; a list of public and private schools starts on page 339 in *Resources*.

ENTERING AND EXITING
Non-Costa Rican Children

In an effort to foil traffic in human beings—child prostitution rings often operate internationally—and to prevent international child abduction, many governments have special rules for minors entering and exiting their countries. For children traveling with one parent, Costa Rica officially requires evidence of relationship and permission for the child to travel from the parent or legal guardian who's not present.

Parents must take this very seriously if they don't want to be refused entry or exit; they might miss their plane while scaring up the necessary forms and signatures. To be on the safe side, parents should carry the child's birth certificate, along with a notarized copy of a letter that says both parents agree to this particular trip.

Costa Rican Children

If your child was born in Costa Rica, or if at least one parent is a Costa Rican citizen, the child will automatically qualify to be a Costa Rican citizen. So even if your child travels on, say, a U.S. passport, if she or he qualifies as a Costa Rican citizen, in effect the child has dual citizenship and will need to comply with entry and exit requirements applicable to Costa Rican children. To exit Costa Rica, she or he will need an exit permit issued by the Costa Rican immigration office. This office may be closed for several weeks during holiday periods.

It is also imperative that if a Costa Rica-born child is visiting Costa Rica with only one parent—even if the child lives full-time in another country and his or her parents are not Costa Rican—the child must have the permission of the absent parent, signed in the presence of a Costa Rican consulate, to leave Costa Rica. Contact the Patronato Nacional de la Infancia (PANI, tel. 506/2523-0700 or 506/2523-0800, www.pani.go.cr), Costa Rica's organization to protect children's welfare, for more information.

Also, if a foreigner in Costa Rica has a child with a Costa Rican, she or he will need the permission of the Tico spouse to take a child under age 18 out of the country.

Parents of kids born in Costa Rica are advised to consult with the Costa Rican embassy or consulate in the United States about entry and exit requirements *before* travel to Costa Rica. Also check the Costa Rican embassy website (www.costarica-embassy.org) for more information.

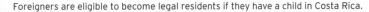

Foreigners are eligible to become legal residents if they have a child in Costa Rica.

Dogs are good for protection—if you can wake them up from their naps.

Moving with Pets

Bringing cats and dogs into Costa Rica is a fairly simple procedure. Bringing cows, horses, and other livestock is a bit more complicated, and if you want your snake or parrot to accompany you, you'll have to jump through some hoops, especially if your scaled or feathered friend is on any endangered species list.

DOGS AND CATS

For dogs and cats, you'll need to prove to both the airlines and Costa Rican customs officers that your animal is healthy. Schedule an exam with your local veterinarian a week or two before your departure date—the vet should fill out a health certificate stating that the animal is disease-free. Dogs need to have been vaccinated against distemper, hepatitis, leptospirosis, parvovirus, and rabies. Cats need to be vaccinated against rabies. The rabies vaccination is supposed to be more than 30 days but less than a year old, and

it's necessary only for animals age four months or older. The health certificate should then be endorsed by a Veterinary Service (VS) veterinarian, but it need not be notarized. The Costa Rican consulate says the examination for the certificate must be conducted within the two weeks prior to travel to Costa Rica, although anecdotal evidence suggests that a certificate up to 30 days old will do the trick.

Pet owners also need to get authorization from the Costa Rican Health Ministry; go through your nearest Costa Rican consulate or embassy to obtain this permission.

When you arrive in Costa Rica, the customs officer will do a visual inspection of your pet and look over the health certificate and the authorization from the Costa Rican Health Ministry. If all is in order, you're through, and you can find a pet-friendly taxi (not an easy task) and stuff your Irish wolfhound in the

Bringing Your Dog or Cat to Costa Rica

Want to bring Fido or Fifi or Steve along when you come to Costa Rica? The U.S. Embassy in Costa Rica advises that your dog or cat must be accompanied by a health certificate issued by a licensed veterinarian and endorsed by a U.S. Department of Agriculture (USDA), Animal and Plant Health Inspection Service (APHIS), or Veterinary Services (VS) veterinarian. That endorsement needs to be done by the APHIS Veterinary Services Area Office in your home state.

You'll also need certificates to the effect that:

- The dog or cat was examined and found to be healthy and free of any signs of infectious disease. This examination should be conducted within two weeks of your departure date.
- Dogs were vaccinated against distemper, hepatitis, leptospirosis, parvovirus, and rabies.
- Cats were vaccinated against rabies.

Note that all animals over three months of age will need to be vaccinated against rabies.

Other tips:

- Use an International Certificate (APHIS Form 7001) for Small Animals.
- Make out the health certificate in duplicate.
- The health certificate does not need to be signed by a notary public, nor does it need to be stamped by the Costa Rican Consular office.

- Animals exported in commercial lot numbers must be accompanied by an Import Permit. Personal pets (dogs or cats) do not need an Import Permit.
- The official rabies vaccination certificate must accompany the health documents and is valid for the period of the vaccine (one or three years).
- The dog or cat and supporting documentation will be inspected upon arrival in Costa Rica.

CHECKING WITH THE AIRLINES

Rita DeVore, who did a lot of work with SASY (Stop Animal Suffering Yes; now with offices in Nicaragua but not Costa Rica), says you should check the different airlines' rules about transporting pets. "If it's too cold or too hot," says Rita, "you can't fly your animal in cargo. Small dogs aren't a problem; some airlines allow between three and six dogs on board in the cabin, where people ride. They have to fit under the seat. A couple of our guests in the past year got their larger dog certified as a service dog so they could ride in the cabin, to help keep them [the people] calm while they fly.

"If your animals fly in cargo, the crate has to be the correct size for the animals; you have to have the right signage, plastic ties, and food and water dishes within the crate. As long as you follow all the airline's instructions to the letter, you'll be fine."

backseat. Some people traveling with pets report that they weren't even asked for their documents, but you can't count on encountering such relaxed attitudes yourself.

If you're missing any documents or the officer decides your pet looks ill and might transmit disease, the animal will either be temporarily released to your care (kind of like being out on bail) or, if the official decides there's a real health risk, kept in a state kennel for up to 30 days, until you work out what to do next—arrange for the necessary paperwork or contact a local vet if your animal needs care.

TAKING PETS FROM COSTA RICA TO THE UNITED STATES

If you're an animal lover who arrives in Costa Rica petless, there are many cats and dogs that need adoption.

You'll need permission from Costa Rica's Agriculture Ministry to bring your horse into the country.

The Asociación Humanitaria para la Protección de Animales (AHPPA, www.animalsheltercostarica.com) is a good resource.

If you adopt a dog or cat in Costa Rica and want to return to the United States with your new pet, you'll just need a Certificate of Good Health from your veterinarian in Costa Rica and an authorization issued by the Costa Rican Ministry of Agriculture (SENASA—Departamento de Cuarentena Animal), located in Barrial de Heredia, Jardines del Recuerdo, 2 kilometers (1.2 miles) west, 400 meters south, Heredia (tel. 506/2260-8300). Normally, your Costa Rican veterinarian can take care of all the required authorizations.

For more information about bringing pets to and from Costa Rica, especially about the fees involved, visit the website of the U.S. Embassy in Costa Rica (http://costarica.usembassy.gov/catsdogs.html).

LIVESTOCK AND EXOTIC ANIMALS

You'll need permission from Costa Rica's Agriculture Ministry's Animal Sanitation Department to bring livestock into the country. Ask your Costa Rican consulate or embassy how to go about getting this authorization, or, if you speak Spanish, call the San José office (tel. 506/2253-5605). More exotic animals, such as lizards, will be allowed in if they have a clean bill of health from a vet—you'll need to check what diseases might affect your particular creature to know what vaccinations will be required.

If your pet is on the endangered species list, the paperwork will be more complicated, from both the Costa Rican end and from your country of origin, which may have even stricter regulations; required information may include the animal's country of origin and permission to take it out of that original country. Such regulations aim to protect against illegal traffic in endangered animals. Again, the Costa Rican consulate in your country of origin is your best source of information for up-to-date specifics.

FLYING WITH PETS

Most likely you'll bring your pet with you on the plane. Most airlines allow guide dogs in the cabin, and some allow small pets to accompany you at your seat. I know a woman who carries her little dog with her in a big purse; sometimes the flight crew doesn't even realize the animal is along for the ride. I never asked this woman what she does about letting the poor creature relieve itself on long flights. Bigger animals (or all animals, on some airlines) will need to ride in the cargo hold or even on a separate cargo flight. Some airlines will not accept pets as checked baggage May 15-September 15, since the cargo hold is not air-conditioned.

Animals checked as baggage need to travel in leak-proof crates that have handles so the baggage handlers will easily be able to lift and carry the crate. The crate should be just large enough for the animal to turn around. Vets say animals should fast for six hours prior to the flight in order to reduce nausea. If the flight is longer than four hours, the animal should eat a few hours before takeoff.

The bottom line is that each airline has a different policy regarding pet transport, and those policies often change. Note that many airlines have blackout periods for pets, times of year they don't allow animals to fly, even if they have all the proper paperwork. Set aside some time before your departure to research which airlines best meet your needs.

PETS IN COSTA RICA

Most buses and taxis do not welcome animals, though they must, by law, accept guide dogs. Some hotels accept pets—check ahead of time. There are plenty of vets in Costa Rica, especially in the Central Valley area. Vets in more rural areas will probably specialize in livestock. Vets will often board pets for around US$10 per day; animals stay in cages but are supposed to be exercised daily.

Pet food is easy to come by in Costa Rica, even upscale brands like Iams and Eukanuba.

Costa Rican Attitudes Toward Pets

Although Costa Ricans love their pets, they think of them differently than do most North Americans. Dogs are valued for their ability to protect people and property and are often not let into the house. The U.S. practice of letting dogs sleep on the sofa or even the bed would be considered in Costa Rica hopelessly *cochino* (literally "piggy," used as a synonym for "dirty").

You won't see many cats out and about in Costa Rica, maybe because the street dogs would consider them tasty morsels. Walk down any street or along any beach with your dog at your side and a motley crew of other canines will rush out to see who dares to invade their territory. In the dog world there is a complicated pecking order that is given freer rein here than in other countries; you'd better not stand in the way as the dogs work out for themselves who's on top. Each block has its neighborhood bully dog, so if you're going to let your beagle roam free, she or he had better be streetwise. There aren't as many mangy street dogs in Costa Rica as you see in other developing countries, but they do exist, and it's best to give them a wide berth—they've had to adapt to a life of people kicking them and throwing rocks at them, so they're not likely to be too friendly.

That said, there are many good things about bringing your pet to Costa Rica. Especially if you move here with children, your dog or cat could be that living, breathing piece of home that helps your kids adjust to their new environment. And there's nothing like a big dog—however sweet-tempered—to discourage burglars and other scoundrels. Dogs also have such keen senses of smell and direction that if you get lost in the forest that is your new backyard, your dog will almost certainly know the way home.

LEAVING WITH PETS

Animals leaving Costa Rica require exit permits. You'll need a local vet to fill out a health certificate; often she or he will accept the original health certificate from your country of origin as proof that the animal is in good health. For a fee, the vet can take care of all the paperwork.

What is likely to be more of a hassle is getting the animal back into your country of origin, which may have stricter regulations about animals entering its territory. It's best to check out your country's regulations even before you leave for Costa Rica.

A note on birds: In 2009, Costa Rica relaxed its rule for bringing birds into the country, but taking that same bird back out of Costa Rica may be next to impossible—check with the ARCR, the U.S. Embassy in Costa Rica, or your nearest Costa Rica consulate (see page 330 in *Resources*).

What to Take

Most people—even adventurous souls who decide to pick up and move to another country—have a lot of stuff that they've accumulated over the years. Even if you consider yourself nonmaterialistic and have made an effort to keep your possessions to a minimum, chances are that what you own is more than you could check as baggage on a flight to Costa Rica.

And this method—bringing in your possessions as checked baggage—is by far the cheapest and easiest option. As long as you can convince customs officials that everything you bring is portable, for your own personal use, and necessary for your enjoyment or for the practice of your profession while in Costa Rica, you will pay no duties (taxes on imported goods) and there will be no bureaucracy save filling out the usual customs form that flight attendants hand out just before the plane lands.

The second-easiest option is to send a small shipment as air cargo (not as luggage

accompanying you on your flight)—at least some of the shipment will be taxed, and there will be forms to fill out and lines to stand in.

The third option is to ship your possessions by boat; the container will arrive at a port on either the east or west coast of Costa Rica. In terms of customs, hassles, and duties, this is the most time- and money-intensive option, but it's the way to go if you really want to bring your entire household with you: books, CDs, stereo, sofa, bed, stove, and refrigerator—even your car can go in the shipboard container.

But why lug your old life with you to a new country, especially when you have to pay so dearly for the privilege? If you've lived in one place for more than a few years, I'll bet that you've been meaning to purge your belongings—to have a garage sale or take a few trips to the Salvation Army drop-off station. It feels good to pare down, and a lot of people who move to Costa Rica do so in part because they

What I Wish I Hadn't Left at Home

Ask expats what they wished they'd brought with them but didn't, and you'll get a range of responses.

- High-quality sheets and towels
- Favorite spices
- Cast-iron frying pan
- Chef's knives
- Vitamins and supplements (usually cheaper in the US)
- Hiking boots (not leather – leather molds in the tropics)
- Camping equipment
- Favorite lotion, makeup, sunscreen, etc.
- Hand tools
- A favorite pillow
- The full 5 liters of booze allowed per adult per trip!

Bottom line: if you love it and feel your life would be diminished without it, stuff it into that suitcase!

want to simplify their lives. You can start simplifying even before you get here by thinking carefully about what possessions you can't live without, then selling or giving away the rest. "I thought about selling all my favorite things, all the great stuff I've collected over the years, and I just couldn't do it," says Mary Ann Jackson, who moved to Costa Rica in 2004. "But I wasn't going to lug it all with me either. So I gave it all away to friends. Now I can visit my stuff in their houses."

You may be tempted to bring your appliances, but I would advise against it. You will pay high duties on these items (sometimes more than 50 percent of the item's value), and it's easy to buy appliances here. You'll probably pay about what you'd pay in the United States, though the selection isn't as good here. The best deals are in the Pacific coast port of Golfito, near the border with Panama. There, Ticos and tourists alike can buy up to US$500 in duty-free goods every six months. Many people hang around the area, selling off their buying rights to the highest bidder. Golfito is near the legendary surf spot of Pavones and close to the Osa Peninsula, home to magnificent Corcovado National Park. You could do worse than to head south for a week of surfing, tapir watching, and appliance shopping.

Furniture is another thing that is easy to come by in Costa Rica. In fact, many newcomers have pieces custom-made for not much more than they'd pay for ready-made items in the United States or Canada. Costa Rica is known for its tropical hardwoods and for its tradition of woodworking. Even if you don't want to spring for a custom-made dining room table or a hand-carved headboard, there are plenty of ready-made items that show the local materials and skills to good advantage. The Central Valley town of Sarchí, for example, is known for its lovely wood-and-leather rocking chairs, which are very comfortable and will look great on your tiled front porch with a volcano view.

ON THE PLANE

As discussed, bringing used goods and personal belongings with you as checked baggage is your first and best option. Some airlines allow you to pay extra and bring a little more than the usual limit. It's worth checking as much luggage as possible, as this is the only way to import your belongings without duties and customs hassles. Everything you bring must be for your own personal use (not intended for resale), be portable, and be a reasonable quantity for the duration of your stay. Most people, even those who plan to stay years, first come in on a 90-day tourist visa, so what you bring in as luggage should look like a reasonable amount of goods for that amount of time.

On the other hand, consider the case of Brenda Burnside, a former professional boxer who moved to the Pacific coast town of Nosara. When she saw the reduced circumstances of the local public school, she wanted to help. Enlisting the help of eight members of her church back home in Nevada, she offered them a free place to stay in sunny Costa Rica if they would fill their luggage with books, school supplies, and sports equipment. When Brenda lugged the precious cargo to the school, the teacher cried in gratitude—she couldn't believe such generosity. Now, a persnickety customs official at the airport could have challenged the travelers' need for so many pens, notebooks, geography textbooks, and soccer balls for a stay of just a few weeks. As luck would have it, all of the do-gooders got the green light at the airport. That's how customs used to decide whose bags to check at the San José airport: You pushed a button, and if the light came up red, they searched your bags. If it came up green, you were on your way without even a glance inside your luggage.

What you're allowed to bring in as luggage includes:

- Clothing, jewelry, purses, umbrellas

- Medicine and medical equipment if necessary for personal use, such as a wheelchair or oxygen tank

- Sporting equipment, including surfboards, kayaks, golf clubs, and fishing poles

- One video camera, one still camera, one zoom lens, one portable tape recorder, one portable computer, one portable telescope, one portable radio

- One portable typewriter, one calculator, one portable printer

- Paint and canvases

- Tools, supplies, and manual instruments pertinent to the trade of the traveler, as long as these do not constitute a complete set for an office or laboratory

- One musical instrument and accessories (no pianos!)

- Books, tapes, photos, CDs, if for noncommercial use

- 500 grams (17 ounces) tobacco, 5 liters (1.3 gallons) of wine or hard liquor per adult traveler, 2 kilos (4.4 pounds) of candy per person

- Baby food in an amount "sufficient for your proposed stay"

- Tent and other camping gear

If you arrive at the airport with items that don't qualify as luggage, don't despair. There's a duty-free exemption of up to US$500. So if you bring, say, two portable TVs instead of one, if the second one is worth less than US$500, you're still OK. Customs will stamp your passport, and you'll need to wait six months to take advantage of that US$500 exemption again. Note that this applies both to casual tourists and to residents of Costa Rica. If you live here, it can save you money when you have items shipped to you in Costa Rica. Many expats use private mail services that

Old Piano Gets New Life

In a second-floor living room overlooking Costa Rica's Lake Arenal, two 20-something Ticos are pulling the insides out of a 1934 Steinway piano. Only pings and twangs come from the instrument at this point, but through the open window comes a different kind of music: insects keen, birds screech, and howler monkeys make their deep-throated call that's somewhere between a lonely dog and an irritable lion.

Before arthritis compromised her hands, the owner of the piano, Sandra Shaw Homer, would sit down to play Chopin Preludes and Schubert Impromptus surrounded by the sights and sounds of her adopted tropical home, where she has lived since 1990. "I felt I had an audience out there in the trees. Even the green here is its own kind of music."

How did Sandy's Steinway L—in size somewhere between a baby grand and a concert grand—end up in Costa Rica in the first place? And why, if Sandy can't play anymore, is she bringing in Esmeralda Gamboa and Pablo Chaves, two Costa Rican technicians, to restore it?

Sandra Shaw Homer's grandmother, Leona Shaw, with the 1934 Steinway piano that Sandra ended up shipping to Costa Rica

Let's take the last question first. The future of this octogenarian piano is less complicated than its past. Sandy, with the help of her husband, Roger Eichholz, and his family organization to promote the arts (The Robert and Mercedes Eichholz Foundation), is overseeing the restoration of the piano, which will then go to a local nonprofit with the unwieldy name of the Association for the Rescue and Promotion of the Musical Arts. This little organization with the big name and mission, founded a few years ago, is dedicated to providing local kids access to musical instruments and instruction. "Roger's family foundation is providing a total of US$15,000, to restore the piano, buy other instruments, hire quality teachers, and offer scholarships to the local kids," says Sandy.

Sandy and Roger have lived in the area for over 20 years. "We know everybody, and everybody knows us," she says. "It's something we want to do for the community, for the children here."

The piano's past is a regular *Red Violin* kind of a story, but the short version starts with Leora Shaw, Sandy's grandmother, in Manhattan. Leora, born in 1899, went to Juilliard, sang religious music in New York City churches, and taught piano and voice to students in Upper East Side private schools. Trailing after its owner, the piano moved around a lot: a couple of New York City apartments, several houses in Albany, New York, and then a few places in Philadelphia.

At this point Leora had moved to an assisted living facility and had made good on a promise to give her granddaughter her beloved piano. Sandy studied piano from a young age, and before the Steinway came into her life, she had been making due with a dilapidated upright. When she moved to Costa Rica, there was no question about it: she would bring her grandmother's Steinway with her. Her possessions were shipped from Philadelphia to the port of Limon on Costa Rica's Caribbean coast, and then trucked to a warehouse outside of San José. When she and her then husband went to claim their possession, they noticed something odd: no piano.

"I thought, my god, it's probably rotting on some dock in El Salvador," says Sandy. But they tracked it down (it was still in Philadelphia), and when the piano finally arrived, they gave it pride of place in their house in Grecia, a small town in the Central Valley. Later, Sandy separated from her husband and moved to the Lake Arenal area. Of course the piano came with her. It spent some time in a little cottage, and then when she and her new husband, Roger, built a larger house, the piano was lifted to its present location by backhoe. "There were five or six guys," Sandy remembers, "tying ropes around the piano seventeen ways from Sunday. The backhoe grabbed the ropes with its claw, and lifted it onto the second floor deck. My heart was in my throat."

But the piano survived yet another move, and now, Esmeralda and Pablo, up from the capital city of San José on their third working visit to restore the piano, are in the next room. They bend to their task, removing and cleaning pins, restringing, and refinishing the cabinet to bring out the mahogany grain. Pablo is studying mechanical engineering and tunes pianos on the side. His dream is to play piano professionally, but that's not an easy path, especially in Costa Rica, where pianos are a huge expense for families of modest means, good teachers are hard to come by, and opportunities to play professionally are limited. Esmeralda, the daughter of the piano technician who several times tuned the very piano she now works on, trained in New York to be an official Steinway technician.

Esmeralda and Pablo are glad to be restoring such a beautiful instrument, and they're excited that the piano will give local kids more to play on than a few guitars and the drums and glockenspiels used in local parades.

"Tilarán is a small town," says Sandy. "People don't have great expectations. There is music education to some extent, but it's very low down on the curriculum. All they need is that the kids can get out there and parade in civic events. But I don't think they've had the chance to be exposed to much good music. This new organization can change that."

Most of the kids here don't make it to university, there's a high rate of high school dropouts, and some of the kids don't even make it into high school; they have to work with their families in the field or in the family-owned business or shop. Oddly, the Canton of Tilarán has one of the highest per-capita incomes in the country, but it's because there are a number of wealthy ranchers. There aren't many opportunities for the kids here, though now that there's more wind power generation here, there's a whole new social strata of engineers and their families, mostly from outside of the area.

Tilarán is only a little over 100 years old. Sandy says, "People came here and carved out farms from the virgin forest; it's a very inward-facing community. Music has not been a priority, and when a child showed interest or aptitude there wasn't really any way to develop it. Now we hope that will change."

Thinking of children playing the piano that was her grandmother's makes Sandy very happy.

"There are moments when you lose yourself in the playing. It's as if Schubert is playing you rather than the other way around. I want the kids here to have access to those kinds of moments."

will track the deduction for you (see page 355 in *Resources*).

If the US$500 exemption isn't enough and you get slapped with some duties, you have two choices: Pay the bill right then and there if you think the amount is fair, or leave the goods in question at the airport (ask for a receipt) and return the following day to argue your case (bring along someone who speaks Spanish).

AIR CARGO

You can send up to 227 kilograms (500 pounds) as air cargo. Duties for items sent air cargo differ from those of items carried into the country as luggage, though personal clothes, shoes, purses, books, hand tools, and some sports equipment will still be duty-free. Everything else will be taxed—each item has its own duty, from paintings to pots and pans. You will even be taxed on the freight charges you pay, and on any insurance, which is why some customs brokers suggest you forgo insurance.

When your shipment arrives in Costa Rica, it will be sent to a bonded customs warehouse. To pick up your shipment, you will need:

• Your passport (copy the main page and the page with your last entry into Costa Rica, proving you've entered the country within the last 90 days)

• The Air Way Bill, which the freight handler you contracted will have given you

• Packing inventory that includes the declared value of the contents

Then you pay the duties assessed, the terminal handling fee, and the bonded warehouse fee. You can do this on your own, hire a customs broker, or bring along a calm, savvy Spanish-speaking friend who can help you out.

Very important: For claiming either an air cargo shipment or a surface (boat) shipment, you need to prove by the stamp on your passport that you have entered or reentered Costa Rica within the last 90 days. If you've been here longer, your shipment will be considered a commercial one, and all hell will break loose. You'll have to pay duties on everything, even books and clothes; a health certificate will be required for used clothing; and you'll need invoices for everything shipped. And if you don't have the necessary invoices and certificates? Good luck trying to claim your stuff.

SHIPPING BY BOAT

If you have a lot you want to ship, you can pay for a quarter, half, or full ocean container, which is a steel box measuring 12 by 2.5 by 2.5 meters (40 by 8 by 8 feet). The box will be loaded onto a ship, which will eventually dock on either the Atlantic or Pacific coast of Costa Rica, depending on where it's coming from. You can fit a great deal in one of these containers—even a car—but every item needs to be numbered and inventoried, including the serial numbers of all appliances and electronic items. And you can't just dump it all in—you need to pack carefully, because it will need to withstand a lot of moving around and perhaps a lot of heat. Experienced movers recommend putting any heat-sensitive items in the middle of the load. Most people hire professional movers and so don't need to worry about packing the box themselves.

It's important that you ship only used items that are more than six months old; otherwise you may end up paying duties on new items, which are much higher. The serial numbers on appliances and electronics allow customs agents to know exactly how old they are and what their average prices are.

If you choose to go it alone, you'll either meet the ship to pick up your possessions or ask that the container be trucked to a warehouse in San José. The documents needed to claim the shipment are:

- Your passport (copy of the main page and of your last entry into Costa Rica showing you've entered the country within the last 90 days)

- Inventory list with declared value of container contents

- Original Ocean Bill of Lading

DRIVING TO COSTA RICA

If you've got some time on your hands, love road trips, and are good at talking your way in and out of rough spots, you might want to drive all the way from North America to Costa Rica. You could load your car or truck with all your worldly possessions, then hit the road and see what happens. You'll pass through some beautiful country and will cross many borders, all of which will be enforcing different regulations concerning what you can and can't bring into their country. It's not for everyone, but it's not a trip you will soon forget. *¡Buen viaje, y buena suerte!* For more information on bringing your car to Costa Rica, see page 230 in the *Travel and Transportation* chapter.

DAILY LIFE
MAKING THE MOVE

HOUSING CONSIDERATIONS

You have a dream, and it goes like this: You'll quit your job, buy a dirt-cheap piece of beachfront property in Costa Rica, then build a little house with your own two hands using driftwood and palm fronds. You've got the skills—you hammered together that tree house when you were 12, and once you fixed a door that wouldn't close. In a few months you'll be spending your days surfing bathtub-warm tubes, reading all the novels you've always meant to read, or just lying in a hammock, swaying in the ocean breeze.

Or maybe your dream is more industrious: you'll take over a down-at-the-heels lodge at the foot of an active volcano. Howler monkeys will hoot you awake each morning, and toucans will serenade you at dusk. With hard work you'll turn the place around, adding an upscale spa, a five-star restaurant, and stables. Soon your place will be featured in *Travel + Leisure* magazine, tourists will flock to you, and the money will roll in.

Hold on a minute. Better yet, hold on a few good months or even years. "Things take a long time to accomplish in Costa Rica," says Brenda Burnside, a former professional boxer who ran a health and exercise center in Nosara. "And sometimes

that's a good thing." If you've done your homework—traveled the country, staying here and there a month or two and longer in the place you think you might like to call home—you'll already know that these scenarios are about as likely as crossing a raging river in a golf cart.

You'll also know that Costa Rica has some of the most beautiful land you've ever seen, and you'll be ready to do whatever it takes to get your own private piece of it.

There are always people for whom price is no object; most of us don't belong to that select club. You *could* pay as much for property here as you would in some of the hotter U.S. markets—we're talking millions of dollars—but most people want to avoid such madness.

How do you keep costs down and still get the house of your dreams? Adaptability and patience are key. If you need to duplicate exactly how you'd live in the United States, you'll pay a high price. But if you're willing to embrace what Costa Rica has to offer rather than concentrating on what it lacks, you're off to a good start. And if you rent for a while in your area of choice, getting to know the ups and downs of the place, talking to people, and observing what properties are going for, you're more than halfway there. Some real estate agents say that property values have doubled in the past decade and are likely to double again soon. That may very well be true in some areas and for some types of property. That doesn't mean you should snap up whatever's on offer. I've said it once and I'll say it again: *Be patient.* "It's easy to buy," cautions Chris Simmons of RE/MAX in Tamarindo, "and not so easy to sell." Which is in itself good news, as it suggests that in Costa Rica right now, it's a buyer's market.

Another piece of good news is that regardless of your nationality or immigration status, you have basically the same property rights as native Costa Ricans. Costa Rica's solid and egalitarian property rights are a big incentive to investing here.

BOOM AND BUST

The new national bird of Costa Rica might well be the crane—the construction crane, that is. This awkward yellow giant is often spotted in the beach communities of northern Guanacaste, on the central Pacific coast, in the suburbs of San José, and in formerly sleepy crossroads towns. The crane's call is a creaking complaint as it swings back and forth accompanied by a cacophony of hammers, drills, and shouts of "Buy now!"

Costa Rica is a country under construction. Developers and individuals have snapped up most of the land around popular beach resorts like Jacó, Tamarindo, and Playas del Coco. Condo towers, malls, and low-rise residential complexes are popping up wherever you look.

With the world economic downturn of 2008, many of the more ambitious real estate projects ran out of money and had to be put on hold. In the places that had seen the most growth, the downturn hit the hardest, and you saw still half-finished condo projects everywhere. Nowadays the real estate market has come back up again, though it may be a while before it hits the pre-2008 prices, which is good news for buyers.

There are distinct regional differences, both in prices and in how the areas weather booms and busts. A realtor on the Caribbean coast says he thinks the market on his side of the country went into the crisis later and came out of it sooner. Real estate on the Pacific coast has had more dramatic ups and downs, with more building and prices rising faster than on the Caribbean coast, which has no high-rise condos or mega-developments and where prices have always been a bit lower.

Even with the boom-bust cycles

an unfinished condo project in Playas del Coco

making one leery of investing, the hot spots are getting hotter: so hot that expats of modest means can't even touch them. Not to mention Costa Ricans—even middle-class and professional Ticos complain that the influx of foreigners has priced them right out of much of northern coastal Guanacaste, some of the central Pacific coast, and the western suburbs of San José.

The good news is threefold. First, there's more housing stock to choose from in the areas of intense development. Two, there may be deals to be had as developers try to minimize their losses where they've overestimated the need for condos and new houses. And three, once you start to explore the entire country—the lush back roads to Arenal, the Caribbean coast, the parts of the Nicoya Peninsula not yet overrun, the San Isidro Valley, and still many lovely towns and rural areas in the Central Valley—you'll see that what at first glance seems to be a countrywide boom is still pretty much contained in a few key areas. Stray off the beaten track and you'll find pockets of the old Costa Rica.

Prices

Real estate prices in Costa Rica are as varied and volatile as they are in the rest of the world. An "average" price one week might be out of date the next. And for any price I quote, there will be people saying, "But I paid much less," or "I spent a lot more." Because Costa Rica has no true multiple listing service (MLS), it's even harder to nail down average prices.

Here's a little history, fodder for the ever-popular "If only I'd bought up a bunch of land way back when" laments. According to the *Tico Times,* in 1968 one *manzana* (about 7,000 square meters/1.75 acres) generally went for the equivalent of about US$1,500. In 1974 the price had jumped to US$12,500. In 2017 prices were all over the map, from under US$50,000 for a modest house in an out-of-the-way town to multimillion dollar spreads on the beach or in the suburbs of San José.

The areas most popular with expats and well-to-do Ticos are the most expensive,

Rent Before You Buy

OK, so all the books on moving abroad say the same thing: Rent before you buy. Live where you think you want to live to see if you really want to live there. You've heard it before, and I know that you are prepared to happily ignore this advice. Sure, it's good for others, but you're impulsive, right? A free spirit. Or you have a friend who bought property on her first trip down, and she's happier than she's ever been.

Maybe so. But for every success story there are many people who tell me, "I wish I'd known. . . ." Here are a few examples of things that, after buying property your first week here, you may wish you'd known:

- See that hill with the amazing views? Half the year it gets winds so strong you'll have to dress like a Sherpa to have a drink on your deck.

- That charming group of expats you met your first week? Well, they don't actually live here full time. In fact, they're hardly ever here. In fact, you'll be the only full-time expat for miles.

- The guy who bought up half the land around town and carved it into tiny, expensive lots is not the only game in town – just the one with the best advertising. You'll find other, better, quieter deals to be had if you hang around long enough to get to know both expats and locals who might be selling or might know someone who is.

- The developer who touts his spread as eco-friendly wouldn't know a watershed if it burbled up in his bathtub. He's digging the septic tank too close to the water and deforesting the hillside, then planting a few "native species" saplings so he can put that in his brochure and on his website. As soon as they catch up with him, all sorts of government and environmental agencies might succeed in shutting him down.

- In the rainy season you'll become a charter member of the "bug of the week" club, as new species hatch in waves and make your house their temporary home.

So, please, rent before you buy. See if you like it here (and maybe you'll try out a variety of "heres"). Live here a while before you commit your life savings and burn your bridges back home. And you might consider that renting can be the most economical and trouble-free option, even if you plan on being here a long time.

both for renting and buying. The hottest spots are the western suburbs of San José, the central Pacific coast area around Jacó and Quepos/Manuel Antonio, and Guanacaste's Gold Coast, which runs from Playa Potrero down to a bit below Tamarindo. In some areas—like the San José suburb of Escazú, the burgeoning surfer burg of Tamarindo, or the easy-access beach town of Jacó—prices can rival those at home, with the larger luxury condos going for more than US$500,000 or US$2,000-4,000 per month in rent, and beachfront or mountaintop spreads fetching millions of dollars. These places tend to rent by the week, always a bad sign if you're looking for a bargain.

At the other end of the spectrum, you hear tales of great bargains: US$35,000 for 9 hectares (22 acres), with a river and spring on the property and good soil to grow fruit. As elsewhere in the world, it's a matter of supply and demand, and of location. Those amazing deals are most often way out past who knows where—you may have to build your own road or lay your own water line. But if you're looking to really get away from it all, you could live like a king on a workingman's budget.

Outside the Central Valley and

You may have to pay extra for the epiphytes growing on the roof.

excluding Jacó-Manuel Antonio and Guanacaste's Gold Coast, prices tend to be lower. There are countless towns, nestled on the slopes of a volcano or down a sandy track on a hidden peninsula, where you can find your own little piece of paradise for under US$100,000, and often considerably less.

If you find something you like, don't rush. Settle in to that area—maybe in an economical hotel or a short-term rental apartment—and look around. Visit the real estate agents in the area, talk to hotel owners and with expats you see in cafés and bars. Walk the streets in the early morning and at night. See how long it takes to get to the next town and what is available there. In short, do your homework and don't be swayed by people urging you to buy right here, right now! The real estate market back home may be just as cutthroat, but it's more regulated and easier to understand.

In Costa Rica, you've got to be more wary and self-reliant. There are no shortcuts to finding the right place at the right price. And in the end, the right place is more important than the right price. Just because something's a bargain doesn't mean you'll be happy there. Choose where you want to be first, then look for a good apartment to rent, a house to buy, or a lot to build on.

The Housing Search

WHAT'S DIFFERENT?

In terms of buying, building, and renting in Costa Rica, a lot of the same rules apply as in the United States and Canada. It takes perseverance and a certain measure of luck to find the place of your dreams. As elsewhere, location is everything: If everyone wants to live there, prices shoot up. The more you know about a place and the people in it, the better deal you're going to get. Would you bluster into a small town in the American Midwest and snap up the first house on offer, just because the price is half of what you'd pay in New York City? Of course not. You'd hang around for a while and get to know some real estate agents and residents. You'd learn that every spring the local meandering creek swells and jumps its banks; the houses nearby have mud marks to prove it. You'd learn that the owner of the best restaurant in town is desperate to sell because she wants to join her daughter in Santa Cruz. You'd hear about the new mall they're putting out on Highway 32, which will increase traffic fourfold on the single-lane road leading to what you'd thought was a pleasantly remote little plot of land.

In a new culture, where laws and customs are different, and where you may not even speak the language, such investigations are doubly important. Some of the major differences you will encounter in Costa Rica are covered here.

- **Real estate agents are everywhere, none of them have to be licensed, and there is no true MLS.**

There are no requirements to be a real estate agent in Costa Rica beyond hanging out a shingle. Some of the bigger realty companies advertise that their agents are licensed in the United States or elsewhere. This may mean that the agents are more knowledgeable, at least about properties and practices in their home country, but it's unclear what that would mean if there were a problem—after all, what sort of jurisdiction would a U.S. organization have in Costa Rica? None at all. As for those with no credentials whatsoever, some of these self-styled real estate agents—many of whom are from the United States, Canada, and Europe—do a fine job. Others are incompetent at best and downright crooked at worst.

Manuel Pinto, who sold real estate on the Caribbean coast, is adamant in his assessment of the situation: "There is *no accountability* for bad real estate agents," he says. He points out that buyers must not only research the areas where they want to live, but also research the real estate agents in that area.

Word of mouth may be all you'll have to go on. You have to be a private eye of sorts—getting as many sides to the story as possible. Realize too that there's a lot of competition and backbiting, especially in small towns; you may have stepped into a family feud, or one real estate agent may badmouth another so he'll get your business. Look for real estate agents who have operated for many years in the same city or town, who have no complaints against them, and who have a good reputation in town and beyond.

To be on the safe side, make sure your real estate agent has the right to work in Costa Rica. Otherwise he or she might be deported in the middle of your deal. Real estate agents who are here on tourist visas are not legally able to work.

And remember that while in the United States few people buy property without using a real estate agent, in Costa Rica, it's more common not to use the services of a real estate agent. Many deals here are still done without a middleman.

But if you want help, check in with the Costa Rican Real Estate Agents Chamber (CCCBR, tel. 506/2283-0191, fax 506/2283-0347, info@camara.cr, www.camaracbr.or.cr). Founded in 1974, the organization lobbies for mandatory licensing of real estate agents. Members must be residents of Costa Rica in good legal and professional standing, and they must take a training course in Costa Rican real estate law. Most real estate agents in Costa Rica are not members of the CCCBR, and lack of membership doesn't mean an agent is a crook. But if the agent you work with is a member, you can complain about his or her conduct to the CCCBR, and the agent may be thrown out of the organization.

The CCCBR also has what they call a multiple listing service (MLS) at www.mls-cr.com. But this isn't at all like the MLS in your home country. Since real estate agents in Costa Rica don't have any licenses to lose and since there is no effective oversight of transactions, any MLS in Costa Rica is going to be little more than real estate agents pooling their listings. And several real estate agents I spoke with said they only had a few listings on the MLS, while they had many more on their own websites. "The majority of Costa Rican real estate agents do not work with exclusive listings," points out Mercedes Castro, former vice president of the CCCBR, so there is little motivation for a real estate agent to list a property on the MLS. They'd rather list it on their own website, hoping to be the one to do the deal and thus earn the commission. In addition, since many properties here are never formally "listed" anywhere, it's unclear how anyone in Costa Rica can claim

a comprehensive MLS. Perhaps in the future there will be a larger, more complete list of properties, along with more effective oversight of real estate agents and their transactions. Until then, buyer beware.

- **When they hear your accent and see your face, the price will skyrocket.**

This may seem unfair, but in the larger scheme of things it makes sense—most North Americans and Europeans who come to Costa Rica have more resources than the locals. But I'm not rich, you may protest. Not by your standards, perhaps, but by Tico standards you're probably pretty flush. Which is not to say you should pay inflated prices. But you should understand and not be personally offended by sellers trying to get as much from you as they can. Is it really any different in other markets, where they won't even look at you unless you've been pre-approved for a loan, and where real estate agents start bidding wars that send costs skyrocketing 50 percent above the asking price? By the way, in Costa Rica buyers almost never bid over the asking price. Bidding substantially lower is much more common. *To avoid paying the gringo price, become a local.* Stick around for a while. Learn the language so you can bargain with the best of them. (For a helpful list of Spanish real estate terms used in Costa Rica, see the *Glossary* on page 337.) Or do what so many newcomers do: Get a trusted local to do your negotiating. When you scan real estate ads in the paper—*La Nación* is a good place to look, especially for Central Valley properties—often a price will be listed. This is a good starting point, and it makes it harder for sellers to double the price once they see they're dealing with an *extranjero* (foreigner).

- **You'll need a lawyer for just about everything.**

Buying and selling property involves a great deal of paperwork, just as it does in the United States. Very few people want to wade through all that bureaucracy themselves, so they hire lawyers to do it for them.

"Forget real estate agents," says one long-time expat. "What you need for buying property is a good lawyer. Or two." (See *Buying Property* on page 133 for more details; lawyers are also discussed in the *Finance* chapter.)

THE TICO HOUSE

It's hard to talk about the average Tico house, which might be anything from a condo in the city to a driftwood shack on the beach or a tree house in the rainforest. Back in the 1800s most Tico houses were made of adobe brick, formed from a mash of mud, grass, and sugarcane waste. Roof tiles were made of soft clay formed on the workman's thigh and left to dry in the sun. Doors and window frames were made of one of the many tropical hardwoods found in this country. Walls were whitewashed, with a wide strip of blue at the bottom to discourage pecking chickens.

Few of these traditional houses remain, although you may see modern houses that adopt some of the traditional elements. Nowadays most Ticos live in small houses of wood or concrete block (making it hard to hang pictures or tack up postcards!).

Tico houses can be as luxurious and well equipped as any you'd find in the world, but most in the mid or lower price bracket will have certain characteristics that may take some getting used to if you're accustomed to North American standards. But whether you're looking to buy or rent, many of the better deals will be Tico-style houses, so it's worth seeing if you can live happily à la Tica.

- **Bars, bars, and more bars**

Even in better neighborhoods of urban areas and in a lot of rural areas as well, there are bars *(rejas)* on every window and usually big iron gates protecting the front of the house and parking areas. Thankfully, you don't see much of the broken bottle-topped fences common in other Latin countries. Still, watching the

Most Tico houses have bars on the windows to protect from theft.

sun rise each morning through barred windows takes some getting used to.

• **Noise**

In Tico neighborhoods and towns, expect to hear roosters crowing, kids playing, music blaring, and car horns honking. Noise pollution is not a known concept here, and it is culturally frowned upon to demand that your neighbor tone down his or her act. The idea is that people need to live their lives, and who are you to infringe on this right? There are upsides to this situation: I've never once been asked to "Keep it down, please!"—not even by my landlord, who lives right next door.

• **Limited hot water**

Often the only hot water to be had in a Tico house is in the shower, and it is not so much hot water as *heated* water, warmed by an electric device attached just above the showerhead. Some of these devices (nicknamed suicide showers) have exposed wires bristling out and seem sure bets for causing nasty shocks or worse, but in practice they usually work well and save a bundle on utility costs. Some modest houses, especially in the hotter areas of the country, have no hot water at all. "Hot water is for wimps," one Guanacasteco (resident of the province of Guanacaste) told me. Washing dishes, clothes, and sometimes yourself in cold water seems strange at first; you'll soon learn that there are special soaps designed to work well in cold water. And there's nothing like a cold shower to make you, well, long for a hot one.

• **No bathtubs**

If you want to soak in hot water, you'll have to rent a room in a hotel geared to North American tastes or head to one of the country's many hot springs.

• **Bare floors**

You won't find much wall-to-wall carpeting in Tico houses. Tile floors are the norm—swept, washed, and waxed each day by the homeowner or, more likely, the maid.

• **Not "up to code"**

North Americans are used to a certain level of quality when it comes to finish work and details. In Tico homes you may marvel at a piece of baseboard or molding that stops a foot short of the corner, or an electrical outlet placed too high for all but a basketball star to reach. An expat couple in La Fortuna was perplexed to find that the lightbulb on their porch would be smashed each time they opened the door. Sometimes closets are nonexistent; other times they are the size of a breadbox or, even stranger, bigger than the room itself. Even in areas with many flying insects, screened windows and doors are an anomaly. When looking at a house to buy or rent, check every detail: water pressure, electrical outlets (do they work? are there enough of them?), windows (do they open? close? lock?), electricity, door locks, toilets, shower, pipes, etc.

Renting

The best way to know if you want to live in a place is to live there, but without investing in property. North Americans are conditioned to want to own, own, own, but renting has a lot going for it. The legal period for a rental lease is three years, but as with so many other things in Costa Rica, theory and practice—what's "on the books" and what's actually done—are separated by a wide gulf. The practice here is that most leases are from six months to a year, with some landlords willing to rent month to month.

Renting month to month, you could live for a few months in the expat-heavy Central Valley suburb of Escazú, then live for a while in the shadow of a highland volcano, then retreat for a season to a beachside haven on either the Caribbean or Pacific coast. (Try to strike a rental deal

on the coast outside of the December-April high season; September and October are good times to negotiate.) After living in a few places, you'll know what sort of weather and ambience suits you.

Get a sense of what's on offer browsing the Costa Rica Craigslist or the *Tico Times* online classified ads.

Make contact with local English-speaking expats and see if they know of any housing available. Most people I talked to found their places by word of mouth. Also try posting on one of the many Costa Rica-related message boards (see page 358 in *Resources*), asking if anyone knows of a place to rent in your chosen area. Home-owning expats just may be looking to rent out their place so they can make a long visit home. You can also ask at language schools, which will have lists of families willing to rent out rooms (although they will give their own students priority, of course). Keep your eye out for For Rent *(Se Arrienda)* signs.

The mechanics of renting here are much as they are in the United States. Landlords often adapt a boilerplate lease according to their own and their tenants' needs. If you're renting an unfurnished apartment, remember that you will probably have to supply your own appliances. In the United States an unfurnished apartment almost always comes with a stove and a refrigerator—not so in Costa Rica. So if you're looking to rent for the short term, your best option is a furnished place. If you opt for unfurnished, it's useful to make a list of what you'll need, estimate the prices, and factor that figure into your decision-making process. Setting up a house or apartment is not cheap.

It's important to check out a potential rental thoroughly. Turn on the faucets

Older Costa Rican houses may have tile floors, cane ceilings, and clay tile roofs.

Deciphering the Classifieds

The classified ads are a good place to start your search for housing. Here are some terms and abbreviations that you may encounter:

2 bñs (2 baños): 2 bathrooms
204m2: 204 square meters
3 dor (3 dormitorios): 3 bedrooms
alfom (alfombrado): carpeted
alquileras: rentals
amplia: wide, spacious
amueb (amueblado): furnished
apartamento: apartment
bñ (baño): bathroom
bodega: storeroom, warehouse
C: the symbol for colones (confusingly, $ is also sometimes used)
casa: house
cerám (cerámica): tile floor
coch (cochera): garage
cocin (cocina): kitchen
comercial: business
condominio: condominium
cta pilas (cuarto pilas): utility room with big sink
c/tel (con telefono): with telephone
dor, dorm (dormitorio): bedroom
edificio: building
exc. ubic (excelente ubicación): excellent location
finca: farm or country estate

gje (garaje): garage
guarda: guard
jardín: garden
lav (lavadora): washing machine
lindo: pretty
local: office
lote: lot
lujo: luxurious
mil: 1,000
millón: 1,000,000
muy seg (muy seguro): very secure, safe
nva (nueva): new
parq (parqueo): parking lot or area
peq (pequeño): small
pisc (piscina): swimming pool
piso: floor, as in two floors (levels)
planta baja: lower floor
playa: beach
quinta: country house
se alquila: for rent
se vende: for sale
tranquilo: peaceful
ventas: sales
vista: view
zona franca: free trade zone
zona verde: green area, perhaps a lawn

For a more extensive list of Spanish words, including real estate terms, see the *Glossary* on page 337.

to check water pressure, see if the water drains out, and make sure the heater attached to the showerhead actually heats up the water. Check to see if there are enough electrical outlets, check the windows and doors for functioning locks, and if there's a phone, pick it up and make sure it works. Try to imagine what you'll be doing day to day and ask questions accordingly: Where's the nearest market, bus stop, bank, running track? When is garbage picked up, and do you have to pay for that service? Can the landlord tell you anything about the neighbors or the neighborhood? Is it safe to walk around after dark? Is it easy to get a taxi?

Legally, landlords are entitled to raise the rent by 15 percent each year, but, of course, if you have a one-year lease, you're also entitled to then opt out of your lease.

If you're thinking of being a landlord yourself, be aware that the law tends to favor renters. A property owner in Manuel Antonio says he thinks long and hard before renting out his places. "There are no zoning laws to speak of," he says. "Tenants could start a disco in your apartment if they wanted to. They could bring in 10 family members and seven dogs, and it would still be hard to get them out. I rented to guy from Oklahoma who thought he was here to save Manuel

Antonio [National Park] from the devil. He decided to move on, but if he hadn't, he'd probably still be in my apartment."

SHORT-TERM RENTALS

Besides a month-to-month lease, there are other options for short-term stays. The San José area has dozens of apartment hotels, some of them quite luxurious. They often cost as much (if not more) than a regular hotel, but they come equipped with a kitchen and other amenities you wouldn't get in a hotel room.

But a comfortable hotel room might suit you as well as an apartment-style room. Before I found my apartment, I was thinking of staying several weeks in a mid-range hotel while I looked for a longer-term place. I arrived in October, which is the low season, so many hotels were empty and quite willing to negotiate. For example, a pleasant hotel advertised at US$35 per night, close to the center of town and offering free breakfast, came down quickly to US$20 per night when I offered to pay by the week and in advance. But don't try this sort of haggling during December, January, or Easter week, when it can be hard to find a room at any price.

Another option is a homestay with a Costa Rican family. These are utilized most often by students in one of the many Spanish-language study programs and are often arranged through the school, but you can also arrange such a stay separate from language study (and living with a Spanish-speaking family is its own sort of language study).

Buying Property

You've rented an apartment or two for a while, have explored the country, and are convinced that this is the place for you. You have an idea of where you want to live and how much you can spend. What's next? You start looking, taking it slow, secure in the knowledge that with patience and perseverance you'll be able to find (or build) the house of your dreams.

WHERE TO LOOK

Look everywhere—in the Classifieds sections of local newspapers, on fences and trees for For Sale (Se Vende) signs. Ask the waiter at your favorite seafood restaurant, talk with hotel owners, surfers, the woman selling fresh-squeezed orange juice on the street. As has happened in other countries, the Internet has revolutionized the real estate market in Costa Rica, allowing you to check out beachfront property as you shiver in Minneapolis. The Web is a valuable tool, but remember that mainly higher-end properties are represented there. The best deals may not even be advertised; you'll find them on the ground, talking to the owner of the *pulpería* or to other expats.

RESEARCHING PROPERTY

So you've found a nice little plot of land, with or without a house on it. Your first step is to check to make sure the person selling the property actually owns it, and that there are no snags such as liens, lawsuits against the property, public road restrictions, water easements, or any other type of restriction.

The steps outlined here can be accomplished by a very resourceful and patient prospective buyer, although most people choose to hire a lawyer to take care of these details. Both methods have their advantages: If you do it yourself, you'll learn a great deal about the country and its laws, and you'll be sure that you've really covered all the bases. On the other hand, and especially if you don't speak fluent Spanish, getting a trusted lawyer to help will save you much time and aggravation.

• **Consult the National Registry.**

You will find information on the property's title at the Registro Nacional (the National Registry, located in San José). You can also access information online at www.rnpdigital.com, although there's no English version of the site, and it's not always easy to get the online resource to yield what you're looking for.

Besides patience, you'll need the name and ID *(cédula)* number of the owner, along with the title number. The property section of the *Registro Público* is supposedly fully computerized and indexed, searchable by the owner's name or ID number or by the title number, but it's best to have as much information as possible.

The title number assigned to each property is known as the *folio real*. It is a six-digit number preceded by a number indicating the province in which the property is located and followed by three additional numbers, which tell you how many people own the property. For example, a title number of 1-240871-000 means the property is in the province of San José (the "1" at the beginning of the number) and that there is only one owner of the property (the "000" at the end of the long string of numbers). Property held jointly by husband and wife will have a -001 suffix, and -002 would mean there are two separate (nonmarried) owners of the property. Condominiums have "F" in the title number: 1-240891-F-000, for example. The certificate of title tells you everything about the property in question, from its dimensions to whether or not there are liens or encumbrances on it.

As with most things in Costa Rica, it's often easier to research the *folio real* in person at the San José office. It's even easier (if more pricey) to have a lawyer or other agent do it for you.

The National Registry report is the *informe registral*, and it provides the name of the title holder, boundary lines, tax appraisal, liens, mortgages, recorded easements, and anything else that would affect title.

Many expats buy homes in gated communities, like this one in Escazú, then rent their places out when they're not in Costa Rica.

- **Get a property map.**

Ask the seller to get you the latest version of the property map. Check to make sure the measurements and boundaries on the map are consistent with the property itself (take a good long walking tour of the property to make sure). If the seller has no map, you can get one at the Catastro Nacional (National Records Office), which is part of the Registro Nacional (National Registry) in San José. If no map exists, get a registered surveyor to draw up a map, and then register it at the National Registry (tel. 506/2202-0800, www.registronacional.go.cr).

- **Make sure the land isn't too close to national borders.**

Only Costa Rican citizens can buy land within 2 kilometers (1.2 miles) of international borders.

- **Look into any zoning restrictions.**

Ask future neighbors and the local municipality about any zoning restrictions, or, if you're really ambitious and thorough, see if you can get answers from government agencies. Ask at the Ministro de Salud (Health Department) and the Instituto de Vivenda y Urbanismo (Housing and Urban Development Department) to see zoning plans that may affect your property. Consult the Dirección General Forestal (Forestry Department) for any land use restrictions. Make sure the property isn't part of a national park or reserve—the Ministro de Recursos Naturales, Energías, y Minas (Ministry of Natural Resources, Energy, and Mines) and the Servicio Nacional de Parques (National Park Service) will have this type of information. If you want to make sure they're not going to build a freeway through your land, check in with the Ministro de Obras Públicas and Transportes. Also consult your local municipality (see *Resources* for more about government agencies).

- **Certify that the seller has paid all past property taxes and assessments.**

- **Make sure any domestic employees you intend to retain have been paid off by the seller.**

seeing what's on offer in the Nicoya Peninsula town of Nosara

Otherwise, you may be liable for any past monies due to them.

• **Check all utilities.**

Does the property have access to water, electricity, telephone lines, and waste disposal? If not, how much will it cost you to secure these services?

• **Check out your neighbors.**

Are they known cranks, water hogs, or drug runners? Ask around.

Tired yet? I never said it was going to be easy. And sure, there are a lot of people who either trust others to do the legwork for them or just slack off and forget many of the steps. You might skip some of the due diligence and be just fine. On the other hand, you might end up with a beautiful piece of land that you can't build on or even access.

RESTRICTIONS ON COASTAL PROPERTY

If you've found some beachfront property that you love and can afford, congratulations! But know that there are different rules for owning and building on this type of land. The Maritime Zoning Law says that no one can *own* the first 200 meters (219 yards) of beach frontage, at least not legally (unless you bought the land before 1977, when the law went into effect). Of those 200 meters of beach frontage, which begin at the high-tide mark, you can't build on the first 50 meters (55 yards)— it's part of the *zona pública* (public zone). The next 150 meters (164 yards) inland is classified as *zona restringida* (restricted zone), which can be built on if the government chooses to grant a lease or concession of the property. Concessions last 5-20 years and can most often be renewed without a problem, says Ryan Piercy of the ARCR.

The Maritime Zoning Law also restricts ownership of concession land. The following are not supposed to acquire concession land:

• foreigners who have been residents of Costa Rica for fewer than five years

• corporations with bearer shares

• corporations based outside of Costa Rica

• Costa Rican corporations incorporated by foreigners

• corporations with 50 percent or more ownership by foreigners

In practice, how strictly these rules are adhered to seems to depend on where you are (How valuable is the land? Are people clamoring to use the *zona pública?*) and how much influence you wield. Tellingly, approximately 300 concessions are recorded in the Registro Nacional, but there are more than 15,000 hotel and tourist developments along the coast that somehow managed to bypass the law.

If you're a multinational corporation with money and lawyers to burn, you probably don't need to worry. For the rest of us, keeping a low profile and not stepping on anyone's toes seems to be the key to avoiding problems. Then again, law enforcement in Costa Rica comes in fits and starts, so it's prudent to operate on the straight and narrow.

If you're building on coastal property, besides getting the usual building permits, you'll need to run your plans by the Instituto Costarricense de Turismo (the Costa Rican Tourism Institute).

TITLE TRANSFER

If everything checks out and you're ready to make the purchase, you or your agent

Buying Real Estate Through a Corporation

Roger Petersen, practicing lawyer and author of *The Legal Guide to Costa Rica*, explains how the old practice of buying real estate through a Costa Rica corporation – a Sociedad Anónima, or Anonymous Society (S.A.) – is changing.

Before 2012, buyers and sellers wanting to avoid the 1.5 percent real estate transfer tax could do so by making sure any real estate deal was a transfer of corporate assets rather than a transfer of property from one individual to another. This qualified the transfer as indirect rather than direct, and avoided the tax.

"People would use S.A.s to hold and transfer property," says Petersen, "and during the real estate boom of 2005, 2006, 2007, developers were basically selling you property by giving you a corporation, which avoided the 1.5 percent property transfer tax.

"Not to have taxed property transfers during the boom was a huge lost opportunity for Costa Rica. What the [Costa Rican regulatory agencies] tried to do in late 2012 was to catch up, although the boom had already passed. They passed a law that says 'We're going to tax *indirect* transfers of property.' 'Indirect' means the transfer of dominion or control of any real estate asset. So if a corporation holding the property transfers it to another owner, that's an indirect transfer, and is subjected to the 1.5 percent transfer tax."

Well-versed in how regulations are passed, ignored, repealed, or reinterpreted, Petersen cautions prospective expats not to panic. "We'll see what sort of workarounds develop," he says, "or if regulators change their minds."

will present the buyer with a written offer and an earnest money deposit. If you and the seller agree that you want a period of time before closing, you enter into either an *Opción de Compra* (Option to Buy) or *Promesa Recíproca de Compra-Venta* (Reciprocal Promise to Buy and Sell); both documents outline the price and timeframe of purchase. At closing, the formal transfer begins.

Property is transferred from buyer to seller by executing a transfer deed (an *Escritura de Traspaso,* often referred to simply as an *escritura*) before a notary public. In Costa Rica, notary publics must also be lawyers, and they can do a lot more than their counterparts in the United States, having extensive powers to act on behalf of the state. The transfer deed will include details of the financing of the property. The notary will then register the sale at the National Registry in San José.

You can buy property individually, jointly with other individuals, or in the name of a corporation *(Sociedad Anónima,* or *S.A.).* For more about forming S.A.s, see page 186 in the *Business and Employment* chapter.

PROPERTY AND MUNICIPAL TAXES

Yearly property taxes are low—0.5-1.5 percent of the declared value of the property. Declared value is often lower than actual purchase price, bringing the property tax figure even lower. Property taxes are assessed yearly (the year runs January 1-December 31) and are collected by the local municipal government, which also collects a general tax that covers garbage pickup, water, and sewage. The amount varies depending on where you live, but it is usually quite low.

"Luxury Home" Tax

At the end of 2009, Costa Rica put into effect a new property tax, called the Solidarity Tax for the Strengthening of Housing Programs *(Impuesto Solidario para el Fortalecimiento de Programas de Vivienda),* or law number 8683 (*Ley* 8683 in Spanish).

Nicknamed the luxury tax and sometimes referred to as the TLH, this tax applies only to houses with a value over 106 million colones (about US$212,000). This includes villas that are part of hotels and condominium complexes in which the shared areas plus the individual unit have a value of more than 106 million. If you own land with no buildings on it, or your house is valued under US$212,000, you are exempt from this tax. The tax is in addition to any other property taxes you are required to pay and is due on or before January 15 of each year.

Revenue from this tax is supposed to help eradicate shantytowns in Costa Rica, one of the richer Central American republics but still with a good portion of its population living beneath the poverty line. This first incarnation of the tax will be in effect for 10 years, through 2020, and may be renewed after that.

The tax is from 0.25 percent of the value of the house up to a maximum of 0.55 percent (for houses valued above 1.6 billion colones) of the value of the home, paid yearly.

REAL ESTATE AGENT COSTS

One of the problems with a country where anyone can be a real estate agent is that each of those middlemen can charge anything they want to on top of the purchase price—if you allow it, that is. It is imperative that you agree, in writing and up front, what the real estate agent's commission will be. Some North America-trained real estate agents follow North American guidelines—3 percent commission for the seller's agent and 3 percent for the buyer's agent. But don't count on that being the case—nail down the numbers ahead of time. Also be aware that the more people

in on the deal (the taxi driver, his brother, and their cousin the barkeep at the local watering hole), the more you'll pay on top of the purchase price, with everyone wanting their cut. Sometimes all the added commissions will double the purchase price, and the seller won't even know it!

CLOSING COSTS

Usually the buyer and seller will split closing costs, but make sure to verify that arrangement. Remember that the various fees involved are calculated according to the *registered* value (rather than the sale price) of the property. Ryan Piercy of the ARCR estimates that most people in Costa Rica register their property at 10-30 percent of what they actually paid.

Fees include a real estate transfer tax (1.5 percent of the price you pay for the property), a public registry fee (0.5 percent), various stamps run about 0.55 percent, and a notary or attorney fee of 1-2 percent of the property's registered value.

If you've arranged for a mortgage in Costa Rica, there will be more fees—mortgage documents require registration fees and documentary stamps. The notary will also charge for drafting and recording the mortgage.

HOUSEHOLD EXPENSES

Household expenses will vary, of course, depending on how large your home is, whether you make do with bare-bones basics or spring for all the amenities, and where you live in the country. For example, high-speed Internet may be available through your phone line for a reasonable fee in the more developed areas, while you may want to spring for satellite Internet in the hinterlands if you don't want to be stuck with dial-up. Or you may live at the beach and feel the need to have the air-conditioning running all the time—this could add hundreds of dollars to your monthly electric bill.

One household expense you'll probably not worry about is a high heating bill.

These figures will vary considerably, and will change often, but in 2017 you could expect to pay monthly fees of about US$10-20 for water, US$20-100 for electricity, US$20-70 for phone service, about US$40 for basic cable TV, and anywhere from US$20 to almost US$150 for Internet. (For details on TV, phone, and Internet installation and billing, see the *Communications* chapter; the companies you'll need to contact are listed in the *Resources* section, starting on page 355.)

For water, you'll contact the National Institute of Aqueducts and Sewage (www. aya.go.cr); for telecommunications and electricity, you'll deal with the National Electricity Institute (www.ice.go.cr).

(For more details on the cost of living in Costa Rica, see page 200 in the *Finance* chapter.)

SQUATTERS

Back in the 1880s, laws were introduced to allow poor farmers to settle on land that was unoccupied or not in use and claim it for themselves. In its usual democratic fashion, Costa Rica wanted all of its citizens to have access to land. The laws sought to prevent a few wealthy and often absentee landlords from owning most of the country, while the majority worked for them as landless laborers.

Known as *precaristas,* squatters here have certain rights. If they occupy and work "abandoned" land for three months, they start to accrue property rights; in a year, they can apply for its expropriation from the absentee landlord. Expats who buy property in Costa Rica and visit just a few times a year need to be aware of this potential problem. It's not common, but that won't be any consolation if it happens to you.

Robert Wells, a U.S. lawyer who has helped many foreigners in conflicts with squatters, said in a *Tico Times* article that landowners should file for an eviction order within the first three months of squatters occupying their land.

"As long as you can prove they've been there for three months or less, the procedure is relatively fast and painless," said Wells. "However, if you wait, the procedure is much longer and more involved."

Shopping for Real Estate

There are hundreds of companies and individuals building houses and condo complexes in Costa Rica. Some of them market their wares aggressively, trolling for clients by phone or email. It's difficult to keep track of all the new players in this game, and it can be hard to know how to evaluate the overabundance of offerings.

Here's a checklist to get you started in your appraisal of what's out there.

WEBSITE AND PROMOTIONAL MATERIAL
Are there real people, with real (full) names, listed on the website or in the brochures?
If not, beware. Why would a company hesitate to tell you who's in charge?

Do they give a physical address for the development?
If not, consider why they might not want you to drop by on your own.

Is a Costa Rican phone number given?
If so, the number will have a 506 area code; you should be able to reach someone on-site if people are living or building there.

How long has the company or developer been in business?
Less than 2 years, be wary. More than 10 years, rest easy.

FINANCING
Is financing being offered by a local bank?
If so, that's a good sign, since banks wouldn't finance a project unless they believed it to be sound. Sometimes developers will offer their own financing, which isn't a bad thing but doesn't give you that extra assurance that another company (a bank) is behind the development.

Where does the initial deposit (earnest money) go?
The best option is to your attorney's or real estate agent's account; also OK would be to a local bank or escrow service. If the money goes directly to the developer or to another individual you don't know, beware.

When can the developer use the deposit?
Best would be not until after closing; fine would be not until certain agreed-upon purchase conditions are met; not so good would be that the developer can access that deposit immediately.

When do you need to start paying the rest of the money?
It's best to spell this out in a purchasing option, a document you draw up before giving any money. Worst-case scenario would be that you start paying immediately, with no milestones or guarantees met.

THE PLACE ITSELF
If you don't know much about construction, you should take someone who does on a walk-through of the development. Here are some basic factors to consider.

Water

Where will your water come from? A private source or well is the best option; water from the city would be the second-best option; last is water from a rural area.

Power

Are there power lines (or underground cables) to the development? To each lot or house?

Telephones and Internet

Will landlines be provided, and if so, how many? What about Internet access?

Roads

How are the roads to and within the development? Concrete roads are best and easiest to maintain. Gravel and asphalt require more maintenance; who will maintain these roads in the future?

Parking

Does the house or condo come with a parking space? Is there sufficient visitor parking?

The Foundation

Does the soil slope away from the house? (It should.) It rains a lot here; how's the drainage? There should be a system to collect rainwater and divert it away from the foundation. Look for any signs of water damage around the foundation.

Walls, Ceilings, Floors

Look for cracks or bulges in ceilings, walls, and floors, which would be signs of shoddy construction or subsequent damage. Check lower corners of windows for discoloration, which could be a sign of water damage. Check for signs of recent repainting (especially in just one spot), which may signal a quick fix of a chronic problem.

Doors and Windows

Make sure doors and windows open and close easily and that they seem sturdy. Locks should engage fully, and doors and windows should not rattle or have a loose fit.

Electrical and Plumbing

Look to see how many outlets there are per room. Outlets should be grounded, with three prongs.

In the kitchen, turn on all the lights and then turn on any appliances. The lights should not dim and you shouldn't blow a fuse.

In the bathroom, check the water pressure. Turn on the shower, and then turn on the sink. Is there enough water pressure for both the shower and sink to have a decent flow?

Where does the water in the house come from, and where does the wastewater and sewage go? If the water comes from a well, what is the diameter of the water main (the supply line to the home)? Ideally it should be 2 centimeters (¾ inch) or larger. If the house is on a septic system, where is the leach field and how large is it?

Use all your senses—does anything smell off, as if the sewage system isn't quite doing its job? Is there the smell of damp in the house?

Thanks to contractor Brian Van Rheenen for his tips on checking construction quality, and to the Tico Times *for some of the other tips.*

Before buying property, do a thorough visual inspection to make sure squatters haven't already settled in. If the seller says there's a resident caretaker, make sure that's what he or she is. Ask to see pay stubs (a caretaker will be paid; a squatter will not).

Record the property on film, and keep records of improvements made so that you can prove the property isn't abandoned.

If you're not going to live on the property full-time, hire a caretaker. Have a written contract with him or her, and keep up-to-date with salary and Social Security payments (so the caretaker won't become a squatter).

Make sure you or someone you trust does a full inspection of the property at least every three months. Nipping this kind of thing in the bud is the way to avoid trouble.

Building a House

If you build your own home, you won't have to adjust to Tico housing styles, which may include low ceilings, no lawns, and odd ideas about finish work. In your own place, you can put the outlets where you want them, install North American-style hot water heaters and window screens, and lay down floors of tropical hardwoods. You can orient the house toward the best view (many Tico houses look inward rather than outward). You can put in a lush lawn or landscape to your heart's content with native trees and flowering shrubs. "You don't really have to plant things here," one gardener told me. "You just stick something in the ground, or you wait (not long) for your yard to be invaded."

In short, you *can* build the house of your dreams for considerably less than you'd have to pay up north. But it won't be dirt cheap, and it will take a lot of sweat and patience. You will need to be scrupulous about paying your workers the minimum wage, which is far lower than it would be in the United States, plus their health benefits (see page 190 in the *Employment* chapter for more details). And most people who've been through the experience say that you really need to speak Spanish, know something about

construction, and be confident you can effectively oversee workers. Those who got the house they wanted tended to be on-site as much as possible, overseeing every little detail.

And be sure your contract with whoever's doing your building is detailed and explicit. Mark Drolette, who moved from Sacramento, California, to near San Ramón, Costa Rica, counts as among the best things that happened to him in Costa Rica "deciding to purchase my half acre." The worst was finding out his house contract "didn't cover the cost of small items like, oh, doors and windows and toilets and sinks."

BEFORE YOU BUY A LOT

Before you buy land that you intend to build on, you need to do a little research. First, make sure the lot has basic services such as water, electricity, telephone, and drainage. If it lacks any of these, get estimates for how much it will cost to install those services. Next, make sure there are no restrictions on the lot that might cause you to be denied a construction permit. Begin by checking with the Public Registry (Registro Nacional), stop in at the Permit Reception Office (Oficina Receptora de Permisos de Construcción)

What You Need to Get a Building Permit

To apply for a building permit in Costa Rica, you or your construction manager will need:

- copies of the construction plans
- the property map or plan *(plano catastrado)*
- the permit checklist *(hoja de comisión)*
- the property deed *(escritura)*
- the consulting contract with your architect or engineer *(contrato de consultoria)*

- approval from the water company (Instituto Costarricense de Acueductos y Alcantarillados, or AYA) regarding availability of water
- the electrical design plan approved by the electrical company (Servicio Nacional de Electricidad, or SNE)
- a permit from your local municipality

Note that applying for building permits for condominium projects or commercial construction requires additional forms.

Plans are filed with the Permit Reception Office (Oficina Receptora de Permisos de Construcción) in San José.

in San José, and consult the municipality *(municipalidad)* where the property is located.

FILING FOR PERMITS

According to Roger Petersen, author of *The Legal Guide to Costa Rica,* requests for construction permits are filed with the Permit Reception Office (Oficina Receptora de Permisos de Construcción) in San José, which is a centralized office that houses representatives from MOPT (Ministerio de Obras Públicas y Transportes—roads), INVU (Instituto Nacional de Vivienda y Urbanismo—housing), ICE (Instituto Costarricense de Electricidad—telephone), AYA (Instituto Costarricense de Acueductos y Alcantarillados—water), SNE (Servicio Nacional de Electricidad—electricity), CFIA (Colegio Federado de Ingenieros y de Arquitectos), and the Ministry of Health (Ministerio de Salud).

By law, the local municipality is responsible for ensuring that all construction complies with building regulations,

so you'll also need a building permit from your municipality. There may be occasional visits to your construction site by the municipal building inspector, who must certify that the construction is proceeding according to code.

Applications for construction permits must be filed by an architect or civil engineer who is a member of the Federation of Engineers and Architects (Colegio Federado de Ingenieros y de Arquitectos, www.cfia.or.cr).

BUILDING COSTS

In general, materials costs in Costa Rica are roughly equivalent to those in North America, while labor costs are significantly less. Total building costs vary a great deal depending on materials used and salaries paid, with estimates ranging from US$25 per square foot for simple construction to up to US$70 per square foot for a luxurious house.

Building in remote areas is often more expensive, since you have to factor in delivery costs of materials.

LANGUAGE AND EDUCATION

Writer and humorist Dave Barry notes that "Americans who travel abroad for the first time are often shocked to discover that, despite all the progress that has been made in the last 30 years, many foreign people still speak in foreign languages."

Of course you're not like those first-timers that Barry lampoons. But even people who've visited Costa Rica many times and are serious about moving here have been known to minimize the language difference. I'd be doing you a disservice, however, if I claimed you could thrive in Costa Rica without at least some Spanish. In fact, working on your

Spanish is the single most important investment you can make in adapting to Costa Rica. And you're in luck—Costa Rica has a great variety of language schools, in locations from very urban to decidedly beachy.

Sure, a lot of people in Costa Rica speak English (though not as many as you might think). ATMs have instructions in English, and English-language TV and movies dominate the media. But before you say, "I'll learn Spanish later, maybe in a year or two," think about how you feel when someone in your home country doesn't try to learn your language. It

Vamos a la escuela (let's go to school).

seems like a lack of respect, doesn't it? The same holds true here.

At the risk of stating the obvious, Costa Rica is a Spanish-speaking country, and if you're going to make this your home, you need to speak the language—if only to greet people politely and thank them for their help. Learning a new language is not easy, but Ticos applaud all genuine efforts. And language is more than just words—it carries with it an entire civilization. Deny yourself the language and you'll never get more than ankle-deep in the culture.

If you have school-age children and are considering relocating to Costa Rica, schools will be a major concern and will probably determine, at least in part, where you choose to live. The Central Valley is rich in educational choices, although outlying areas have an increasing number of viable options as well.

Many expats send their kids to private school. As parents research schools, they'll want to ask whether or not the schools follow the same calendar as schools in their home country, what the primary language of instruction is, and whether the diplomas granted will allow students to apply to the colleges and universities they're interested in.

In Costa Rica there are good private schools that follow the Costa Rican model (ending at the 11th grade), others that grant U.S.-style high school diplomas, and yet others that offer the IB, or International Baccalaureate, which allows students to apply to European universities and can sometimes count toward first-year credit at a U.S. university.

This chapter tells you a little about learning Spanish as well as describing the Costa Rican school system, both public and private. Note that there are extensive and detailed lists of Spanish schools and schools for your kids in the *Resources* section, starting on page 339. You'll also find a *Spanish Phrasebook* on page 359, and a *Glossary* of Spanish terms on page *337.*

Learning the Language

Spanish is the first language of the Americas, and learning it will serve any New Worlder well. Costa Rica is an excellent place to learn, with friendly people with whom to practice and a national tendency not to pronounce the *rr,* the rolling *r* that foils so many nonnative speakers.

How hard is it to learn Spanish? Well, consider the U.S. State Department rankings. That governmental agency groups languages for their diplomatic corps according to learning difficulty. The State Department says that the easiest languages for speakers of English are in Category 1, requiring 600 hours of classwork for minimal proficiency. Spanish is in this category, as are most Romance languages, for its straightforward grammar and pronunciation and for the ease with which North American English speakers can be exposed to the language. (Category 2 languages, requiring 1,100 hours of classwork, include Persian, Hebrew, and many African languages. Category 3, the most difficult, requiring 2,200 hours of study, includes Arabic and Chinese languages.)

Unlike English, which has many irregular spellings, Spanish has a strong correspondence between the sound of a word and the way it is spelled. And Spanish has just five pure vowel sounds, while English has at least twelve. If you learn the five Spanish vowel sounds (roughly "ah-eh-ee-oh-oo"), you'll be able to sound out any word in Spanish.

Other differences between Spanish and English include the fact that Spanish words are gendered, meaning that any given word will be either masculine or feminine. Masculine words usually (though not always) end in *o,* while feminine words usually end in *a.* Masculine words require a masculine article (*el* or *los*), while feminine words require a feminine article (*la* or *las*).

There is no rhyme or reason as to which words are masculine and which feminine. Why should "ears" *(las orejas),* for example, be feminine, while "lips" *(los labios)* are masculine? The gender of words is something you pick up as you go along, though you'll be further flummoxed by

Despite claims to the contrary, you can't assume people here will speak your language.

Language Learning Tips

- Don't be shy. How will you improve your conversation skills if you never say anything? Remember, extroverts learn speaking skills faster than introverts do. Not an extrovert? See the last bullet point.

- Ask the native Spanish speakers around you to correct your errors, and then keep reminding them. They'll probably hesitate at first for fear you'll feel bad if they tell you you're doing something wrong.

- Keep a notebook on you and jot down all the new words and phrases you encounter. Try to look up the new words every evening, and then use them in conversation at least five times the next day. This can get tricky if the phrase in question is X-rated.

- Immerse yourself in the language and the culture but realize you'll need to take breaks now and then. You'll start to go crazy, with your Spanish not yet fully functional but your English getting as rusty as an old machete. Do what you need to do to come back to yourself – I like to watch *Six Feet Under* reruns or reread a chapter of *Pride and Prejudice* – then dive in again.

- Understand that at first you won't be able to convey all of who you are in the new language. Are you a brilliant conversationalist with a sharp wit? You won't be in Spanish, at least not at first. Get used to having the verbal resources of a toddler. This is a good time to remember that a smile and goodwill often get you farther than perfectly formed sentences.

- Your Spanish-speaking self will be different from your English-speaking self. Learning the language and constructing a persona in Spanish gives you an opportunity to emphasize parts of your character that are dormant in your native language. I know people who are much more relaxed and fun in Spanish than in English, for example, and others who are more exacting and precise. Who do you want to be in Spanish?

For a helpful list of Spanish phrases, see the *Spanish Phrasebook* on page 359.

DAILY LIFE
LANGUAGE AND EDUCATION

the rare exceptions when words that end in *o* are nonetheless feminine (like the word for "hand," *la mano*).

REGIONAL DIFFERENCES

Sure, Ticos speak Spanish, and you'll find a portable Spanish-English dictionary worth its weight in gold if you plan to converse with anyone outside of gringo enclaves. But Ticos also speak Costa Rican, using terms that you'll never hear in Madrid or Mexico City.

Even pronouns are different. *Tu* (the familiar form of "you"), so prevalent in other Spanish-speaking countries, is not used in Costa Rican Spanish. But due to the influence of Mexican television and to non-Ticos who can't stop *tuteando* (the

practice of using the informal *tu*), Costa Ricans are familiar with the pronoun, and sometimes even use it themselves.

It wouldn't matter so much except that *vos* and *tu* require entirely different verb conjugations, and those who've learned a *vos*-free Spanish probably won't have learned how to conjugate for that pronoun. For instance, "You want" with *tu* would be *tu quieres,* while "you want" with *vos* would be *vos querés.* (For more on how to use *vos,* see page 362 in the *Spanish Phrasebook.*)

But if you already speak Spanish with *tu,* don't worry about immediately crossing over to the *vos* side. After a time in Costa Rica, you'll probably start picking it up. And if not? Well, you still speak

Spanish, and Costa Ricans will no doubt appreciate that.

There are also differences within the country. For example, you may hear English patois as often as you'll hear Spanish on the country's Caribbean coast. Many of the Costa Ricans on that coast are descendants of workers from the English-speaking Caribbean islands, especially Jamaica, who came to work on banana plantations or build the railroad.

LANGUAGE SCHOOLS

There are as many ways to study Spanish in Costa Rica as there are students who want to learn. Sign up for a 12-week intensive course with six hours a day of rigorous instruction, or arrange for a leisurely hour of private instruction each morning before heading for the beach. You could combine language study with volunteering or enter a specialty program geared to your profession, like courses for Spanish teachers or classes that focus on medical terminology.

The biggest leaps in learning often come when you least expect them, and if you take care to mix mostly with Spanish speakers, just going about your daily business will be a crash course in the language. The best motivation for improving your skills is the genuine desire to communicate with someone who speaks only Spanish, so get out there and meet the locals.

Choosing a Language School

Especially if you're a beginner, it's a good idea to sign up for a course, preferably one that meets every day for at least a few weeks. Language study benefits from daily reinforcement, and it's good to get a base of grammar and verb forms. After that, you can design your own course of study, which might include reading at least one article in the newspaper every day (dictionary at the ready), watching Spanish-language soap operas, or falling in love with someone who doesn't speak a word of English.

Most language schools are based in or near the capital city of San José, but there are also programs in beach towns and other tourist centers. Most schools offer some combination of language study and cultural activities, from day trips to nearby volcanoes to salsa dancing lessons. The fewer side perks, the cheaper the school usually is.

Business travelers will want to look for a program or tutor well versed in business vocabulary and knowledgeable about business practices within the country. Business Spanish can be as much about learning a new professional etiquette as about conjugating verbs.

When choosing a school, call or visit the school's website to learn more details about programs offered. Competition has benefited the industry; be sure to shop around and ask about any special deals—for students, for senior citizens, professionals, or off-season visitors, or for longer stays. Prices change often; make sure you obtain up-to-date prices from any schools you are considering.

(A detailed list of Spanish language schools begins on page 345 in *Resources*.)

Staying with a Host Family

Most schools can arrange homestays for their students. This usually means a single room in a local family's home and often includes two meals a day and laundry service. The nature of the housing and the neighborhood it's located in vary considerably; some schools even offer both "standard" and "deluxe" homestays.

Homestays are a great way to get to know the people of Costa Rica. You'll get a crash course in Tico culture, learning how family members interact, when meals are served, what they do for fun, and how they treat their dog.

Wendy Tayler, who first came to Costa Rica in 1973 on an exchange program with Lewis & Clark College, liked her host family so much she became a part of it. She fell in love with her host family "brother" and married him. Their kids grew up bilingual in Costa Rica. Now she paints and sells silk scarves and wraps with scenes from her beloved adopted country.

Even if your homestay doesn't have such dramatic consequences, staying with a family will radically improve your Spanish. Whether playing cards in the living room, waiting your turn for the bathroom, or sampling your host mother's cooking, you'll hear nothing but Spanish, Spanish, and more Spanish. If you need to ask how to get to the grocery store or let them know you'll be traveling for a few days, guess what you have to do? Tell them in Spanish. Most language learners agree that this kind of immersion is as important (if not more so) than more traditional approaches like grammar and vocabulary drills.

Education

A strong commitment to education is one of the defining characteristics of Costa Rican culture. The 1948 decision to abolish the armed forces meant that Costa Rica could spend more on infrastructure, health care, and, perhaps most important of all for the country's future, education.

PRIMARY AND SECONDARY EDUCATION

In Costa Rica, schooling from grades 1 through 11 is free, and for kids ages 6-14 (through the ninth year in school), attendance is compulsory. Consequently, Costa Rica has one of the highest literacy rates—96 percent—in Latin America, second only to Cuba, and a culture that values education as one of the pillars of national life. The first two heads of state were elementary school teachers. Costa Rica is the most stable and democratic society in the region, and its emphasis on education has a lot to do with that status. On Election Day, in fact, schoolchildren participate in mock elections in their classrooms, and the results are published in the national papers. This early introduction to participatory democracy may have something to do with the fact that voter turnout in Costa Rica is traditionally high—hovering around 80 percent for the last three decades. More recently, turnout rates have started to drop as a mistrust of politicians (always a part of the national culture) increased and people lost faith in the government's effectiveness.

The country's commitment to education didn't begin in 1949. In 1821, the government, newly independent from Spain, established the University of Santo Tomás, and in 1825, a law was passed requiring every municipality to found a public school. Both sexes were guaranteed equal instruction in 1847, and education became free and compulsory for primary grades in 1869.

Public Schools

The good news is that Costa Ricans value education highly. The bad news is that you wouldn't necessarily know it from looking at the country's public schools.

By law, 6 percent of the GDP must be set aside for education, and often many times that amount is spent. Article 78 of the 1949 constitution states that "general education" (through grade 9) is free and obligatory for all Costa Ricans; in 1992

Understanding Costa Rica's Schools

Deciphering the Costa Rican school system can be a challenge. The following table outlines the public school system as governed by the Ministry of Public Education (Ministerio de Educación Pública, MEP), but many private schools follow the same model and use the same terminology. Public high schools end at grade 11, while private schools geared to foreigners will usually offer a 12th year, with either a U.S.-style high school diploma or the International Baccalaureate (IB). The cycles (ciclos in Spanish) are the MEP's grouping of school years; in each cycle the MEP outlines what it thinks students should learn and how they should learn it. For example, in Cycle III, most schools teach physics in the 7th year, chemistry in the 8th, and biology in the 9th year. There are national exams at the ends of Cycles II, III, and IV, corresponding with the end of grades 6, 9, and 11. The last exam is the terminal exam (bachillerato); students do not graduate without passing this exam. The Spanish equivalents of English terms are given in parentheses.

SECONDARY SCHOOL (SECUNDARIA) OR HIGH SCHOOL (COLEGIO)

Grade/Year	Student Age	MEP Cycle Subdivision
11th year (undecimo año)	16.5	IV Cycle or Diversified Cycle
10th year (decimo año)	15.5	IV Cycle or Diversified Cycle
9th year (noveno año)	14.5	III Cycle
8th year (octavio año)	13.5	III Cycle
7th year (septimo año)	12.5	III Cycle

MEP Exam at End of Year

Terminal Exam (bachillerato)		IV Cycle
Ministry Exam		III Cycle

PRIMARY SCHOOL (PRIMERIA)

Grade/Year	Student Age	MEP Cycle Subdivision
6th grade (sexto grado)	11.5	II Cycle
5th grade (quinto grado)	10.5	II Cycle
4th grade (cuarto grado)	9.5	II Cycle
3rd grade (tercer grado)	8.5	I Cycle
2nd grade (segundo grado)	7.5	I Cycle
1st grade (primer grado)	6.5	I Cycle

MEP Exam at End of Year

Ministry Exam		II Cycle

PRESCHOOL (PRE-ESCOLAR). ALSO KNOWN AS PREP (PREPA).

Grade/Year	Student Age
preparatory (prepatoria)	5.5
kindergarten (kinder)	4.5
pre-kindergarten (prekinder)	3.5
nursery (maternal)	2.5

Many thanks to Kirt Wackford for this information.

legislators went even farther, asserting that education is not only the state's obligation but a fundamental human right.

The school year is usually divided into two terms, February through July and August through November or December. The longest break comes between November and January and used to be associated with the coffee harvest (so kids could help), but now it is seen more as a lengthy Christmas holiday. There is usually a two- to three-week break in July as well. National standardized exams are administered during the 6th, 9th, and 11th grades; students must pass them to advance to the next level and, in the case of the exam after the 11th grade, to graduate. This holds true for both public and private schools, as the Ministry of Education's policies apply to both types of education.

Public school begins with kindergarten and runs through what in the United States would be 11th grade. From there some students go on to local universities; the University of Costa Rica (UCR) in San José is the largest (about 39,000 students) and the most respected. Primary school *(primaria)* is kindergarten through 6th grade; secondary school (or *colegio*) consists of grades 7 through 11.

Unfortunately, public education in Costa Rica is in a time of crisis. While nearly all children attend primary school—with a growing number attending preschool—the schools can be pretty basic, and the system breaks down at the high school *(colegio)* level, where the dropout rate is growing. According to the *Tico Times,* only about 40 percent of the population earns a high school diploma, with most dropping out for work or family-related reasons before they reach the 11th grade (the final year).

In the past few decades, budget deficits have led to cuts in the funding of social services, and education has not been spared. Schools have had to make do with less money even as they try to educate a growing population. And while public education is technically free for students in Costa Rica, the price of supplies, uniforms, books, and other costs can be prohibitive for many poor families.

Most public schools have outdated textbooks, if they have textbooks at all, few if any computers for student use, no extracurricular activities such as drama and art, and no school sports or sports facilities.

Salaries for the country's teachers have never been high, and recently pensions were reduced, causing fewer qualified people to be attracted to the field.

With public schools in crisis, private schools have rushed in to fill the gap.

Private Schools

Many expat families choose to send their children to private schools, as do many Costa Rican families who can afford it. Kirt Wackford, who taught science at Saint Paul College, says it's more common here than in the United States for families of modest means to send their kids to private school. Ana, Kirt's Tica wife, comes from a family of seven. Her father was a shopkeeper and her mother a housewife, and yet they made the sacrifices that would allow all seven kids to attend good private schools. Most of them went on to public higher education at the prestigious University of Costa Rica.

The San José-area phone book lists more than 300 private elementary and secondary schools. There are Catholic schools, evangelical Christian schools, Jewish schools, German, French, and Japanese schools, and dozens of bilingual English-Spanish schools with wildly varying ratios of which language is used more often.

It's a good idea to start researching schools as soon as you know you'll be moving to Costa Rica. Ideally, both you

Expat Experiences: Schools

The Central Valley of Costa Rica, where you'll find the capital city of San José, is known to have the highest concentration of high-quality private schools. But what do you do if you live in outlying areas, like at the beach? Or what if you're in the Central Valley but have some qualms about private schools?

SOUTHERN CARIBBEAN COAST

According to Manuel Pinto, the schools in the southern Caribbean coast are good for younger children, not as good for teens. Pinto, owner of a vacation rentals business in Playa Chiquita, moved with his wife Emmanuelle to Costa Rica in 2002, when his daughter was three years old. Soon their daughter was attending a small private Waldorf-style grade school (Centro Educativo Playa Chiquita, tel. 506/2750-0754) right next door to her parents' realty office. Manuel also speaks highly of Mi Jardin, another primary school in the area.

"This is a paradise for little ones," says Pinto. "As a parent, if you want to come to Costa Rica, don't wait for your kids to get old. Do it now. I'd do it all over again with my eyes closed."

But Pinto thinks that parents who live on the southern Caribbean coast should "get their kids the hell out when they become teenagers."

When his first daughter (he now has two) finished up at the local private grade school, Pinto wasn't happy with the options open to her. "We sent her to school in the city of Limón, but it's an hour and a half each way, so she was getting up before sunrise and getting home after sunset, never seeing the daylight. It just wasn't working out." They considered moving part-time to San José, where there are many well-regarded private high schools, but decided that wouldn't be ideal either.

Costs Rica's southern Caribbean coast "isn't a place for teenagers," he continues. "Sure, kids can get in trouble anywhere. The issue is finding positive opportunities to balance the potential for trouble. Kids here can get into gardening, or surfing, but after that there is nothing for teenagers. There are no sports activities in schools. And the level of education is not great from the seventh grade up."

Pinto had been very involved in the community, spearheading community policing initiatives and serving as vice president of the Chamber of Tourism and Commerce. But he felt he was sometimes serving community at the expense of family. Then his mother and brother in Boulder, Colorado, suggested that his older daughter attend high school in that town. Pinto and his wife agonized over it but finally decided to let their daughter go with the understanding that they would be in Boulder as much as they could, maybe three or four months of every year. "For that stage in her life," says Pinto, "she would be in a great town with great values."

NICOYA PENINSULA

There are many schooling options on the northern Nicoya Peninsula, but fewer as you travel farther south. When Country Day School (CDS) in Escazú opened a branch in Playa Brasilito, near Tamarindo, in 2003, they billed their facility as a "serious school at the beach" because it was one of the very few in the area that had a U.S.- or European-style curriculum and accreditation that would allow graduates to go straight to universities in the States or Europe. That school later became the independent Costa Rica International Academy, and now there are other high-quality private schools in the area, like Lakeside International in Playas del Coco and La Paz School in Playa Brasilito.

It's a different story down the coast in the remote town of Playa Junquillal (although with the improvement in roads, "remote" is becoming a relative term). When Swiss-born Alice Iten, who runs Guacamaya Lodge, decided she wanted to send her half-Tica daughter to the local public school in tiny Junquillal, she got to work. Alice, who has lived in Costa Rica since 1993, solicited the help of the Swiss embassy, who donated money for supplies, and she worked with the Ministry of Education to create a school that she terms satisfactory, if basic (no physical education, music, or art). After attending public school in Junquillal, Iten's daughter attended high school in Santa Cruz, 56 kilometers (35 miles) inland.

TORTUGUERO
On the northeastern coast, in a small town with no cars but plenty of boats, there are no private schools, and the local public school, according to nature guide and hotelier Daryl Loth, is "just OK." The school system "has some good teachers but seems to send some inexperienced teachers or problem ones to Tortuguero" as a training ground or a kind of exile, as the town is quite remote.

Loth moved from Toronto to Tortuguero in 1994, and he runs Casa Marbella Bed & Breakfast with his Tica wife, Luz Denia. Their two children went to the local public school for the first part of grade school, but then their parents enrolled them in a private bilingual school in Guápiles (Colegio Bilingüe San Francisco De Asís), two hours away by boat and then bus or car. According to Loth, the private school "isn't expensive for the primary school portion but gets expensive as the students get into the high school. The children of banana plantation and regional office managers of Central Valley-based companies go there, and the school teaches four subjects in English." His children are now in a new public bilingual high school that provides an excellent English program suited to their advanced level of fluency.

The daily commute would have been a killer, so Daryl's family bought a prefab house in Guápiles so their kids could go to school there. Luz Denia stays with the children, and Daryl commutes often to visit and run supplies to the hotel. There are sacrifices, but it's worth it for the children's education. Their Guápiles house also serves as a pit stop and inn for Loth's extended family. When someone needs medical attention, for instance, they stay here to be close to the hospital in Guápiles.

Despite the fact that Loth's children aren't going to school in Tortuguero—where there is now a proper high school that he helped to build through donations from tourist groups and a few NGOs—he has participated on the high school board in Tortuguero for more than 12 years. He says he wants to be part of the solution when it comes to local public education. "We now have 120 high school students with hopes and dreams in Tortuguero— that didn't exist a decade ago. The children are our future" says Loth.

ESCAZÚ, NEAR SAN JOSÉ, IN THE CENTRAL VALLEY
Uwe Kreuzahler, who grew up in Holland and Germany, is married to a Tica and has three daughters. He runs 3D.CR, which provides three-dimensional visualization services for the architectural and interior design industries. He and his family live in Escazú, near San José, close to many very good private schools. And yet, Uwe and his wife decided to send their girls to public school. Why?

Blame it on arrogant rich kids. Uwe and his wife have met their share. "We wondered, Is it worth paying and putting them in that position, where they're thinking, *my daddy makes a lot of money and now I'm better than everyone else?*" So they opted for public school, with a lot of instruction at home. His girls speak perfect Spanish and English, and the two older ones speak French as well. His eldest is already working at HP (Hewlett Packard).

"I think kids need to learn that life is tough. If they always get what they want, how can they survive if something happens to me and my wife? The other day, one of our daughters tells us she needs a new bikini. We say ok, but you need to work it off. You can give the dogs a bath, you can do some LinkedIn for me (for his business). I think it's lazy if parents just give kids everything for free, instead of really listening to them and spending time with them. Some parents say to themselves, I'm taking care of my kid because I'm paying $1,000 a month for the school. But the kids need time with their dad and their mom more than they need an expensive school; that's what parenting is all about.

and your children will make a scouting trip to visit campuses and talk to school administrators months in advance of your arrival. Parents agree that it's a good idea to arrive a few weeks before school starts, so kids can get used to a new house and area before having to adapt to a new school. Arriving too far in advance, however, may be a bad idea, since kids can begin to feel at loose ends when their days have little structure.

"First and foremost," advises a long-term expat who has taught at several private schools in the San José area, "parents must ask themselves what they want for their kids. They especially need to think about what sort of qualification the child will leave the school with. Tico-style private secondary schools may be very good, but they end at the 11th grade—fine if you want to go to university here in Costa Rica, insufficient if you want to go to college in the United States, Canada, or Europe. U.S.-style schools go through 12th grade, and European-style schools mostly offer the IB, the International Baccalaureate, which will get the kids into European universities and can sometimes count as first-year university credit in the United States. Another issue is language. Do you want your kid to speak mostly English, Spanish, German, or Japanese? Schools that call themselves bilingual are all over the map. Make sure you know which language is emphasized."

(Check out the list of private primary and secondary schools beginning on page 339 in the *Resources* section.)

HIGHER EDUCATION

The prestigious University of Costa Rica (UCR) was founded back in 1940; former President Laura Chinchilla is an alumna. Three other important public institutions joined its ranks in the 1970s: the National University in Heredia, Cartago's Institute of Technology, and the State University's Distance Learning Program. Recently, a fifth public university, the Technical University (UTCR), opened in the city of Alajuela. The government funds public universities, and tuition is on a sliding scale.

UCR's main campus is in the San José suburb of San Pedro; there are branch campuses in Alajuela, Cartago, Turrialba, and Puntarenas. The National University, based in Heredia, also has regional centers in Liberia and Pérez Zeledón. The State University's Distance Learning Program has 32 regional centers scattered around the country. People who live far from urban centers can hear lectures on the radio or on TV, or meet once a week with professors who make the rounds of the rural outposts.

Private Versus Public Universities and Colleges

The number of private universities and colleges is growing; they may have more relaxed entrance requirements or offer programs similar to those at public institutions but at a more rapid pace and with greater flexibility in terms of when students attend classes. Some private institutions, like the tiny Universidad del Diseño (University of Design), have excellent reputations both nationally and internationally. Others seem to be run strictly as businesses and are dismissed as degree mills. Concerned with the declining quality of instruction at some private universities, numerous professional guilds, like the Lawyers Guild, now require prospective members to pass an exam rather than simply present their degree.

In 2010 the National Council of Rectors (CONARE) released figures that showed approximately 83,000 students enrolled in the five public universities, 40,000 of them at UCR, with another 100,000 or so taking classes at private colleges. Public universities are more prestigious, but they're harder to get into, and there isn't room for everyone who wants a college degree. That's why enrollment has gradually shifted in favor of private universities.

One of the internationally best-known private universities in Costa Rica is the University for Peace, an ironically well-fortified compound in the rolling hills outside of Ciudad Colón. Established by a United Nations resolution in 1980, the university serves hundreds of students from over 100 countries. Many students come here to work toward master's degrees in international law, human rights, peace studies, sustainable development, and gender and peace-building, to name a few concentrations.

Continuing Education

Many public universities offer courses and talks that are free and open to the general public, advertised in local newspapers like *La Nación*. A sampling of recent offerings at the UCR-San Pedro campus includes a talk on the history of film in Costa Rica, a discussion of Latin American literature (in English, by a U.S. professor), a panel discussion on urban development in San José, and a volcanology seminar. In short, there's a wealth of continuing education options, especially in the San José area, with events either free or very reasonably priced. Most are in Spanish, but what a great way to improve your language skills!

STUDY ABROAD IN COSTA RICA

Besides the dozens of language-learning options mentioned in this book, there are many other study-abroad opportunities in Costa Rica. You can immerse yourself in tropical biology with the Organization for Tropical Studies (www.ots.ac.cr), volunteer to work with marine mammals in Drakes Bay (www.vidamarina.org), or work out a program through your high school or college to get academic credit for a custom-made study-abroad stint.

There are also many educational vacation opportunities. Global Exchange (www.globalexchange.org), for instance, offers two-week trips focusing on subjects such as ecotourism and sustainability on the Caribbean coast. Elderhostel (www.exploritas.org), renamed Exploritas and not just for older travelers these days, has, among other offerings, an unusual cultural interaction through soccer trip. The possibilities are endless. A good place to begin your search is Transitions Abroad (www.transitionsabroad.com).

(Also see page 195 in the *Employment* chapter. For a list of volunteer organizations, see page 353 in *Resources*.)

HEALTH

Costa Rica is a healthy place, and a large number of people come here at least in part for their health. Some are suffering from stress- and work-related conditions that often clear up after a few months of this country's saner pace (outside the congested Central Valley) and salubrious environment. Others have no specific complaint but are drawn to the high-quality medical care, which is cheap if, as a resident, you become part of the country's socialized medicine system, and is still affordable if you opt to go the private route. A place like Costa Rica, which considers health care a fundamental human right, looks very good to refugees from countries where basic health care is not a societal guarantee.

According to the United Nations, an impressive 98 percent of Ticos have access to health care; as recently as the 1960s, the figure was 15 percent.

Costa Rica spends a lot of money to keep its people healthy, and statistics reflect this commitment. Life expectancy is high, at over 78, and infant mortality is low at about 8 per 1,000 births—figures that put most other Latin American countries to shame.

Before You Arrive

VACCINATIONS

Epidemic diseases have mostly been wiped out in Costa Rica, and the country requires no proof of vaccination upon entry. But travelers or potential residents planning to rough it should consider vaccinations against tetanus, polio, typhoid, and infectious hepatitis. For the latest information on epidemics and vaccinations, contact the Centers for Disease Control and Prevention in Atlanta (U.S. tel. 800/311-2425, wwwnc.cdc.gov/travel/page/vaccinations.htm).

MEDICAL RECORDS

If you have any preexisting medical problems, carry a letter from your doctor describing the condition and any prescription medications you need, including the generic name of the prescribed drugs. Better yet, request your medical records before you leave home and carry them with you. If you can get them in digitized form, all the better—carry them with you on a jump drive, or email them to yourself so you can access them anywhere there's an Internet connection.

Make sure any medication you bring is still in its original container, clearly labeled. You don't want customs inspectors to think you're trafficking in prescription drugs.

INTERNATIONAL MEDICAL COVERAGE

If, after reading about the health care options within Costa Rica, you decide you'd like to continue to use the health insurance you have in your home country, or if you want to look into an international policy, you have some advance work to do. Before moving to Costa Rica, learn what medical services your current health insurance will cover outside your home country. If your policy provides international coverage, be sure to carry your insurance identity card; nowadays claim forms are usually available for download from company websites. Clarify whether your insurance will come through with payment while you're in Costa Rica or if you have to save receipts and then file claims when you get home. If you know you'll be in Costa Rica for a while, it's a good idea to research the various forms of insurance that have international coverage. The best-known private clinics in San José work with international insurers and often have a separate claims department that will tell you what your particular company covers.

Medical care in Costa Rica is very good, and it's unlikely that you'll want to be flown back home for treatment, but if you do, it'll cost a small fortune (US$10,000 or more), so you might consider a policy that covers medical evacuation back to your home country.

Kaiser will cover only emergency medical care while its clients are out of the United States, and even with that, you'll need to pay out of pocket, and then submit the claim when you get home. Aetna and Blue Cross/Blue Shield international policies get good marks from both customers and health care providers, but there are dozens of other companies that offer similar coverage (see page 351 in *Resources* for a sampling). Do your homework and ask the hard questions. By law, Costa Rican hospitals and clinics must accept any and all patients who need emergency care. But if your problem doesn't qualify as an emergency but still needs attending to, you'll be much better off with good health insurance.

Traveling for Treatment

Medical tourism, the practice of going abroad for medical or dental care, is becoming more and more common. It usually involves patients from developed countries traveling to developing countries, like Thailand or Costa Rica, for cheaper procedures. The Centers for Disease Control (CDC) writes that "medical tourism is a worldwide multibillion-dollar phenomenon that is expected to grow substantially in the next 5 to 10 years."

Costa Rica is one of the countries often mentioned in articles about this new trend; doctors here are well trained, and two of the three major private hospitals in San José are internationally accredited.

The motivation for getting on a plane to get your health care is simple, at least for U.S. citizens: You save money—often tens of thousands of dollars for the more expensive procedures. Costa Rica's National Tourism Board (Instituto Costarricense de Turismo, or ICT) has reported that the majority of Costa Rica's medical tourists come from the United States for treatments not covered by their insurance back home—and that they save 50-70 percent off what they'd have paid in their country for the same care. That may be a bit of an exaggeration. In asking U.S. citizens who come here for medical and dental work what they think they saved, I find that most say they paid about 30 percent less for procedures performed in Costa Rica.

People come to Costa Rica for dental implants and crowns, face-lifts, LASIK eye surgery, cardiac surgery, joint replacement, breast augmentation, and gastric bypass surgery, to name just a few of the more common procedures.

The CDC says that most medical and dental tourists rely on private companies or "medical concierge" services to identify foreign health care facilities, but the intrepid can cut out the middleman, choosing their own doctor or dentist and recovery facility through Internet research, word of mouth, and, in some cases, pre-surgery visits to get the lay of the land. I know many people from the United States who used a medical middleman for their first visit, then—seeing that making the arrangements wasn't rocket science and gaining valuable contacts—did it on their own for subsequent visits (major dental work, and other procedures, may require several visits over a period of months). Since the middleman tacks on an often hefty fee, making your own arrangements can save you a lot of money.

If your current insurance has no international coverage, and you plan to be in Costa Rica for just a short time, traveler's insurance may be the way to go. Such coverage often includes health and baggage insurance, along with insurance against cancellation of a prepaid tour or flight.

Types of Health Care

PUBLIC HEALTH CARE: THE CAJA

In 1943, the Costa Rican government created a health insurance program for workers that has, over the years, grown to cover more than 90 percent of the population. The big mama of an agency that makes this possible is the Caja Costarricense de Seguro Social, otherwise known as the Caja (www.ccss.sa.cr).

Today, a person can be insured as a worker, as part of the worker's family, or simply by paying into the system independently. And according to the immigration reforms of 2010, expats with legal residency (in programs like the *pensionado*

GETTING GOOD CARE

The CDC's travel health guide has a section on medical tourism (http://wwwnc.cdc.gov/travel/yellowbook/2016/table-of-contents) that provides tips on getting good care. The guide explains, "In recent years, standards have been rising in other parts of the world even faster than prices have surged in the United States. Many physicians abroad trained in the United States, and the Joint Commission International applies strict standards to accreditation of offshore facilities. Those facilities use the same implants, supplies, and drugs as their U.S. counterparts. However, a heart bypass in Thailand costs US$11,000 compared to as much as US$130,000 in the United States. Spinal fusion surgery in India at US$5,500 compares to over US$60,000 in the United States."

In Costa Rica, prices might be higher than those in India or Thailand, but then again, Costa Rica is a lot closer, at least for North Americans.

The American Medical Association (AMA) advises those planning a surgery abroad to check if medical facilities have been accredited by recognized international accrediting bodies such as the Joint Commission International (JCI, http://jointcommissioninternational.org/JCI-Accredited-Organizations). Two of the three major private hospitals in Costa Rica—Clínica Bíblica and Hospital CIMA—are JCI accredited. Hospital la Católica's accreditation was withdrawn in October 2012. Newcomer Hospital Metropolitano is accredited by the Accreditation Association for Ambulatory Health Care.

AFTERCARE

The AMA says that prior to travel, patients should arrange local follow-up care. With increasing numbers of medical tourists arriving in Costa Rica, more aftercare facilities are springing up, most of them close to San José, where the major private hospitals are located. CheTica Wellness and Recovery Center (www.cheticaranch.com/) in the hills north of San José and Las Cumbres Surgery Retreat (www.surgery-retreat.com) in the western suburb of Escazú have both been around for a while and have good reputations. Rates are usually around US$100 per day, including after-surgery medical care and meals.

DAILY LIFE
HEALTH

and *rentista* [nonretired] categories) now must enroll in the Caja. The monthly fee for Caja is usually 7 to 11 percent of the person's monthly income, with a dependent spouse covered under that payment. The Caja offers good medical care, probably the best in Central America, and just about everything is covered.

The Caja system extends to every corner of the country, although the majority of well-regarded public hospitals—including San Juan de Dios, Hospital Calderón Guardia, and Hospital México—are in San José, and outlanders routinely journey to the capital for specialized services.

Due to a general downturn in the economy that began in the 1980s, social services have suffered budget cuts, with the Caja taking its share. Although the system is overburdened, it still delivers an admirable level of care to people who could not otherwise afford it. Still, Ticos and resident foreigners who can afford it often choose to use the Caja as a backup to private care, which they pay for out of pocket or through international or national insurance.

Though many expats are happy with the routine care or scheduled procedures at public hospitals and clinics, where life-threatening emergencies are concerned, public hospitals don't get such high marks.

THE INS

The Costa Rican Instituto Nacional de Seguros (INS; http://portal.ins-cr.com) used to be the only authorized dealer in health insurance in Costa Rica, although implementation of CAFTA (the Central American Free Trade Agreement) opened the field to private competition. Currently, INS rates depend on age, gender, and physical condition. INS policies are usually more expensive than the Caja, while cheaper than international policies. With INS insurance you can choose your own doctors and go to private clinics, which have better reputations than public hospitals, and the INS covers 70-80 percent of the bill.

MIXED MEDICINE

Some Ticos and resident foreigners use both public and private health care. I met a man in the waiting room at Hospital Calderón Guardia, a public hospital, who was fully covered under the Caja but had up until then paid for private care—he wasn't crazy about the Caja's bureaucracy and long waits. But now he needed an operation on his hand, and he couldn't afford to have that done by a private doctor in a private clinic. So he'd returned to the Caja fold and was trying to schedule his operation within the next decade. If he had the money for the operation, he said, he wouldn't be there.

Other people will use the Caja for routine care—minor ailments, blood tests, and medication—but turn to private care when the going gets tough. One reason many people use the Caja until things get serious is that the sicker you are, the harder it is to navigate all the forms in triplicate you'll need to see Caja specialists, and the more taxing will be the hours of waiting you'll endure at every turn. Another reason to go private is to engage a respected specialist who doesn't work in the Caja, although many doctors have a private practice and also work for the Caja, and they can schedule their private patients' surgeries there, thus eliminating hospital expenses but not the surgeon's fees.

If you need surgery but it's not an absolute emergency, the Caja may assign a surgery date many months from diagnosis. And while some Caja delays are unavoidable, given the system's scant resources, other delays are the result of sheer incompetence and may have lethal results. Take the May 2003 case in which 81 patients at San Juan de Dios Hospital in San José waited more than eight months for biopsies to ascertain whether or not they had prostate cancer. Orders for the necessary medical equipment were approved but then got lost on some bureaucrat's desk. No hospital official followed up on this incredible lapse until patients and journalists pressed for an investigation.

Such incompetence is the exception rather than the rule, and similar outrages have no doubt occurred in health facilities the world over. Still, there's no denying that public hospitals here, though the facilities are adequate and the doctors often very good, are not cheery places. Nurses are overworked, and rooms are small and often shared with three or more other patients. You'll find no telephones, TVs, or privacy in these rooms. Some public hospitals lack basic supplies like toilet paper.

PRIVATE CARE

Doctors in Costa Rica, whether they work for the Caja, in private practice, or in a combination of the two, are in general very well trained. Many have studied in the United States, Canada, or Europe. They keep up with developments in their field and often have access to the latest technology. Some doctors who work privately are associated with private clinics;

CIMA is a large private hospital near Escazú.

others are not. Either way, they can send you to private clinics for tests or operate on you there.

The best private clinics are in San José, and they are very good indeed. Prices at private clinics are often beyond the reach of the average Costa Rican, but resident foreigners—who tend to have greater financial resources and are accustomed to higher prices—find the fees refreshingly low. Part of the reason prices are lower is that malpractice lawsuits are rare here; when damages are awarded, they're usually only enough to cover hospital bills and other expenses.

Many of the private hospitals in Costa Rica market themselves to international patients, aka medical tourists. These hospitals are going after their share of this multibillion-dollar world industry, and in some cases they've created special websites in English and toll-free numbers in the United States to answer questions about procedures and insurance (see page 349 in the *Resources* section at the back of the book for full contact information).

Hospital CIMA

Located just off one of Costa Rica's few stretches of superhighway, CIMA is nothing if not modern. The clinic opened in early 2000 near the upscale suburb of Escazú. Rumor has it that CIMA was built to work as a hotel if it failed as a hospital, and with its marble-floored foyer, glass-bricked administrative offices, and the white tablecloths in the cafeteria, CIMA does indeed resemble a tasteful, upscale chain hotel.

Downstairs, you'll find the emergency room, the outpatient clinic, and the big guns of medical technology: a cardiac catheterization lab, CAT scan, sonogram, and X-ray equipment, and an open MRI machine.

Upstairs, the patient rooms feature everything that most San José private clinics offer—cable TV, phones, adjustable beds, private baths, safes, and daybeds for overnight guests—but on a grander scale. Of 58 beds, 4 are equipped for neonatal care, 6 are in the intensive care unit, and 6 are suites; all patient rooms are private.

CIMA (tel. 506/2208-1000, fax

506/2208-1001, cima@hospitalcima.com, www.hospitalsanjose.net) is near Escazú. It works with all major international insurance companies as well as with INS. Its website for medical tourists is www.cimamedicalvaluetravel.com.

A smaller branch of CIMA opened in Liberia, the capital of Guanacaste Province, six miles from the Liberia international airport.

Clínica Bíblica

Founded in 1929 by Christian missionaries from Scotland and Ireland, the Bíblica, as it's known, takes up more than a city block in downtown San José. A new wing that opened in 2006 has 9 new operating rooms and 25 new private patient rooms with the same amenities as rooms in the old building but with the addition of flat-screen TVs and Wi-Fi access. On the clinic's second floor you'll find a small chapel, and there's a rack of religious tracts near the front desk.

The older wing has 80 beds, 16 examination rooms, 5 operating rooms, and modern ultrasonography, mammography, radiology, CAT scan, and MRI equipment. The clinic's cardiology and maternity units are well known.

The "old" clinic has sky-blue walls and tiled floors; each of the rooms has a private bath, cable TV, a phone, a safe, and an electric bed. Rooms also have either a rocking chair or a recliner, along with a sofa bed so that a friend or family member can stay overnight. Other visitors are allowed 9am-9pm.

The Bíblica works with many international insurance providers.

The Bíblica is on Calle Central, between Avenidas 14 and 16 (tel. 506/2522-1000, U.S. toll-free tel. 866/665-6433, centrodecontacto@clinicabiblica.com, www.clinicabiblica.com). It also has smaller branches in Heredia and near the Liberia airport in Guanacaste.

Clínica Católica

Founded in 1963 by Franciscan nuns, La Católica was bought in 2006 by a private company, Grupo Sama, that renovated and expanded the hospital and added an aftercare hotel on the premises, right where the convent used to be. Located in the quiet suburb of Guadalupe, just north of San Pedro and the University of Costa Rica, the clinic has about 70 beds; most are in single rooms, but there are also a few shared rooms, which cost less, and several suites.

Although well regarded, La Católica had not been as geared toward foreign patients as CIMA and the Bíblica. In 2012, La Católica lost its JCI accreditation, though it still seems to be going strong.

The clinic is in San Antonio de Guadalupe, a suburb of San José (tel. 506/2246-3000, fax 506/2283-6171, info@clinicacatolica.com, www.hospitallacatolica.com).

Hospital Metropolitano

Founded in 2010, this relative newcomer to the private hospital roster is getting some good reviews. There are two locations: one in downtown San José, the other in the suburb of Tibás. Rumor has it that doctors from CIMA, frustrated with a profit-sharing program that never made good on its promises, started this new enterprise.

The downtown branch is located at Avenida 8 and Calle 14 in San José, while the Tibas branch is 400 meters east of the Catholic Church in Tibás. Both facilities are private, but they accept national insurance (INS). Contact them at 506/2521-9595 or www.metropolitano.cr.

PHARMACIES AND PRESCRIPTIONS

Pharmacies in Costa Rica (called *farmacias*) are on every other corner, and most are well stocked. If you bring a

kiosk selling herbal remedies

by pharmacists in different parts of the country, and every time, the medication prescribed cleared up the problem in short order. Most pharmacists will even give injections for a small fee.

Prices are usually reasonable, but do shop around, and know that prices will be higher in heavily touristed areas. In San José, for instance, the pharmacy at Clínica Bíblica and the Fischel chain of pharmacies are known to be well stocked but much more expensive than lesser-known shops.

ALTERNATIVE MEDICINE

Alternative medicine—such as acupuncture and homeopathy—is popular in Costa Rica, especially in the Central Valley and in beach towns, where arrivals from other countries have brought with them their interest in all things holistic. You'll have no problem finding massage therapists, health-food stores, or yoga classes. The best way to find a reputable practitioner is through word of mouth.

Especially on the Caribbean coast, you will hear about native healers—called bush doctors (usually of African heritage) or *sukias* (of indigenous heritage). The healers don't have websites or phones—this is one place where you definitely need a personal recommendation. But if you're in a place for a while, you'll no doubt hear stories, some of them true.

"Alternative" birthing methods—using midwives or giving birth at home with a trusted friend or relative—used to be the norm, but over the past half century hospital births have become the only way to go, with cesarean sections promoted even when a vaginal birth would have presented no hazard to mother or baby. Recently, there has been a renewed interest in midwives and natural birthing practices, although you'll have to look hard for this small but growing movement, especially because practitioners operate

prescription from outside the country, make sure it is for generic rather than brand-name medication—generic names are common to all countries, while brand names are not. And unless you're looking for narcotics or psychotropic drugs, you often don't even need a prescription, and many antibiotics don't require a prescription. You can tell the pharmacist what you're looking for, or, if you're not sure what you need, the pharmacist will diagnose you and suggest appropriate medication—thus saving you the price of a doctor's consultation.

A pharmacist's diagnosis is especially helpful when you're far from a doctor, but of course you shouldn't expect the pharmacist to have specialized knowledge of arcane ailments. For simple problems, however, it's a godsend that in this country pharmacists have more power than their counterparts back home. I've had skin problems, ear infections, and stomach ailments diagnosed and treated

Expat Experiences: Health Care

Expats who are legal residents in Costa Rica must enroll in the national health care system called the Caja (CAH-hah), which gives them low-cost access to neighborhood clinics, pharmacies, and public hospitals.

Some expats are satisfied with Caja (public) care; others opt to supplement or replace it with private care, paid out of pocket or through national or international health insurance. Note that even if you decide not to use Caja services, you still need to pay its monthly premium. Nonresidents are not supposed to sign up for the Caja.

MIXED MEDICINE

San Ramón-based expat Stephen Duplantier, born in 1945, is a Caja fan, with reservations. He happily uses the Caja for nonurgent care and tests but had found that "for certain diagnostic tests such as ultrasound and X-rays, it is much faster to use private clinics than the sometimes long waits with CCSS [the Caja]. Private clinics are very reasonable, and we barely notice the costs of out-of-pocket expenses. Routine lab tests of blood and urine are fast and efficient.

"For major surgery, I faced a dilemma: we had an excellent Caja urologist who was ready to perform surgery, but the operating room for urologic procedures was booked longer than I wanted to wait, so I opted for private clinic surgery. This was much cheaper than returning to the States and using Medicare." For another matter, Stephen's wife, Kathleen, broke her wrist, which was set so badly by a local Caja doctor that weeks later she had to have emergency surgery. The couple opted to have the procedure done at newcomer Hospital Metropolitano; they were happy with the results.

CAJA FOR ROUTINE CARE; PRIVATE CLINIC FOR SURGERY

I agree with Stephen that the Caja can be great for routine care, but when I found I needed surgery, I moved from the public to the private realm. Then 41, I'd been part of the Caja system, happily using its neighborhood clinics for routine care and medications. But when it became clear that I would need a major procedure, I went to look at Hospital Calderón Guardia (a public hospital) in San José, then defected to private care, opting to pay out of pocket (I'd let my U.S. insurance lapse). I'd heard that there could be long waits in the Caja for nonemergency surgery, and my reconnaissance of Calderón Guardia had shown me crowded wards that didn't look that clean.

I was happy with the care at private Clínica Bíblica, although the final price for my stay, while low in comparison to U.S. prices, was still more than twice what I'd been quoted in a formal estimate. They wouldn't let me leave until I'd paid the bill in full.

They allowed a friend to sleep on the couch-bed in my room for no extra charge, which was a great comfort during my hospital stay.

A MOTORCYCLE CRASH IN THE ZONA SUR

Matt Hogan is cofounder of Finca Bella Vista, a sustainable tree-house community near the Osa Peninsula. In 2009, when he was 34, Matt had a motorcycle accident and was taken to the newly opened public hospital in Ciudad Cortéz. "All the newspapers had been boasting about the brand-new state-of-the-art facilities and medical equipment, 300 clean new beds, and the rest," says Matt. What the newspaper accounts failed to mention,

in a legal gray area and are not likely to advertise. In Costa Rica, one is a certified midwife only through a specialization after obstetrical nursing studies, and officially, midwives are allowed to attend births only in an emergency. Otherwise mothers must go to the hospital. But there are ways around these restrictions.

According to Uva Meiner, a German-born birth assistant, the handful of

according to Matt, was that all those new beds were serviced by only a few doctors who showed up only once in a while. Matt says he suffered serious neglect and misdiagnosis (they told him he was fine).

Feeling anything but fine, he had himself driven by ambulance to San José and checked himself into private Clínica Bíblica. There he was found to have one collapsed lung and the other in mid-collapse, as well as severe internal bleeding in his chest cavity. The doctors at Bíblica said that if Matt had waited another day to seek proper care he most likely would have suffocated.

Matt was very happy with the care he received at Bíblica, adding with a smile that "all the nurses were very attractive young Ticas."

SERIOUS BURNS IN ARENAL

In another example, Alaska native Alex Murray, 72 at the time of a fire that burned more than 20 percent of his body, endured an extended hospital stay that allowed him to compare private and public care in Costa Rica.

After the fire, Alex was taken to a clinic in nearby Tilarán, and then moved to the public hospital in Liberia, about an hour north. Doctors there decided to send him to the burn unit at San Juan de Dios, a public hospital in San José, four hours away.

"Arriving in San José," says Alex, "we should have directed the driver immediately to Bíblica or Católica [two private hospitals], but, ignorant of the quality of the public hospital and anxious to get treatment, we let the driver take us to the teeming mystery that is San Juan."

Three Days at a Public Hospital

Alex spent three days at San Juan de Dios. "In our three days there," says Alex, "no doctor ever consulted us, though one led a group of students into my room each day. The nurses, male and female, sometimes seemed like the proverbial five or six workmen who stand around a pothole gabbing while one guy fills the hole. For the most part, they were not dedicated, not attentive, not very competent, and not sympathetic. A friendly nurse assigned to draw blood samples spent three days drilling mostly dry holes all over my landscape, partly due to my extremely low blood pressure. In the not-very-clean bathroom, Alex's wife found bloody bandages in a corner.

Seventeen Days at a Private Hospital

Alex and his wife decided that they needed to move him to a private facility.

"When I was admitted to Clínica Bíblica," says Alex, "I recognized immediately that here was a competent staff. The emergency room nurse quickly found a vein and soon had a set of color-coded vials filled with my blood. All staff were purposeful and attentive.

"Three doctors tended me at Bíblica, one a burn doctor, one a plastic surgeon who moved skin from my thigh to my hip, and one a staff doctor. They each came by almost every day to talk with us. The nursing staff was a no-nonsense but friendly and attentive group.

"And throughout my stay, my wife was permitted to sleep on a narrow built-in bed or cot in each room."

midwives in Costa Rica are mostly foreign-born, with a strong sense of mission. Uva herself provides extensive "spiritual, emotional, and physical" preparation for the expectant mother and makes house calls every day for one week postpartum and three times the following week. Some midwives use a portable birthing pool or a birthing chair, depending on the expectant mother's wishes.

SENIOR CITIZENS

U.S. citizens need to know that Medicare does not provide coverage for hospital or medical costs outside the United States. If you've bought other coverage to supplement Medicare, that policy may pay for up to 80 percent of your care abroad, as in the absence of Medicare it becomes your primary coverage. Among other organizations, AARP offers Medicare supplement plans that include foreign medical care coverage.

Nursing Homes and Continuing Care Communities

There are more than 150 nursing homes in Costa Rica, with thousands of senior citizens (known in Spanish as *personas de la tercera edad*, or "people of the third age") making use of these facilities, either residing there or coming for meals and activities.

There are no figures available on how many foreign-born seniors make use of Costa Rica's nursing homes, but I would guess that it's not a high number. For many seniors, the language and the culture would be barriers to feeling at home.

High life expectancy and a decline in childbearing have made people over age 60 the fastest-growing segment of the Costa Rican population. In 2009, 1 Tico in 15 was over age 65; by 2025 the figure is expected to be 1 in 7 or 8. And many foreign residents who live in Costa Rica come in their later years. Although only a small percentage of Tico seniors live in such centers, the existing facilities barely keep up with present demand and certainly will not be sufficient in years to come. There are also a fair number of North American expats who are (or may be soon) in need of assisted living situations.

The market is starting to catch up. In 2013, a high-end private assisted living facility, Verdeza, opened in the San José suburb of Escazú, in Trejos Montealegre,

one of the most North-Americanized neighborhoods in the Central Valley. It has 61 units, a "restaurant-style dining hall," and various fee plans, from independent living to Alzheimer/dementia care.

At-home care, for seniors and others in need of help, can be very reasonable here compared to how much it would cost in the United States or Canada. For example, in 2017, a couple in San Ramon in need of help caring for the wife, who was in a wheelchair and in the early stages of dementia, hired a local young woman for 40 hours a week at just under $5/hour. The helper had no formal medical training but caught on quickly to the needs of her patient.

ACCESS FOR PEOPLE WITH DISABILITIES

In 1996 the Costa Rican Legislature passed the Equal Opportunities Law for People with Disabilities, an ambitious directive that aimed to provide Costa Rica's more than 200,000 residents with disabilities equal access to work, health care, transportation, and public space. More than 20 years later, some progress had been made: more special education programs in schools, ATMs with braille, some curb ramps built or repaired, a few "sonorous stop signs" installed for the sight-impaired, and about 10 percent of public buses modified to accommodate wheelchairs.

But if you've ever seen an individual in a wheelchair try to negotiate San José's torn-up streets or the sandy tracks of a beach town, you know that the country has a long way to go. It's heartening to see friendly strangers pitch in, helping people in wheelchairs up and down curbs or over rough spots. But the government's push to improve conditions is still in its infancy.

Disabled-rights activists say the problem is that the 1996 law has no teeth and is hard to enforce. There are proposals in

Expat Experience: Costa Rica from a Chair

Kathleen Duplantier

Kathleen Duplantier moved to Costa Rica in 2004 after taking early retirement from her job teaching school in Louisiana. Kathleen has multiple sclerosis (MS), a disease of the central nervous system with symptoms that may include loss of balance, spasticity, and partial or total paralysis.

Kathleen uses a wheelchair, and she and her husband custom-built their home in San Ramón to accommodate her chair. They chose San Ramón in part because of its cool climate—hot weather tends to exacerbate the symptoms of MS.

I asked Kathleen about getting around Costa Rica in a wheelchair. She said it was a challenge but that it hadn't been much easier back home.

"I'd ask at a café or restaurant (in Louisiana) if they had a bathroom I could use. If they said no, I'd say, 'Well, then, do you have a mop?'"

Kathleen has been impressed by how resourceful and helpful people are here in Costa Rica. "My wheelchair broke in Grecia. I had a huge number of people who came to help. One guy said, 'We'll take you to a bicycle shop,' which was a good idea, because they have the right sort of tools there. So they carried me in my chair to the bicycle shop, brought out a little stool, and I sat there while they fixed my chair. They didn't charge me anything."

Stephen, Kathleen's husband, adds, "Wherever I'm transferring Kathleen from the car to the chair, people run over to help—the other day, it was a little old lady. They ask how they can help, and I'll say *empuje sus nalgas* ('push her bottom'), and they don't mind. They know that's what it takes. Sometimes they're overly helpful and can knock her off balance."

the works that may make enforcement more of a priority and also provide incentives to private businesses that hire people with disabilities and who make their facilities accessible to all.

More and more hotels, restaurants, and tour companies are making things easier for their customers with disabilities, especially where wheelchairs are concerned. Two popular tourist attractions—the Rainforest Aerial Tram and Poás Volcano National Park—are now wheelchair accessible, and the hope is that other attractions will follow suit.

Health Hazards

DRINKING WATER

Water quality is one of the biggest differences between Costa Rica and other Latin American nations. Often people don't believe it until they arrive, but it's true: You can drink the water! Something so basic has profound implications, not the least of which is that it feels like the natural world is working with rather than against you, offering up an abundant and untainted supply of the most essential of elements. Anyone who's lived in a place where they can't even wash vegetables or brush their teeth with what comes out of the tap knows what a blessing this is. Clean water also eliminates most waterborne diseases, such as cholera, typhoid fever, and dysentery. Also rare in Costa Rica are the less dangerous but still annoying intestinal upsets from tainted water so familiar to Third World travelers. The country has a few areas—such as remote parts of the Talamanca Mountains and (ironically) the upscale San José suburb of Escazú—where the drinking water is suspect. Sometimes water quality worsens with heavy rains, as debris is washed into water supplies. Ask around, and if there's any question, stick with bottled water. Otherwise, turn on the tap, fill up your glass, and enjoy.

FOOD

You might get sick of all the rice and beans, but you won't get sick *from* the rice and beans. Food hygiene standards in Costa Rica are high. And you can get cheap and filling food at *sodas,* informal and inexpensive restaurants that usually serve Costa Rica's national meal: the *casado.* Named after the word for "married man," these full plates of food offer fish or meat, rice or potatoes, sometimes beans, and a small salad, often made of shredded cabbage.

You'll want to take the usual precautions: Think twice about buying food from street vendors, and be careful about raw fish and shellfish (where cholera bugs like to hang out). That said, I wouldn't trade my ceviche (raw fish marinated in lime juice) for anything. I just make sure to go to established restaurants, which have a vested interest in keeping their customers healthy and happy. The usual Third World warnings—wash it, boil it, peel it, or forget it—don't really apply in Costa Rica, at least not in the Central Valley or the more developed tourist destinations. I don't have an ironclad stomach, and yet I've eaten every salad served to me here with no ill effects whatsoever. In fact, I wish I would encounter more salads—they're not easy to come by in this starch-loving nation. Most traditional meals will boast two, three, or even four starches—usually rice, potatoes, and fried plantain, with some yucca, chayote, or a few tortillas thrown in for good measure. If good salads are hard to come by, there's no such problem with fruit. You'll want to try all of Costa Rica's astonishing variety of fruits, from the heart-shaped *annona* to the purple-fleshed *zapote.*

SMOKING

Costa Rica has passed an array of anti-smoking laws that utterly changed the landscape for smokers. You used to be able to smoke in bars and pretty much anywhere the owners of an establishment allowed it. Now smoking is banned in all public spaces, including bus and taxi stops, public buildings, restaurants, and bars. The laws also outlawed the sale of individual cigarettes; banned cigarette ads, required that cigarette packages carry health warnings, and added more tax onto cigarette purchases.

Costa Rica became the 10th Latin American country to pass laws that followed guidelines set by the World Health Organization for smoke-free public spaces.

The Costa Rican Social Security System estimates that just over 14 percent of Costa Ricans smoke, most between ages 20 and 39. It remains to be seen if the laws will discourage new smokers and encourage current smokers to quit.

CARS AND TRUCKS AND TRAFFIC

Without a doubt, the biggest threat to your safety here comes from cars and trucks speeding along city streets and highways. The risk of motor vehicle-related death is generally many times higher in developing countries than in the United States (no haven of safety itself), and Costa Rica is no exception to this rule. Automobile accidents are the leading cause of death here for people under the age of 50.

Some observers suggest that the national character—which is one of avoiding conflict and smoothing things over at any cost—does a flip-flop when Ticos get behind the wheel, with drivers asserting every bit of the hostility they repress in other parts of their lives.

Michael Kaye, owner of Costa Rica Expeditions, has a whimsical take on the situation: "Driving in Costa Rica is inspired by the ancient tradition of the bullfight. The driver who cuts you off is not insulting you; she's playing with you. The best way for you to handle this is the same as for newcomers to all games. Play, but play by local rules, don't play too intensely, and expect to lose."

Be prepared to lose that game of chicken, but take care not to lose your life.

Every day the newspapers report on the previous night's wrecks and on the pedestrians who've been *aplastados* (flattened, or run over). Most of the country's roads are atrocious, and as for walking, there's a public service announcement on TV that urges pedestrians to wear white and to step off into the dirt whenever they see a car coming. No mention is made of the fact that the country could use a few more sidewalks, and that drivers should be on the lookout for "obstacles," especially in rural areas where cars share the road with horses, oxcarts, and whole families walking to weddings, baptisms, and funerals.

In Costa Rica, the car is the *patrón* and the pedestrian the *peón*. The culture here is that cars stop for nothing—not an old woman limping across the street, not a stalled car, not a group of schoolchildren trying to get to class on time. In many cultures, people are taught to drive defensively. In Costa Rica, parents teach their kids to *walk* defensively. Ticos on foot know to treat cars (and their drivers) as the unpredictable animals they are. Follow their lead and don't expect cars to stop just because there's a stop sign or a red light. And if you're wondering how you're ever going to cross that busy street, watch what the locals do. Shadow them; walk when they walk. And watch out for potholes—not just in the road but on the sidewalks.

In the past few years, there's been an increase in pedestrian signals in larger cities; hopefully in years to come the environment for pedestrians will become friendlier.

If you can avoid driving at night, do so. Eighty percent of insurance claims come from nighttime accidents. In rural areas, be on the lookout for cows or dogs lying in the road, and for people who consider the bank of a highway a good place to hang out and socialize.

Fruits of Costa Rica

Chances are you've sampled a fair number of tropical fruits even if you've never lived in the tropics: bananas, coconut *(coco)*, pineapple *(piña)*, and most likely mango and papaya. All of these are wonderful in Costa Rica, as are more familiar species like oranges *(naranjas)*, watermelon *(sandia)*, and blackberries *(mora)*. But what about some of the lesser-known delights of Costa Rica's fruit universe? You owe it to yourself to try every fruit you can find.

Note than many of Costa Rica's fruits are enjoyed as *refrescos naturales*, refreshing fruit drinks to which sugar is added and that are prepared either *en agua* (in water) or *en leche* (in milk), the latter resembling a thin and fruity milk shake. Milk-based fruit drinks here are also sometimes called *batidos*.

Costa Rica's abundance of tropical fruits even inspire new Tang flavors; maracuyá is passion fruit.

One writer called the interior of **maracuyá** (passion fruit) "a disgusting-looking spewdum of goo," and while it does look and feel a trifle gelatinous, for my money this plum-size hard-skinned yellow-orange fruit is one of the most delicious in all of Costa Rica. Try it as a water-based *refresco natural* or just scoop out the flesh and enjoy it raw, seeds and all. Rolf Blancke, author of the encyclopedic *Tropical Fruits of the World*, tells me that the jellylike flesh can be frozen and will retain its flavor for up to a year.

THE NATURAL WORLD

Threats like cars and their drivers are the most serious hazards; what comes at you from the natural world pales in comparison. Still, it's a good idea to know what kinds of creatures you'll find here and how the environment might affect you.

Bugs

Many people are drawn to Costa Rica for its amazing abundance of animal life. Most species are harmless if left unmolested, but there are a few exceptions to every rule.

In and around the Central Valley, the higher altitude means fewer bugs. You hardly ever see houseflies, spiders are of reasonable size and lead discreet lives, and even the ants don't seem as aggressive as in other areas.

In lowland and more humid areas, you'll find more quantity and variety in the insect department. Some, like the enormous Hercules beetle or the bright blue morpho butterfly, are stunning but harmless. It's the more prosaic insects like mosquitoes that do greater harm, occasionally transmitting dengue fever and, more rarely, malaria—mostly in wet lowland areas with poor sanitation. Malaria is rare enough in Costa Rica that few doctors suggest taking chloroquine pills along on your trip. But cases have been reported, and the best prevention against both malaria and dengue fever is to guard against mosquito bites. Wear long sleeves and long pants, use insect repellent containing DEET, and sleep under a mosquito net. Some suggest that spraying your clothes

Granadilla looks and tastes a lot like its cousin, the *maracuya,* but has a more pronounced stem coming out of the fruit.

The **guanabana** (soursop) looks like a spiky green football and tastes like heaven. Its creamy white flesh is full of black seeds and hard to enjoy straight from the tree, but mixed with milk for a *batido* (a thin milk shake), it's almost worth the price of the plane ticket down.

Carambola (star fruit) is pretty–it's often used as garnish on a plate or in a glass–but shockingly sour. **Caimitos,** another star-shaped fruit, are more palatable and taste a bit like Asia's mangosteen.

Mamón are the size and color of limes but have a harder, smoother skin and a single large seed inside that is covered with sweet, almost translucent flesh.

Mamón chino (rambutan, hairy lychee) are not native to Costa Rica–they come from Asia originally–but they've adapted well, and you see the small red fruits everywhere, their soft red spines making them resemble a pile of fat headless caterpillars. Inside, a large seed is covered with delicious white flesh that tastes a bit like grape flesh.

Tamarindo (tamarind) are the seeds inside the tamarind tree's long, skinny pod. A paste is made from the seeds that is then mixed with sugar into a refreshing drink that tastes a little bit like tart and grainy apple juice.

Guayabo (guava) are small spherical fruits with yellow skin and soft flesh that is either white or pink. The acidic fruit is mostly mixed with lots of sugar and made into jam and jelly. Early Spanish settlers complained that eating the raw fruit set their teeth on edge.

Cas is a small round fruit that starts out green and ripens to yellow. This tart-sweet fruit makes a delicious *refresco natural* that tastes faintly of guava (*cas* is in the guava family).

The **nance** (NAN-say) is a small strong-smelling fruit that's often cooked as a dessert or made into syrup or a rum-like liquor called *crema de nance.*

with the insecticide permethrin will guard against dengue fever.

Africanized bees have arrived in parts of Costa Rica and are as aggressive here as they are elsewhere. Experts advise running in a zigzag pattern if they come after you, getting under a sheet, or submerging yourself in water if there's any available.

Some areas have scorpions. I heard of a woman who, when she washed her family's clothes, made sure to put them away inside out. That way, when they dressed, they'd have to turn everything right side out and thus would be automatically checking for bugs that might have hidden in the armpit of a shirt or in the leg of a pair of jeans. Despite her precautions, one day her husband found a scorpion crawling out of his sleeve. Then he noticed the seams on his shirt—it was still inside out. In scorpion areas, make sure you shake out your clothing and shoes before getting dressed in the morning. This will help with snakes too, which love nothing better than to curl up in a warm, odoriferous boot.

Snakes

Costa Rica has more than 100 kinds of snakes, including venomous ones such as the much-feared fer-de-lance, which accounts for 80 percent of all snakebites in the country, and the yellow-bellied, black-backed sea snake, which paddles along in the Pacific Ocean with its oar-like tail. Despite the variety of snakes here, death from snakebite is rare. Most bites occur when snakes are stepped on—watch where you're going!—or if you harass or try to handle a snake. Leave snakes alone and they'll return the favor. Be especially careful in long grass, and remember that many snakes are arboreal—the tree branch you grab onto for balance just may be alive. Snakes also like to hang out in bromeliads, so be careful when looking inside these tightly wound whorls of stiff leaves and brilliant flowers. If you are bitten, move as little as possible. If the bite is to a limb, apply a tight bandage (not a tourniquet) above the bite, and release it for a minute or two every 15 minutes. Apply ice if available, and keep the bitten limb elevated while getting to a hospital or clinic. Don't try that old remedy of cutting an X over the bite and sucking out the venom. Some snake venom contains anticoagulants, which will make any cut bleed like crazy.

Sun

What people come to Costa Rica for can also be their downfall. The sun can be like a molten hammer, especially around midday. Sunscreen, a wide-brimmed hat, sunglasses, and a long-sleeved light-colored shirt may make you look like your typical gringo in the tropics, but that's a small price to pay for guarding against sunburn, skin cancer, and heatstroke. Don't forget to drink a lot of liquids, and I'm not talking beer, which goes right through you. Take it slow at first, especially in areas of high humidity. After you've been here for a while, you'll adjust to your chosen area's weather. In the most sizzling areas, early mornings and late afternoons are the best times to be out and about. There's a reason hot countries invented the siesta, that midday break that gets you out of the sun and into a hammock. Do as the locals do and spend the early afternoon swaying on the front porch, a cool drink within reach.

Safety

CRIME

The good news is that Costa Rica does not suffer from political violence, has no army, and its police are not to be feared, as some Latin American police forces are. "This is one of the few countries," says French-born Emmanuel Pinto of Caribe Sur Real Estate near Puerto Viejo, "where I'm actually glad when I see a cop."

Violent crime here is less common than in many other places, including the urban United States, but it's on the rise. Robbery, assault, and even armed home invasions have increased in the last 15 years. The U.S. State Department says that tourists are frequent victims of crime in Costa Rica and advises "the same level of caution that one would exercise in

major cities or tourist areas throughout the world."

The country is trying to improve the situation. In 2006 the government created specialized tourism police—many of whom speak English—to assist visitors and to help combat sex tourism. It's hard to gauge how effective this new police force has been, but I have to say I've seen tourist police all over the country, including on a rather remote and rainy stretch of road in the Lake Arenal region. The friendly officer on a motorcycle seemed alarmed to see a woman walking on her own and asked if I needed a ride. I thanked him but said I was fine.

Besides the tourist police, there's the Fuerza Pública (Public Force), the regular uniformed officers you're likely to see

Police in Costa Rica routinely wear bulletproof vests.

department get the basics. Over the years I've heard more than a few stories of people calling the police only to be told that if they want police service, they need to come get the officers or send a taxi.

But the police situation in Costa Rica has definitely improved lately. The average police officer is better trained, better equipped, and makes a better salary. One police officer in San José who I spoke to said that starting in 2000, the police force has become more and more professional and effective. Just walking around San José I see more police than I used to, and they look better turned out and somehow more confident (maybe owing to their mandatory bulletproof vest).

Still, there are many neighborhoods and towns where the police presence is so minimal that people take matters into their own hands. Expats soon learn that they need to take precautions to protect their home, property, and family, and prudent expats know not to flaunt their wealth in any way. And whether it's the men in the little kiosks you see in urban and suburban neighborhoods, the guards and dogs patrolling hotel grounds, or caretakers living in the houses of absentee owners to prevent break-ins, this country has "an army of private security guards," according to Arturo Condo, professor and dean at INCAE business school near San José. Most experts agree that there are probably more private security guards in the country than police.

All those bars you see on windows are there for a reason, as break-ins are on the rise and are becoming more brazen, with thieves entering a house while the occupants are at home. Gated communities are successful in large part because they offer better security. Big dogs are very popular as four-footed guards that make a lot of noise; from many accounts I've heard, dogs are even more effective than elaborate locks and bars.

on the street or in their cars. Their role is crime prevention. Then there are the officers from the Organization of Judicial Investigation (OIJ), plainclothes police who are in charge of investigating crimes after they've occurred and occasionally respond to high-profile crimes-in-progress like bank robberies. There's also a transit police force, which imposes fines and comes when you call if you have a car accident (see page 348 in *Resources*, where contact information for all the police forces is also available.)

In the past, even if the police weren't to be feared, they didn't necessarily inspire confidence either. There were simply too few police officers in Costa Rica to do an effective job, many officers were not well trained, and, especially in areas outside of the Central Valley, police departments didn't even have enough funding for a police car. In some towns the community has raised funds to help the local police

A Woman Alone in Rural Costa Rica

When Emily moved from the United States to Costa Rica in 2009, she arrived with a husband and a dream of a self-sustaining farm. Tapping her savings and employing all of their ingenuity and capacity for hard work, the couple built their own home, their own roads, and their own water and power systems. They nursed their previously neglected acreage back to life, planting everything from coffee to bananas to shade trees beloved by monkeys and sloths. They still had much to do, but things were really coming together.

Six years after they arrived, Emily's husband, in the United States for a few months of seasonal work, emailed that he wanted a divorce. He said he wouldn't be returning to Costa Rica.

A year and a half later, I spoke with Emily (not her real name) about the transition from being coupled to pursuing the dream on her own, about how secure she feels as a woman alone in a rural environment, and about any advice she might offer women (especially women alone) thinking about making the move to Costa Rica.

HOW HAS IT BEEN, LIVING HERE BY YOURSELF?

I'm ok now, but it started out pretty rough. When I got my husband's email, I was distraught. And right around that time, in our very quiet community, a local man was murdered in front of his wife and child, and two friends of mine, older expat women, experienced an armed home invasion. In the middle of the afternoon, the women were in their yard. Out of the trees come three masked men, dressed in black boots and black clothes, with only their eyes showing. They were organized, even tactical; some people speculate that these kinds of things are somehow tied to the police. Anyway, these guys had flashlights and guns; they had one woman with a gun to her head. The men got money, jewelry, electronics, and three guns that the women owned. The women weren't physically hurt but you can bet they're traumatized.

So I felt pretty insecure and alone, like there's a tree down, and I have to get out the chain saw. Or I can't cross the creek to get to the main road because the water's too high. These things happened when my husband was here, too, of course. But now I had to deal with everything on my own.

In terms of security, you have to pay attention, always. You can't just let go and let God, or whatever it is they say. I looked around my house and property and assessed everything from a security standpoint. We'd built with security in mind, with lots of metal bars, so that was good. I started letting the dogs in the house, because that made me feel safer. I lock the door every time I go out, even just to take a walk around the property. I have a big flashlight here on the counter; if someone gets in I can shine it in their eyes. I have mace, a Taser, and a billy club. I don't want a gun; you always hear that robbers get the gun and use it against you. With the ladies who were home invaded, those robbers now have three more guns than when they started. Those guns could be used against me or anyone else. But I do have a slingshot near my bed. I practice. I'm pretty good.

When you're out and about, you need to be aware of those around you. Once you get a feel for the country and its people, you'll be able to recognize potentially dangerous situations and ease out of them gracefully. Until then, be wary. Petty theft is on the rise, especially in San José. Keep your bags close at all times, and don't be flashy with money, jewelry, or cameras. Make photocopies of important documents—passports, visas, and plane tickets—and keep the originals at home or in a hotel safe. Cars are broken into on a regular basis—don't leave anything of value in your car, and if possible, park your car in a garage or a guarded lot or make an arrangement with the orange-vested

In terms of making a living and getting help, I found online work and also started taking in volunteers to help on the farm, through the web site HelpX.net. It's nice to have help, and it's nice to have people around. I've had volunteers from all over. The Romanians are the hardest workers.

TELL ME ABOUT YOUR COMMUNITY AND YOUR NEIGHBORS.

Luckily, I have very good neighbors. I'm in a rural community of about 500 people. We're not in a touristy area; the place is quiet and has its own beautiful charm. The closest bus service is 3 kilometers away, but even that bus doesn't come very often.

When I first got here, we were an anomaly: the only gringo couple. They must have thought, What are they doing here, of all places? But most people now know me by name or at least by sight because a few years ago, I started a baseball team for kids from 5 to 13. One of the teachers at the local school helped; in class we taught about the baseball diamond and the rules of the game. So everybody knew me through their kids—everybody here has kids. I was the lady doing baseball. Suddenly you're not just the gringo on the hill.

As soon as I knew my husband wasn't coming back, I told my nearest neighbors: I said, "I don't want to broadcast this, and I don't want everybody to know, but I'm alone. If you don't hear from me for a little while, you might think to check on me. My nearest neighbors still call me twice a week. I take them limes from my tree and carrot cake. If I get lonely or bored, I can go down and sit on their porch and play with the kids.

We all see each other at kids' birthday parties and at funerals, which are three-day events. I'm part of the community, and they are my support system. One neighbor regularly helps me with my water supply. We both have water that starts near the same spring. A lot can go wrong.

ANY ADVICE FOR WOMEN THINKING OF MOVING TO COSTA RICA?

Even if you come down with a partner, given that half of relationships don't work out, think ahead about what you would do if you ended up alone. For women alone, it's easier to live in a community where you can have friends close by and go out, and where you don't have to worry about leaving your place unattended. There's strength in numbers. There's a reason people in this country live together—it makes things easier, both practically and emotionally.

But there are also benefits of being alone. It's a Latin thing for men to say to women, "Hey, let me help you with that." I never played that card, but now I realize it's not a card; it's just this little dance, that's what they want to do anyway. Being down here, in a different culture, and now being alone, it's brought out different parts of me. It's made undiscovered parts of my character flourish. I do need help, and I need to be OK with getting help.

DAILY LIFE
HEALTH

man on the street who specializes in looking after people's cars. His job depends on satisfied customers, so even though we North Americans aren't accustomed to this form of makeshift security, it has been surprisingly effective for me and others I've talked to.

SCAMS TO WATCH OUT FOR

Costa Rica is also the land of scammers, many of whom will look like you and speak your language. Scams range from low-tech—someone spilling a drink on you and relieving you of your wallet while "helping" you clean it off— to more sophisticated schemes that ask for investments of tens of thousands of dollars. In late 2002, for instance, hundreds of expats and Ticos lost an estimated US$200 million when a financial entity known as Ofinter S.A. (aka the Brothers) closed up its offices overnight and fled the country, taking investors' money with them. Clients had been lured by promises of 3.5-4 percent interest a month (that is, 42-48 percent a year), and the Brothers had indeed delivered on those promises for years, supporting many an expat in high style. But then the goose laying those golden eggs flew the coop, and investors were left in the feather-strewn mud.

Call center scams are common. Between 2002 and 2013, for example, a huge and long-running scam, based in part in Costa Rica, defrauded thousands of U.S. citizens—most over the age of 55—of almost US$20 million. The perpetrators of the scam were U.S., Canadian, and other English-speaking expats living in Costa Rica. The scammers, claiming they were calling from the well-respected insurance company Lloyds of London, convinced mostly elderly retirees in the United States that they had won hundreds of thousands of dollars. To claim their prize, they only needed to pay a "refundable insurance fee" directly to "Lloyd's of London of Costa Rica." Scammers who manned the phones earned 20 to 40 percent of what they brought in—as much as US$3,600 in cash weekly. Their targets lost an average of US$1,200 each to the fraud. Nearly 50 defendants in the case have been convicted in the Western District of North Carolina; the case is still ongoing.

There are many other such schemes still in operation—beware of investments that seem too good to be true. The maxim "If you wouldn't do it at home, don't do it here" isn't nearly strong enough, since there's less effective government oversight of financial dealings here than there is in North America or Europe.

DRUGS

The North American appetite for recreational drugs has helped make Central America a conduit for marijuana, heroin, and cocaine moving up from South America. Drug trafficking and money laundering are on the rise throughout the isthmus, including Costa Rica. Thwarted smuggling attempts have revealed a variety of attempted vessels, including underwear, surfboards, tires, submarines, sharks, and wigs. Who knows what the successful smugglers are using—perhaps coffee beans or the baseballs stitched in Turrialba?

What all this means to the average visitor or foreign resident is that Costa Rican police, assisted by the U.S. Drug Enforcement Agency (DEA), are on high alert. The United States and Costa Rica signed a treaty in 1998 on joint air and sea patrols to crack down on drug smuggling. The DEA's Central American headquarters, in fact, is in San José. Big guns are trained on this little republic, and anyone suspected of participating in international drug trafficking will be dealt with harshly.

As for personal use, if you tend toward addiction and have dabbled in recreational drugs, be especially careful in Costa Rica. Amphetamine use is on the rise, and marijuana and cocaine, including crack, are easy to come by and tend to be less expensive than they are back home. Many an expat has been brought low by the availability of crack in particular. I've heard stories of gringos ending up broke, on the street, in jail, or worse.

Alcohol is another drug that expats may abuse when they move to Costa Rica. The stress of adapting to a new culture, coupled with feelings of isolation and boredom, drives many newcomers to drink. "If you have a drinking problem," advises an expat who has lived here for a few decades, "don't come to Costa Rica—it'll just get worse." Costa Ricans also like their liquor, which is no good thing but has a silver lining: There are Alcoholics Anonymous meetings in almost every neighborhood and town in the country. Recently I saw a small-town meeting where attendees had arrived by pickup truck, quad, and horse. Some meetings are in English, but don't worry if the meeting is in Spanish and you can barely say *"Hola."* The camaraderie of such gatherings transcends language.

PROSTITUTION

There are tens of thousands of prostitutes in Costa Rica, and the majority operate well within the law. Yes, prostitution is legal here, and working girls are supposed to have special ID cards (*carnets de salud* or "health identity cards") proving that they are disease-free. There are brothels in most towns and hundreds of them in San José, as well as bars known as gathering places for prostitutes and potential clients. The age of consent in Costa Rica is 16, but it is illegal for young people under age 18 to work as prostitutes; anyone who engages the services of an underage prostitute is at serious legal risk.

SEXUAL EXPLOITATION

Prostitution is legal in Costa Rica if the prostitute is a consenting adult over 18, but sexual exploitation—of underage or unwilling partners—is most definitely illegal. Many of the prostitutes in Costa Rica are brought in from other countries, including Colombia, the Dominican Republic, and the nations of Eastern Europe, and, while they may be of age, there's often more than a whiff of them having been railroaded into their current situation.

Underage prostitution is also a big problem. In 2000, ABC's *20/20* broadcast a report that Costa Rica was second

only to Thailand in underage sex tourism. Since then, there has been increased awareness of the issue and heightened police vigilance. The Costa Rican government formed the Commission against the Sexual Exploitation of Children, and private organizations also lend a hand to try to rectify the situation, offering job training for young people who might otherwise be drawn to the "easy" money of prostitution, or providing rehab and employment opportunities for those already in the life. And you'll now see signs in the airport and in some cities that tell you that you're in for trouble if you have sex with underage Costa Ricans.

But it's unclear just how effective these efforts have been. One indication that Costa Rica has a long way to go is that the respected Ethical Traveler website (www.ethicaltraveler.org), which uses a variety of criteria to name the top "ethical travel" destinations each year, in 2010 bumped Costa Rica from its list because of the sex tourism situation here. They had in years past "strongly encouraged travelers to bring their commerce to Costa Rica—a country top-rated by many important indicators." They've since changed their minds, stating that, "Unfortunately, [we] now consider Costa Rica among the world's most notorious destinations for sexual predators, with an unusually large number of sex tourism venues in operation. According to Casa Alianza, more than 3,000 girls and young women work in San José's 300 brothels. Now rivaling Thailand and the Philippines as the world's leading sex tourism destination, Costa Rica is credited with having the region's largest child prostitution problem and has thus been flagged by INTERPOL, as the country is fast becoming the hemispheric capital of sex tourism."

ARRANGEMENTS

Beyond the straightforward sex-for-money world of prostitution lies a wide gray area of "arrangements." In this country, where women (as elsewhere in the world) are at an economic disadvantage, and where it is not uncommon for men to abandon their wives and children (desertion is called "the poor man's divorce"), women may actively seek out relationships with expat men in the hopes of garnering support for themselves and their families.

Some of these Tica women and girls are quite desperate or underage, but there are always men, often three or four times the girl's age, willing to take advantage of the situation. The slimiest of these are lampooned as "sexpats" or members of the "dead pecker brigade." Other women know exactly what they're getting into and may even qualify as the exploiter in the situation. But in both cases, the women believe that most expat men are well off, and by Costa Rican standards, most are.

Expat men looking for such arrangements should go in with their eyes wide open. Exploiting underage girls is illegal, exploiting desperate women is creepy, and even if your potential honey is neither underage nor desperate, things can get complicated. Think twice when a beautiful young woman claims that she truly prefers a man three times her age.

That said, marrying or hooking up *por interés* (for money, or security) here is not uncommon, and it's not limited to Tica women looking for foreign sugar daddies. In terms of world history, marrying for love is a relatively recent development, and in poorer countries marriage is still seen as an economic contract as much as a romantic one. There's nothing wrong with that, as long as you don't confuse a mutually beneficial arrangement with true love.

HIV/AIDS AND OTHER STDS

Sexually transmitted diseases, including HIV, are less prevalent in Costa Rica than in many other nations. Even though Costa Rica has done a decent job with HIV/AIDS education, and the country's public health system cares for people living with the virus, it's still very important to be careful, especially if your plans here include casual sexual contact.

Prostitution is legal, and prostitutes are supposed to be checked regularly for disease, but some prostitutes aren't registered and don't get checked and are therefore at high risk of contracting HIV and other STDs and of passing diseases on to their clients. Even if your partner is nonprofessional, know that Costa Rican men usually prefer not to use condoms, and Costa Rican women don't tend to insist. Practice safe sex, and use condoms every time.

SAFETY NOTES FOR WOMEN

North American and European women may get a lot of attention in Costa Rica, especially if they're young or blond. Some women appreciate the attention; many do not. You may hear wolf whistles, hissing, or suggestive comments as you walk down the street. If you speak fluent Spanish and are one of those lucky people who always think of the right thing to say at the right moment, by all means, attempt a witty comeback. The easier option is to ignore unwanted attention and to walk on by with purpose and confidence.

Most guidebooks advise women to dress like the local women do, but if you did that in Costa Rica, you'd draw even more attention, since most Ticas favor skin-tight pants or skirts, plunging necklines, and high heels. If you dress conservatively, you'll get less attention, but not that much less. Costa Rican men seem to believe that North American and

European women—whether in miniskirts or overalls—are easy conquests. This may have some basis in truth, as many visiting women enjoy brief beach flings or choose the optional night tour with their nature guide. There's nothing wrong with that if everyone's a consenting adult, but remember that you are in unknown waters here.

Even supremely confident and experienced women probably don't know the ins and outs of dating etiquette in an unfamiliar place. For your own safety, it's best to lay low at first, taking it all in but not acting impulsively. Costa Rican tradition says that *las mujeres deben de ser deseadas y no sobradas,* which basically means women should be desired but not show desire—not flirt, put themselves on display, or be bold in their approach to men. While modern-day Ticos have to some extent moved beyond that double standard, tradition dies hard, and some women are still judged harshly for being too forward.

Wherever you fall on the boldness spectrum, be sure to observe the same commonsense precautions you would in any new place: Don't walk alone in remote places, and don't hang out late at unfamiliar bars unless you're with friends who'll keep an eye on you and make sure you're OK.

DAILY LIFE
HEALTH

BUSINESS AND EMPLOYMENT

Self-starters will do well in Costa Rica. It's actually easier to establish your own business here than to get a decent job working for someone else. Compared to many other countries, which put up obstacles to foreign-owned enterprise, Costa Rica welcomes foreign investment, especially businesses that create jobs for Ticos.

Tax breaks are offered to new ventures related to tourism, reforestation, and low-income housing, and specially designated free trade zones *(zonas francas)* offer further tax breaks for businesses located within their boundaries. You don't even need residency to start that rafting business, flower shop, or production plant you've always dreamed of. Since most businesses here are owned and operated by a corporation (in Costa Rica called an S.A., or Sociedad Anónima), you can even start and run a business on a tourist visa.

A few decades back, the average North American living in Costa Rica—well past midlife, living off a pension or investments—wasn't looking to work or start a business. More and more, however, those who move here are still smack in the middle of their working years. Some have been laid off; others have cashed in or dropped out. They come to Costa Rica

to escape, to reassess, and to start over. If they decide to stay, most of these sojourners will, sooner or later, need to think about how they will support themselves.

You *can* support yourself here, but it will take more than picking up coconuts, sticking a straw in them, and selling them to tourists—that job is taken. And it's not a place to come to get rich quick, or to get rich at all, for that matter. Those who do best simply want to live here and do what it takes to make that happen. Lance Byron, co-owner with Adrienne Pellizzari of the ever-expanding Café Milagro in Quepos, says loving the country and its people are essential to success in business. "And when I say success," he clarifies, "I mean not only monetary, but spiritual as well. Some foreigners manage to make enough money to survive, but they're miserable," complaining about the bureaucracy and their workers to whomever will listen. Lance and other business owners emphasize that it's the newcomer who must adapt, not the other way around.

Even though you'll naturally want to turn a profit or make a decent salary, it's good to keep things in perspective. Costa Rica offers visitors the benefits of living in a nation that has made long-term investments in peace, social justice, and the environment. It abolished its army in 1948, has put aside one-quarter of its territory for national parks and wildlife refuges, and continues to put money into the country's infrastructure and social services. Think of all the sacrifices this tiny nation has made to transform itself into a place where all are entitled to health care and education, where despite problems the country basically *works,* and where a disproportionate share of the world's biodiversity has been given a fighting chance at survival.

Add to all that a slower, more humane pace, and you're already enjoying a host of advantages that money can't buy. Factor these into your balance sheet, and listen to the expats who note that those interested only in money seem to do worse here than those with broader goals. Whether you choose to teach English, start a bed-and-breakfast, or run a tour company, you'll do better and be happier if you want to contribute to Costa Rica rather than wring from it everything you can.

Being a contributing member of your new society and earning money are not mutually exclusive. It's not only possible to make a living here, it's often easier to start and run a business in Costa Rica than it would be in the United States or Canada. Making money hand over fist is another story.

And there's a lot to learn quickly. You're in a new environment, often using an unfamiliar language, and different labor laws apply. Legal and cultural differences come into high relief as you contract a lawyer to do the paperwork, hire staff to help you, and try to carve out your niche with tools you're not even sure how to use yet. It's easy to get discouraged. The successful business owners I've met all have their tales of struggle and woe, but they tell them with a comic twist rather than with bitterness. And it's a sense of humor—along with good planning, experience in the field, hard work, and just plain sticking to it—that makes a business work here (much like elsewhere in the world). It's the couple who buys a hotel though they don't know the first thing about running one, or the tourist who thinks doing business here will be like taking an extended vacation, who lose their shirts and often their affection for the country.

The Job Hunt

Costa Rica is like the United States in that it has one of the strongest economies in its geographical area, and so it attracts people who need work. If your home country is in bad economic straits with high unemployment—think Peru or Nicaragua—Costa Rica may look very good. "It's easy to make a living here," a Peruvian living in Liberia told me, "as long as you're ready to work hard. But at least here you find something to work hard at."

For North Americans used to making a good wage or salary, however, Costa Rica is no haven. North Americans don't usually come here for job opportunities; they come because they love the country. Those who need to generate income can do so, but that income won't approach what you could make back home. Sure, the cost of living is lower here, but not that much lower. Rent is less; food is about the same. Buses are a bargain, but cars and gas are more expensive here than in North America.

You can't legally work without a work permit, and they're not easy to get. Sometimes employers will arrange for permits or give you a letter of employment so that you can hire a lawyer to apply for the permit.

Most of the jobs are in the Central Valley, the economic engine of the country. Yes, there's a lot of tourist activity on the coasts and in some inland areas like Lake Arenal. But there's also a lot of competition for those tourism-related jobs. How many wanderers stumble into cool little beach towns and decide they want to stay? Too many. These areas can only absorb so many massage therapists, surf instructors, real estate agents, and bartenders. And Ticos will always be hired before you—it's only fair. Says the owner of a large Pacific coast hotel, "Eighty percent of [foreigners] who move to Manuel Antonio seem to be looking for work. They usually don't find it, because it's very hard for businesses to hire foreigners. If it were easier, the whole tourist industry would change."

If you do get a job in a tourist town, it will probably end when high season does—in April—or even before. The few North Americans I met who had managed to land jobs in resort areas spoke of low wages, lack of shifts, and (for waiters) no tips.

The government would really rather you start your own business and provide work for others. To get an idea of how foreigners are encouraged to open businesses but discouraged from holding jobs, consider this: The most common categories of foreign residency—*rentista* and *pensionado*—allow you to be a business owner but not an employee. Understandably, Costa Rica wants to protect its own workforce.

But there are foreigners who work at salaried jobs, some even legally. What do they do, and how do they do it?

Some work for multinational corporations with branches here—those jobs are usually arranged before they get to Costa Rica. By law, these companies are allowed to fill 10 percent of their positions with foreign workers; in practice the percentage is much lower. There are many qualified Ticos to fill the positions, and they are likely to work for lower salaries.

Some foreigners work for nongovernmental organizations (NGOs). Others with specialized skills, like electricians, plumbers, or finish carpenters, get hired because there may be few people in the

Most jobs are in or around San José, the economic engine of the country.

area with their skills, especially outside the cities.

Probably the most common job for expats is teaching English, especially in the Central Valley. English teachers don't make a lot of money—maybe US$10 per hour. The bigger, more successful English schools can often give teachers enough hours a week to make a living wage, but smaller or struggling schools may only have a few slots available. Be wary of promises. A young woman I met in Monteverde had communicated by Internet with an English school there, which promised her work along with room and board. When she arrived, she found that the room was a hovel, the board not available, and she only got paid for teaching if students signed up for classes, which seemed to be a rare occurrence.

"If they don't know you," cautions Peggy Windle, who has taught at several schools in Costa Rica, "they won't give you a full-time job. They'll try you out part-time, and if they like you, maybe in four or five months they'll give you enough work to live on. Bring money."

She also advises bringing your actual physical credentials with you—diplomas, teaching certificate, et al. "They wanted my sheepskin from college," says Peggy. "Not the transcripts, but the piece of paper that says I graduated. They're very into pomp and circumstance here. I had to call my son and get him to FedEx everything down."

I asked Peggy if would-be teachers should do a lot of advance work before they arrive in Costa Rica. "You can email or call if you want," she says. "But the schools will only believe you really want a job when they see the whites of your eyes."

You could start your search by scanning the jobs posted on Craigslist and other overseas job forums, but it's important to get to know the country and where you might want to live before applying for any jobs.

Some English-speaking foreign residents also teach in bilingual primary and secondary private schools, most of which are located in or around San José. Kirt Wackford, who has a PhD in ecology, taught science at Saint Paul's College in

Expat Experience: River Guide Makes Good

In the spring of 1978, New York-born **Michael Kaye** and his Salvadorian wife, **Yolanda,** were riding the rails in the wilds of Costa Rica. They'd been living in El Salvador, but that country was heading toward civil war. Both had heard good things about peaceful and democratic Costa Rica, though they had no idea how they'd make a living if they were to move themselves and their two small children here.

At that time the train still ran from San José to the Caribbean coast. "We were the only tourists," says Michael. Though wildly scenic, the route was also "the real deal, the local transportation, the way people got around. When the train ceased running, it caused a lot of ghost towns."

Writer Paul Theroux took that same ride the very same year and wrote about mountains "so precipitous that the train has to descend through tunnels (screams, exalted yells in the cars, and the odor of damp walls) to a cliff-side that brings us so near the river the spray hits the windows. Then up again, along a cut, to switchbacks and bridges."

Michael and Yolanda's train clung to a high cliff. On the left was a sheer rock wall; on the right was nothing at all.

"I went out between cars to get a better view," says Michael. He'd been a river guide and had owned a rafting company in the United States, so he knew that "when it just drops off, it usually means there's a river down there."

Indeed there was a river down there. Through a deep gorge flowed the mighty Río Reventazón (Exploding River), a riot of Class V rapids that leapt over boulders and sent up plumes of mist. Emerald-green rainforest crowded the river's banks where the rocks allowed.

Above the water's distant roar and the metallic clack of the train, Michael heard the voice of his wife. "She was yelling at me, telling me I was crazy to be out between cars just to see a river. I yelled back, 'No me jodas. Este rio nos va a dar comer.' (Don't bug me. This river's going to put food in our mouths.)"

So Michael had an idea of what he might do if they moved to Costa Rica: lead river-rafting trips down what looked like a thrilling run of rainforest-fringed white water. But the couple wasn't yet convinced that Costa Rica was the place for them.

NOT YOUR USUAL LATIN AMERICAN COUNTRY

After their trip to the Caribbean coast and a glimpse of the Pacuare, another gorgeous and raftable river, the couple returned to San José, and Michael went looking for topographical maps.

"My experience of river exploration in Latin America was that the only topo maps available were for military use – they were considered state secrets. I once paid a bribe to spend almost two weeks in a dark, airless room in the Military Geographic Institute in Guatemala, tracing maps, each of which was numbered and controlled. We were going to do these very steep, remote rivers, and you need to be able to get in to start the run. And if anything happens, you have to know how to walk out."

Michael headed for Costa Rica's National Geographic Institute, fully expecting either to be turned away or solicited for a bribe. But a democratic country without a military has a different way of doing things.

"I walk into the institute," Michael recalls, "and they're selling the topo maps I need for two dollars apiece. That impressed me. Then I thought, so I can get the maps, but I'll probably have to bribe them to get aerial photos. In Guatemala they wouldn't even let me look at aerial photos. In San José, I asked, 'How much are the aerial photos?' This was before satellite photos, and it turned out the photos were from the United States Geological Survey (USGS). They told me, 'The aerial photos are also two dollars apiece.' That impressed the hell out of me. I thought this place is really different."

Yolanda still wasn't convinced. It would take a parade to change her mind. Luckily, their visit coincided with May Day. Michael wanted to go to this celebration of workers; Yolanda not only didn't want to go, but was also convinced that if Michael went, he'd be hurt or worse. "In El Salvador," says Michael, "workers would go and march, and then a lot of people would get shot. I'd heard that that didn't happen in Costa Rica, but I wanted to see it with my own eyes."

Michael went to the parade, and saw that "the workers were joking with the cops, and the cops were unarmed. I went back to Yolanda and said, 'Well, since I didn't get killed, we're going to move here.'"

COSTA RICA EXPEDITIONS IS BORN

The couple returned to El Salvador and began preparations for the move. Michael arranged for rafts to be shipped to Costa Rica and began running rivers almost as soon as they arrived. He named his enterprise Costa Rica Expeditions, and more than three decades later, the company is still going strong. It's known not only as one of the first tour companies in Costa Rica, but also as one of the most prestigious and successful outfits in the country's ever-expanding ecotourism sector.

Back in the late 1970s, however, the company still had some growing to do. "My idea," says Michael, "was that I could make some money here if I had a commercial rafting outfit. But it soon became obvious that no matter how good the rivers were, people wanted to do other stuff. To get them to come here, I needed a wider group of attractions. There was all this great wildlife, protected in national parks. I'd done stuff in Guatemala, and it wasn't the unrest that got me; I was taking people to primary forest that kept disappearing. I was losing the product. I kept telling people on one trip about this place, the highlight of the trip. When I got there, it had been clear-cut."

Forward-thinking Costa Rica had already committed to protecting its rainforests and rivers and oceans, and the resulting wilderness and wildlife was—and still is—a powerful draw for tourists. And so Costa Rica Expeditions expanded its offerings tenfold, taking travelers all over the country to experience its multifaceted flora and fauna.

The company still runs rivers these days, but it focuses mostly on small private trips—there are plenty of outfits offering the large-scale summer-camp sort of river experience. Michael says the company offers a variety of multistop trips, from pampered luxury to high adventure. And he's always coming up with new ideas, like the "Side by Side but Worlds Apart" trip that debuted in 2013. Meant to compare Costa Rica and neighboring Nicaragua, the trip starts in San José, which, according to Michael, is "a city that has adopted many characteristics of North American cities and then made them worse." Travelers soon leave that city behind, heading for the carless hamlets of Tortuguero and even more remote San Francisco on Costa Rica's north Caribbean coast. Then it's a boat up the fabled San Juan River, the fluid border between Costa Rica and Nicaragua, a waterway with a history that includes U.S. industrialist Cornelius Vanderbilt running a steamship company transporting East Coasters to the gold fields of California in the 1850s, using the San Juan as a trans-oceanic canal. Michael says the trip may only appeal to diehard adventurers, but he's not worried—after decades of running a highly successful tour company, he can afford to indulge his personal passions.

San Rafael de Alajuela. The school emphasizes English instruction as well as other academic subjects, and Kirt taught his classes in English. Full-time teaching earned him about US$1,000 per month before taxes.

Teachers I spoke with said they had a hard time adjusting to some aspects of the Costa Rican classroom. The biggest was noise level and a certain lack of respect for the teacher. "Kids will talk away while you're trying to give your lecture," says one teacher. "And the culture here is to just let them."

Starting a Business

With a stable political environment, an educated workforce, and few limits on foreign control of corporations, Costa Rica is a good place for foreign residents to do business. Costa Rica considers that it protects itself against exploitation by protecting its workforce. Labor laws are strict and well enforced. The government makes it easy for foreigners to do business here in part because it wants more jobs created for Ticos.

For a few specific kinds of enterprise there are further incentives, which include tax exemptions that can last for more than a decade. You'll need an experienced and up-to-date lawyer to tell you which of the many incentive programs you might qualify for and to guide you through applying for them.

If your company qualifies for Free Zone (export processing zone) incentives, your company may be able to receive exemptions on import duties on raw materials or components, on export taxes, and on taxes. If your company relates to tourism or reforestation, there are other incentives to be had, and some investments may even qualify you for residency.

SOCIEDAD ANÓNIMA (S.A.)

Get used to the two letters *S.A.*; You'll be seeing a lot of them, especially if you want to start your own business. A Sociedad Anónima (Anonymous Society)

is a corporation, and in Costa Rica, everybody and their dog seems to have one. The main feature of an S.A. is limited liability. If something goes wrong, it's not you who owns the company or enterprise; it's the corporation. Liability is limited to how much money you've put into the S.A.

To form a Costa Rican corporation, two people appear before a notary public and execute the articles of incorporation, and they subscribe to at least one share of stock each. The incorporators don't have to be citizens or even residents of Costa Rica; citizens of any nation are free to form a corporation here. An S.A. also needs a board of directors, with a minimum of three members: president, secretary, and treasurer. The two incorporators often play two of these roles, drafting a friend or relative to play the third. That third director needn't appear before the notary public if he or she sends a letter accepting the position.

Forming a Corporation (S.A.)

To form a corporation, you'll need to:

- Execute the articles of incorporation before a notary public.

- Publish legal notice of the corporation in Costa Rica's official newspaper, La Gaceta—this is to give people the chance to object to the corporation

Expat Experience: Mead, Honey, Goat Cheese

Back in 2013, **Michael Lindeman** and **Alejandra Arraya** were sitting on their front porch in Alajuela, Costa Rica, singing the praises of honey wine. Their own wine, to be exact, made with honey from their very own bees. Michael's blue eyes flashed with enthusiasm; Ale smiled as she folded her hands across her very pregnant belly. Both seemed happy but still a little bemused that after fifteen years of working demanding jobs in the United States – which had nothing at all to do with bees – they were back in Costa Rica, the proud owners of 20 beehives and a spare bedroom full of fermenting tanks and bottles.

Keeping bees and making mead wasn't just the couple's latest passion; it was also their new business. And they were in good company: handcrafted libations were gaining popularity in Costa Rica. Wine culture was growing, with a greater selection of imports every year and two schools in San José offering sommelier classes. Craft beer brewing was also on the upswing. In July 2011 a handful of microbreweries and a store that sells beer-making equipment banded together to form Costa Rica's first craft brewing association.

TROPICAL *TERROIR*

Michael and Ale projected that each of their hives would produce an average of 30 kilos of honey per year. "We've done the math," said Michael. "With 20 hives we can make about 2,000 bottles of wine per year." They also planned to buy honey from other beekeepers to augment that number and to experiment with different flavor profiles.

Mead tastes of the flowers the bees have tapped for the honey. Coffee flower honey, for instance, produces a brightly flavored mead with mild stimulant properties, while honey from tropical flowers like maracuya (passion fruit) creates mead with a heady fruitiness. Michael explains it in terms of *terroir*. The French term refers to how the soil and weather of a particular place interact with a plant's genetics. *Terroir* is expressed in everything from wine to coffee to chocolate to honey.

HOW IT ALL STARTED

The couple met in 1995, when Michael was teaching English in Costa Rica and Alejandra was a student. "She wasn't *my* student," Michael clarified with a smile. But the two fell in love, and when Michael had to return to Champagne, Illinois, to finish his ESL degree, Ale went with him.

"We arrived in Illinois on a cold, dreary, January day," Michael recalled, "It was the first time Ale had experienced subzero temperatures." For someone who'd grown up in sunny Costa Rica, it was quite a shock. But Ale adjusted quickly, enrolling in school, earning an engineering degree, and landing a good job with Caterpillar Industries. Michael secured a faculty position at the University of Illinois, now their shared alma mater.

"Then we had Sofia," said Michael. "She rocked our world, in a good way."

"We started re-evaluating," said Ale.

After 15 years in the United States, the couple and their toddler returned to Costa Rica in March 2011, hoping to make a living related to sustainable agriculture and organic farms. They enrolled in a course at the National University's Centro de Investigaciones Apícolas Tropicales (CINAT), the Center for the Study of Tropical Bees. The course culminated in visits to local hives, which they documented in videos now posted on YouTube under Michael's name. Then they enrolled in a honey winemaking course.

Soon thereafter, Costa Rica Meadery was born. Their plan was to sell honey, mead, and goat cheese. And that's what they're still doing, years later, along with winning prizes at fairs, teaching classes, and being part of a vibrant microbrew, mead-making, and farm-to-table scene in Costa Rica. Check out their Facebook page for more information: facebook.com/CostaRicaMeadery.

name being recorded, if, for instance, the name is already taken.

- Register the company at the National Registry (the notary public who executes the articles of incorporation usually does this).

- Legalize the corporation's books: a set of three accounting books—daily, main (mayor), and inventory and balances—and three "legal" books—shareholders' record, shareholders' assemblies, and board of directors' meetings—are presented to the Ministerio de Hacienda for its initial authorization by the Book Legalization Department. Once legalized, these books will register all internal affairs of the company as well as stock transfers and are kept privately by the shareholders.

The incorporation process usually takes a few months to complete, though I've heard of people in a hurry completing the process in a matter of weeks.

In 2012 banking regulations were passed that may make it a little more complicated to get a bank account in a corporation's name, if you've formed it just to hold property, for example. Roger Petersen, practicing lawyer and author of *The Legal Guide to Costa Rica,* explains: "There's the presumption that if you have an S.A., it's a commercial entity, so the bank says, 'Well, show me your balance sheets.' And you say, 'Well, the S.A. just holds a house; it has no balance sheets.' We still don't know just how these new banking regulation will play out." Regulations also require anyone attempting to open a bank account in Costa Rica, whether as an individual or corporation, to "provide very in-depth information about the source of your funds," Petersen continues. "You're required to hire a Costa Rican CPA to certify all your financial records. Without that CPA certification, the bank won't even look at you."

(For more about the banking regulations, see the *Finance* chapter.)

Corporation Tax
The fiscal year in Costa Rica runs from October 1 through September 30, with tax returns due by December 15. A corporation is taxed only on income earned within Costa Rica, and tax rates vary from 10 to 30 percent, assessed on the difference between gross income and allowable deductions. Businesses will need to charge customers and then pay sales tax *(impuesto de ventas),* also known as a value-added tax. The current rate is 13 percent, and the tax is on goods and services not deemed basic necessities. If your business imports goods, there will be those tariffs to deal with as well. Anita Myketuk of the Buena Nota in Manuel Antonio notes that a store owner needs to figure import taxes into her balance sheet. "A lot of the items in my store are imported," says Anita. "That's why, for instance, sunscreen is so expensive here. There are a couple of brands made in Costa Rica, but no one wants them, because they're not name brands—Coppertone or Hawaiian Tropic. But some things don't have import taxes or have very low taxes, like sporting gear."

In April 2012 legislators passed a law imposing an additional yearly fee on corporations.

Hiring Help

Education in Costa Rica is free and compulsory through ninth grade, so there are lots of good, qualified people here who are ready to work. But the country knows what it has, and it protects its workers with a series of regulations that you should study carefully before hiring *any* employee. Lawyer Roger Petersen cautions, "What people need to realize is that when they hire someone in Costa Rica, the benefit of the doubt will always be with the employee, not with the employer. Understand that, keep the Caja [national health insurance] off your back, and you'll be fine."

LABOR LAWS

Whether you hire 1 person to clean your house or 30 people to sew stuffed monkeys, the same basic labor laws apply. The Labor Code of 1943 is the basis for the lengthy document now in effect, which seeks to minimize conflict between employer and employee by spelling out every detail of that relationship. These regulations are taken very seriously, workers generally know their rights, and if there is a conflict, labor court judges often decide in favor of the employee.

In brief, the regulations specify that:

• Employers must make Social Security (Caja) contributions for each employee and also deduct a percentage of the employee's pay for further contribution to the Caja.

• Forty-eight hours is the maximum workweek; hours beyond that are paid as overtime.

• Minimum wages and salaries for most jobs and professions are set by the Caja.

• Employers must notify the local Caja office within 8 days of a hire.

• The first 30 days of employment is a trial period; after that, employees must be given notice *(pre-aviso)* if they are to be fired, and they have the right to severance pay *(cesantia)*.

• Employers must provide employees with paid vacations.

• Employers are obligated to pay a Christmas bonus (called the *aguinaldo*).

• Employers must provide for maternity leave.

• Employers must pay employees for nine holidays off per year.

These rules are covered in more detail in the following sections.

Social Security (Caja) Contributions

The Caja Costarricense de Seguro Social (the Caja) pays for workers' health care, sick leave, and disability, but employers are expected to do their part. An employer must calculate 26 percent of a worker's gross salary and pay that amount to the Caja. Employers also need to deduct 9 percent of a worker's wages and pay that additional amount to the Caja. As an example, let's say that a cashier at your bookstore earns US$400 a month. Twenty-six percent of that salary is US$104, which is the employer's contribution to the worker's Social Security. Nine percent of the salary is US$36; the employer deducts that amount from the employee's pay (leaving the worker with a salary of US$364) and pays that additional amount to the Caja.

The Workweek

The maximum workweek is 48 hours, 10 hours is the maximum day shift (8 hours for hazardous work), and 6 hours is the maximum for a night shift. Managers and executives can be asked to work 12-hour days. Anything exceeding these limits is overtime and must be paid at time and a half.

Minimum Wage

Almost all jobs in Costa Rica have a minimum wage, set by the National Council on Wages. In 2017, minimum wages ranged from about US$17.55 a day for unskilled laborers to US$1,125 a month for some professions that require a *licenciado* degree (roughly equivalent to a master's degree). Remember that these are minimums—to attract and retain quality workers, many employers pay more. In Spanish the list of wages is called the Decreto de Salarios Mínimos and can be obtained at Social Security offices or from most bookstores. A detailed outline is available online at www.mtss.go.cr, the website of the Ministerio de Trabajo y Seguridad Social (Ministry of Work and Social Security).

If laborers here are earning about as much per day as their counterparts in the United States would make in a couple of hours, what does that mean? Well, that workers here have a harder time making ends meet, and that if you want to work in Costa Rica, you won't be getting the salary you're accustomed to. It also means that as an employer your money will go farther here, whether you're paying someone to build your house or keep it clean.

The minimum wage for a domestic worker does not include meals and board. Food and lodging provided to a live-in domestic is considered "in-kind" payment equivalent to 50 percent of the worker's wages, and it must be factored in when calculating severance pay or the mandatory Christmas bonuses. What that means is that if you pay a live-in gardener or maid a salary of, say, US$300 a month, the real total, with which you would calculate severance or bonus, would be US$450.

Notification of Hire

You must notify the Caja within eight days of hiring someone. This is to limit the employer's possible liability as well as to start the paperwork moving. If an employee registered with the Caja is injured on the job, the Caja pays most of the medical bills—the employer's liability is limited to four days' salary. But if the worker isn't registered with the Caja, the employer could be liable not only for the worker's medical bills, but also half of his or her salary while the employee is injured or sick.

Length and Cessation of Employment

The first 30 days of employment is considered a trial period, with both employee and employer having the right to end the relationship without notice. After 30 days, unless an employee's termination is for just cause, employers must give advance notice of dismissal and are liable for severance pay. An employer can fire an employee and have no further responsibility to that worker only under very specific circumstances, outlined in Article 81 of the Labor Code. Just causes for dismissal range from deliberately damaging an employer's property to being thrown in jail. In Costa Rica, it is the employer's responsibility to document reasons for dismissal and to be ready to argue his or her case.

Pre-Termination Notice (Pre-Aviso): If termination is not for a cause listed in the Labor Code (maybe business is slow and there isn't enough for an employee to do), an employer must give advance notice of dismissal, and the amount of time is dependent on how long the worker has been on the job. If the worker has been with you for more than three months but less than six, one week's notice is required. Employment of six months to a year requires two weeks' notice. One month's prior notice is necessary for workers who have been employed for one year or more. In lieu of notice, an employer can pay the wages that would have been earned during the notice period. Notice may be in written form or may be delivered orally in the presence of two witnesses.

Severance Pay (Cesantia): If an employee is terminated without just cause, he or she is entitled to severance pay. If an employee has worked more than three but fewer than six months, he or she receives seven days' wages. Employees who've worked from six months to a year get 14 days' wages. Employment of a year or more requires between 19.5 and 22 days' wages for each year, depending on the number of years worked.

What If the Employee Quits? If an employee quits for just cause (also outlined in the Labor Code), the employer has the same responsibilities that he or she would have to a worker terminated without just cause. If, however, the employee has no just cause for quitting (maybe she got a better offer elsewhere), the employer's responsibilities end with the employee's departure.

Paid Vacations

Employers must provide workers with 2 weeks of paid vacation for every 50 weeks worked.

Unused Vacation Pay: When a worker is terminated without just cause, unused vacation pay is due him or her. Workers get 2 weeks of paid vacation for every 50 weeks worked. If a worker is terminated before a year is up, he or she should be paid for one vacation day per month worked.

The Christmas Bonus (Aguinaldo)

Law mandates this bonus, sometimes known as the 13th month of pay. Every worker who has been on the job at least a year is entitled to an extra month's wages to be paid between December 1 and 20. If a worker is fired before December, the aguinaldo must be prorated and paid to the employee at the time of termination: Take the total wages paid to the worker from December 1 through November 30 and divide the amount by 12.

Remember that to calculate aguinaldo for live-in domestic servants, you must add 50 percent to the salary for in-kind payment in the form of room and board.

Maternity Leave

Pregnant employees are entitled to one unpaid month off before the baby is born and three half-paid months off afterward. During those three months, the employer pays full salary, with half going to the worker, half to the Caja.

Paid Holidays

Employers must either provide paid time off for the following nine legal holidays or pay workers (if they agree to work) double their usual wage. Legal holidays fall on January 1 (New Year's Day), April 11 (Juan Santamaría Day), two days during Easter week (Holy Thursday and Good Friday), May 1 (International Workers Day), July 25 (Annexation of Guanacaste),

Expat Experience: A 3-D Life

Uwe Kreuzahler has a faded tattoo of Che Guevara on his forearm. The six foot, three inch Dutch German "mixed breed" is making coffee in the kitchen of his spacious home in Escazú, an upscale suburb of San José. "That's from a long time ago," he says, checking the tattoo as if consulting a wristwatch.

Guevara, the Argentine-born poster child of the Cuban revolution, would have approved of the radical change Uwe made back in 1996, upending his life to move to Costa Rica and marry a local girl he met on a business trip to San José.

"She was working at the pizza place next to the hotel," says Uwe. "I couldn't speak Spanish and she couldn't speak English. But I couldn't get her out of my mind, and when I came back, I wrote down how to say, 'How are you? Would you like to go to the movies?'"

They made it to the movies, and not long after, they made it to the altar.

Since then, Uwe says his life has been less about grand gestures and more about daily pivots and compromises. He's had to adjust to doing business in an unfamiliar language and culture, and to negotiate the challenges of a cross-cultural marriage, complete with three daughters and Tico in-laws.

WORKING FROM HOME, WITH CLIENTS ALL OVER THE WORLD

But on this beautiful Costa Rican morning, Uwe doesn't seem to be suffering too much. He's dressed for work–shorts and a loose shirt–if your work is on your terms, in a light-filled home office a few steps from his living room. His wife and daughters will be home soon. "They're what makes it all worthwhile," he tells me.

Uwe is the driving force behind a firm called 3D.CR (www.3d.cr), which provides three-dimensional photorealistic visualization services for the architectural and interior design industries. Previous to launching that company in 2009, Uwe worked with Costa Rica's Digital Factory, which provided similar services, and which went under, along with so many other companies, during the worldwide economic downturn in 2008. "When the crash came," says Uwe, "everything changed. Now you have competition from people in India, China, and the Philippines. They'll work for $20 a day. Costa Rica is one of the most expensive countries in Latin America, so I can't work for so little."

Instead, he upped his game and now provides renderings of such quality that people are willing to pay a premium. "Most of our clients need photorealistic renderings of buildings not yet built, for presale purposes. In the United States, they also need such images for environmental reports."

Pushing his craft further has served him well, but it also means that he's priced himself beyond most Costa Rican companies, which are still recovering from the downturn. He has one project in Costa Rica: a US$150 million development in the beach town of Jacó. But most of Uwe's clients are from outside of Costa Rica. "Maybe 65 percent of my clients are from the United States or Canada, 20 or 25 percent from Europe, a few Australian clients, and a few from Argentina and Brazil."

Uwe gets help from a partner, nine employees, and a stable of freelancers. Some of his coworkers live in Costa Rica, but most don't. "My partner is based in Texas. Then there's a Swedish guy in Sabanilla," a neighborhood in San José, "plus two Italians in Italy, a French guy, a German guy, a Belgian, a Canadian, and a guy in Venezuela who I'm training. I get two or three CVs every week, which shows me how the market is growing."

QUALITY OF LIFE

For several years, Uwe kept an office in Escazú, but when a locally based employee asked to work from home, Uwe took a look at how much the office was costing: US$2,500 a month in base rent, plus Internet, utilities, and security. What clinched his decision to move the office to his home was the traffic. He lives in an outlying area of Escazú called Guachipelín, but getting to "downtown" Escazú can take 45 minutes. "The traffic down here is a major problem," he says.

So now he gets up in the morning, makes coffee, and walks a few steps to the office. "Most of my friends hate their jobs. I've been doing what I do for 20 years and I still love it. I feel blessed, waking up in the morning with a smile on my face."

JUST SAY NO TO SEGWAYS

I asked Uwe if he had any advice for non-Costa Ricans who want to do business in Costa Rica.

"Don't try anything new," he says. "Ticos are very settled in what they like and want. A friend opened a place that served Dutch food. Delicious! I could have gone there every day. But he had to close because Ticos didn't like the food. Actually, they didn't know whether or not they liked it because they wouldn't try it.

"Or learn from the guy who brought in 150 Segways. Ticos don't have the money for that kind of thing. You have about 4.5 million people in the country, plus illegal immigrants. About 10 percent are the people running businesses. The others, what's the average monthly salary? Maybe US$500 or $600. How can they afford to pay US$25 an hour to rent a Segway?

"And even if they can afford it, they won't know how to use it. And another thing about Ticos is they don't want to make fools of themselves. So they won't even try it, because they're afraid of failing, of falling down, and of people laughing at them.

"So don't expect to bring something amazing and new down here. Check to see if there's a market already, either national or international, and don't expect to make the market accommodate your great idea."

YOU CAN TAKE THE TICA OUT OF COSTA RICA, BUT . . .

Uwe confides that over the past two decades "there have been moments when I got very sick of Costa Rica." In 2002, he took his family to live in Argentina, and then they lived nine months in a small German city, where his wife and girls really felt the racism. Then they tried Spain.

"Bottom line? I realized I couldn't take my wife away from her parents. Costa Rican families are very tight. Europeans and Americans, not so much—it's OK if you don't see your family for years. And we were at the point, either we get a divorce or we all go back to Costa Rica."

They came back. "My advice to people considering a cross-cultural relationship? Think twice. It seems incredible at first, old guy gets young girl—my wife is 12 years younger than I am. But for a relationship to work, and not just be about the money, you have to understand the culture and the Costa Rican family. And you make a lot of compromises."

Good advice, no doubt. But when Uwe's family comes home, whatever compromises he's made don't seem to have compromised his enjoyment of his wife and three daughters. His face lights up, and so do theirs.

September 15 (Independence Day), and December 25 (Christmas).

Unpaid legal holidays include August 2 (celebration of the country's patron saint, the Virgin of the Angels) and October 12 (Day of Cultures—formerly Columbus Day).

CULTURE CLASHES

It seems to be an international pastime to complain that you can't get good help anymore. Costa Rica's version of that game includes grumbling that Ticos lack initiative and a sense of personal responsibility. The Beisanz family writes in *The Ticos* that the "emphasis on dignity and courtesy often takes the form of saving face for others as well as oneself. Ticos rarely accept blame for mistakes and usually take care not to embarrass others, especially in public." To save face and to make the moment agreeable, Ticos will tell you whatever they think you want to hear: that your check will clear soon; that they'll be there this afternoon, for sure; or that they know which of those wires is live.

Ticos want to *quedar bien,* which means to make a good impression and to get along with others. They want to be respected as individuals and to be treated with the same consideration that they extend. Being scolded or corrected, especially in front of others, is not something a Tico will easily forgive.

A hotelier told me, "You have to charm people here in order to get them to want to help you. And never, ever yell at anyone or get nasty. North Americans are used to yelling; it's not the end of the world. Here it *is* the end of the world."

A developer in Guanacaste described how he learned to deal with the Tico tendency to nod and say yes even if they don't know what's being asked of them. "I say to my worker, 'Go over there and dig a hole.' And I leave, and come back, and

Many expats open restaurants, like this vegan restaurant over a butcher shop in Puerto Viejo.

he hasn't done it. Then I think, maybe there's something he didn't understand. I tell him again. 'Please, go over there and dig a hole.' And this time I ask, 'Did you understand what I said?' And he nods yes, but later I come back and he still hasn't done it. Finally—and this took a long time—I tell him what to do, and then I ask him to repeat back to me what I've just said. Usually he'll hem and haw, but then he'll say, 'OK, tell me again.'"

The culture values harmony—even if it's a superficial sort of harmony—over honesty, an approach that makes for a polite society but can be frustrating for those who prefer candor and are counting on people to keep their word.

Lateness is common, to the extent that when making plans one needs to specify *hora tica* (Tica time, which means an hour or two after the appointed time) or *hora*

DAILY LIFE
BUSINESS AND EMPLOYMENT

Americana (American time) or *hora exacta* (exact time).

Still, with all the frustrations (and there's no doubt that Ticos are frustrated with foreigners' idiosyncrasies at least as much as the other way around), many of the expat employers I spoke with were happy with their employees. Many think they got lucky, and they claim to have the best cook, clerk, or carpenter in all of Costa Rica. But it seems that a great many employers "got lucky," which suggests that Ticos are essentially good workers, especially if you're a good boss and make it your business to learn about cultural differences that may affect the employer-employee relationship.

In the end, it's all about people. Many foreigners move to Costa Rica because things here are on a more human scale. Personal relationships are paramount, even in the business world. Lance Byron of Café Milagro in Manuel Antonio tells of a local girl who worked in the café. "Silvia worked for us during her high school vacations, went off to college, and then got a great job with Procter & Gamble International, who sent her to the United States several times as one of their prodigies. We'd see each other once

in a while, and she'd always tell us Café Milagro was her favorite job. Whenever Adrienne [the café's co-owner] and I would sit and dream of the day we'd export coffee, Adrienne would have an implementation panic attack and ask, 'But who's going to run it?' I'd calmly reply, 'Silvia.' Well, wouldn't you know it, after a few years in the multinational corporate world, Silvia comes back to us and says she's tired of being 'a number.' So we created the export manager position for her, and she's been working on Café Milagro's export logistics."

Costa Rica is like a small town. You never know who will leave the *pueblo* only to circle back into your life again. This kind of coziness comes as a shock to vagabonding, job- and city-switching North Americans, who may launch and then jettison a dozen different lives before they hit middle age. In Costa Rica it's a bad idea, both personally and professionally, to burn too many bridges (in Spanish it's called *quemar sus barcos*, to burn your boats). A good rule of thumb here is to treat everyone as if you'll have to see him or her every day. It might turn out that you actually do.

Volunteering

Although many think of volunteering as giving something for nothing, seasoned volunteers see it differently. Besides the satisfaction of knowing you're helping where help is needed, volunteering often gives you a crash course in an unfamiliar subject, from the life cycle of the butterfly (if you're a guide at Monteverde's Butterfly Garden) to how to build a house (if you're helping out at Habitat for Humanity). Some organizations even provide room and board for their

volunteers, though most require you to pay your own way.

Volunteering also significantly expands your social circle, often hooking you up with people whose politics and priorities are similar to yours. Sometimes volunteer positions lead to paid work within the same field, as when Robert Durkin volunteered for Habitat for Humanity and later became a paid employee, organizing the agency office in Ciudad Colón. He says at Habitat, volunteers not only

Volunteering to Protect Wildlife

In Spring 2016, something extraordinary happened in the world of the highly endangered great green macaw: a chick hatched in the wild, the offspring of birds who had been bred in captivity and then released to their former range.

It happened high in a Mountain Almond tree, on a hill overlooking Costa Rica's Caribbean coast. It probably wouldn't have happened without the efforts of The Ara Project, a nonprofit founded in 1982 that is reintroducing great greens to their former habitat in the tropical forest along Costa Rica's Caribbean coast. And nonprofits like The Ara Project wouldn't be able to do their work without local employees and international volunteers, like Buffie Biddle, a writer, illustrator, and wildlife lover from Philadelphia.

Buffie just happened to be on her second volunteer stint with Ara when the chick, named Pewe, started getting his feathers and just generally learning how to be a macaw.

Volunteer Buffie Biddle keeps her eyes on the great green macaws.

"The exciting thing is that Pewe has macaws teaching him how to be a macaw," Buffie told me on my visit to Ara's great green macaw refuge near the beach town of Puerto Viejo. "His captive-bred parents sort of had humans teaching them how to be macaws, even though they're free to fly wherever they want and do what they want."

So what qualifies a writer and illustrator from Philadelphia to be at ground zero, witnessing and nurturing this important development for an endangered species? Her willingness, mostly. Not to mention her capacity for hard work, and her love of animals. This isn't her first volunteer rodeo. Besides two stints volunteering for The Ara Project (this second visit will last six months), she has also volunteered for a jaguar conservation program in Tortuguero. Back in her hometown of Philadelphia, she volunteered at the local museum of natural science. "What I love about working with environmental nonprofits is that I can contribute to important research and species conservation without having, say, a degree in biology." Not only does Buffie hold down the fort at the site and teach visitors—tourists, locals, and groups of schoolchildren—about macaw and rainforest conservation; she also keeps records of the birds' behavior that will contribute to our understanding of how these reintroduced great greens are doing, and what could be done to make them do even better.

pay their own way, but often give financial contributions as well. "It probably started with church groups, who give of both their time and financial resources. But it seems to have also extended out to individual volunteers."

ORGANIZATIONS

Just about every agency in Costa Rica that is working to improve society and the environment could use dedicated volunteers. If you have a special area of interest, contact organizations

ACCESS TO WILDLIFE

Buffie says that without her volunteer stints, her experience of Costa Rica would have been much more superficial, and she wouldn't have seen half as much wildlife. At the Ara center, she routinely sees howler, squirrel and white-faced monkeys. Agoutis are everywhere—"I always seem to get photos of their butts," she laughs. The other day, there was a kinkajou in the tree outside her cabin. And a few weeks back, she had the rare pleasure of seeing a puma. She was sneaking a cigarette on the road; she says she didn't want the macaws to see her; she didn't want to be a bad influence. "Out of the corner of my eye," she says, "I think I see someone's golden retriever. I look over and my god, it's a puma! It walks along the road and then bounds up that hill there. It was the most beautiful thing I've ever seen. That night, I'm FaceTiming with my father, and I get teary-eyed, I was so excited."

Her experiences move her in different ways. Working in jaguar conservation in Tortuguero, for example, she saw an iguana hanging out in a tree, which inspired her to write and illustrate a children' picture book (Pura Vida, Maje) about a chill iguana. Another book is in the works, and she also does freelance writing and illustration, something she can keep up with while she volunteers at The Ara Project, where she has Internet and lots of time on her hands.

ADVICE FOR POTENTIAL VOLUNTEERS

Buffie's advice if you want to volunteer at a wildlife project in Costa Rica is know that there's going to be some physical labor. "There was more in Tortuguero," she says. "Here at Ara there's work, but it's not that physical. You have to be ok with roughing it a little. In Tortuguero we only had electricity four hours a day. We had to use it to charge the computers and run the wells. You also have to be OK with being with lots of people (like in Tortuguero) or with being on your own a lot (like at The Ara Project Caribbean coast site)."

In a landscape where there are a lot of ways to give of your time and expertise, Buffie says it's important to research the places that call for volunteers. "Talk to people who've done it, if you can," she says.

Part of the satisfaction comes, of course, from helping out. And sometimes it takes people with their basic needs already met to pitch in and help. Amy Robertson, author of *Volunteer Vacations in Latin America*, points out, "In developing countries, wildlife conservation is often left behind in the basic struggle for survival." Volunteering in such environments can support and draw attention to local efforts that address these issues, she says, not to mention that such work transforms a tourist into a participant and advocate.

"Travel becomes transformative when it is about sharing experiences and integrating with the people, culture, and environment of the place," says Robertson.

And as climate change deniers in powerful global positions take aim at hard-fought regulations that protect the environment, this kind of hands-on work is all the more important and satisfying.

For more about macaws, The Ara Project and Buffie Biddle, see "Saving the World, One Bird at a Time," on page 326.

working in that field. (See the list in the *Resources* section for ideas.)

CREATING YOUR OWN OPPORTUNITIES

Although there are many ready-made volunteer positions, you may prefer to do good in your own way. It can be as simple as identifying the needs of your community and then organizing the effort to fill them. Maybe your neighborhood has no place for kids to play. What would it take to build a playground or even a community center? What kind of help could you get from local and national governments, from private organizations, and from your neighbors?

In rural areas, even basic necessities like garbage pickup and a reliable water supply may be lacking. In Tortuguero, the local Women's Association took on their Caribbean town's trash problem. "Every tourist, and every person who lives here, produces a mountain of trash—Coke cans, cigarettes, juice containers. We took on the responsibility of picking up all that trash." But they found they couldn't do it alone, and they have begun charging a small fee per house and business (much like any trash-collecting enterprise) and soliciting funds from government agencies. Their project is still a work in progress, but it shows what a small group of people can do.

Look around your town. Does the local health clinic need a vehicle so doctors and nurses can make house calls? Is the nearest preschool or library hours away? Do a lot of people drown every year at the local beach? If you're a problem solver, maybe you can help fix these things.

The best part about getting involved, one volunteer told me, is that "it gets you to the heart of things. You're right in the middle of town life. It can be frustrating, trying to get things done, but sometimes it all comes together, and you get to help change the face of the place for the better."

FINANCE

"Money is better than poverty," quips Woody Allen, "if only for financial reasons." Allen's smile-provoking maxim rings true wherever you are, although in Costa Rica your money will go a little farther, and your financial dealings will be just different enough from what you're used to that you can't coast along on automatic pilot. There are subtle and not-so-subtle differences in how money, that universal language, is spoken here in Costa Rica. Yes, you can open a bank account, but the process won't look like it does back at your neighborhood Bank of America. Shopping, tipping, and taxes will all need to be explored from a Tico vantage point.

You *can* live in Costa Rica for less than what you'd be spending in the United States or Canada, but not without conscious effort. What helps is that most people who move down here want to pare down, to let go of all they've accumulated over the years. They want to own less, work less, spend less, and enjoy life's simple pleasures. With this approach, it's not hard to live economically.

Cost of Living

What most people thinking of moving to Costa Rica want to know is, "Can I afford it?" Some have heard you can live like a queen on next to nothing; others say rumor has it that it's as expensive to live here as it is up north. As always, the truth is somewhere in between. Calculating the cost of living is by no means an exact science—so much depends on where you live and on your personal definition of what is essential. Some can't live without everything they came to rely on in their life up north, from expensive cars to gourmet food. Those looking to create an exact replica of their U.S. life here in Costa Rica will find life very expensive indeed. Those who are more adaptable will be able to live well on a lot less. Most budget-conscious expats end up compromising—living a life that is frugal but with a few frills. They take buses but splurge on restaurant meals twice a week. Or they live in a small house in a modest neighborhood but take a beach vacation every month.

"When I was married to a lawyer in San Francisco," says Victoria Schwarz, who moved here in 2002, "we had a combined income of US$450,000—and that was in 1990! I had a US$150,000 line of credit, and I used it. Sometimes I miss that life, but mostly I don't. I purposely did not transplant my U.S. life down here, as I notice many gringos do. I would say that I live better than most Ticos but far 'lower' than I lived before in the United States. I count my pennies. If I see something I want, I wait three to five weeks, then look again to see if that item would really enhance my life. With this technique, it's amazing how little is necessary. It's been good for me to not just go out and buy whatever I think to buy. It feels good not to consume."

What about the numbers? Again, it's hard to pin these things down, but from my observations of many foreign residents, I would say that a frugal person could live on as little as US$1,300 per month. This would mean not owning a car (vehicles are very expensive here), eating mostly at home, and shopping at farmers markets. The frugal-with-a-few-frills types will need more like US$2,000 a month to live well. These are budgets for single people—if you're a couple, add another 40 percent to the figure, although this may be an overestimate, since often two can live almost as cheaply as one. Rent is shared, food prepared at home isn't that much more expensive for two, and—if you like each other—you can be your own entertainment.

Of course, there are foreign residents who spend four or five times as much per month, and more power to them—they often throw excellent parties. But the point is, if you need to live on less, you most certainly can. Some things that will drive your budget way up are an expensive private school for your kids, luxury cars with high insurance rates, gambling habits or bad investments, child support (laws here are strict), and high drug or alcohol consumption. Know thyself, and you will know thy budget.

(See the *Housing* chapter for more details on housing costs, and the *Health* chapter for details on health insurance costs.)

SHOPPING

Newcomers are often surprised to see the vast U.S.-style supermarkets and upscale malls that have sprung up all over the country, but especially in the Central Valley. The megastore of megastores,

Household Help

Having household help is more common in Costa Rica than in North America, and many expats of even relatively modest means hire a cook, a gardener, or a housekeeper. Nannies, often from Nicaragua, are common in both expat and Tico households, especially those in which both parents work. Wages for household help are low (think US$4-5/hour) but are regulated by the government. As with any employee, employers are required to provide holiday and vacation pay for household help. (For more information, see page 189 in the *Employment* chapter.)

Hipermas, is like a big SuperTarget. You can load your cart with toaster ovens, mattresses, Häagen-Dazs ice cream, and fresh pineapple (from Costa Rica or Hawaii!), get your day's exercise just walking from one end of the store to the other, and pay with your U.S. credit or debit card. Prices are often disconcertingly similar to those in the United States, though careful shopping will yield some bargains. Soon you'll learn that the local ice cream, Dos Pinos, is quite tasty and costs a fraction of what imported brands do. Or you'll figure out that you can get cheap sheets and towels in downtown San José rather than pay Hipermas prices. But if you want everything under one roof, price be damned, these megastores are for you. There are several other grocery store chains with branches all over the country, from the well-stocked Perimercados to the barebones Palí.

In the past several years, Wal-Mart has bought up most of the supermarket chains in Costa Rica, including Palí, Mas X Menos, Maxi Bodegas, and Hipermas.

In terms of nonfood shopping, the pedestrian-only Avenida Central in downtown San José gives you a chance to get a taste of Costa Rica, or you can enter the world of the mall, where it feels like you could be anywhere in the world: In the Central Valley, you've got Multiplaza West in Escazú, Multiplaza East in Curridabat, Terramall on the road from San José to Cartago, Paseo de los Flores in Heredia, and Mall San Pedro in San Pedro, to name a few. There are even five PriceSmart stores (in Alajuela, Heredia, Llorente, Zapote, and Escazú), this country's answer to membership shopping.

Bargaining

Travelers who know the vast public markets of Mexico, Guatemala, and other developing countries may be surprised to see few such places in Costa Rica. Western-style malls are more the norm, and bargaining is a very different matter. Forget offering one-quarter of the asking price and then settling in for 20 minutes of animated haggling, including the old ruse of pretending to walk away so that the merchant will call you back with a better deal.

In Costa Rica you pretty much pay the asking price. There's a little bit of room to move, but be careful and don't insult the merchant or her wares. You might ask if there's a discount for volume or, if you're in a more upscale shop that accepts credit cards, if there's a discount for paying cash. Merchants here pay up to 7 percent to credit card companies for each transaction, so they may be motivated to give you a 5 percent cash discount. For services—tours, hotels, and the like—ask if there's an off-season rate, a midweek rate, or any discounts offered to senior citizens, Costa Rica residents, or ARCR members. It's best to do this with a light touch and not to insist—merchants may prefer to lose the deal than to keep haggling with someone they perceive to be difficult. And if you do negotiate a good price, be sure to get it in writing if it applies to something in the future, like a trip or a car repair, as

Farmers Markets *(Ferias)*

In almost every town or neighborhood there is a weekly farmers market offering up mounds of onions, whole hands of bananas, and row upon row of head lettuce. Quality is often better and prices a lot lower than in supermarkets, and shopping at a farmers market is a lot more satisfying than choosing from among plastic-wrapped cucumbers at the local supermarket. Organic produce is becoming increasingly available, even in the supermarkets. The farmers markets are social occasions, with housewives chatting with neighbors or the vendors they've come to know. Cheese, meats, and fresh juices are often available, as are plants from hardy daisies to delicate orchids. Arrive early in the morning for the best selection, and bring your own bags or a cart.

Prices for fruits and vegetables are much lower at farmers markets.

people here have a tendency to forget what they've promised.

TIPPING AND SALES TAX

Unless tax and service are included in the price of the dishes you order, in restaurants the bill will be 23 percent more than you expect it to be, with 13 percent added for sales tax and 10 percent for service. In many restaurants you'll see two rows of prices, one that excludes taxes and service fees; the other that includes those charges and represents the actual final price.

When you pay a restaurant bill, most often you've really already paid the tip; outstanding service may warrant a little extra, but most Ticos don't leave any additional tip.

The 13 percent sales tax is on all goods and services except fees to doctors, lawyers, dentists, and most other independent professionals. The sales tax on airline tickets is 5 percent. The sales tax on hotel rooms is the usual 13 percent but with an

additional tourist tax of 3 percent, for a total of 16 percent.

Taxi drivers are not usually tipped (unless they are especially helpful or friendly), although you'll want to tip bell boys (about US$1 per bag), hotel maids (US$1-2 per day), and tour guides (depends on service, the length and cost of the tour, and how many people were on the tour, but a good measure is to think what you'd tip someone in the same position in your home country).

An experienced tour guide once gave me a rundown on which tourists tip and which don't. Guides are always happy when they get a group from Canada or the United States, as these travelers are known to be generous tippers. Most European tourists and domestic tourists (Ticos traveling in their own country) don't tip very much, my informant told me. If you're North American, then, your countrymen and women who have come before you have set certain expectations.

The Song of the Street Vendor

On any given day in cities and towns all over Costa Rica, you'll see and hear the evidence of what economists call informal commercial activity but what most people know as street vendors. Compared to shopping in malls full of multinational chains, street vendors make for a quirkier and more intimate experience of buying and selling.

Rickety kiosks offer a little of everything: banana chips, fruit, batteries, dirty magazines, and hair barrettes. A man with an orange squeezer mounted on a shopping cart calls out *jugos!* Vendors spread their stuff on the sidewalk, everything from *rrrrricos mangos!* (delicious mangoes) to Winnie-the-Pooh paraphernalia (here the ever-popular bear is just Winnie-Pooh).

A gravel-voiced man hawks *tarjetas telefonicas* (phone cards), a lottery ticket vendor sing-songs *chance para hoy!* (your chance for today). A guy with a Barry White baritone tries to interest you in cigars, while a slippery-eyed fellow (keeping an eye out for cops, no doubt) offers *lentes para mil pesos* (sunglasses for 1,000 colones).

Roving vendors are sometimes called *polacos,* after the Eastern European Jewish immigrants who arrived in the 1920s and often made their living peddling wares from house to house. Especially on weekends, ambulant vendors go up and down urban and suburban streets: ice cream carts with their bells chiming, vegetable vendors, knife grinders, and the ubiquitous little old man pulling his cart piled high with simple wooden furniture.

Banking

CURRENCY AND EXCHANGE RATES

Costa Rica's currency is called the colón (plural is colones), named for the explorer Christopher Columbus (his name in Spanish is Cristóbal Colón). Often the U.S. "cents" symbol (¢) is used to denote colones, but sometimes "$" is used, which can make it difficult to know if colones or U.S. dollars are meant. But if a car is priced at over one million, or a cup of coffee at 1,000, you know you're in colón country.

The bills you'll most often see are in denominations of 1,000 (red, often called a *rojo*), 2,000 (blue), 5,000 (yellow), and 10,000 (green). The bills vary slightly in size but are close to the dimensions of U.S. notes. Coins vary in size; you'll most often see denominations of 500, 100, and 50. Money is sometimes called *pista* or *plata,* and loose change is *menudo.*

Since 2006 the exchange rate has stayed between 500 and 600 colones per U.S. dollar. In the past several years it has been around 550 colones per US$1.

Counterfeits

Counterfeit bills seem to be more and more common these days, with the most commonly counterfeited denominations the 2,000 and the 20,000-colón bills.

Many merchants have small light tables that allow them to quickly check for fakes. The low-tech method of checking for counterfeits even has its own tagline: *toque, mire, y gire.* People are encouraged to touch *(toque)* the bill to make sure they feel raised elements, to look at *(mire)* the bill and find the faint watermark, which should be a ghostly reproduction of the historical figure featured on the bill, and to turn *(gire)* the bill to make sure the omnipresent map of Costa Rica changes color when viewed from different angles.

Once when I tried to pay for a bag of *pan dulce,* the bakery owner pointed out that the design on my 1,000-colón note was totally off register, and so it was—the counterfeiter had been quite sloppy. I did what a Tico would do—kept the bill and paid a taxi fare with it later that night. Money is just a collective hallucination, after all—a consensus that these scraps of paper mean something. The off-register bill will be someone's change in that taxi, and it will make its way around the country much as any legitimate bill would. Maybe it's a metaphor for the world economy: If you don't look too closely, everything works just fine.

GETTING CASH

The U.S. dollar is much in evidence in Costa Rica. Upon arrival, you needn't hurry to change money (forget changing money on the street—you'll get ripped off) since taxi drivers will accept dollars as will many businesses, especially in tourist areas. Often they won't accept soiled or torn U.S. bills. Note that these service providers and businesses will give your change in colones, but not necessarily give you a great exchange rate.

It'll save you money to operate with the national currency, and the easiest way to get colones is to withdraw them from one of many ATMs, using your U.S. or Canadian bank card. Watch out for fees, both from your own bank and the bank you're withdrawing from in Costa Rica.

ATMs are much in evidence in cities and medium-size tourist towns, and they are usually well stocked. If you're going to be in the outback or in small towns, stock up on cash before you go.

Occasionally I won't be able to get dollars but will be able to get colones (you can only get dollars out of an ATM if you're pulling from a dollar account, whether that account is in Costa Rica or abroad.) Sometimes the "system" is down and the machine spits my card out. Sometimes the system is down for a few days, which means I have to go inside the bank and get an advance on my credit or debit card. This can take time, and the transaction is more subject to human error.

Note that Costa Ricans often write numbers using a decimal point where North Americans would use a comma, and use commas where North Americans

There are often long lines to get into banks.

would use a decimal point. For example, what we know as $3,000.00 would be written $3.000,00 and 1.9 million would be 1,9 million.

HAVING MONEY SENT TO COSTA RICA

You can have money wired to banks here for a fee, but it might take a while for the wire to go through. It's usually quicker (but more expensive) to have money wired through Western Union (www.westernunion.com), which operates within many different businesses, including Coopealianza and Servimas, which are often found within supermarkets. You can also use MoneyGram (www.moneygram.com), which operates in (among other places) HSBC banks, Banco de Costa Rica, and BAC San José.

PayPal (www.paypal.com) also makes it possible to send and receive money to and from a variety of countries.

GETTING YOUR U.S. FEDERAL BENEFITS IN COSTA RICA

These are questions asked frequently of the Federal Benefits Unit (FBU) at the U.S. Embassy (costarica.usembassy.gov/fbusanjose.html) in Rohrmoser, a neighborhood in San José. The FBU offers help by appointment only. To set up an appointment, call them at tel. 506/2519-2228 between 8am and 11:30am Monday-Friday, except for the first and third Wednesday of every month, when the FBU is closed.

- **I was receiving Social Security benefits in the United States. Can I receive them in Costa Rica?**

Yes, if you are the direct beneficiary. If you are the child, surviving spouse, or dependent, please contact the embassy's Federal Benefits Unit.

- **Is there direct deposit with Costa Rica-based banks?**

Yes. Monthly federal benefits payments can be directly deposited into the beneficiary's Costa Rican bank account. This system increases the speed with which you can receive your benefits (almost always by the fifth day of the month) and is more secure than the mailing of paper checks, which are subject to theft and loss. The local banks available for direct deposit are Banco Nacional de Costa Rica and Banco de Costa Rica. Note that it has become more difficult for nonresidents to open bank accounts.

- **Can I use a U.S. mailing address to receive my Social Security checks while living in Costa Rica?**

According to Social Security Administration regulations, you cannot use a U.S. mailing address unless you are physically present in the United States.

- **If I work outside the United States, will this affect my benefits?**

Only after age 65 may you work without your earnings affecting your pension.

- **How soon can I apply for my retirement benefits?**

Three months prior to your 62nd birthday.

- **Do I need to travel to the United States to apply for Social Security benefits?**

No, you may apply at the embassy's Federal Benefits Unit. You can also apply for Social Security benefits online at www.ssa.gov.

A Jungle in Your Wallet

Costa Rica bank notes

Costa Rica's paper money is as riotously colorful as the country itself. Each denomination not only sports its own size and color scheme, every bill is also a lesson in history and a showcase for Costa Rica's flora and fauna. On the front of each note is a historical figure; on the back you get an entire ecosystem.

The back of the 2,000-colón note, for instance, is devoted to the endangered coral reef. Pictured in full color, we have a bull shark, a sea star (aka starfish), two types of coral, sea turtles, and sea plumes.

In the past several years the exchange rate had hovered around 500 colones per US$1, so to make a rough colón-to-dollar exchange, people often just double the colones, then take off all the zeros. For example, with a 2,000-colón note, doubling that amount gets you 4,000. Take off all the zeros and you have 4, which means that 2,000 colones is worth (very approximately) US$4.

The bills come in these denominations (conversions are approximate):

- 1,000 (1 *mil*) = US$1.80
- 2,000 (2 *mil*) = US$3.65
- 5,000 (5 *mil*) = US$9
- 10,000 (10 *mil*) = US$18
- 20,000 (20 *mil*) = US$36
- 50,000 (50 *mil*) = US$90

Family Members

- **I am married and would like my spouse to receive survivor Social Security benefits on my death. Can he or she?**

Your spouse would be eligible at age 62, if she or he had been married to you for more than one year and had not remarried. Please contact the Federal Benefits Unit of the embassy for specific requirements.

- **While in Costa Rica, can I apply for Social Security numbers for my children?**

Yes, but they must be either U.S. citizens or legal residents of the United States.

- **Can my non-U.S. citizen spouse receive a Social Security number?**

Only if she is a legal resident of the United States. He or she may apply for a Tax Identification Number (TIN) at the U.S. Embassy.

- **How does the U.S. government tax Social Security benefits sent to Americans living abroad?**

If you are a U.S. citizen or U.S. resident, up to 85 percent of the Social Security benefits you receive may be subject to the federal income tax—it depends on your income level. If you are not a U.S. citizen or a U.S. resident, federal income taxes will be withheld from your benefits. The tax is 30 percent of 85 percent of your benefit amount.

Medical Care

• **Can I use Medicare in Costa Rica?**

No, there is no Medicare coverage in Costa Rica, not even for emergency services.

• **Who handles claims for foreign medical treatment under the Veterans Administration?**

The Denver Veterans Affairs office handles the claims. It may be reached at U.S. tel. 303/331-7590, U.S. fax 303/331-7803. The embassy cannot process these claims. For more information, visit the Veterans Benefits and Services website (www. va.gov).

• **I am a full-service U.S. veteran. Can I receive coverage over here for my service-connected disabilities?**

Yes, you can be reimbursed for medical treatment, but this is limited to service-connected disabilities only. The Veterans Administration Foreign Medical Program Office in Denver sets the protocol on how to approve claims.

COSTA RICAN BANKS
History

Up until 1949 most of Costa Rica's banks were private and owned by U.S. citizens. Early efforts to nationalize banking didn't go well. In 1914 President González Flores was ousted by wealthy Ticos and U.S. oil interests for his attempt to open a state bank. But decades later, a nationalized system became part and parcel of Costa Rican identity, offering up loans on the basis of social responsibility rather than profit. National banks helped fund infrastructure, health, education, and rural development. These banks were the only ones authorized to offer checking accounts and time deposits, and the Central Bank was in charge of national monetary policy.

Despite the benefits of public banks, there were also major drawbacks. Critics complained of inefficiency, misuse of public funds, and cronyism—it was thought almost impossible to get a loan unless you knew someone high up in the bank hierarchy. National bank employees were (and are) essentially government employees, and it's nearly impossible to fire them, no matter how incompetent they might be.

The industry began to change in the early 1980s, in part because the United States Agency for International Development (USAID) threatened to halt new grants and loans to Costa Rica if the banking system didn't move toward privatization. By 1996, private banks were given the same rights as public ones—the ability to offer checking and savings accounts, for example.

The Present Day

Now there are both public and private banks in Costa Rica, and neither are models of efficiency. The three public banks (Banco Nacional de Costa Rica, Banco de Costa Rica, and Banco Crédito) at least have branches all over the country. If you live out in the sticks, it might be easier to deal with one of these entities. Also, the National Banking System guarantees deposits in government-owned banks. National banks are known to be extremely slow and bureaucratic, with checks often taking weeks to clear and wire transfers taking up to a week to register in your account.

Service at private banks may be a bit less inefficient, with slightly more possibility of getting a loan or a mortgage. Fees are often higher as well. And even in private banks, it seems to be a matter of whom you know. One long-term foreign resident half-jokes, "If you want decent service in any bank, you need to woo the manager, charm the pants off the tellers, and even make friends with the guard who stands by the door."

Tips on Banking in Costa Rica

• Each of the country's approximately two dozen banks has different processes and different requirements for opening an account. And just like banks back home, they offer different kinds of accounts and services with different fees. You can also apply for credit cards.

• You can choose to do business with either a public or a private bank. Public banks are generally thought to be slower and more bureaucratic, but deposits in state-owned (public) banks are guaranteed by the government, while deposits in private banks are not. On the other hand, private banks tend to have a wider array of services and choices than public banks.

• You can choose to keep your money in either colones or U.S. dollars. Having a dollar account protects you against colón devaluations, while having a colón account protects you against dollar devaluation.

• Most banks are open Monday-Friday 9am-4pm. Some branch offices have longer hours; some private banks are open Saturday mornings.

• You may wait a very long time—an hour, say—for even simple transactions. Sometimes you'll see people lined up outside of banks even before they open. Bring a good book.

• Try to avoid banking on the second and last Friday of the month. These are paydays for many Costa Rican workers; lines might snake out the front door and down the block.

CREDIT CARDS

Credit cards are widely accepted, especially by upscale or tourist-oriented businesses. Visa is the most widely accepted card, with MasterCard a close second and venerable American Express a distant third. Conversion is at the official exchange rate, though merchants may tack on a surcharge to offset the 6 or 7 percent they're charged by credit card companies for each transaction. You can use your credit card to buy colones or dollars at a bank (there may be a minimum, often US$50). You can also get cash advances on your credit card via an ATM, provided you have arranged for a PIN.

Income Tax

COSTA RICAN TAXES

If you have a job or a business (including a vacation rental) in Costa Rica, you're on the hook for **Costa Rican** taxes. Employment income is taxed in the form of a monthly withholding ranging from 0 percent to 18 percent, depending on how much you earn. For the self-employed, tax rates are from 10 percent to 25 percent. The fiscal year runs from October 1 to September 30, with tax returns due before December 15.

You do not have to pay Costa Rican taxes on your Social Security income, pension, or investment income.

U.S. TAXES

The U.S. Internal Revenue Service (IRS, www.irs.gov) has long arms, and they're not for hugging. The United States is one of the few developed countries that taxes its citizens and resident aliens while they live overseas. In the words of the IRS, "Your worldwide income is subject to U.S. income tax, regardless of where you reside."

A small number of expats around the world have quietly given up their U.S. citizenship, in part to avoid the tax burden (including inheritance taxes) that the IRS imposes on all Americans, no matter where in the world they live. Still, there are a few minor tax advantages for citizens living outside the United States.

Automatic Filing Extension

The first advantage is that the April 15 deadline is automatically extended to June 15. The IRS says that although you have until June 15 to file your return, you must pay any tax owed by the original deadline of April 15. It doesn't say how you would

know how much to pay if you haven't yet prepared your return. If you don't pay by April 15, you may end up paying interest or penalties. You can request an additional extension to October 15 by filing Form 4868, with a corresponding increase in potential interest.

You can file your income tax return through the U.S. Embassy in San José or online, or you can mail your return to an address in Texas (see the "U.S. Citizens and Resident Aliens Abroad" section of the IRS website for more information).

Foreign Earned Income Exclusion

The second potential advantage for U.S. citizens living outside the United States is the Foreign Earned Income Exclusion. If you pass the IRS's "bona fide residence test," you'll be able to exclude from taxation a portion (or perhaps all) of what you earned while abroad. In 2015, the amount you could exclude before paying U.S. taxes on it was US$100,800; the amount is adjusted for inflation each year.

The exclusion doesn't apply to interest, dividends, capital gains, pensions, annuities, or gambling winnings. You need special forms to apply for this exclusion, and the rules are complicated enough that you'll probably want to hire a tax professional. Even if you qualify for the exclusion, you still need to file a return. Also look into the housing exclusion or deduction; sometimes you can also deduct moving expenses.

For more information, search the IRS site for the comprehensive "Publication 54: Tax Guide for U.S. Citizens and Resident Aliens Abroad."

Lawyers in a Nonlitigious Country

Lawyers (*abogados* in Spanish) permeate many aspects of Costa Rican life. You'll need them for, among many other things, real estate transactions, residency permits, and forming a corporation (Sociedad Anónima, or S.A.). One exasperated local jokes that you can barely get out of bed in the morning without a lawyer filing a *tramite* (the general term for "legal papers") on your behalf.

It is imperative that you find an honest and effective lawyer, if not several. Personal referrals are the best way to go, though even with a recommended lawyer you need to be vigilant – reading over all the documents he or she will file with various agencies (errors abound) and keeping on top of dates and deadlines (because he or she might not). It's also helpful to know the basic prices for various services to make sure you're not being overcharged – ask other expats and other lawyers.

Though the country is rife with lawyers, Costa Rica is not a litigious society, probably because lawsuits can take seven years to come to trial, and monetary awards are limited.

Investing

There are many investment opportunities in Costa Rica—everything from pineapple processing to stocks traded on the National Stock Exchange (the *bolsa*). Costa Rica's *bolsa* (www.bnv.co.cr) was established in 1970 and offers stocks from national companies such as the *La Nación* publishing empire, coffee producer Café Britt, and Durman Esquival, seller of PVC products.

Land development is big business, with megamalls, hotel and condo spreads, and housing developments springing up all over the country. For those who don't want to go the real estate route alone, there are Real Estate Investment Trusts (REITs, or *fundos immobiliários*), companies that buy and rent out real estate and then distribute the profits among their investors.

Everything you read about investing in Costa Rica, along with every hard-luck story you hear from bilked expats, tells you to be very, very careful when parting with your hard-earned money. A lot of people seem to think, sure, lots of people get ripped off in Costa Rica, but *I'm* too

sharp for that. Rest assured that the criminals out to defraud you are even sharper. It's their business to know exactly what will make you want to turn over your cash, and there are not many people trying to stop them, at least in the initial stages of the game. The investment climate here, says financial consultant Alan Weeks in one of his newsletters, is largely unregulated. "For every person who has struck it rich," he warns, "there are dozens of people left behind to tell the sad story of a lifetime's worth of savings . . . down the drain."

Besides the real estate scams, the teak farms that don't exist, and various and sundry swindles, there are also many financial firms offering high-yield investments that seem too good to be true, and indeed they usually are, as the fall in recent years of two of the largest entities demonstrates. Ofinter S.A. (aka "the Brothers") offered returns of 3.5-4 percent interest per month (42-48 percent per year) and got around the regulations by claiming investors were "friends" of the man who headed the firm, Luis Enrique

Villalobos. Loaning money to friends is not regulated here (nor is it in most countries). In late 2002, some of the Brothers' accounts were frozen while they were being investigated for money laundering. Shortly thereafter the company heads skipped town with an estimated US$200 million that had belonged to their many "friends." A similar thing happened with Savings Unlimited (aka "the Cubans") in early 2003.

Many of these firms' investors were foreign residents who didn't ask many questions about how they were able to earn such astronomical interest. When the rocket shook apart in midair, however, many investors blamed the Costa Rican government for their losses, sharply criticizing the loosely regulated financial environment that had allowed them to earn such impossibly high rates in the first place.

An article in *La Nación* diagnosed the problem as "an explosive mix of excessive trust, tempting high profits, and lack of regulation." Speaking of Ofinter and Savings Unlimited, former Central Bank president Eduardo Lizano said, "I do not know of traditional investments with such high returns." A *Tico Times* editorial asked, "With gray areas, who needs corruption? Costa Rica needs urgently to get clear about what's legal and what's not, and to enforce its laws."

The problem wasn't and isn't limited to the Brothers or the Cubans. Almost every week you'll see headlines in the local press like "Another Financial Firm Under Scrutiny" or "Another Fraud Suspect Caught." The unregulated environment attracts a great many scamsters, many of whom are on the run from financial trouble up north or across the sea. Another headline you'll see frequently is some version of "Fraud Suspect Extradited to the U.S." Con men and women come to Costa Rica thinking they'll be able to ply their trade unfettered, and indeed they often do, sometimes for decades. With all the people getting caught, you have to wonder how many more are still doing brisk business. But some are nabbed and whisked away to Miami, Toronto, or Bartlesville, Oklahoma—wherever there's a warrant out for their arrest.

It's all mildly entertaining unless you happen to have invested with one of these snake-oil vendors; then it's not so funny, and it could have devastating consequences if you're relying on that income for living expenses.

I don't want to scare potential investors, but I do want to stress the dangers of trusting one's savings or pension checks to suspect enterprises. Costa Rica is an extraordinary place, but basic common sense still applies here. Do your homework, ask the hard questions, and don't invest in risky ventures unless you can afford to part with that money. You've heard it before, but I'm going to say it again: If you wouldn't do it at home, don't do it here.

For more on financial scams, see "Scams to Watch Out For" in the *Health* chapter, page 175.

COMMUNICATIONS

Internet, phone, mail, and shipping: in my nearly two-decade relationship with Costa Rica, these services have improved by fits and starts, and then, more recently, by leaps and bounds.

It's no accident that so many multinational corporations choose this country for a Latin American branch office—they're drawn by the solid infrastructure.

The high concentration of call centers and sports books (online betting agencies), with their reliance on phone lines and Internet, tells you that the system is working.

As for the public mail system, well, it's not ideal, but many expats use private mail and shipping services, which rival the service you can get at home.

Telephone Service

Landlines are on the wane, but cell phone use has exploded. As of 2015 there were fewer than 100,00 landlines in this country of nearly 5 million people, while (according to the *CIA World Factbook*) there were 7 million cell phones, with the number increasing every day. Almost everyone you see—on the street, waiting for the bus, drinking coffee in a café—seems to be checking their bag to see if that's their phone (or one of their several phones) ringing. Costa Rica has one of the highest numbers of phone lines per capita in Central America, and even in all of Latin America.

LANDLINES: YES, THEY STILL EXIST

Why would anyone even want a landline these days? One, cell phone reception doesn't extend to every corner of the country. And two, in case of an emergency, if cell phone towers are down or overburdened, landlines can be useful. You can also get Internet service through your landline. You're supposed to be a legal resident to apply for a new landline. The best case scenario is that you inherit one when you rent or buy a place to live. Otherwise, you could wait months for one to be installed. If you're out in the sticks, you might have to wait until they get around to putting up poles and stringing wires. Locals know tricks to speed up the process—like requesting a commercial line if a residential one seems slow in coming.

The Instituto Nacional de Electricidad (ICE, pronounced EE-say) is the government agency that provides not only electricity but also residential and commercial phone lines. ICE does things at its own pace, but implementation of CAFTA (the Central American Free Trade Agreement) means that parts of the telecommunications sector (broadband Internet service, cell phone service, and private data networks) are gradually opening to private competition, which is mostly good news for consumers.

PHONE TIPS FOR TRAVELERS AND POTENTIAL EXPATS
Will your U.S., Canadian, or European cell phone work in Costa Rica?

Probably. Most GSM phones work here; often cell phone carriers list which phones will work in given locations. Some phones (like my Samsung Galaxy S4) can operate as both a CDMA phone (the mode I use for my U.S. Sprint account) and a GSM phone (the mode I switch the phone to when I go to Costa Rica).

Will your calls and texts cost you an arm and a leg?

Not if you do some advance research, making sure you have the best international plan your present carrier offers. Most will cost you, but not as much as roaming charges would set you back if you simply tried to use your phone without signing up for your carrier's international plan.

In the United States, this is one of the few areas where Sprint shines. If you sign up for their Open World program (at no charge), you get free calls and texts within Costa Rica and from Costa Rica to the United States. The plan also comes with 1 GB of data (you can pay for more). With the Open World plan, if you're in Costa Rica with your U.S. phone and want to dial a Costa Rican number, you dial 506 (the country code), then the eight-digit

Costa Rican number. Although you are dialing from a U.S. number to a Costa Rica number, you don't need to bother with the international access code from the US (011) if you are physically in Costa Rica.

If you're dialing from your U.S. phone in Costa Rica to a number in the United States, you don't need the international access code (001) from Costa Rica; just dial 1, the U.S. area code, and the U.S. phone number.

If someone is calling you in Costa Rica from the United States, they just dial 1, your U.S. area code, and your number; no international access code needed.

AT&T, Verizon, and T-Mobile all have different options for international travelers, none of them free. Scour their websites and then call to ask detailed questions about their plans. Be sure to ask about roaming charges. It's a hassle, but it's better to be safe than charged hundreds or even thousands of dollars you weren't planning on.

CELL PHONE RECEPTION IN COSTA RICA

I was frankly amazed on a recent trip that I had reception almost everywhere I went, from Caribbean coast beach towns to misty cloud forests.

Note that remote eco-lodges, windy mountaintops, and far-flung small towns may have spotty reception or no reception at all.

WHISTLE WHILE YOU WI-FI

If you know that most of the places you'll be staying at in Costa Rica have free wireless Internet (there are a lot of them from fast-food joints to airports), you could opt to forget the whole phone service conundrum and just stick with VOIP services like Skype or FaceTime. Wi-Fi also lets you use Twitter, Facebook, Instagram, and What'sApp.

LEAVE YOUR PHONE AT HOME, BUY ONE HERE

Another good option is to leave your phone at home, then buy an inexpensive one in Costa Rica at a Kolbi counter in the San José airport or in countless stores all over the country. At the San José airport, there are two Kolbi counters, one at the baggage claim area (for people arriving in Costa Rica), and one at Gate 9 for passengers leaving the country. The four

Cell phone stores are common in cities and towns.

cell phone carriers in Costa Rica are Kolbi (state-owned), Movistar, Claro, and TuYo (all private companies). You can buy a low-end phone from any of these carriers for around US$25, then purchase a prepaid SIM card for texting, calling, and Internet use. Some say a 5,000-colon (US$9) prepaid SIM is sufficient for your average vacation; you can also add to the amount (on your phone itself or in a store). Note that international calls from Costa Rica eat up your card balance quicker than you can say "I'm fine, Mom."

FOR RESIDENTS AND POTENTIAL RESIDENTS

People who will be here longer than your average vacation will want to look into cell phone plans—which work pretty much the same way they work back home. Some people who settle here are content to keep going the prepaid SIM route. It's easy and there's no commitment.

BRING AN UNLOCKED PHONE WITH YOU, BUY A PREPAID SIM CARD

You could also bring an unlocked phone from home and then buy a SIM card in Costa Rica (also available at the Kolbi airport kiosk or in stores around the country), which gives you your Costa Rica phone number.

Once you buy your prepaid SIM from a store, kiosk, or street vendor, you pop it into your phone (put the old SIM card in a safe place, and put it back in your phone once you get back home), then follow the activation instructions. Usually activation involves dialing a number and punching in a few codes.

Don't throw out the plastic card or sleeve your SIM card comes in or on. It has the unlock codes you'll need when you activate the card.

If all that sounds like too much, the clerks at the carrier stores or kiosks are usually happy to help.

If you're about ready to run out of money on your prepaid SIM, you can usually add to it from your phone (by credit card). You can also have the SIM card recharged at those same stores or kiosks that sell the SIM cards. Look for signs that say *Recargas.*

You could also just buy a new prepaid SIM, toss the old one, and go through the activation steps again.

MAKE A FELLOW TRAVELER'S DAY

Prepaid SIMS lock up after a month of disuse, and after three months, they are automatically deactivated and the number reassigned to another person. So if you have money left on a prepaid SIM and you're heading back home, give the card to a fellow traveler or a Tico who uses prepaid SIM cards. Don't forget to give them the plastic sleeve that the card came in—they'll need that to activate the SIM card on their phone.

Now that everyone has a cell phone, you'd think that pay phones would be a thing of the past. But there are still plenty of these throwbacks around. If you're not getting reception on your cell phone, you'll be glad.

The easiest and cheapest way to use a pay phone is to have thought ahead and bought a calling card. They are available in many amounts; remember that using them to call outside of Costa Rica will eat up your balance quickly. Calling within Costa Rica is inexpensive. You can get the cards in many stores, even little street-side kiosks, and it's as simple as scratching off the code, then following the directions, which are usually in both English and Spanish.

Some pay phones are still coin operated but most require phone cards. Though some pay phones have a place

pay phones in downtown San José

for you to swipe phone cards, usually this won't work, and you'll need to punch the numbers on the back of the card into the keypad and make your call that way.

Dial 116 for an English-speaking operator and to make a collect call (called *por cobrar* in Spanish).

In tiny villages, there may be only one pay phone, usually at the *pulpería* (general store). Often you can't access the phone unless the store is open.

PAYING YOUR BILL

If you have a service plan for a landline or a cell phone, you'll get a monthly bill, just like back home. Most people pay their telephone bills online, but if you still receive a paper bill, you can usually take care of it at the bill-paying window of your local supermarket (you can also pay water and electric bills there). If you live in a more remote location, you'll need to find the place designated as a payment point. It won't always be an ICE office; it could very well be the local *pulpería* (corner store).

To pay your bill, however, you first need to receive it. Ask locals how and when telephone bills are delivered in your area; in some cases you may need to go pick up your bill at a central delivery point. If you've inherited the line, it will be in someone else's name (it's hard to transfer the account to a different name, so many people just pay on an account that isn't in their name), which may complicate things further.

In ICE's eyes, not receiving a bill is no excuse for not paying it, and nonpayment of bills will, of course, lead to your phone line being shut off. The burden is on you to make sure you receive your bills and pay them on time. When in doubt, call or visit the nearest ICE office and check on your account.

BRINGING YOUR LANDLINE PHONE TO COSTA RICA

The landline system here, down to the jacks, is the same as it is in the United States, so if you want to bring your favorite phone down, just pack it in your suitcase.

You'll find Wi-Fi even in some far-flung jungle cafes.

Email and the Internet

INTERNET ACCESS

Costa Rica has fully embraced the digital age. As of 2015, there were 2.9 million Internet users in Costa Rica, accounting for almost 60 percent of the population. In 2012, the figure was 1.5 million users, which means Internet usage almost doubled in just a few years. For comparison, note that in 2015 in neighboring Nicaragua, just 20 percent of that country's population were Internet users.

Most government agencies have extensive websites, which are an excellent (if dizzying) introduction to how the country works. It's easy to get English translations of the sites through Google Translate. Costa Rica's Internet country code is cr.

Used to be you had to go through the state-run RACSA (Radiográfica Costarricense, part of ICE) to get Internet. These days, there are many more options. Is service better? Sort of. If you don't compare it to the speed and reliability you had back home, you'll do fine. Depending, of course, on where you live, if there are outages that day, and whether or not the tech support guy who says he speaks English actually does.

Different Internet providers have popped up in different parts of the country—ask your neighbors for the best local providers. Smaller providers aside, the main national players are Cabletica (cabletica.com), RACSA (racsa.co.cr), Kolbi (kolbi.cr), Tigo (tigostar.cr), and Movistar (movister.cr). Cabletica gets the best reviews among people I've spoken with, though they are not trouble-free. Plans run anywhere from $15 a month for basic and slow service, to over $100 for fast service. Really fast Internet is only available in certain parts of the country, like the Central Valley.

INTERNET CAFÉS & WI-FI

There are scores of Internet cafés in the greater San José area, and you'll also encounter them in tourist towns like Tamarindo, Montezuma, and Puerto Viejo. The access points in San José tend to be cheaper because there's so much competition—sometimes prices are as low as US$1 per hour. In remote areas prices can be higher, since often the café is the only game in town. Many hotels, even low-end backpacker hostels, now offer free Internet access (on their computers), and Spanish-language schools often provide their students free access.

As for free Wi-Fi, Costa Rica is a bit behind Europe and North America, but you can find hotspots in many hotels, schools, and some restaurants. There is free Wi-Fi at the airports in San José and Liberia. Remember, if you're using free Wi-Fi, nothing you send or receive is private or secure.

Mail

EL CORREO

The national mail service can at times surprise you with its efficiency. Say you're swinging in a hammock outside your rather remote home near the beach when a man on a dirt bike roars up your gravel drive. Don't be alarmed—it's just the mail carrier, his pouch slung across his shoulder and his fat-tired motorcycle perfectly suited to his potholed route. It's like a modern-day Pony Express, and when he hands you an envelope with a New York postmark of just five days back, it feels like magic.

It's true that mail service has improved in recent years. Some expats say they have little trouble, even when they order (small) things from Amazon or eBay. A woman who ships hand-painted floor cloths to customers all over the world says she relies on the certified mail option at the national mail service and has never been let down. Others still tell tales of postal woe that would make you run to private mail services.

For my part, I think that as long as you marvel when the postal system works and don't have to rely on it, you'll be fine. Most letters arrive in a timely fashion (5-7 days from the United States; 10-15 days from Europe), but some take a lot longer, and parcels more than two pounds in weight or larger than a magazine-size envelope are often held at customs until you come and pay the outrageous duties (often 100 percent of perceived value). Both receiving and sending packages can be complicated and expensive, and safety is an

the main post office in San José

issue. Theft is not uncommon—don't send valuables through the mail.

Sometimes the lack of addresses and house numbers in this country seems to stymie even experienced mail carriers. Mail sent to my San José address (which is a long recitation of turn this way and that, and look for the pink house) from across town never arrived, though bills always made their way into my *buzón* (mailbox). Many people like to pay the small fee for a post office box at their local post office. Depending on where you live, there can be a long wait to get a PO Box.

PRIVATE MAIL SERVICES

Many foreign residents swear by private mail services. You get a post office box in Miami, the U.S. city closest to Costa Rica, and from there the company couriers your letters and packages to you in Costa Rica. Plans generally have a monthly fee (starting at around US$15) that covers, say, 3 kilograms (6.5 pounds) of mail a month. Excess weight is charged at various rates.

Companies to consider for mail service include Aeropost (www.aeropost.com) and Jetbox (www.jetbox.com).

Shipping Options

There are many ways to ship packages within Costa Rica and from Costa Rica to the United States, Canada, or Europe. It's a competitive market, with rates and services changing rapidly to meet customer needs; be sure to confirm rates and time frames with a call or a website visit.

(For more on shipping your household goods to Costa Rica, see page 120 in the *Making the Move* chapter.)

NATIONAL POSTAL SERVICE

The cheapest way to send packages is via the *correos,* the national post office, though it only guarantees arrival time on parcels sent within Costa Rica. Go to the nearest *correos* branch, or visit the website www.correos.go.cr, which will have the latest rates and services available. The post office provides no packing materials.

When I sent three heavy book-filled boxes (approximately 15 by 12 by 10 inches) from Costa Rica to California, it cost me about US$65—a bargain compared to what I would have paid with a private shipping company. The boxes arrived in about three and a half weeks.

It's not advisable to send anything of great value or that you can't afford to lose through the *correos.* I sent my books because, well, who wants books these days?

PRIVATE SHIPPING SERVICES

Many private shipping services are available in Costa Rica, including familiar international companies like FedEx. New services come on the scene often, and certain services may be available only in certain areas—be sure to ask locals which company they use and how they like it. No private service is perfect, but most provide an easier and more secure shipping experience than the national post office. Many companies will pick up packages from your home. Of course, you'll pay for all these perks.

There are also a host of unofficial shipping options, especially when you need something sent within Costa Rica—deals with truck drivers to bring your new furniture along with their weekly delivery of vegetables, for example, or sending a package with a bus driver whose route takes him through the little town where your friend lives.

DHL

DHL has offices in Liberia (Guanacaste), Limón, Alajuela, Ciudad Quesada, Puntarenas, and in the San José neighborhoods of Cariari, Rohrmoser, and Paseo Colón. Its Costa Rican headquarters are in Heredia. It can get your package to other points in Central America or to Miami overnight, to the rest of the United States in one or two days, and to Canada and Europe in three days. Boxes are available at DHL offices. Rates change frequently; for more information go to www.dhl.co.cr.

FedEx

FedEx has many different ways to send packages within, from, and to Costa Rica. Its website has a lot of information on shipping internationally and on customs procedures, as well as a list of the many shipping points within Costa Rica. Heredia has a FedEx office, and in San José there's an office on Paseo Colón (tel. 800/239-0576, www.fedex.com/cr_english), 100 meters (110 yards) east of the León Cortéz statue and right next to the Iberia Airlines office.

UPS

UPS's main office in the Pavas area of San José (tel. 506/2290-2828, www.ups.com) has a good selection of boxes, tubes, and other packing materials. One new service is the TicoPak, which offers shipping directly from souvenir shops in Costa Rica to homes in the United States, with special CoffeePaks, HammockPaks, and MachetePaks to accommodate the most frequently bought keepsakes.

Media

Freedom of the press has long been an essential feature of Costa Rican culture. It began with the founding of local papers in the early 19th century and was formally declared a fundamental right in 1948. More recently, in 2016, Costa Rica ranked high in a study of press freedom conducted by media watchdog group Reporters Without Borders (RWB). Of 180 countries around the world, Costa Rica ranked 19th in press freedom! That impressive figure is up from 19th place in 2012 and 30th in 2007. "Never has freedom of information been so closely associated with democracy," RWB has noted.

The media landscape is changing rapidly here, and as in much of the rest of the world, print media is on the wane while online media is exploding. The venerable *Tico Times* shut down its print edition in 2012, ending that weekly's 56-year run as the English-language paper of record for Costa Rica. The "paper" still has an online presence, but many expats miss the weekly ritual of buying the paper and reading it cover to cover (see the sidebar on page 222 for more on this newspaper and its history.)

SPANISH-LANGUAGE NEWSPAPERS

Costa Rica has at least eight major Spanish-language newspapers, and one of them, *La Gaceta* (www.gaceta.go.cr/gaceta), belongs to the state. New laws are made public in *La Gaceta* and go into effect six months after the publication date. *La Nación* (www.nacion.com) is the largest and most widely read daily paper. *El Financiero* (www.elfinancierocr.com),

newsstand in Puerto Limón

owned by the *La Nación* publishing empire, is a business weekly. *La Nación* also owns *Al Día* (www.aldia.cr), known for its sports section.

As for the non-*Nación* papers, there's the daily *La República* (www.larepublica.net), *La Prensa Libre* (www.prensalibre.cr), and *Diario La Extra* (www.diarioextra.com), with photos of half-naked women and bloody bodies to lure readers. Along those same lines is *La Teja* (www.lateja.co.cr). *Teja* is the Spanish word for a terracotta roof tile and was slang for the old green-and-orange 100-colón bill. *La Teja* got its name because it used to cost just 100 colones.

A great way to get in the spirit of Costa Rica (even if you're in the United States) and to practice your Spanish is to check out the local papers' websites. Not only will you know which government ministers have resigned and which bridges have washed out, you'll also keep up to date on daily temperatures and fluctuations in the exchange rate. Many of these sites also have background information on Costa Rica and links to other excellent sources of information.

ENGLISH-LANGUAGE NEWSPAPERS AND MAGAZINES

The bad news is that the main English-language newspaper, the *Tico Times*, no longer puts out a print edition and has far fewer reporters to create a viable online version. The good news is that there are more and more online publications in English that might be of interest to the English-speaking expat, like AmCostaRica.com, InsideCostaRica.com or The Costa Rica Star (they snagged a great url, www.news.co.cr). A quick Web search will yield dozens more, many of which come and go.

All over Costa Rica you'll find regional publications, such the *Tamarindo News* (www.tamarindonews.com); the *Voice of Guanacaste* (www.vozdeguanacaste.com/en) with special sections for Nicoya, Samara, and Nosara; or *Quepolandia* (www.quepolandia.com), covering the Quepos-Manuel Antonio region. There

The Life and Times of the *Tico Times*

It began in 1956 when a group of high school seniors wanted to learn journalism. It ended in 2012, an object lesson in how the Internet can turn print media on its ear. In between, the award-winning newsweekly *Tico Times* was a clear and ringing voice in a region of muffled press freedoms. It was a mainstay for expats in Costa Rica, Ticos learning English, and readers abroad who wanted locally based English-language reporting on Central America. Publisher Dery Dyer noted recently that the paper was "a sort of binding force in the English-speaking community in Costa Rica . . . a focal point that held the community together."

A NEWSPAPER IS BORN

The paper began when a group of Lincoln College students asked Elisabeth "Betty" Dyer, who'd been a journalist in the United States, to teach them the trade.

"The best way to learn about journalism is to put out a paper," Dyer told the students at what has become one of the most prestigious bilingual high schools in Costa Rica.

And so the *Tico Times* was born. The first edition, printed on letterpress, came out on May 18, 1956. It was eight pages long; the two cover stories were "Costa Rican Fruit and Coffee Threatened: Fruit Fly Invades Plantations Here" and "Oil May Be Exported from Here." Early advertisers included the Gran Hotel Costa Rica, La Gran Via supermarket, and TACA Airlines, who touted the novelty of flying to the United States in "just one day."

From the start, the paper had a varied readership: English-speaking expats, Ticos who read or were learning English and wanted a different perspective on their own country, and readers abroad – who often had the dream of moving to Costa Rica.

The *Tico Times* made a name for itself with investigative reporting on topics ranging from secret runways in Costa Rica used by the Contras to illegal shark finning and poaching in national parks. Guido Fernández, publisher of leading Spanish-language daily *La Nación*, credited the *Tico Times* with introducing the country to investigative reporting. One *Tico Times* reporter, Linda Frazier, lost her life in the 1980s in pursuit of the story of the rising Sandinista revolution in neighboring Nicaragua. She and several others were killed when a bomb went off during a meeting with Edén Pastora, the Sandinista's "Commandante Cero."

In 2006, after 50 years of publishing, the paper was at its height, with a circulation of 15,000, a staff of 60, a pull-out section on Nicaragua (the *Nica Times*), an abundance of advertisers, and a paper of 48-56 pages that came out every Friday.

are also scores of Facebook groups dedicated to areas and aspects of Costa Rica, both in English and Spanish.

TELEVISION

While more than a dozen broadcast stations here have programming mostly in Spanish, many cable channels are in English (sometimes with Spanish subtitles, sometimes without). Cable services are extremely popular, and even lower-middle-class households pay for the privilege of choosing from among dozens of channels, including ones in French, German, Italian, and Japanese. But English rules, and even the Spanish-language stations reveal the influence of English and of U.S. culture. During a long series of commercials (as in Europe, commercial breaks here are longer but less frequent), you may hear "Ya regresamos a *Dexter*." ("We will return to *Dexter*.") Even if there's not an English syllable within shouting distance, the U.S. influence is often obvious, as in a local KFC commercial that has a cartoon colonel speaking Spanish with a horrendous gringo accent.

THE END OF THE PRINT EDITION

But by 2012 the paper's circulation had dropped by more than half, its staff was down to 16 overworked people, and advertising revenue had declined precipitously. Editor David Boddinger said the laid-off staffers were working on a volunteer basis to keep the paper's website going.

"The reasons for the print edition's demise are many," wrote publisher Dery Dyer (Betty's daughter) in the paper's last print edition on September 28, 2012. The print edition's eventual demise became apparent following a crisis in advertising that began in 2008, coupled with a drop in the value of the colón against the U.S. dollar. She mentions the Internet revolution, "the global recession that clobbered our principal advertisers" such as real estate companies, as well as "our lack of long-term vision and a series of fatal decisions." The proliferation of websites focusing on Costa Rica meant that the print edition of the *Tico Times* was no longer the community focal point it once was.

So in September 2012, Dyer told the staff that the print edition was no longer sustainable. "To keep alive and improve upon a brand that has existed in Costa Rica for more than a half century, the print product needed to go," the paper reported on its own demise. "The digital world moved too fast for a family-run newspaper with a shrinking staff." A few weeks after the shut-down, a For Sale sign hung on the facade of the old *Tico Times* building.

I'll miss the ritual of buying the paper every Friday at 7th Street Books in downtown San José, then splurging for an overpriced cappuccino at the café inside the rococo National Theater. I'd spread the paper out on the marble table, paging through national and regional news, scanning Ed Bernhardt's "Home Gardening" column, and checking the "Community Connection" page for word on surf contests, restaurant openings, and expat bingo games in small towns all over the country. The events calendar gave me ideas on what to do that week – maybe a production of the Little Theater Company, an art exhibit of sculpture made of beach trash, or an outing with the Birding Club. The paper's ads made me chuckle, as they were such an accurate portrayal of the expat community's needs: Spanish-language schools, real estate agents, tax lawyers, therapists, and cosmetic surgeons. After another week of struggling in a foreign (if beloved) country, reading the paper felt like coming home. Long live the online edition.

Some Ticos worry that so much foreign influence is eroding the national character and filing away the rough edges of local lingo. Still, it's unlikely that this country will do what France has done, trying to protect its language by mandating that a certain percentage of cultural offerings, like films, must be homegrown.

Ticos watch a lot of TV, and they don't seem bothered by the flood of foreign programming. Just as the radio is left playing all day as background noise and electronic companionship, so too is the TV on almost everywhere you go. In restaurants, bars, doctors' waiting rooms, and corner stores you'll see CNN en Español, *Mr. Ed* reruns dubbed in Spanish, old *Munsters* episodes, soap operas from Mexico and Venezuela, and the ubiquitous soccer games, punctuated by the announcer shouting an impossibly drawn-out "go-o-oal!"

Network TV

Teletica (channel 7) is the local favorite. Founded by the Picado family, the station went on the air in 1960 and has been offering news, sitcoms, variety shows, movies, and reality programming ever since. State-owned Channel 13 has cultural programming, with news at 9pm. Repretel launched in 1993 and now runs channels 4 (kid's shows and movies on weekends), 6 (similar to Teletica's channel 7), and 11 ("on the air from midnight to noon with live footage of events occurring at night.").

Cable and Satellite TV

Craving your CNN, BBC, or ESPN? Many expats go with satellite service Sky TV (tel. 506/4055-4646 or 2239-9759, www.skycostarica.com). Also check out cable providers (who also have Internet and phone service) TigoStar (www.tigostar.cr) and Cable Tica (tel. 506/4700-7777, www.cabletica.com). Many plans run about US$40-70 per month. Basic packages offer CNN, ABC, NBC, and CBS. HD channels and sports channels usually cost extra.

There's also the possibility of getting a big dish and pulling in content from the United States.

RADIO

Radio is king in Costa Rica, and you hear it everywhere you go—in homes, workplaces, buses, and taxis. Radios outnumber televisions by two to one, and there are over 100 radio stations in this tiny country, broadcasting talk shows, sports, humor, news, and

popular music from Latin America and the United States. Golden oldies in English are omnipresent, and many expats listen to Radio Dos (99.5 FM), especially the morning show with Margie Flaum-Scott from Philadelphia.

Ticos seem to have a high tolerance for noise, and you may be surprised when a friend keeps the radio blaring while you're trying to have a conversation. Get into a taxi and you may have to shout above an earsplitting soccer match to tell the driver where you're going. Public buses sometimes play dance music so loudly it makes your fillings throb. Maids, housewives, and other homebound folks may keep the radio on all day for company.

Radio is a traditional link between the capital and the provinces, and a community service in many small towns. On local stations you'll hear neighborhood news and even pleas for Juan to call María at 5pm from the local pay phone.

Widespread ownership of radio receivers also makes the medium a natural for distance learning. In 1973 the newly founded Costa Rican Institute of Radio Education created *The Teacher in Your House,* a program that broadcasts primary and secondary school lessons from 12 noncommercial stations around the country. Many farmers living in isolated rural areas have taken advantage of the program, enrolling in courses that led to certificates of completion.

TRAVEL AND TRANSPORTATION

Nestled in the elbow of the isthmus connecting North and South America, Costa Rica is about as centrally located as the western hemisphere allows. Getting here is easy, and getting around is simple if not always smooth. The fabled potholed roads may slow things down a bit, but the country has cheap and efficient buses that go just about everywhere. Driving yourself around, whether as a visitor or resident, is an acquired taste, but a real feeling of accomplishment comes with negotiating Costa Rica's challenging but beautiful byways. Small planes are another viable option for getting around.

More than two million people visit Costa Rica each year, and the vast majority fly, landing at the two international airports—the largest in San José, the other in Liberia. You can also arrive by sea, either on a cruise ship or on your own boat, or come in overland. The car or bus trip from the United States takes you through five countries, all with their own laws, visa requirements, and border-crossing protocol. It's a journey not to be undertaken lightly, but you'll remember it for the rest of your life.

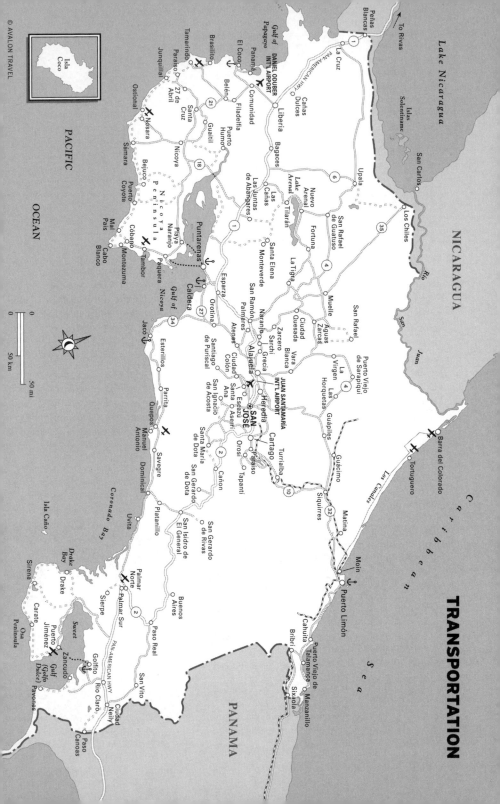

Getting to Costa Rica

AIR

Back in the 1950s, TACA, Central America's regional airline, boasted in an ad that their flights allowed you to reach North America "in only one day." These days, Costa Rica is less than three hours by air from Miami, about five hours from New York City, seven hours from Los Angeles, and eight and a half hours from Toronto. Dozens of international flights arrive daily at Juan Santamaría International Airport, half an hour northwest of San José, and in Liberia, in Guanacaste Province. Every year carriers add more flights, and more carriers get in the game. Coming from North America, you can choose from Aeroméxico, Air Canada, American, Avianca, Delta, Frontier, Spirit, and United, not to mention charter flights that come and go as demand dictates. In May 2013, TACA eliminated many of its nonstop flights to Costa Rica; now its planes fly under the banner of Avianca. Charter flights seldom show up when you do Internet searches for the best airfare deals—it's best to make direct contact with package tour companies for these fares.

Prices vary widely, but from U.S. hub cities fares run about US$450-900. Fares are the most expensive in December and January, especially during the Christmas holidays. The cheapest fares I've found were in September and October, two of the rainiest months in Costa Rica (except on the Caribbean coast).

Direct flights to San José are available from many cities, including Atlanta, Charlotte, Chicago, Dallas-Fort Worth, Fort Lauderdale, Houston, Miami, Newark, New York, Los Angeles, Phoenix, Toronto, and Washington DC. Most other cities require a brief stop and

sometimes a plane change, although every year it gets easier to get to San José or Liberia quickly and painlessly.

Airports

Costa Rica's main airport, **Juan Santamaría International Airport** (arrival and departure information tel. 506/2437-2400, http://fly2sanjose.com/en), is in Alajuela, 16 kilometers (10 miles) northwest of downtown San José. The airport occupies an attractive glass-and-steel terminal with fast-food options, wireless Internet access, TVs, gift shops, cell phone kiosks, and a money exchange counter.

After your plane arrives, you'll go through immigration and customs, usually a fairly painless procedure. A taxi ride from the airport to downtown San José costs US$20-25. If you've arranged a rental car, many companies will either pick you up at the airport or bring your car to the airport so you can take off from there.

Getting to the airport from the San José area is a matter of hailing or calling a cab, or arranging for a shuttle (see page 233 in the *Getting Around* section). Leaving by air, travelers may be liable for a US$29 exit tax (payable in colones, U.S. dollars, or a combination of the two). I say *may,* because starting in 2014, the exit fee was supposed to be included in airline tickets. But since some airlines have been very slow in adopting this practice, the only way to know whether you've been charged for the exit tax is to look at the price breakdown of your plane ticket. Check it out so you won't have to pay twice. If you know you do have to pay the exit tax, factor that in to your airport timing. The line to pay that tax is separate from all the other lines, and it can be long.

The line to pay your exit tax at Juan Santamaría International Airport; check first to see if the exit tax was included in your airfare, as some travelers unwittingly pay the tax twice.

Baggage limits change occasionally and can be different depending on the airline you fly—check with your airline. Airline policies on surfboards also vary; call ahead.

You'll save a lot of time at the airport if you check in online up to a day in advance of your flight and print out your boarding pass.

Tobías Bolaños Airport—six kilometers (four miles) southwest of central San José in the suburb of Pavas—handles local flights to places within Costa Rica and to neighboring Nicaragua and Panama.

Flights to **Daniel Oduber International Airport** (tel. 506/2668-1010, www.liberiacostaricaairport.net) in Liberia deposit you in the northern province of Guanacaste, about 40 minutes from Playas del Coco and a little over an hour from Tamarindo. For those heading for the northern Pacific coast, flying into Liberia eliminates a car or bus ride from San José, which can take four or five hours.

BOAT

An increasing number of cruise ships are making Costa Rica a port of call, if only for a few days or even hours. Passengers may disembark for some shopping and sightseeing, a hike, or a river-rafting jaunt. Hundreds of thousands of cruise ship passengers dock in Costa Rica every year. More than half disembark in the Caribbean port city of Limón, the rest in the Pacific coast ports of Puntarenas, Caldera, and Golfito. Many of these journeys are part of multicountry tours that often include the Panama Canal. The cruise ship (*crucero* in Spanish) season is October to June on the Caribbean and September to May on the Pacific coast.

Smaller boats are more flexible about where they can dock, stopping at beach towns such as Guanacaste's Playas del Coco or the Los Sueños marina in Herradura, near Jacó. There are also marinas in Quepos and Golfito, among other port cities.

Boats like these come from San Carlos, Nicaragua, up the Río Frío River to the Costa Rican town of Los Chiles.

Ports of Entry

If you're coming on your own boat, there are several official ports of entry with immigration and customs stations. On the northern Pacific coast you have Playas del Coco; the central Pacific has Puntarenas and nearby Caldera; farther south there's Playa Herradura (north of Jacó), where you can put in at the private Los Sueños Marina; farther south still there's the expanding port at Quepos; and the southern Pacific has facilities at the old banana port city of Golfito. Boaters arriving on the Caribbean coast go through immigration and customs at Puerto Limón and dock at nearby Moín.

There are inland routes by river as well. The most established is probably the border crossing at Los Chiles in northern Costa Rica. If you're coming from San Carlos, a Nicaraguan town at the confluence of the Río Frío, the Río San Juan, and enormous Lake Nicaragua, you'd take a boat (there are both public and private options) down the Río Frío to Los Chiles. There's a checkpoint midway down the river, where soldiers with big guns paw through your luggage, but the immigration office itself is in the small Costa Rican town of Los Chiles. This is one of the more hassle-free border crossings I've experienced, and I saw more wildlife on that trip than I did on a "wildlife tour" farther south on the same river.

Commercial Ports

Costa Rica's main commercial ports are Caldera on the central Pacific coast, Golfito on the southern Pacific, and Limón and Moín on the Caribbean coast. The ships that come and go from Caldera traditionally carry agricultural products. Those in Golfito are stacked with the electronics and appliances sold at the Deposito Libre (duty-free store) in that ex-banana town; Limón is now the banana port, among other things, and Moín is associated with the oil that runs in a pipeline from the Caribbean coast to the Central Valley. Puntarenas used to be a big commercial port but now receives only cruise ships.

LAND
Arriving by Car

The most direct route from the United States to Costa Rica is from the Brownsville, Texas, border crossing and runs about 2,250 miles through five countries. These won't be highway miles—you'll be on winding mountain roads and potholed desert tracks, occasionally making your way through sleepy one-horse towns or congested cities.

When I was a kid our family drove from California to Guatemala in our blue Ford station wagon. A hotel was a splurge, and I can still remember the smell of our old canvas Army tent, mildewing in the tropical humidity. It was an amazing trip, full of sights and sounds I'll never forget. I plan to do a longer version of that same trip soon, with me at the wheel this time, seeing just how much trouble I can get into and (hopefully) out of.

Travelers who have made the trip more recently have mixed reports. Some feel that all those border crossings, bad roads, and national police forces (which love to stop foreigners) added up to a very big headache. Others say it was the trip of their lives.

Let's say you do it, taking the popular Pacific coast route through Mexico, Guatemala, El Salvador, Honduras, and Nicaragua. Driving from Nicaragua into Costa Rica, you'll cross the border at Peñas Blancas on the Pan-American Highway. Peñas Blancas is not a town; it's simply the border post, open daily 6am-8pm.

Your first step in crossing the border by car is to pay a few dollars to have your car fumigated: An official will spray a white liquid on the underside of your vehicle. This happens before you get to the border proper.

The Costa Rican and Nicaraguan immigration offices are 4 kilometers (2.5 miles) apart. Once inside Costa Rica, you'll park, go to one window for an entry stamp (a few dollars), then take your passport and car title to the Aduana window.

You'll also need to buy insurance for a minimum of one month; Costa Rica is one of the few Central American countries where insurance is mandatory. Officials will provide three forms: Certificado de Entrega de Vehiculos, No Comerciales Importación Temporal; Instituto Nacional de Seguros; and Recibo de Dinero, and then you're on your way. There are several checkpoints just beyond the border area; show all your papers, and they'll let you pass.

Before you get to the border, make sure you have your passport and all vehicle documentation, and be prepared to stand in one line after another. There are lots of kids who will run up to you and offer to speed you through the process. Veteran border crossers advise caution, but I've had good luck picking a kid who looks street-smart but not yet like a full-fledged criminal. These helpers will show you which line to stand in first, and then hurry you to the next window, rattling off advice in Spanish that you may or may not understand. The kids expect a tip of at least a few dollars for their efforts.

I've crossed the border in a private car, by bus, and on foot. I've sped through the border and have also had to wait hours in the pouring rain. Be prepared for delays, bring an umbrella, and try not to take out your frustration on border officials, lest they return the favor. If you can help it, don't change money at the border—the freelance moneychangers with their bills fanned like an enormous hand of cards don't tend to offer a good exchange rate.

One advantage of coming by car is that you can load up with all that you need to start your new life—there's no weight limit on luggage coming overland. But be sure to do your due diligence on any import duties you may be slapped with at any of the various borders you'll be crossing.

Arriving by Bus

Busing the whole way is cheap and easier than driving in terms of bureaucracy (no licenses, insurance, or traffic cops to deal with). It also can be harder on the body. Most long-distance Mexican and Central American buses are as comfortable as Greyhound buses in the United States, and some are positively deluxe, with movies, clean restrooms, and snacks served. But some buses still fit the stereotype of rickety haulers of the unwashed masses and their livestock; you'll probably find yourself on one or two during your trip, maybe for that 13-hour stretch with only pork rinds to eat and no restroom breaks. Those with delicate stomachs and weak bladders need not apply. Costa Rica-based Tica Bus (www.ticabus.com) has daily buses to and from San Salvador (El Salvador), Tegucigalpa (Honduras), Guatemala City, Managua (Nicaragua), and Tapachula (Mexico).

Getting Around

AIR: PUDDLE JUMPERS

Domestic airlines use small planes to make their short hops (20-60 minutes) to places like Tortuguero, Golfito, Nosara, or Tamarindo. Recently they've also been offering flights into southern Nicaragua and northern Panama with air and hotel package deals, such as three days and two nights in Granada, Nicaragua. Planes carry 4-40 passengers. Fares are always changing, but in general they're reasonable. If you're short on time, these flights are a downright bargain, saving you hours in travel time and perhaps saving you the bother and expense of renting a car. Locals and expats who are legal residents pay significantly lower fares.

Sansa (www.flysansa.com) is the domestic branch of TACA, and it flies out of Juan Santamaría Airport (its terminal is 200 meters from the international terminal). Nature Air (www.natureair.com) flies mostly out of Juan Santamaría Airport as well, with a few of their flights

Deplaning at Daniel Oduber International Airport in Liberia

Long-distance buses in Central America are often like Greyhound buses in the U.S.

leaving from Tobías Bolaños Airport in the Pavas section of San José, a short taxi ride from the international airport.

COSTA RICA BY BUS

Costa Rica has a great bus system—cheap, extensive, and often on time. You can get to just about any place in the country for less than US$15. It's also a great way to see the country without the expense or hassle of a car, and to make contact with locals, who use buses as their daily transport. Popular destinations—like Jacó, Liberia, and Limón—are served by both direct *(directo)* buses and those that stop a lot along the way (called *normal* or *corriente*). Routes from San José to crossroads towns like Liberia often leave every hour from early morning to late evening, while less-visited destinations may be served by just one or two buses per day. Buy tickets a day or two in advance—seats sell out fast. Popular routes are served by buses with comfortable seats and decent legroom; many resemble Greyhound buses in the United States. Urban or shorter-distance buses

may be renovated U.S. school buses, with those unpadded seats that hold two small children but only one and a half adults.

In San José, there's no central bus station; instead there are many departure points throughout the city. The tourist office downtown (one block north of the National Theater and then one block west on the pedestrian-only Avenida Central) has free booklets that list where a variety of long- and short-distance buses leave from and arrive. Most points are in decent areas, but be especially careful at the central San José bus depot, known as the Coca-Cola (near Avenida 1 and Calle 16)—your bags can disappear in the time it takes to check your watch.

City Buses

Most urban routes cost between US$140 and 360 colones ($0.25-$0.65), to be paid in cash and as you enter the bus. Check the bus's front windshield for the fare. When you want to get off, either pull the cable or—if there is no cable—call out *"la parada, por favor"* ("next stop, please").

Bus stops often have shelters (essential

during the rainy season) or battered signs that say the route name or number. Route numbers seem not to be much use, though: I once asked the driver parked at the Route 66 sign if that route went to my neighborhood. He looked at me quizzically—he'd never thought of his route as having a number. Buses are known for their destinations: the Desamparados bus, for example, or the bus to the university.

Shuttle Bus Companies

Interbus (tel. 506/2283-5573, www.interbusonline.com) will take you to more than 40 destinations in air-conditioned vans. Routes leaving from San José pick up passengers at hotels and other locations throughout the city; one-way fares range US$39-55. Also check out Gray Line Tours (tel. 506/2220-2126, United States or Canada toll-free tel. 800/719-3905, www.graylinecostarica.com). Other options include Caribe Shuttle (tel. 506/2750-0626, toll-free from the United States or Canada tel. 800/274-6191, www.caribeshuttle.com) and Easy Rider (tel. 506/4033-6847, www.easyrydercr.com). If you want more comfort than you'd get on a regular bus, these shuttle services can be very useful, although they're not always as reliable as you'd like. Especially if you're catching one in a town outside the Central Valley, check and double-check departure times, and book ahead (it's easy to book online). Most companies also offer airport shuttle service.

URBAN TRAIN

After decades of disuse, the old train tracks in and around San José have been pressed back into service, much to the delight of train aficionados and working stiffs alike. As of 2013, three commuter lines, known collectively as the *tren urbano* (the urban train), are running strong and pretty much on time.

The train lines are geared to students and working people; most run daily 5:30am-9am and then 4pm-8pm. But riding the urban rails is also an excellent way for a potential expat to learn the lay of the land without having to fight the traffic on the Central Valley's clogged highways. Fares are low—rarely more than US$1—and the routes take you through territory few tourists will see.

For train schedules, visit www.trenurbano.co.cr.

History

At one time trains were crucial to the economic development of the country, transporting coffee and bananas, once Costa Rica's top exports (see the sidebar on page 40 for more on the early history of trains in Costa Rica).

But freight trains were eventually displaced by trucks running on improved roads, urban train tracks were abandoned or paved over in favor of cars, and both freight and passenger trains were further compromised by a serious earthquake in 1991 that inflicted severe damage on the country's tracks and railroad bridges.

In 1995 the rail system was dealt another crushing blow when then-president José María Figueres closed the Costa Rican Railroad Institute (INCOFER) except for basic rail maintenance and limited grain transport. The decision was a popular one at the time, as INCOFER was seen as a bloated bureaucracy that siphoned funds from a cash-strapped government. During the 1980s, INCOFER's personnel swelled to an all-time high of 3,000 workers. By 1994 the number of employees had dropped to 1,250. In 2005, when the urban trains began to be reintroduced, INCOFER had just 42 employees to maintain the country's 400 kilometers (250 miles) of train tracks.

Much of the country's rail system is still severely damaged and neglected, but restoring the urban rails have long been a priority for city planners looking to alleviate ever-increasing traffic in the Central Valley.

Growing Pains for the Tren Urbano

In 2005, the route from Pavas to San Pedro (two outlying districts of San José) opened to much fanfare. Far from high-speed rail, however, the line resurrected an old diesel-fueled locomotive that takes close to an hour to run its 15-kilometer (9-mile) route through the neighborhoods of La Sabana, Plaza Víquez, Barrio Luján, Los Yoses, and Barrio Escalante. Still, students and workers immediately adopted this new mode of transport, leaving cars at home or vacating their seats on crowded city buses.

In 2009 the Heredia-San José line started up again. In its first two weeks of operation, the train hit a car, derailed twice, took a lot longer than its touted 28 minutes, and was even blocked for hours by protesters in Santa Rosa de Santo Domingo. But the kinks were soon worked out, whittling the travel time back down to about half an hour. It now transports an estimated 4,500 to 5,000 people per day.

When ribbed about the problems, Miguel Carabaguíaz, executive president of INCOFER, said that they were part of the learning curve.

"What?" he asked. "Trains don't derail in the United States? Look, it's like a child who's growing up and you have to help him a little along the way. It's all a process, and I think so far, it's working really well."

On the subject of collisions, of which there have been several, he said, "People need to understand that the train has the right of way, and in the case of an emergency, it cannot stop as quickly as cars do." There are very few signals or gates that keep cars and trucks off the tracks when the trains are passing, and engineers have taken to blasting their horn continually when they reach heavily populated areas.

Houses built along the tracks, for years silent, are suddenly having to cope with the noisy passing of up to 15 trains a day. On the outskirts of urban areas, shantytowns grew up around (and sometimes directly on top of) the tracks, and for many people, the rails were a ready-made path through the city or the country. Locals have had to relearn the caution necessary when living alongside a conduit for hurtling, belching masses of glass and steel.

Newer lines have had fewer problems. In 2011 the San José-San Antonio de Belén train began running again. The ride from the Estación del Pacífico in downtown San José to the eastern suburb of Belén takes about 35 minutes. In rush hour traffic, traveling that distance in a car would take from 60 to 90 minutes.

The San José-Cartago route debuted in May, 2013, a 23-kilometer (14-mile) route with four stops: two in the eastern San José neighborhood of Curridabat, one in Tres Ríos (west of Cartago), and one in downtown Cartago.

Other routes, like one from San José to Alajuela, the city closest to the international airport, are still in the works. Officials hope that many of the new routes will be powered by electricity rather than diesel.

WITHIN COSTA RICA BY BOAT

The Caribbean coast north of Puerto Limón is riddled with rivers and swamps, which have made it tough to build roads. This is perhaps one of the few areas in the country where boat travel is the daily norm, with motorized *canoas* (canoes) making runs from one tiny town to the next carrying people and freight. Boats can be hired from Moín, just north of Puerto Limón, and from Caño Blanco, among other ports.

Ferries and Launches

There are three major ferry crossings in Costa Rica, all of them carrying people or vehicles between Puntarenas and the southern end of the Nicoya Peninsula. Two of these—the Tambor Ferry and the Ferry Peninsular—go from Puntarenas to Paquera, and the third runs between Puntarenas and Playa Naranjo. All take about an hour. The trip is scenic, and fares are reasonable (about US$25 for a car and driver, and less than US$2 for a walk-on). It's a great way to start a trip to Montezuma or Mal País. Check out www.nicoyapeninsula.com/general/boat.php for ferry schedules.

There used to be a ferry across the Tempisque River in Guanacaste, but it shut down in 2003 on completion of the Taiwan Friendship Bridge.

On the southern Pacific coast, there is sometimes a passenger launch that goes across the Bahia Dulce, connecting Golfito and Puerto Jiménez on the Osa Peninsula. The trip takes about 90 minutes.

Anywhere there's water to be crossed, you can often find a guy with a boat. You may have to track him down, wait around, and pay more than you'd like for passage, but with patience and perseverance, you'll get where you need to go.

CAR
Renting

Although it's expensive to rent a car here and the roads are quite a challenge, having a car in Costa Rica gives you a great deal of freedom and lets you see every nook and cranny of the country. You don't have to worry about bus schedules or packing light—just load up the car and take off into the wild green yonder.

You'll probably want to rent a four-wheel drive with high clearance, unless you're sure you'll be on major roads for your entire trip. In my experience it pays to rent a medium-size vehicle rather than the smallest four-wheel drive—you'll appreciate the extra weight when you're trying to ford a river. My favorite car for driving around Costa Rica is a Rav 4, and, no, Toyota isn't paying me to say that. The Rav 4 is big enough but not too big, it gets decent gas mileage, and I like the way it feels on the road.

Be sure that if you're quoted a rate, the insurance you need is included in the price.

One good thing about renting a car in this country is that some companies will deliver the vehicle to your door, especially if you live far from a rental office. In Guanacaste's Playa Negra, I had a four-wheel drive delivered to the door of the rather remote place I was staying. The company sent two cars so that the fellow driving my car would have a ride back.

No car-rental companies here will allow their cars to be driven out of Costa Rica.

Renting a Motorcycle

If you want to rent a motorcycle and two-wheel it around the country, it'll cost US$55-150 per day. The price depends on the model (Harleys cost the most) and usually includes standard insurance, taxes, and helmet rental; weekly or month-long rentals mean a lower per-day cost. Most companies require a hefty deposit, usually ranging from US$700 to more than US$1,000. Wild Rider (www.wild-rider.com) rents Hondas and Suzukis, while Costa Rica Motorcycle (www.costaricamotorcycletours.com) rents BMWs.

Rental Insurance

When you rent a car in Costa Rica, you need to pay for mandatory basic insurance, which doesn't give very much coverage and usually features a high deductible. Most renters opt to buy more insurance; this expense can almost double the cost of renting a car.

Dos and Don'ts of Costa Rican Driving

- **Do** try to avoid driving after dark – that's when most accidents occur.
- **Do** wear your seat belt – it's the law. A selectively enforced law, but a law nonetheless.
- **Do** wear a helmet and reflective clothing if you're on a motorcycle; if you don't you might be ticketed and fined.
- **Do** make sure you have a valid license from your home country, along with a valid passport with an up-to-date entrance stamp.
- **Do** consider renting a four-by-four with high clearance, unless you're sure you'll be on major roads for your entire trip.
- **Do** get gas as often as possible when driving outside main cities (gas stations are known as *bombas*).
- **Don't** try to bribe your way out of a traffic ticket. Take the ticket, smile, and pay it later (they'll tell you where you can do that). Although I have to admit that in this case, I don't always take my own advice . . .
- **Don't** leave the car if you have an accident or break down. Call the Transit Police (tel. 800/TRANSITO – 800/8726-7486). You can also call 911 and ask to be

If you have a car insured in your home country, there's a possibility that that policy may cover you while driving another car in another country. Call your insurance company and ask for details.

Some drivers get the basic insurance only and let their credit card cover the high deductible (often US$750-1,500) that goes along with basic insurance. Be sure to check that your card indeed offers this benefit. And be ready for surprises—a friend thought American Express would cover him, but he found that there was a clause that said the coverage didn't hold if the driver went off-road—that is, on un-paved roads. Since most of the roads in Costa Rica are unpaved, he ended up having to pay a few hundred dollars to repair a small scrape.

Call your credit card company and get the lowdown on what it covers, if anything. The insurance associated with my Visa card, for instance, covered physical damage to the rented vehicle along with vandalism and theft. It did not cover personal liability (damage

to another vehicle or property), loss or theft of personal belongings, or injury to self or others. That's a lot not covered. And as with my friend's American Express card, the coverage was good only if I didn't drive off-road.

Rental-car companies charge for the minutest scratches, so be sure to look over the car very carefully before driving off the lot. Things like rearview mirrors and tires are often not covered by insurance; you pay if they get ripped off. That's why it's so important to park the car in a safe place.

Owning

Due to high import tariffs, cars in Costa Rica are expensive. If you try to get around that by bringing in a car from outside, you'll confront another set of problems. You could import a car to use for the time on your tourist visa (three months plus a three-month extension) without paying high fees or tariffs, but after that time expires, things get complicated. Of course, you have to get the car here first—which

- **Don't** neglect insurance when you rent a car. There is mandatory basic insurance, which doesn't give very much coverage; most renters opt to buy more insurance, while some let their credit card cover the high deductible (often US$750-1,500) that goes along with basic insurance. Be sure to check that your card indeed offers this benefit.

- **Do** be ready for surprises — a friend thought American Express would cover him but found that there was a clause that said the coverage didn't hold if the driver went off-road — that is, on unpaved roads. Most of the roads in Costa Rica are unpaved! He ended up having to pay a few hundred dollars to repair a small scrape.

- **Don't** forget to look your rental car over very carefully before driving off the lot. Rental car companies will charge for the minutest of scratches.

- **Do** park the car in a safe place, like a guarded lot at your hotel. Things like rear view mirrors and tires are often not covered by insurance; you pay if they get ripped off.

connected with whatever agency you need, including the Red Cross if there are injuries. If you're in a rental car, call the rental agency as well.

means driving it through five countries or shipping it by container. Shipping from Miami or New Orleans to Puerto Limón is the cheapest option, but it still might cost you over US$1,000, and that's before you pay any of the various taxes and fees to pick it up on this end. You can also ship from the west coast of the United States or Canada to Puerto Caldera on the west coast of Costa Rica, but that's even more expensive.

Note also that most shipping insurance covers the car if it is lost at sea but not if it is damaged within the container. And many new car warranties become invalid if you take the car out of the country where you bought it.

If you want to make your car a Costa Rican native after the six-month grace period has expired, the process is long and costly. You'll pay 60-85 percent of the car's appraised value in duties, and then there will be lots of paperwork, stamps, and miscellaneous fees. It's easier to buy a car down here; if it's used, get it checked out by a reputable mechanic, as you would in the United States.

If you're driving around in your own car, be sure you have a valid driver's license, along with the originals (not copies) of the car's registration and title.

(For information on buying a used car, see the sidebar on page 238.)

Driving

The U.S. State Department's assessment of roads here starts diplomatically: "Costa Rican road conditions can significantly differ from those in the United States." But before you can say "Different doesn't have to be bad," you read about "large potholes with the potential to cause significant damage," unclear lane markings, farm animals, pedestrians and stalled cars surprising you around a bend, and the fact that "rural roads sometimes lack bridges, compelling motorists to ford waterways."

It's all true. The roads are riddled with potholes (if they're paved at all), signage is woefully inadequate, torrential rains can make some routes impassable, and all the aggression Costa Ricans repress in their daily lives comes out when they get behind the wheel. And yet I love driving in

Buying a Used Car

Given the high cost of importing and shipping your car to Costa Rica, it makes sense to buy a car once you're here. New cars in Costa Rica, however, cost significantly more than what you'd pay for the same make and model in the United States; import taxes and other fees jack up the price of a new car by about 30 percent.

Consider looking for a used car. Costa Rican roads are hard on cars, it's true. On the other hand, because cars are so expensive, Ticos tend to take good care of their vehicles, to better maintain their resale value.

Where Should You Look?

Try online first to get a sense of what your preferred makes and models are going for down here. Check out Craigslist, TicoCarros.com, CRAuto.com, the TicoTimes.net, and the classified section, both in print and online, of *La Nación* (http://nacion.com), the daily newspaper.

If you know what you're looking for and what you're willing to pay, and you stand up well to pressure, you could also visit some of the car dealerships in San José. Dealers are legally obligated to offer a 30-day guarantee on the car's transmission and motor. They'll do the paperwork, might take another car as trade-in, and they often offer financing if you're not ready to pay full price at the outset. The *Tico Times* suggests that the following dealers are established and reputable: Purdy Motor, EuroAutos, Vetrasa & Veinsa, and Datsun.

Expats who are moving back home are often motivated sellers.

What's the Best Car for Costa Rica?

You'll probably want four-wheel drive and high clearance, although hundreds of thousands of Ticos do without (you'll wait for them as they take speed bumps at 2 mph).

Japanese or Korean cars—Toyota, Honda, Suzuki, Mitsubishi, Daihatsu, Hyundai, and Kia—do well here and are popular enough that mechanics have the parts you'll need and will know how to work on the cars. The French brand Peugeot is also becoming popular.

Many of the Japanese and Korean makes and models sold here are made with Costa Rican roads in mind, with engine size, tuning, and suspension calibrated to the conditions here.

Dos and Don'ts

- **Do** get a reputable mechanic to check out the car before you put the money down.

- **Do** make sure the car is registered in Costa Rica, or you'll end up paying the sky-high import taxes. If you don't pay the duties, your car could be impounded.

- **Do** check that the car has passed the required annual Riteve technical inspection.

- **Do** make sure that the car has no encumbrances (*gravámenes*) or infractions recorded in the National Registry. Check online at www.registronacional.go.cr/bienes_muebles/muebles_consultavehiculos.htm.

- **Do** check that the car's *marchamo* (annual circulation permit) has been paid for the year. A sticker displaying the current year should be affixed to the windshield. When you buy or renew your *marchamo,* part of the fee goes to mandatory personal liability insurance. The coverage is very basic; many people get additional insurance.

- **Do** check into the *traspaso* (transfer of registration) fee, which varies depending on the car's value.

- **Don't** meet a seller in an isolated area—you could get robbed.

- **Don't** hand over any money until you're sure you want the car.

Roads have been improving over the last several years, but you'll still find the occasional bridge that looks like it wouldn't support even a bicycle.

Costa Rica! It's an extreme sport, one that kills far more people than canyoneering or zip-lining. But after a week or two on the back roads of Costa Rica, negotiating corrugated dirt tracks and fording rivers, the highways back home will seem impossibly wimpy.

Costa Rica has about 38,000 kilometers (23,600 miles) of roads; fewer than 8,000 kilometers (5,000 miles) of them are paved. And paved is sometimes worse than unpaved—a gravel road can be well graded and in excellent repair, while a "paved" road may be riddled with deep holes.

Things really are getting better, however. Each time I travel around the country I think, wow, the roads have improved! OK, not all of them. But a lot of places have smooth and well-maintained roads now; as of 2016, the Panamerican Highway from Liberia almost to Puntarenas is an actual four-lane highway!

Still, a driver in Costa Rica must be ready for anything—trucks passing on a hill, potholes big enough to do your vehicle real damage, and cops hiding behind the next palm tree. Police here have radar guns, and they love to use them. Speeding tickets can be very expensive—up to US$500! Pay attention to speed limit signs, even if it seems that there's no one else on the road. Speed traps are common on the most-traveled routes to tourist areas.

Costa Rican drivers have developed a way of signaling to other drivers that there is trouble up ahead—they flash their lights at oncoming cars. Of course, this can also mean "turn off your brights," but if someone flashes you, slow down and be on the lookout for an accident, a damaged roadway, or a police car. If you're behind someone and they flash their lights, it can mean "The road is clear for you to pass," but be aware that what Costa Rican drivers consider a safe distance to pass is a fraction of what most North American drivers deem necessary.

Wear your seat belt—it's the law. A selectively enforced law, but a law nonetheless. Motorcyclists are supposed to wear helmets.

The Fine Art of Honking

The language of the car horn in Costa Rica is a rich one that may take years to master. Ticos don't tend to lean on their horns like some Type A people back home, but they don't ignore them either. Only long-term residents, however, can tell the difference between the "Get out of my way!" honk and the "What a pleasure to see you, my friend, on this same stretch of road where I see you every morning and evening" honk.

There's also the "Hey, baby" honk, the "I'm a taxi and I'm available" honk, and perhaps most maddening, the "I'm here! Come out of your house and say hello!" honk, which can go on for a long time, especially if no one's home.

After you've been in Costa Rica for a while, you'll start to recognize even more varieties, maybe even inventing a few of your own. After all, what occasion—no matter how humble—is not enhanced by the sound of a car's horn?

Even as you try to drive by the book, other drivers will be throwing that same book out the window—turning across two lanes of traffic without signaling, hoisting a bottle while passing on a blind curve, or realizing that, yes, they really should have had the brakes fixed last week.

Traffic enforcement in Costa Rica is the responsibility of the Transit Police (Tránsitos), who wear light-blue shirts and dark-blue pants and drive light-blue cars or motorcycles equipped with blue lights. (Regular police drive dark-blue cars.) Transit cops often wave vehicles to the side of the road for inspection, asking drivers for their driver's license, vehicle registration, and insurance information. Fines are not supposed to be collected on the spot, although reports of officers attempting to collect money are common.

You can drive with a valid license from your home country for the first three months you are here, as long as you have a valid passport with an up-to-date entrance stamp.

Motorcyclists must wear helmets and special reflective clothing or risk being pulled over and fined. Children riding in cars must be strapped into approved carrier seats.

Accidents and Breakdowns

If you have an accident or the car breaks down, try to stay with your car until the police arrive. If you're out in the middle of nowhere or in the middle of a highway, this is impractical, of course. But if it's possible to wait, do so, so as not to open yourself up to liability.

Call the Transit Police (tel. 800/TRANSITO—800/8726-7486, www.transito.go.cr). You'll also need to call the National Insurance Institute (INS, tel. 800/800-8000 or 506/2287-6000, http://portal.ins-cr.com). You can also call 911 and ask to be connected with whatever agency you need, including the Red Cross if there are injuries. If you're in a rental car, call the rental agency as well. It will often send a tow truck, and it may bring you another vehicle, depending on where you are and what the problem is.

While you wait, get the names, license plate numbers, and *cédula* (ID) numbers of those involved, along with the same information for any witnesses. Make a sketch of the accident.

If you have reflective triangles, place them to warn oncoming cars. Many Costa Rican drivers improvise with piled-up leaves or branches to alert other drivers of trouble up ahead.

Being able to read Spanish comes in handy when the sign says "Danger—Road in Bad Condition."

Stranded foreigners in nice cars, especially those carrying expensive luggage or sports equipment, can attract the wrong sort of attention. Most people who try to assist you will be doing so out of kindness, but be wary of helpers who want to relieve you of your possessions.

When officials arrive, they may or may not speak English. They may be very concerned and helpful, or they may sullenly perform the bare minimum that their office requires. Keep your wits about you, write down everything, and don't neglect any of the steps (like contacting the INS, which is crucial if you want to make an insurance claim of any sort).

Most accidents occur at night—do what you can to avoid driving after dark. Most roads are unmarked and unlit. Fog and torrential rains can make the way even rougher.

Gasoline

Both the regular and super sold at gas stations (or *bombas*) here is unleaded—the super has more octane. Diesel is also available. Gas is more expensive here than in the United States. When driving outside main cities, get gas as often as possible. In remote areas there may be no station, or the station may be open very limited hours. In some small towns you can find a local who sells gas out of his backyard, with the kind of crazy markup that comes with being the only game in town.

Maps and Signs

As you navigate Costa Rica's roads, don't expect signs to alert you to where you need to turn off, even on major highways to popular tourist spots. And if there is a sign, sometimes it will point in the wrong direction. Coming from Puntarenas to San José, there's an important turn that I've gotten wrong three or four times. I keep thinking, "By now the sign must point the right way," but each time I am mistaken.

Getting around in cities and larger towns is an even bigger challenge (see the sidebar on page 74 in the *Planning Your Fact-Finding Trip* chapter).

Most people these days navigate by GPS. Tico drivers also swear by Waze, which began in an Israeli start-up and was then acquired by Google. The largest crowd-sourced real time navigation app, Waze is a godsend in a place like Costa Rica, with poor signage and unpredictable road conditions, Download it for your iPhone or Android phone. But old-school maps still have their fans (like me). As you make your way through the urban maze and along winding mountain roads or sandy coastal routes, your best bet is to consult a variety of good maps—the more the merrier, as each tends to have its own strengths. I have not found one single map that did not have errors in it,

How to Talk to a *Taxista* (Taxi Driver)

Take me to . . . *Lléveme a . . .*
Straight ahead *Directo*
Stop at the corner *Pare en la esquina*
Take a right *A la derecha*
Take a left *A la izquierda*
A block *Una cuadra or cien metros*
Half a block *Cincuenta metros*
North, south, east, west *Norte, sur, este, oeste*
At the intersection *En el cruce*
Next to *Al lado de*
Across the street from *Frente a*
Around the corner *A la vuelta de la esquina*

The next street *La proxima calle*
Are we lost? *¿Estamos perdidos?*
Stop here *Pare aquí*
Stop there *Pare allí*
Wait for me *Espéreme*
Taxi meter (in Costa Rica) *María*
Please use the meter *Use la maría, por favor*
How much to take me to . . . ? *¿Cuanto cobra por llevarme a . . . ?*
How much do I owe you? *¿Cuanto le debo?*

but usually the other maps in my collection set me straight.

Security

Whether you're driving your own car or a rental, seek out a secure place to park it overnight. Car theft is common, and the deductible on rental-car insurance policies can be as much as US$1,500. Many hotels provide secure parking, or you could seek out one of the many freelance car or neighborhood guards and take your chances by giving him a few bucks to look after your vehicle. Never leave anything of value in a parked car.

In looking for a place to live, it's important, if you're a car owner, to find a place with a secure garage. In my middle-class neighborhood in San José, no one ever left a car on the street overnight.

TAXIS

In the San José area, taxis are plentiful. Official taxis are red, with the taxi's ID number in a yellow triangle on the door. Taxis should have meters (called *marías*), and drivers should use them—otherwise you'll have to haggle, which is hard to do when you don't know how much the fare should be.

There are thousands of taxis in the San José area, and it's easy to flag one down from just about any corner, unless it's raining at rush hour. While local men tend to ride up front with the driver—perhaps to show they're just folks—foreign residents, especially single women, should probably ride in the back.

Most taxi drivers are friendly and helpful, and they will sift through your broken Spanish with a smile. They know that foreigners have different ways of thinking of addresses (like street names and house numbers) and are good about helping you figure out where you need to go. You don't need to tip the drivers, though I do if they help with bags or go out of their way for me.

Besides all the official cabs tooling around the city, there are also thousands of *piratas,* pirate cabs that may be red and even have a *maría* but are not registered. The proof is in the ID number on the door—if a car doesn't have it, it's not an official cab. In outlying areas (like Escazú), *piratas* are the norm, and residents come to know the drivers who wait at the central square for fares. If you have the option, take an official cab. Some *piratas* aren't really taxis at all, but criminals cruising for marks. Women traveling alone should be especially wary, but everyone needs to stay alert.

Cabs waiting outside hotels or discos will often charge you several times the normal rate. Ask before getting in if there's a *maría;* if there's not, either negotiate the fare before entering the cab or look for another cab.

Taxis outside the greater San José area are a different story. They're usually high-clearance four-wheel-drive vehicles, for starters, because provincial roads are so bad. Few have meters, and they charge whatever the market will bear. You'll pay through the nose until you know the area and the usual fares from one point to the next. That said, the occasional taxi can be a good alternative if you're traveling around the country but don't want to rent a car. If you take buses whenever possible, it won't break your budget to hire a taxi to take you where buses don't go.

Cabbies don't like to break large bills. They also complain that North Americans have a nasty habit of slamming car doors. Prove them wrong: Be gentle.

Hiring a Taxi Driver

When you get serious about looking for a place to live, hiring a taxi driver by the hour or day is a good way to explore. Especially in the Central Valley, there are so many little towns down so many little roads that it helps to have a driver who knows his or her way around. Sure, you could rent a car—for about the same price as hiring a taxi for the day—but you'll spend most of your time trying to figure out where you are or how to open the gas tank.

Most taxi drivers will charge about US$15 an hour or US$100 a day. If you're going to need a car for several days, you can probably negotiate a lower rate. Hotels and travel agents can suggest reliable English-speaking drivers, or you can ask

foreign residents for their recommendations. These drivers often double as translators and cultural informants, and they might end up as friends. Buy them lunch and listen to their advice.

UBER

Uber came to Costa Rica in 2016. The company's entry into Costa Rica wasn't smooth. Taxi drivers went on strike, and some taxistas went out of their way to harass or even beat up Uber drivers and passengers. Uber hit back hard with aggressive ad campaigns and political savvy. It looks like the company that wants to rule the world's roads is here to stay. Most people in the country seem excited to have an alternative to driving their own cars or hailing a taxi. "It's not just tourists that the taxi drivers rip off," a Tico friend told me. "They screw us locals, too."

Until self-driving cars become a reality, Uber provides thousands of drivers with a way to make a living. Uber drivers rely on Waze, the crowd-sourced navigation app. Bring up Google maps to an Uber and you'll get snorts and frowns and cursing—apparently that app just gets you lost in Costa Rica.

HITCHHIKING

Costa Rica has a good bus system, but in remote areas the bus might come only once a day. Local people routinely hitch rides, and if you have a car you may be asked for a ride or be inspired to offer one. The longer you stay in an area, the more you're likely to become part of this informal ride-sharing system.

In general, ride-sharing is not dangerous, but use your judgment. Drunks with machetes may not be a good risk, although carrying a machete in the *campo* (countryside) doesn't mean you intend to use it for anything more than weed-whacking.

For female hitchers and drivers: Many guidebooks describe the ins and outs of hitching and picking up hitchers, then add a line, almost as an afterthought, urging women to not do any of this, ever. Experienced solo women travelers and women who live alone in Costa Rica know the situation is a bit more nuanced than that. There are times you need to get somewhere and there's no bus in sight. And if you're driving an air-conditioned car along a hot and dusty back road, it can seem criminal not to pick up women carrying babies or kids trying to make it to school in the next town.

I have hitched alone and have picked up hitchers when I was driving alone, but I am very, very careful about when and where I do this, whom I accept rides from, and whom I pick up. Sometimes I'll approach a safe-looking car full of people (at a restaurant, or stopped on the street), introduce myself, and let them know where I need to go, offering to help out with the gas. I accept rides mostly from families. I give rides to women and children and sometimes the men with them. The only time I felt even a shiver of danger was when I picked up a father and his small son; the father kept asking for money in a way that suggested that giving voluntarily might prevent the situation from escalating to the next level. I gave him a little money, and then stopped to let them out. Ironically, I wasn't driving alone that time. I was with a male companion, who couldn't believe I would pick up hitchhikers.

PRIME LIVING
LOCATIONS

OVERVIEW

The chapters in this section describe the characteristics and appeal of the different regions of Costa Rica, also outlined in brief here. The areas profiled are by no means the only desirable ones, but they are places where a number of expatriates have decided to make their homes. For such a small country, Costa Rica has an astonishingly varied terrain. Guanacaste in late April (the end of the Costa Rican summer) will be hot and dry, its fields and rolling hills blanketed in deep yellows and browns. Just a few hours away, mountain towns like Monteverde—or La Fortuna, in the shadow of Arenal Volcano—are still wet and green. Puerto Viejo, on the Caribbean coast, will be its usual humid and rainy self, while the weather near peaks south of the Central Valley will be downright frosty.

Deciding where to live is a very personal exercise, a process of self-discovery and of getting to know your adopted country. You may love to vacation at the beach, for instance, but find that after two months there, you're bored stiff. You may think you want to be far from other expats but then realize how much you need an occasional dose of your own kind. Or the opposite may occur—you begin in an expat-heavy area and then, as your Spanish gets better and you feel more at home in the culture, decide you want to move

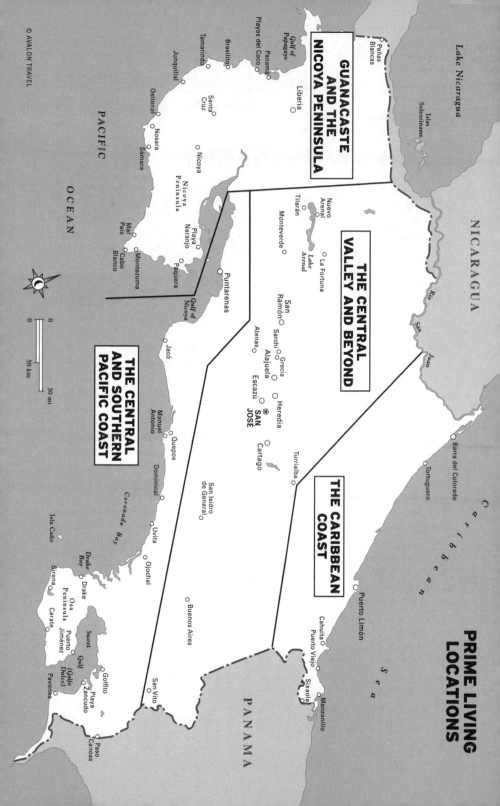

PRIME LIVING
LOCATIONS

the Southern Zone's inland valley

farther afield, into a more truly Costa Rican environment. As I suggest elsewhere in this book, the best approach is to rent houses or apartments in a variety of locales, seeing which place suits you best, before settling in.

As you review the basics, like real estate prices and climate, also ask yourself how you might contribute to the towns that make it onto your short list. What will you do there? Who will you *be* there—the owner of a thriving business that employs a dozen locals? The founder of the new town library? Or the sour-faced gringo on the hill who complains about the roads and starts drinking before breakfast? Such considerations are not solely altruistic; it's well known that to successfully relocate, a person must forge new roles and new relationships. You'll be a happier camper if you not only make friends with the locals (both Tico and expat), but also become an integral and valuable part of your adopted community.

OVER- AND UNDERDEVELOPMENT

A caveat: When you hear that a beach town in Costa Rica is overdeveloped, take that designation with a grain of salt. It's all relative, and what for some might seem touristy will for others seem enchantingly rough around the edges.

Of greater concern is the underdevelopment of so many beach towns. Places whose popularity has skyrocketed in the past decade often cannot keep pace with the basic needs of visitors, not to mention residents. We're talking woefully inadequate roads, water, electricity, phone lines, garbage pickup, and sewage treatment.

But many towns are rising to the occasion, forming residents' associations to figure out what the community needs and then lobby for it, either asking the national and local governments for help or getting locals to pitch in and do it themselves. Whether it's Danish students organizing beach cleanups in Playas del Coco or hotel and restaurant owners in Tamarindo commissioning a sustainable growth plan, it's often foreign residents who spearhead such efforts. Which is only fair—it's the influx of foreigners who overtax the system and who often hope to make a living off that same influx. It makes sense that they should give something back to their adopted communities.

Not that Costa Ricans aren't deeply involved in improving their own communities. Take the example of a bus driver in Ciudad Neily, not far from the Panama border, fed up with the rutted roads and how long it was taking the Ministerio de Obras Públicas y Transportes (MOPT, the agency in charge of the highway system) to fix them. He loaded his pickup with cement and sand and spent his days off filling potholes on a 28-kilometer (17-mile) stretch of road that was especially damaged. No one paid him; he just decided to take the initiative and improve the road he had to use every day. The government's slow response to community needs has had the side effect of forcing people to be more self-sufficient. This is also why, perhaps, people who live outside the Central Valley, where all the best services are concentrated, feel more identified with their town or area than with Costa Rica as a whole.

THE CENTRAL VALLEY AND BEYOND

The beautiful and fertile basin called the Valle Central is home to 70 percent of Costa Rica's population. At the heart of this highland plain (1,150 meters/3,770 feet) lies the capital city, San José, the nation's undisputed political, economic, and cultural center. Here is where you'll find the museums, the theaters, the government buildings, and the University of Costa Rica, the country's largest and most important institutions of higher learning. Costa Ricans from outlying areas are drawn to San José for better job opportunities, and many expats are sent here to work at branches of multinational corporations.

Temperate weather is one of the area's main draws. For those who don't do well with heat or humidity, the Central Valley's mild and dry climate is a godsend. It never gets very cold or very hot here—temperatures average in the mid-20s Celsius (high 70s Fahrenheit).

Some of the most popular expat areas around San José include Escazú, where the U.S. ambassador makes his home; nearby Santa Ana, with its lovely old stone church and upscale restaurants; Alajuela, a reasonably priced town near the international airport; and Heredia, larger and more congested but still worth a look. Farther afield you'll find Grecia, 30 minutes from San José but a world apart—it was voted "cleanest town in Latin America" and boasts an interesting sheet-metal church in its quiet main plaza; Cartago, the original capital of the country and home to Costa Rica's most stunning church; and Sarchí, a center for arts and crafts.

North of the Central Valley and over the mountains of the Cordillera Central lies the highland plain of San Carlos, home to Arenal Volcano, Lake Arenal, and a temperate climate that draws "non-beachy" expats. Northwest of San José are the mountain towns of Santa Elena and Monteverde, the latter founded by Alabama Quakers in the 1950s and now an interesting mix of long-term expats and native Costa Ricans, many of whom have intermarried and speak both Spanish and English at home.

South of the Central Valley is the Valle de El General, an oft-overlooked zone that includes the bustling inland town of San Isidro de El General and the smaller San Vito, settled by Italian homesteaders and now the center of one of Costa Rica's most fertile coffee-producing areas.

Range of Motion

What it takes to make it in Costa Rica is not unlike what it takes to make it in any new environment—those who've been through the experience agree that flexibility is key.

But you may not even know how inflexible you are until you try to do the cultural equivalent of touching your toes. (Let's not even talk about the backbends and head-stands you'll be called on to perform as you adapt to your new world.)

In our everyday life, within our own familiar culture, we often stay within fairly narrow confines, from the route we take to work to the emotions we allow ourselves to feel. Our range of motion, both physical and otherwise, is quite limited. As we age, this becomes even more pronounced, as bodies stiffen and thoughts and feelings travel along familiar paths.

But one can consciously fight against this closing in by exercising the body and mind to increase all forms of "range of motion." And if deliberately stretching your boundaries while in your own culture is good exercise, moving to a new country and adapting to a new culture is an extreme sport. You need to train for it—to read up on the culture, to prepare yourself mentally for a period of upheaval, even to physically build up a resistance to all the new microbes that will invade your system.

Adapting to a new culture is not easy, but the rewards are immense. Increased flexibility and range of movement mean you travel through the world with more grace and plea-sure. You will look back on your old life, your old frame of reference, and it will look small.

GUANACASTE AND THE NICOYA PENINSULA

Guanacaste, with its dependable December-April dry season and seemingly endless supply of beaches, is the preferred choice for lovers of sand and surf who want to escape the rain and snow back home.

Most of the beaches are on the Nicoya Peninsula, which is 150 kilometers (90 miles) long, averages 50 kilometers (30 miles) wide, and lies almost entirely within the province of Guanacaste. The southernmost tip, where you'll find off-beat Montezuma and the surfer haven of Mal País, is part of Puntarenas Province. But provincial boundaries don't mean much here; the Nicoya Peninsula is all of a piece, though the northern part, dubbed the Gold Coast, is experiencing a build-ing boom that makes it look a lot differ-ent from the more laid-back towns farther south.

Driving Guanacaste's potholed back roads (most of the area's roads qualify as back roads), you'll see barbed wire looped around gnarled and crooked tree trunks, improvised fences that keep the pale, humpbacked Brahmin cattle from wan-dering off. In the dry season, trees blaze with bright yellow and orange blossoms made even more dramatic because they grace bare branches before the trees leaf out. The evergreen Guanacaste tree has a full, spreading, often perfectly symmet-rical crown that provides welcome shade during hot afternoons. The tree's long dark pods curl like ears, which is why the original inhabitants of the area called it *quauhnacaztli,* from the Nahuatl words *quauitl,* "tree," and *nacaztli,* "ear."

As you move toward the Pacific, you'll catch glimpses of the sea through branches or across scrubby fields. Arrival at the westernmost edge of the country is an inspiring experience, and Guanacaste's beaches seduce even non-beach lovers. From white-sand Playa Hermosa up north to rocky Cabo Blanco down south, there's something for everyone. Most expats in

trees witth buttressing roots

Guanacaste live (or try to live) off the tourist trade, running hotels, restaurants, Internet cafés, or real estate offices. Land prices around the most popular resorts are high, but then again, there's an entire coastline to be discovered—you needn't limit yourself to developed areas such as Tamarindo and Playas del Coco. Long-term expats warn of a lack of health care facilities and a dearth of culture—most go to Liberia or sometimes San José for more serious medical problems, and some might drive hours just to see a movie or try out a new restaurant. Still, most agree they wouldn't have it any other way—they didn't move to the beach for state-of-the-art medical care or to be able to see the new James Bond movie the day it debuts in New York.

THE CENTRAL AND SOUTHERN PACIFIC COAST

The grouping together of the central and southern Pacific coasts makes sense geographically, but the two areas couldn't be more different in terms of ambience and density of settlement. The central Pacific coast, located between Puntarenas to the north and the Osa Peninsula to the south, is one of the most visited and most developed parts of the country. It is anchored by the resort towns of Jacó and Quepos-Manuel Antonio: Jacó is famous for surfing—international contests are held on its long palm-shaded beach—while the Quepos area is a sportfishing mecca and home to Manuel Antonio National Park, where sloths and monkeys hang out in trees that border some of the country's prettiest white-sand beaches.

As in most areas outside the Central Valley, expats who come to this area and need to make a living tend to work in the tourist trade. In fact, the majority of hotels and restaurants in Jacó and Manuel Antonio are owned and operated by non-Ticos. Industries not based on tourism include vast plantations of oil-producing African palms, which line the road from Jacó to Quepos, extending inland and often planted where bananas used to grow before that industry was destroyed by blight in the 1950s.

Stages of Culture Shock

According to many psychologists who specialize in cross-cultural transitions, culture shock is a very real phenomenon, with identifiable stages.

- **Initial euphoria:** This is the "honeymoon" feeling that usually comes with being exposed to so many new, strange, and interesting things. It doesn't really matter that the visitor can't always understand all of it, because there is so much to see and do.

- **Hostility:** This is a feeling of rejection and alienation when real differences are experienced but not understood. People in this stage understand that things are really different, but they also can't help feeling they are also wrong. It just doesn't feel natural to them.

- **Gradual adjustment:** With time, people begin to learn skills that make them culturally competent, like language fluency and putting cultural practices in the proper context.

- **Biculturalism:** In this phase, visitors may not function like natives, but they fit in relatively well to the host culture. And they can move back and forth, from culture to culture with some ease.

In the excellent *Survival Kit for Overseas Living*, L. Robert Kohls offers these wise words on the value of culture shock: "Be ready for the lesson culture shock teaches. Culture is a survival mechanism which tells its members not only that their ways of doing things are right but also that they are superior. Culture shock stems from an in-depth encounter with another culture in which you learn that there are different ways of doing things that are neither wrong nor inferior.

"It teaches a lesson that cannot be learned by any other means: that one's culture does not possess the single right way, best way, or even uniformly better way of providing for human needs and enjoyments. Believing it does is a kind of imprisonment—from which the experience of culture shock, as painful as it may be, can liberate you."

The central Pacific coast has a wet season (May-November) and a dry season (December-April), but this area's dry season is not nearly as dry as that of Guanacaste, where virtually no rain falls. The farther south you go, the wetter it becomes. Temperatures hover around 30°C (86°F) in the dry season, a little lower in the wet season.

The coastal road south from Quepos has improved considerably, and you'll see some developments scattered amid the palm-tree plantations. About 40 kilometers (25 miles) from Quepos is the still-funky town of Dominical, known for its surfing and popular with foreigners looking to buy property on the coast but away from big resorts.

The southern Pacific coast is dominated by the hook-shaped Osa Peninsula and the vast, tranquil Golfo Dulce (Sweet Gulf), which borders the Osa's eastern shore. Termed Costa Rica's Amazon, this area is wetter, hotter, and more lushly verdant than the central coast. It's also wilder—less populated and less developed. Up until the early 1980s, the area had a lawless Wild West feel, with gold prospectors making and losing fortunes daily. Old-timers say that everyone carried a gun and prostitutes were paid in gold nuggets. The Osa Peninsula's Corcovado National Park was formed partly in response to mining that was destroying the country's biggest and best example of coastal rainforest. Now the park—almost

There are no cars in the town of Tortuguero.

42,000 hectares (103,800 acres)—protects 139 species of mammals and 400 species of birds, including the brilliantly plumed scarlet macaw.

Bigger towns in the area include Puerto Jiménez, where a good number of expats have settled, and Golfito, a port that was United Fruit's company town until the banana producer pulled out in 1985 after a series of labor strikes. Golfito today is most famous for the Deposito Libre, a duty-free shopping compound where Ticos can buy appliances and other goods without paying the duties that can tack up to 50 percent onto purchase prices.

The southern Pacific coast is also known for excellent surf spots, including Pavones, home to what some call the longest wave in the world.

THE CARIBBEAN COAST

In a country where each new province seems a world apart, the Caribbean coast of Costa Rica might just qualify as another universe. Nearly all of the country's black citizens, most of its Chinese inhabitants, and a good part of its indigenous population can be found in the Zona Caribe, as it's known in Spanish. Though these minorities make up only a few percentage points of the total national population, the fact that most live in the sparsely populated Caribbean province of Limón means that this area is the most ethnically diverse in the country.

The Caribbean coast is where the colonizing Spaniards first arrived, but it is its more recent arrivals, the Jamaicans, who have had perhaps the biggest impact. Along with people from other Caribbean islands and a number of Chinese people, they migrated here in the late 19th century to work on the railroad and in the banana fields, and Caribbean culture now dominates the area. What this means is that reggae overtakes salsa, spicy island-inspired concoctions offer welcome relief from bland *casados,* and a lilting Caribbean English is heard as often as Spanish.

Puerto Limón (often simply called Limón, which is also the name of the entire province) is the biggest city in the area, a laid-back port that has more economic than aesthetic appeal. North of Puerto Limón, swamps and rivers dominate the area. Waterways are the zone's roads, and boats outnumber cars. In the little town of Tortuguero, at the entrance to the famed Tortuguero National Park, there are no roads. Paved and unpaved paths connect the wood-frame houses built on stilts to guard against flooding, and almost everyone has a dock and a boat or two in their front yard. South of Limón is one decent coastal road linking the beach towns of Cahuita, Puerto Viejo, and Manzanillo, where most expats tend to settle. Inland, the heavily forested Talamanca Mountains are home to several large indigenous reserves, among them the Bribrí and the Talamanca.

It rains more here than in most other parts of the country, and the humidity is higher. The beaches south of Limón look like a South Seas fantasy, the water tending toward turquoise when the seas are calm, coconut palms arcing out over coral-protected coves. Limón is the poorest province, and you won't see many upscale shopping malls or luxurious resorts here. What you will see are ramshackle villages, wildlife-rich rainforests, and beautiful beaches.

THE CENTRAL VALLEY AND BEYOND

It's upon returning from the humid Caribbean or the dry northern Pacific coast that you really start to appreciate the charms of the Central Valley, where the great majority of both Costa Ricans and expats choose to make their home. It's not hard to see why. Drive up from Guanacaste in the dry season and you'll go from flat expanses of dry grass to a rolling panoply of every shade of green. Stands of trees alternate with deep-green patches of coffee growing up the hillside. You'll see pine trees next to palms and bright-yellow daisies at the foot of enormous stands of bamboo. Bougainvillea,

hibiscus, and roses—yes, roses—add dashes of red, and stately trees burst with fiery orange and yellow blossoms.

But the big story is green, and to see the morning light illuminate the most delicate yellow-green all the way to the deepest emerald is to know that you're in one of the most fertile areas of a fertile country, rich in volcanic soil and irrigated by rivers, streams, and the rain that comes down in brief afternoon downpours during the green season. Of course, the closer you get to San José, the faster the pace will be and the slower the traffic. Each year the roads become more congested. Choosing to live

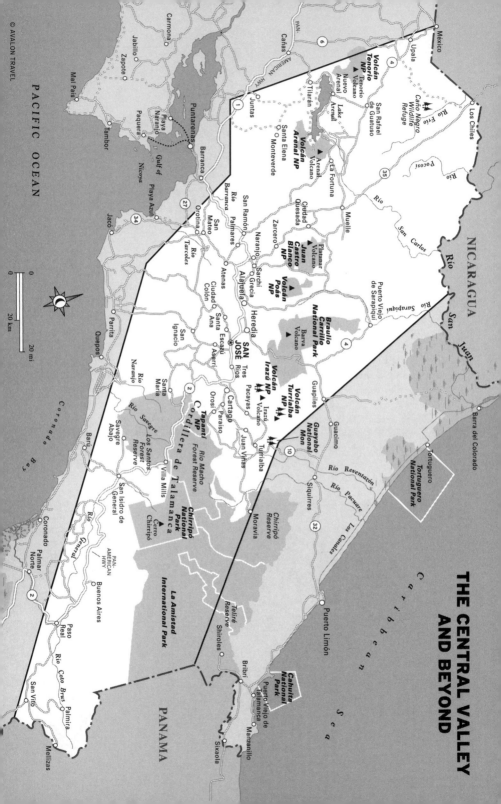

in the more populated parts of the Central Valley means you'll constantly be weighing whether the amenities and opportunities are worth the cost.

The Lay of the Land

The area's scenic beauty owes much to the dramatic juxtaposition of imposing peaks and gentle valleys. To the north the Central Valley is encircled by the soaring Cordillera Central with its chain of volcanoes, including the active cones of Poás and Irazú. The Cordillera Talamanca forms the area's southern perimeter. Measuring 80 kilometers (50 miles) east to west and 40 kilometers (25 miles) north to south, the plateau is actually two separate valleys split by the Cerros de la Carpintera, which marks the Continental Divide. The Río Virilla drains the valley to the west, and the Río Reventazón—well known in rafting circles—plummets down the eastern slopes of the Cordillera Central.

Elevations within the Central Valley range from 900 to 1,787 meters (2,953-5,863 feet), with weather at lower elevations suggesting perpetual summer. As you ascend the volcanic peaks that ring the valley, the air becomes a little cooler. Temperatures in the heart of the valley are mild year-round, averaging around 21°C (70°F). Moisture levels also weigh in at a happy medium. If you've been to a humid area, you'll find the drier air here a great relief, and if you've been in dry heat, your skin will drink greedily of the increased moisture in the air.

The most densely populated part of this area, however, is growing by leaps and bounds and becoming less and less appealing to those who appreciate peace and clean air. Called the Great Metropolitan Area (Gran Área Metropolitana or GAM), it includes the cities and suburbs of San José, Alajuela, Cartago, and Heredia.

With about 2.6 million inhabitants, it is home to approximately 60 percent of the country's people, while accounting for just a little over 4 percent of its area. It's the most developed and populated area of Costa Rica.

PRICES
San José and Environs

"Average" real estate prices in a country without a true multiple listing service are notoriously hard to come by. That said, I'll plunge into the perilous world of generalizations, starting at the high end of the market.

In white-hot spots like the San José suburb of Escazú, larger condos and single-family homes go for US$300,000-$900,000, with monthly rent very high for Costa Rica—up to US$7,000 per month for luxurious places. Escazú and nearby Santa Ana are still some of the most expensive places to live in the Central Valley, with Escazú a bit on the wane (there's not much room left) and Santa Ana on the rise. Foreigners and upper-middle-class Ticos come to these two areas for the high-rise condos, the full-service malls, the country clubs, and the good restaurants. Escazú's popularity means that the basic infrastructure of this one-time small town has been stretched almost to the breaking point. The narrow roads can hardly accommodate all the cars of the new residents.

La Sabana and Rohrmoser, neighborhoods near La Sabana Park in east San José, were hot spots 20 years ago and still have some very nice areas (former President Arias lives in this area), where spacious homes can rent for over US$3,000 per month. Parts of the area have become run-down and now rent for significantly less.

San Pedro, in western San José near the University of Costa Rica, and nearby Los Yoses still have affordable student-style housing for perhaps US$200-500 per month, with more luxurious places going for US$700-900. North of San Pedro is Sabanilla, a middle-class neighborhood where rentals go for a little less.

The middle-class areas of Zapote, San Francisco de Dos Ríos, and Curridabat offer up housing that can be as cheap as US$200 per month up to a few thousand per month for luxury condos in the better parts of Curridabat.

North of San José, the middle-class neighborhood of Tibas is affordable, with rentals going for US$300-500.

In other middle- or working-class areas (there are a lot of these), houses can cost less than US$100,000, and rent will be lower, maybe as low as US$200-300 per month.

The city of Heredia, to the north of San José, is cheaper than San José's western suburbs, with condos or small houses starting from under US$200,000 and with rents of US$300-900 per month. The city of Alajuela, closer to the airport, has similar prices.

Zona Norte and the Southern Inland Valleys

Prices outside the Central Valley will more closely resemble the lower end of San José-area prices, with the popular Arenal area a touch more expensive (but not nearly as expensive as San José suburbs like Escazú) and the southern inland cities of San Isidro and San Vito significantly lower.

Where to Live

SAN JOSÉ

It's not just the climate that draws people to the Central Valley area. Everything is here, much of it in and around the capital city of San José—jobs, government offices, the best public hospitals and private clinics, shopping malls, restaurants, and theaters. Bill White, a music lover who in the early 1990s founded an artists' colony in Ciudad Colón, said that when he arrived, he drew a circle around the National Theater in downtown San José and only looked at property within a half hour's drive of the ornate building that hosts the national symphony. San José does have a lot to offer. On any given night you can choose from a dozen plays (some in English), opera, dance performances, classical and popular music, and dozens of movie screens on which you'll find some of the latest films, often premiering just a few days after their U.S. release.

While San José isn't known for its 24-hour antics, the city has a pleasant buzz. That it's the literal center of the country adds to the draw; all roads lead to San José, and residents of outlying areas come here to find what can't be found in the hinterlands. They may come for a better selection of building supplies, a hip new pair of shoes, or just to stroll down the Avenida Central, a bustling pedestrian mall great for window-shopping and people-watching. At the far end of Avenida Central is the Central Market, a jumble of stalls and smells, where you'll find no Tommy Hilfiger (unless it's a knockoff) but plenty of fresh fruit, dried bunches of medicinal herbs, and whole pigs on hooks.

People love to complain about San José—the traffic, the crime, and all those KFC franchises—but I find it an agreeable city, if you know where to go and where to avoid. The excellent and inexpensive public transportation puts my hometown of San Francisco to shame. You can find pretty much anything you need, from showerheads to CDs, and there are lots of opportunities to soak up culture or make some of your own. English-speaking activities are plentiful—from theater clubs to self-help groups.

As for safety, you'll want to take the same kinds of precautions you would take in a similar-size U.S. city. Petty theft is common and assault is on the rise, especially at night. Awareness is the key, and the more people there are flowing around you, the sharper you'll want to be. I probably don't need to tell you that you shouldn't take your wallet out in the middle of the Central Market and count just how many colones you have left. Any sort of flash is ill advised—keep your new digital camera under wraps, and leave your grandmother's sapphire pendant in the safe-deposit box. Thieves will choose another target if you look like you know where you're going. Of course, you'll have

to be a good actor to pull this off; with the utter lack of street signs in San José, it's unlikely that you'll even know where you are.

Those expecting a historic jewel of a city will be disappointed. It's the rare building that is more than 100 years old, and San José boasts its fair share of remarkably ugly modern edifices. Still, the city grows on you. You find your own favorite attractions, from the guy selling fresh orange and carrot juice on the corner near the bus stop to the shady out-of-the-way park at the foot of the city's only all-metal (and all-yellow) building. It's a city of neighborhoods, and if you walk just 10 or 15 minutes from the jam-packed downtown, you'll hit quiet, often upscale neighborhoods in every direction.

The suburbs of the city and the outlying towns range from wealthy and Americanized to working-class and *puro Tico,* but all share a truly spectacular setting perched at the foot of, or climbing up, hills carpeted with the glossy green of coffee plants or, even higher up, towering cedar and pine. The flora here is not what newcomers expect. While there is a definite tropical undercurrent, the hills

PRIME LIVING LOCATIONS
THE CENTRAL VALLEY AND BEYOND

Plaza de la Democracia in San José

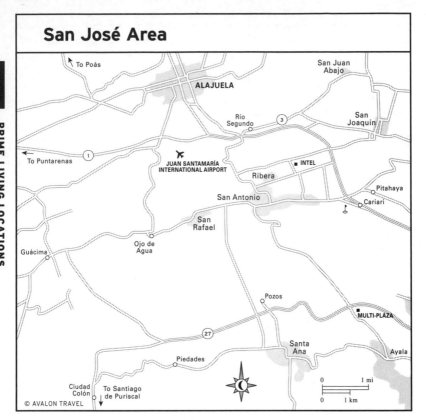

San José Area

above San José look more like summertime Switzerland than the Amazon basin.

Getting to know the Central Valley can be a challenge. Just figuring out where all of the towns are will take a few months, and exploring them could take half a year of weekend jaunts. The fact that roads are so poorly signed doesn't help matters. Luckily, getting lost can have its rewards, not least of which is discovering a tidy little town halfway up the slopes of a dormant volcano or terraced fields cascading down the mountain and nurturing everything from potatoes to ornamental plants.

For each town described in this chapter, there are literally dozens of others waiting to be discovered. The places I've focused on tend to appeal to foreign residents, and there are often good reasons for their popularity. Still, I encourage those serious about living in the area (especially if you plan to buy property) to take their time to explore the densely settled and enormously varied Central Valley.

Los Yoses, San Pedro, and Barrios California, Escalante, and Dent

East of downtown and west of the university, you'll find a handful of residential neighborhoods where the houses range from middle-class modern to gracious old estates tucked behind lovely gardens. Los Yoses has a quiet energy during the day; several government buildings are located on the neighborhood's western edge, and nearby restaurants serve lunch

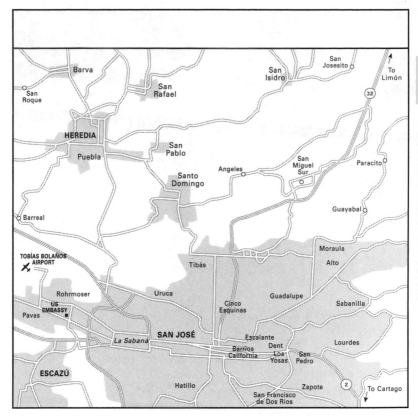

to civil servants in suits and ties. At night, the area all but shuts down.

The neighborhoods dubbed California, Escalante, and Dent, all north of the main drag, an extension of downtown's Avenida Central, are quiet and low-rise but are on the upswing in terms of restaurants and bars.

San Pedro is the liveliest neighborhood of the lot by day and especially by night. The presence of the large University of Costa Rica guarantees an abundance of bars, clubs, cheap restaurants, and funky clothing stores. When school is in session, the streets around campus bustle with activity, with small businesses catering to student needs—copy shops, pizza-by-the-slice joints, and kiosks selling pens, notebooks, and single cigarettes. At night,

people come from all over the city to hang out at the bars, restaurants, and clubs.

San Pedro was once its own town. The village church and square (just a few blocks from the university) now stand across from the Outlet Mall. Despite its name, the mall offers no cut-rate bargains but four floors of upscale clothing boutiques, music and electronics stores, multiple movie screens, and plenty of mall food.

Foreign residents who live in these areas appreciate that they are integrated into the life of the city but also have a quiet place to close the door and regroup. In Los Yoses, the North American Cultural Center organizes conferences, film series, art exhibits, and theater. Even if you don't want to enroll as a full-time student, the

pedestrian street in San José

University of Costa Rica is a great place to study Spanish or brush up on your art history.

Lomas de Yarco Norte

East of San Pedro, on the road to Cartago, Lomas de Yarco Norte is a few minutes from the Terramall shopping center. Because of the good roads, private schools, banks, and high-speed Internet available, some real estate agents say this area is the new Escazú, with prices to match.

Rohrmoser and La Sabana

West of downtown, the streets get wider, and green areas start to crop up with more regularity. Though not usually thought of in recreational terms, the large General Cemetery does provide a break from the surrounding hubbub, with marble mausoleums and special sections for *obreros* (workers) and *israelitas* (Jews). Down the street and quite a bit livelier is La Sabana, San José's largest park, which used to be the national airport and now is one of the few places in town where you can jog without having to fight traffic. You can also play basketball, volleyball, or tennis; swim in an Olympic-size pool; or take one of the free aerobics classes offered on weekends. On the park's southeast corner is the National Gymnasium; on its northwest corner is the National Stadium, recently rebuilt by a crew of Chinese laborers working day and night. (For more on Costa Rica's relationship with China, see page 29 in the *History, Government, and Economy* chapter.)

The park is a big draw for people who like to be in the city but within walking distance of a little piece of the country. Add to that many good restaurants and cafés, upscale strip malls, and proximity to downtown, and you've got a very desirable area.

The best known of the neighborhoods around La Sabana is Rohrmoser, northwest of the park and home to many upper- and upper-middle-class Tico families. It's also a favorite of expats, who perhaps feel at home where there seems to be a foreign embassy on every corner.

Reverse Culture Shock

If you stay in Costa Rica for a while and then go home for a visit or to stay, you may find that reverse culture shock can be even more jarring than culture shock. In a new culture, you expect to feel out of place, but you don't expect to feel that sense of dislocation in what used to be home.

Brenda Burnside went home to Las Vegas for a three-week visit after a year and a half of living in the Pacific coast town of Nosara. "I was miserable," she said. "People there don't know how to live. You say hi to them and they look at you like, 'What do you want?' My friends had all the best new electronic equipment, flat-screen TVs, and killer stereos—all in these dinky little apartments. They work all the time to be able to afford the stuff. I went to see a friend and she didn't even have time to talk to me—she was too busy showing off her new TV. I'd rather have nothing but have time to sit around and talk to my friends."

Gina Hyams, who returned to Oakland, California, after four years in the Mexican state of Michoacán, has some interesting things to say about going home. In her essay, "Before and After Mexico," in the book *Expat: Women's True Tales of Life Abroad*, she writes: "Perhaps we've become permanent expatriates—neither fish nor fowl, forever lost no matter our location. But the fluidity also means that we're now like mermaids and centaurs—magic creatures who always know there's another way."

Barrios Amón, Atoya, and Aranjuez

These three contiguous neighborhoods to the immediate north of downtown boast some of the oldest and most interesting buildings in the city. There's a feeling here you don't get in the rest of San José— namely, that the city has a history, and remnants of it are still visible if you take the time to look. Exploring these streets, I have seen dozens of gorgeous old wood-frame houses that cry out for loving restoration. Hand-carved wooden latticework graces roof eaves, and the wraparound front porches remind me of grand old houses in the U.S. South and Midwest. Architects and historians may cringe, but if pressed, I'd dub these charming buildings Caribbean Gothic.

These neighborhoods are uphill from the center, which gives them a feeling of being above and beyond all the downtown bustle. The area's northern perimeter is the Torres River, which is best seen from the cliff that marks the abrupt end to Barrio Aranjuez.

Zapote, Curridabat, and San Francisco de Dos Ríos

The neighborhoods to the southeast of downtown San José are a varied lot, but in general they are pleasant middle-class areas that are drawing more and more foreign residents. Those who want to be close to the action of the city center and don't want to pay the higher prices of upscale western suburbs like Escazú have quietly moved in, and it's not uncommon to see gringos (including lots of families) going about their daily business at the supermarket or running track. There's a great kid-friendly park in San Francisco (Parque Yokohama), where the kids of foreign residents swing on the swings and mix it up with the locals on the soccer field.

The Curridabat neighborhoods of Pinares and Fresa have many condos on offer, less expensive than those in Escazú.

All of these neighborhoods are beginning to take off. There's a lot of recent commercial development in the area, from Multiplaza East in Curridabat to the Terramall on the highway to Cartago.

RE/MAX real estate agent Les Núñes calls it a "lead-lag situation," explaining that "commercial development leads off, and residential follows." Though this area is now on the rise, he believes the price differences among neighborhoods will remain constant. "The way it works is the west side [Escazú, Santa Ana, etc.] levels off, the east side picks up, and then the west side will take off again."

WEST OF SAN JOSÉ
Escazú

One of the oldest settlements in the country, Escazú is also one of the most up-to-date and sophisticated. This is arguably the most prestigious place to live in Costa Rica, and residents love that they're only 15 minutes from San José (in the rare event that there's no traffic) but worlds apart in terms of atmosphere. I can't tell you how many successful lodge and hotel owners I meet all over Costa Rica who tell me that their real home is in Escazú.

The town climbs the lower slopes of the surrounding mountains, the highest of which is 2,455 meters (8,054 feet), and the air is usually a few degrees cooler than it is in San José. Tucked amid the foothills you'll find impressive individual homes, gated condominium complexes, fine hotels with manicured grounds, and even a few affordable apartments. There's a well-regarded K-12 English-language school called the Country Day School, and not one but two country clubs. Despite the fashionable shops and restaurants, parts of Escazú still have a surprisingly rural feel. Next to a high-end furniture store you might see a couple of cows grazing in front of an adobe hut.

In proper terms, Escazú is not one but three towns, each with its own church, central plaza, and prefix (San Rafael de, San Miguel de, and San Antonio de). There are about 56,000 people living in the greater Escazú area. As tends to

happen in burgeoning areas, what were once separate areas started to bleed together, and soon it was hard to tell where one stopped and the other began. Now the different towns function more as different neighborhoods, with the air growing clearer and the streets more tranquil the farther up the hill you go. San Rafael de Escazú is the lowest, close to one of the few stretches of superhighway in the country and home to most of the modern shopping malls and services. This area's busy strip offers up the chance to drop a small fortune on an imported suit or handmade tile for your kitchen, or to sample Italian, French, or Argentine cuisine, among many other international options. Although the tenor of the place is undeniably upscale, there's still room for more down-to-earth establishments such as supermarkets, health clinics, gas stations, and, of course, a McDonald's or two.

One kilometer (0.6 miles) up the road is San Miguel de Escazú, which centuries ago began life as a crossroads between indigenous villages and later, in the 1700s, became a Spanish settlement that served the area's cattle ranchers. A few remaining cobblestone streets can be found around the village square, with its lovely red-domed church painted at its base with a strip of color to ward off *brujas* (witches). Despite such precautions, Escazú, traditionally known as the witch capital of the country, hasn't lost its power to captivate and enchant. Some residents seem to soak up that ability; a local *bruja* suggests that any woman who lives long enough in Escazú becomes a witch in her own right.

Still farther up the hill is San Antonio de Escazú, the most rural of the three Escazús and home to the annual Oxcart Drivers Day festival. The slopes above San Antonio are planted in coffee bushes, until even these give way to cloud forest. Just minutes from town you can be walking along a remote trail, maybe heading for the 15-meter (49-foot) iron cross on a nearby peak, with nothing but trees and the occasional dairy cow to keep you company.

Driving around the hills above town you'll see sprawling homes that combine a dizzying array of architectural styles; a starkly modern building might sprout Greek Revival columns or a quasi-Victorian turret. Closer to Escazú's neighborhood centers, the municipality usually requires new construction to conform to a more traditional style.

There are a lot of gringos in Escazú, some in gated communities that allow them to leave for months and not worry about security, others more integrated into the community. Real estate prices are among the highest in the country.

Socially there's a lot going on in Escazú, and the number of expats here ensures that you'll have plenty of potential playmates who speak your language.

Santa Ana

Unlike Escazú, which is spread out and has many "centers," nearby Santa Ana has one heart: the 1870 medieval-looking stone church. Even on a Saturday night the church will be packed to its wooden rafters, worshippers dressed to the nines, throwing flirtatious glances between the call-and-response of six o'clock mass. It's a place to see and be seen, with young men and women dolled up as if for the disco, which is indeed where they'll probably be later in the evening.

Across the street the soccer field will be lit up, with teams of 12-year-olds playing as if the World Cup were at stake. Within a radius of a few blocks, you can find Peruvian ceviche, American steakhouse fare, or local specialties like wood-grilled chicken with fried sweet onions.

The town is famous for its ceramics, and there are at least 30 independent pottery shops in the area. An 8,000-hectare (19,800-acre) forest preserve and bird sanctuary above town ensures that Santa Ana will always be bordered by nature.

Santa Ana used to be billed as the next Escazú, with lower prices and a more traditional Tico feel. From what I can observe, though, it's not far from Escazú in terms of real estate prices, fancy restaurants, and expat presence. Santa Ana is a little lower in elevation than Escazú, so it's a few degrees warmer.

Ciudad Colón

Eight kilometers (five miles) west of Santa Ana is Ciudad Colón, which feels farther from San José than it actually is. Even the weather is different—warmer and a touch more humid. It feels more tropical.

In 2009 the long-awaited San José–Puerta Caldera highway opened, an alternate route to Pacific coast resorts like Jacó. The highway, which passes by Colón, means that people living in places in the western suburbs of San José can now reach the beach in about an hour (the trip used to take double that).

Atenas, San Mateo, and Orotina

On the older route to the Pacific coast resort of Jacó, you'll pass through some very pleasant country as the road gradually loses elevation and the foliage becomes slightly more tropical, but the weather retains a mountain freshness. The town of Atenas, 50 kilometers (31 miles) from San José, was said by *National Geographic* magazine to have the best climate in the world. It also has several gated communities and a safe, small-town atmosphere. At 800 meters (2,625 feet) in elevation, this town of 6,500 hovers between spring- and summertime temperatures and is known as an excellent orchid-growing area. Aside from weather, Atenas and nearby San Mateo (population 2,500) and Orotina (population 8,700)

Cartago's basilica

are clean and appealing towns, with lots of trees and some interesting old wooden houses. There's a sense of *there* there; the towns have a pleasing density that speaks of history and of gradual, organic growth. These aren't non-towns strung out along a highway, and in fact the road slows considerably as it meanders through narrow streets and past town squares. There are a growing number of expats here, as there are everywhere, but these towns have Costa Rican souls.

SOUTH AND EAST OF SAN JOSÉ
Cartago

Twenty kilometers (12 miles) southeast of San José by a four-lane highway lies historic Cartago, a city of about 150,000 best known for sheltering in its cathedral the stone statue of La Negrita, Costa Rica's patron saint. Only 20 centimeters (8 inches) high and supposedly found amid the rocks beneath what is now the basilica, La Negrita has pride of place in the Cathedral of Our Lady of the Angels, attracting pilgrims from all over the country each August 2. On the tourist circuit, Cartago is famous for Las Ruinas (the ruins), the remains of the *parroquia* (parish church) built in 1575 and damaged many times before its final destruction in the earthquake of 1910.

Earthquakes are not the only type of natural disaster Cartago has had to endure. The town is only a few kilometers from the steep slopes of Irazú Volcano. In 1723, the volcano erupted, destroying the city, which at the time was little more than a collection of adobe huts and a single church. Since then, Irazú has seemed content to burble and boil and periodically shower Cartago with a fine layer of volcanic ash.

Cartago is one of the oldest Spanish settlements in the Central Valley; it was the nation's capital until shortly after the 1823 civil war. Central America had just declared its independence from Spain, and the subsequent battle in the Central Valley was over whether to join with other former Spanish colonies in a federation or to declare Costa Rica its own independent republic. The cities of San

The Patron Saint of Cartago

The city of Cartago has Costa Rica's most famous church, a soaring, cupola-topped basilica to which pilgrims flock every August. All year round, the faithful bring gifts: flowers by the truckload, piles of pencils used in exams, medals in the shape of body parts, even bridal veils. The ceaseless tribute is aimed at a diminutive stone statue the pilgrims call La Negrita.

La Negrita is the "little black woman," which may sound condescending in English but conveys nothing but affection in Spanish, for this is the nickname of the beloved Virgin of the Angels, Costa Rica's patron saint, a 20-centimeter-tall (8-inch-tall) stone statue that inspires the yearly pilgrimage, with some of the faithful walking for days to demonstrate their faith.

The story of La Negrita goes back to 1635, when Cartago was more a scattering of crude huts than a city. One day a mestiza (woman of mixed blood) named Juana Pereira saw a strange light coming from between the trees on the path she took every day. Following the light to its source, she found a small black stone in the shape of the Virgin nestled in the recess of a much bigger rock. Delighted, she took the figure home, but twice La Negrita found her way back to her place of birth. Even when Juana gave the statue to the town priest for safekeeping, La Negrita returned once again to the rock from which she had come. The Virgin's attempts to escape captivity were interpreted as a desire for a basilica of her own, to be built where Juana had first found her.

And so the Basílica de Nuestra Señora de los Ángeles was constructed, and today its vaulted hardwood ceiling, stained-glass windows, and flower-painted walls host all who come to visit the shrine of La Negrita. They come steadily all year long but arrive in the hundreds of thousands for the Día de la Virgen de los Ángeles, a national holiday on August 2, when the pious make the old story new again.

The story has some unexpected twists. For instance, in recent times, late April and early May have seen spikes in the national birth rate. It seems that the pilgrimage is one of the few times "good girls" are allowed to stay out all night, and the religious revelry can turn carnal. If you walk the 22 kilometers (14 miles) from San José to Cartago the night of August 1, you'll see pilgrims with flowers in one hand and a beer in the other.

Even back in 1782, the party sometimes got out of hand. That year, a priest ordered the statue moved from the basilica to a local church called El Carmen, so that La Negrita wouldn't have to witness how her day had been taken over by drunken carousing. Partying now takes a back seat to devotion, but the tradition of moving the statue to El Carmen has endured, and from August 3 to September 7, La Negrita takes a post-party vacation in the parish church.

Now, what about those offerings – the pencils, the charms, and the wedding veils? They're fervent thank-yous for miracles performed: prayers answered, exams aced, bodies made whole again, and husbands delivered to the altar. And what becomes of those countless tokens of gratitude, too much by half to fit into a church, even one as large as the basilica?

The flowers are used to decorate the church. The nonrusting medals are put in glass cases in a side chapel, while the lower-quality ones are kept in some unspecified back room. And the bridal veils are cut up to make veils for poor girls about to undergo their first communion. Call it the recycling of miracles, short work for La Negrita.

José and Alajuela favored independence; Heredia and Cartago wanted to be part of the larger federation. Those seeking independence won the day, and Cartago lost its capital-city status to San José.

Cartago feels more traditional and reserved than the current capital. This growing city has not attracted as many foreign residents as places like Escazú and Santa Ana. But that may change, as

Cartago seems a very livable place indeed and is not yet so "hot" that property values are rising daily.

Turrialba

About 40 kilometers (25 miles) east of Cartago and 65 kilometers (40 miles) from San José lies the small but bustling town of Turrialba. Not yet a magnet for foreign residents, the town is pleasant, and the surrounding cane fields, coffee farms, and dense forest are beautiful. The drive from San José, up to Cartago, and then down to Turrialba reveals new shades and textures of green at every turn, with mist drifting down from the higher ridges. You'd never pick this town out as the place where Rawlings manufactures the baseballs used in Major League games in the United States, but it is.

Twenty kilometers (12 miles) north of Turrialba is Costa Rica's best-known archaeological site, Guayabo National Monument, where you can study the workmanship of a 3,000-year-old cobblestone street or watch water rush through an equally ancient aqueduct system that still functions today.

Walk around Turrialba and you'll see some gringos, the majority of whom are here to run the Reventazón and Paquare Rivers and one or two of whom actually live here. As San José continues to sprawl, places like Turrialba, not far from the capital but far enough to avoid its fumes and grit, will become more and more attractive for relocators.

In recent years, nearby Turrialba volcano has been very active. At one point the volcano sent ash and hot rocks 1000 feet into the air, and ash from its throat-clearings have closed down the airport in San José more than once. So far, though, Turrialba's eruptions haven't done any large-scale or lasting damage.

NORTH AND NORTHWEST OF SAN JOSÉ
Heredia

Founded in 1706 at the foot of Barva Volcano, Heredia is home to the National University, whose student body, the second-largest in Costa Rica, injects into the town a good measure of youthful energy. There are also several Spanish language schools in this city of over 200,000, and the students—mostly from Canada and the United States—add to the cosmopolitan feel of the place.

The town's tree-shaded central park is a first-rate place to people-watch and listen to free live music on the weekends. The nearby Cathedral of the Immaculate Conception was built in 1797 and has managed to withstand several earthquakes since then. Another historic building, El Fortín, is a lesson in how not to build a fortress. Alfredo González Flores, president of Costa Rica from 1914 to 1917, designed the gun slits on the circular tower so that they easily allowed bullets in but made it nearly impossible for soldiers to shoot out.

With its proximity of just 11 kilometers (6.8 miles) to San José, Heredia has attracted its share of expats, though many tend to settle in and around nearby small towns—Santa Barbara is set in the heart of coffee country, while San Joaquín de Flores is known for its upscale residences and lively Easter week processions. Santo Domingo de Heredia, a quiet, bougainvillea-draped town, is an easy 20-minute bus ride from downtown San José. A gleaming white and silver basilica presides over the soccer field and the weekly farmers market. Just outside town is Casa Zen (www.casazen.org), founded in 1975 and, as far as I know, the only Zen Buddhist community in the country. Casa Zen has ties to Zen centers in Vermont and Toronto.

Heredia is slightly higher in elevation than San José, so it's a little cooler and greener all year long; towns farther up the slopes of the volcano are even cooler.

Alajuela

The City of Mangoes, a bustling city of about 160,000, is often called a mini San José, but it's warmer than the capital in both senses of the word. The temperature is consistently higher. Shaded by enormous mango trees (hence the city's nickname), the city's Parque Central is where it all happens. Local teenagers cruise, money changers trade colones for dollars, and the town's substantial population of North American retirees comes here to trade information about available apartments, where to find a good masseuse, or the current price of a round-trip ticket home. The talk slows when professional musicians file into the park's bandstand and begin to tune up for a program of classical or popular music.

Every April 11, the Parque Central is the center of a raucous party celebrating Juan Santamaría, Alajuela's native son and Costa Rica's beloved national hero. Also known as El Erizo (The Hedgehog) for his bristly hair, Santamaría set fire to the invading enemy's barracks after a ragtag army chased them out of Costa Rica and over the Nicaraguan border. The enemy happened to be William Walker, a pintsize Nashville native drunk on Manifest Destiny. Dreaming of a Central America firmly under U.S. control, Walker and his band of mercenaries invaded Nicaragua in 1855, then turned their sights on Costa Rica. Santamaría, who died in that final battle, became a symbol of Costa Rica's capacity to oust foreign invaders. Even so, everyone—regardless of nationality or secret desire to rule the world—is welcome at the town-wide fiesta celebrating the Hedgehog's bravery.

On Saturdays, there's an excellent farmers market. During the rest of the week, there's no shortage of supermarkets and *pulperías*, the corner stores where you can find at least one of everything.

Grecia

Aside from the oddly columned structure at the turnoff to this town, Grecia feels about as Greek as a scarlet macaw. In the 1820s, shortly after Costa Rica won its independence, the towns of Grecia (Greece) and Atenas (Athens) were named to honor the Greek struggle for independence from Turkey. Grecia is a pretty little place, just 30 minutes from San José's international airport, small enough to be safe and friendly and large enough to have a critical mass of expats and some decent services. The road into town winds past coffee *fincas* (farms) and fields of sugarcane, which looks like enormous clumps of grass topped with pale yellow tassels. Every bend in the road reveals stunning views of gently sloping valleys and steep volcanic peaks.

At the center of town is, of course, the church, in this case made of an unlikely material: metal. Constructed of steel plates imported from Belgium in 1897, the church is prettier than it sounds, with stained-glass windows and an attractive tiled floor. Streets around the church and town square are wide and pleasant. Locals like to remind you that the town was voted "cleanest town in Latin America" not once but several times, and indeed Grecia does have a tidy and prosperous feel. Expats (along with everyone else in town) congregate in the palm-shaded main square or shop for fresh fruit and vegetables at the nearby Central Market. If you need a little excitement, you can always visit a must-see attraction just east of town: El Mundo de los Serpientes has a living collection of 300 snakes from around the world, including some of Costa Rica's most beautiful and deadly.

Expat Experience: Making a Living

Laurel Anderson in her studio

Laurel Anderson arrived in Costa Rica in 1977 at the age of 23. She took the bus from California, through Mexico and Central America, with no particular destination in mind. In El Salvador, a young American woman heading for Cahuita, on Costa Rica's Caribbean coast, got on the bus. Laurel thought she might as well go there, too. Laurel got off the bus in Costa Rica, and she never looked back.

At that time, Cahuita—and all of Costa Rica—had little or no tourist infrastructure. "It was mostly people coming down because they liked to do something, maybe river rafting or sport fishing. Then their friends came down. Then they all tried to figure out how to make a living, so they could stay."

In her dedication to staying in Costa Rica, over the years Laurel has made a living in so many ways it would make a high school guidance counselor's head spin. But look for the through lines, and they're there: art, organization, adaptability, and a kind of "Well, why not?" attitude. Why not make a hobby—hand-painting dresses and bags—into a cottage industry employing eight local women? That's what she did in Cahuita; the women worked from home because their husbands didn't want them to stray far from the kitchen. Why not buy land, grow trees to make into lumber, then build houses for other expats moving to Costa Rica? (This was with her husband, another American she met in Cahuita, and with whom she had two kids. Their son now builds houses with his father in Cahuita; their daughter works in Amazon's Costa Rica call center, training Spanish-speaking service representatives.) Besides these early enterprises, Laurel has also grown and exported ornamental plants, and she's traveled the country with her surfboard and fluent Spanish, repping everything from organic soymilk to greeting cards and hammocks. She's taught English and Spanish, and, in her spare time, has managed other people's companies and real estate holdings. She loves to garden and paint and read.

"I tend to have a lot of balls in the air," she admits.

These days, Laurel lives on a hilltop overlooking the Central Valley in Santa Barbara de Heredia, half an hour from the international airport but a world away in its peace and quiet. She lives in a small house, works in a large studio, and rents out houses on her property, mostly to people who come to study Spanish or earn a TESL certificate at one of two nearby schools.

She's circled back to her love of painting, this time applying it to a new canvas, so to speak: hand-painted custom floorcloths.

On a recent visit, Laurel showed me her studio, so well equipped and spacious it makes you want to dive into all those jars and tins and yoghurt containers of color and see what you might make. An enormous plywood table provides a surface so vast it would be the envy of anyone who dreams of really spreading out with their projects. The high ceiling consists of sloping sheets of corrugated metal set on raw wood beams, no doubt noisy in a rainstorm. In fact I've timed my visit to avoid the afternoon rains–during the regular downpours, Laurel tells me, you can barely hear yourself think, much less hear another person telling you their life story.

There is order in the accumulation of supplies: shelf after shelf of paint; bouquets of brushes, handles down in jars; shoeboxes filled with stamps and sponges; rolls of canvas. The table is filled with half-finished floorclothes in various sizes and patterns, which hardly make a dent in all that delicious horizontal space. Underneath is a faded medley of all the paint that's ever spilled or splattered in here, an accidental masterpiece of its own.

"Floorcloths are a very old art form," says Laurel. "U.S. colonists brought them over from Europe. In colonial times, they made them from old sails, then put them on their cabin floors. I thought it was a fabulous idea for Costa Rica; it's hard to find nice rugs here, and you can't really have a regular rug if you live at the beach or have dogs in all the time, like I do. But the floorcloths, they don't absorb the hair or sand, and you can just wash them with soap and water.

"I start with cotton canvas," she says. "I use house paint for the design, with varnish on top. I'll seal the underside of a floor cloth that will be used where there's a lot of water, like next to the shower."

Lined up against the walls are completed floor cloths, rolled and ready to be shipped. She also creates place mats and hand-painted canvas bags, which hang from hooks along one wall.

She's becoming better and better known, showcasing her work at trade shows and shipping her handiwork to clients around the world. Naysayers of Costa Rica's mail service will be surprised to learn that she ships certified through the Costa Rican mail; she says she's never had a problem.

"I never thought of myself as an artist," she says, "I just painted on things. But then I saw that some people hang my floor cloths on the wall. They also ask me to paint their furniture and murals. And people tell me that what I've been doing all along is art. With that kind of feedback, I'm starting to become more confident as an artist."

She is grateful to live in such a beautiful environment and to have the time to work on her art. She's also happy that fellow expats are so open to her work. "Expats are more likely to buy my work than Ticos. Costa Ricans are slow to embrace new ideas," says Laurel.

"Think of the people coming to Costa Rica," says Laurel. "They sell their house, they come here to live in a new culture and learn a new language. They're already adventurous. You give them a new idea, like the floorcloths, and they're like, 'Sure, why not?'"

Laurel herself continues to ask, Sure, why not?–exploring new designs, colors, and techniques, and thinking up new ways to be in a country that she landed in as a result of that very same spirit.

See Laurel's work at http://laurelsoriginals.com.

Sarchí

A few kilometers northwest of Grecia is the crafts center of Sarchí. Famous for the brightly painted oxcarts that are one of Costa Rica's most visible examples of folk art, the town is now on the tourist map, with crafts emporiums offering everything from miniature oxcarts to handmade wooden furniture. In fact, Sarchí rockers—simple but attractive chairs combining hardwood and leather—have become famous, with the added advantage of being collapsible and thus easy to transport.

The main street, which connects Sarchí Sur with Sarchí Norte, is lined with somewhat tacky tourist shops (avoid the area on weekends during high season, when tour buses clog the road). Beyond this unpromising introduction, however, the town is quite charming. Whitewashed buildings and the bridge into town are painted with the intricate geometric designs originally found on oxcarts—the colorful patterns remind me of Pennsylvania Dutch motifs found on barns in that state, but amped up a notch or two until they hit tropical exuberance. Equally festive is Sarchí Norte's church: birthday-cake pink with bright turquoise trim. Inside are vaulted hardwood ceilings and striking carvings made by local artisans. The town's setting can't be beat—it's surrounded by hills blanketed in coffee and sugarcane, and has spectacular views of higher peaks farther off.

San Ramón

About an hour west of San José on the highway to Puntarenas, San Ramón is beginning to attract a few expats but is still undiscovered by the masses. The small city (or large town) has an interesting history. In 1870 a local priest published a satire of those who couldn't find the time for church. The book's fame drew other writers, and San Ramón became known as the City of Poets as well as the City of Presidents; former heads of state José Figueres Ferrer and Rodrigo Carazo were born here.

Nowadays, the José Figueres Ferrer Cultural Center organizes weekly events, from art exhibits to readings, and the nearby San Ramón Museum offers up an interesting re-creation of a traditional *campesino* (peasant) home.

ZONA NORTE

There are several routes north over the peaks of the Cordillera Central, and all offer spectacular views and a glimpse of a Costa Rica the casual tourist rarely sees. Narrow roads rise up out of the Central Valley, winding past mountain towns and highland farms before dropping down to a fertile plain that extends all the way north to the Nicaraguan border.

Comprising the Llanura (Plain) de San Carlos and the Llanura de Guatuso, this 40,000-square-kilometer (15,400-square-mile) area has been called the breadbasket of the nation, though it'd be more accurate to call it a rice bowl. Ticos eat rice with every meal, including breakfast, and most of the rice consumed in Costa Rica is grown here in the Zona Norte (Northern Zone). Three great rivers and their tributaries irrigate the region, flooding during heavy rains and creating the swampy conditions ideal for rice cultivation.

I've heard the area described as a tropical Tuscany and as a steamier Oregon. Boulder-strewn streams alternate with lush farmland. You pass fields of knee-high pineapple plants, a single fruit at the center of each burst of bladelike leaves, and papayas growing on small trees, all the fruit hanging from the central stalk. Bean fields give way to paddy fields and banana groves.

Rising up out of this lush plain like a whale breaching the ocean's surface, Arenal Volcano is one of the most dramatic sights in the country—if you can see it, that is. Arenal is so often shrouded in clouds that some tourists wonder if the steep-sloped gem really exists or is just a clever figment of a tour agency's imagination. (One local guide reports that a tourist asked if they turned on the volcano at night.)

Whether or not you see it, you can always hear the volcano, grumbling deep in its fiery throat and just generally making sure you never forget that although it slept through the colonial times and most of the modern era, when it woke in 1968 its eruptions wiped out two towns. Not quite as furious now, it still coughs up smoke and truck-size cinders, and on a clear night you might see red-hot rocks bouncing down the mountain. There's nothing like soaking in the hot springs at the foot of the volcano, a light cool rain pocking the water, secure in the knowledge that if Arenal blows again like it did in '68, you'll have about nine minutes to get out of the danger zone.

Around Arenal are two seasons: wet and really wet. Theoretically, there's supposed to be less rain February-April, but locals rarely go out without a rain hat or umbrella. During the really wet season,

they don't go out without heavy-duty slickers or ponchos. When it rains here, it pours, and it's part of local hospitality to offer you dry clothes if you arrive soaked.

La Fortuna

A town built in the shadow of Arenal Volcano, La Fortuna has become something of a tourist hub. More than a dozen tour agencies line the main street, as do souvenir shops, whose most appealing wares come from Guatemala, Panama, and Indonesia (Costa Rica isn't known for its crafts). At the center of this town is not the usual soccer field (that's down the street, near the high school) but a plaza dominated by a basketball court, the backboards neon-orange advertisements for a rent-a-car company. Taxis line up along one side of the plaza; local buses stop along another. The inevitable Catholic Church is unremarkable save for the view of the volcano as you look up from the main steps: The white cross on the church's roof is like a tattoo on Arenal's huge green shoulder.

Visitors on their way to Caño Negro Wildlife Preserve, windsurfers heading for Lake Arenal, or those who come to catch a glimpse of the volcano all pass through

La Fortuna

Expat Experience: The Fruits of Costa Rica

Steve Duplantier, farmer, writer, idea-spinner, and accomplished cook, takes a break from dinner prep to help his wife take a sip of her Old Fashioned. The drink is made with artisanal small-batch bourbon his U.S.-based kids brought down on their last visit to what the family had come to call Rancho Relaxo, a 1-hectare (2.5-acre) spread at about 1,219 meters (4,000 feet) in Costa Rica's Central Valley, above the town of San Ramón.

Steve Duplantier spreads freshly roasted coffee to allow it to cool.

Steve's wife, Kathleen, needs help wrapping her fingers around the glass and then bringing it to her lips. She's in a wheelchair with late-stage MS. Still, she relishes her cocktail, beaming a smile that lights up the room.

You can't get Kentucky bourbon like this in Costa Rica, much less in the roadside liquor store near the Duplantier's house. But almost everything else Steve will put on the table tonight is not only locally produced (from their own land, in most cases), but also carries the story of the Duplantier's passionate and hands-on engagement with their adopted land.

Steve puts me to work pitting the parboiled chayote he'll make into a casserole with baked ham and prawns in a creole sofrito. They've grown the chayote here on their property, but Steve and Kathleen were already familiar with the mild squash from living in Louisiana, where it's called mirliton, or vegetable pear. The baked ham in this casserole wasn't raised on the premises, but a few months ago it might have been; Steve bought and raised a pig he named Rosie. Kathleen's grandfather raised hogs in Louisiana and that inspired him to try, but ultimately he decided that hog farming wasn't sustainable.

"We've tried all sorts of things," says Steve, running through the attempts on their farm to grow taro commercially (he had a good crop, but the size wasn't uniform and the buyer turned up his nose), raise pigs (the sensitive and emotional Rosie got sad and self-aborted her piglets), and even breed koi and fantailed goldfish. "I sold hundreds of dollars' worth," he says, "but the pond doesn't hold water well enough, and it cost me $50 a month to fill it with spring water. "The idea of Rancho Relaxo is that we make the place sustainable, but sustainable means no work or as little as possible."

The name may be more aspirational than accurate. Steve still has dozens of irons in the fire and is animated by a seemingly endless supply of ideas, not to mention the muscle-toning follow-through. He and his neighbor Juan have planted taro, rice, maize, beans, huge squashes, ginger, turmeric, bananas, and plantain, to name a few local crops. He roasts his own San Ramón coffee using a popcorn popper, gas mask strapped to his face, and windows opened wide to let out clouds of white, oily smoke from the roasting. "Here's where we get to see how a dream is coming along, ten years after we built the house," says Steve. "Warranties run out before imagination does, like the fan on our expensive Spanish stove hood. I can't get the parts to fix it."

He's worked hard to reforest the farm hectare that had been cleared for agriculture. "The re-foresting principle is if you think you have enough plants, you don't. Just keep planting. That's how it works in nature." Steve just keeps planting, and the soil and weather tell him what will thrive. A surprise has been that he's been able to grow a lot of plants that forestry experts insisted would not grow at 1,219 meters (4,000 feet) at the edge of the cloud forest.

One example is the balsa tree. "It's a coastal, sea-level tree," says Steve. "But I wanted to see if it would grow here. Its big leaves are great for shade, and I needed the shade to starve out this really noxious invasive exotic that they call pasto, or pasturage. It's African Elephant Grass *(Pennisetum purpureum)*, it's beautiful and gets 3.6 meters (12 feet) tall, but it's aggressive and crowds out everything else. But it doesn't like shade, so shade trees are a no-work Rancho Relaxo way of dealing with it." The balsa trees have thrived, and the pasto is on the wane.

"As global warming sends temperatures rising up into the mountains," says Steve, "people who've lived here all their lives say, 'Oh, I've never seen anything like this before.' Maybe it's an unfamiliar bird or insect or a plant that hasn't grown here before. It's more common these days to see surprises with the world weather patterns changing."

The Duplantiers come from Louisiana, and they know what changing weather patterns can do, though since they've arrived in Costa Rica in 2004, they missed Hurricane Katrina (August 2005), the costliest natural disaster in the history of the United States.

They dodged that swirling nightmare, and they made good on a long-standing dream. "We sold our house in Abita Springs, Louisiana, for US$200,000," says Stephen. "With that money we bought the land here from a local farmer, built the house, and were well-staked for 18 months." Prior to their move, Steve made documentary films about Cajun food and music and taught at Southwestern Louisiana University. Kathleen taught grade school, taking early retirement when she contracted Multiple Sclerosis (MS). They built a spacious Mediterranean-style house with a view of the valley and nearby mountains. The wide doorways and open atrium design allows easy access for Kathleen in her wheelchair. On a prior visit a few years ago, Kathleen was still very sharp mentally, and she told me great stories about her teaching days when she got into trouble with the school board for her creative style of teaching. Her innovations and grant writing led to her becoming a Christa McAuliffe Educator with the National Foundation for the Improvement of Education. She traveled widely and inspired teachers across the United States.

Nowadays, Kathleen's memory and physical health are in decline. Steve has help from a local young woman who comes 40 hours a week to care for Kathleen. Steve says she is a godsend. He pays her about $US5 an hour, a good wage for a nonprofessional in rural Costa Rica. They also count on support and friendship from Tico friends and local expats.

But back to dinner. We're getting close now, and the house has filled with delicious aromas, caramelized vegetables, slowly roasting pork loin, and fresh-baked bread. When we sit down to the meal, each bite is a revelation.

On the table is the herbed pork roast, falling-off-the bone delicious. But it's the sides that steal the show: garlic cheese grits soufflé, the grits hand-ground from maize grown a few hundred feet from where we sit; buttered African yams with sugar cane syrup; baked spiny chayote casserole with smoked ham and prawns; and fresh bread—slowly fermented for 24 hours—baked in a clay Dutch oven. The yams, called ñame locally, and the chayote were grown here, too.

We've switched to wine now, a dry red from Chile, and we raise our glasses.

"To the cook!"

"To not working when you don't want to."

"To having a dream and mostly making it happen."

"To Rosie!"

We dig in.

and often stay in Fortuna. To accommodate the influx, everybody and their dog seems to be building small hotels or tourist *cabinas,* some of which are little more than huts in someone's backyard. The place seems quite prosperous given that three decades ago it was hardly a bump in the road. Real estate is still reasonable (especially when compared to other parts of the country), but Fortuna is changing so rapidly that it's hard to predict how long that will last.

Most, but not all, business opportunities revolve around the tourist trade. Foreign residents run a variety of enterprises, including an adventure-tour agency, an Internet café, a massage parlor, various restaurants and hotels, and at least one art gallery.

There are some very pretty places to live just outside town, especially near the river on the road to La Catarata, the local waterfall.

Nuevo Arenal

Although it's often called simply Arenal, the *nuevo* (new) in this town's official name reminds us that the old town is at the bottom of lovely and pristine Lake Arenal, a 32-kilometer (20-mile) reservoir created in 1973 when the Costa Rican Institute of Electricity (ICE) built a dam at the eastern end of the valley. ICE also erected wind turbines along the new lake's southwestern shore, taking advantage of the stiff 30-80 kilometer-per-hour (20-50 mph) winds that blow almost constantly and make Lake Arenal one of the world's best windsurfing spots.

Thankfully, Nuevo Arenal is more protected and is a pleasant, prosperous-looking town built on the lake's upslope shore. Perhaps because it was a planned community, it looks more spacious and less haphazard than most Tico towns, though some newer construction seems

to be slumping along in usual Costa Rican fashion.

One guidebook says this town of a few thousand inhabitants has "nothing of tourist interest," but what draws tourists is not always what draws new residents. Though residents hope the area will never be as popular (or as expensive) as some of the Pacific coast beaches, it is nevertheless experiencing its own boom, with real estate prices rising and more people arriving all the time. Views of the lake from town are stunning, and the weather is temperate. Lakefront property is not subject to the same restrictions as beachfront property; if you find your Eden on Arenal's shores, you can own it outright rather than having to lease it from the state. Much of the land around town has quietly been changing hands over the past decade or two—from Tico to German, Swiss, Italian, U.S., Canadian, and other nationalities.

Tilarán

Although it's only a few dozen kilometers from Nuevo Arenal to Tilarán, the unpredictable state of the highway means the trip could take anywhere from 30 minutes to well over an hour. Sometimes you'll fly along on what appears to be well-maintained blacktop, but don't be fooled—around the next bend may be a lacework of potholes or a mudslide blocking the way. Take your time and enjoy the view. The road skirts the north end of Lake Arenal and is the site of an increasing number of hotels, lodges, and private homes. Five kilometers (three miles) after the road heads west, away from the lake, it arrives in Tilarán, a pretty highland town with a population of around 25,000, including a number of expats. At 550 meters (1,800 feet) above sea level, Tilarán is high enough to have pine trees as well as palms in the town square, and the temperate climate, springlike and drier than Arenal, is a big draw.

Tilarán sits atop a hill with the land sloping away to the west, down to the Guanacaste flats, and climbing a little more to the east, up to gorgeous Lake Arenal. The streets are wide and immaculate, and the soaring church tower is flanked by two tall monkey puzzle trees. Last time I was in town, traffic slowed to let an iguana cross the street from the churchyard to the main plaza. In the shadow of the church is the town's vocational center, complete with horse and cattle stalls—ranching is one of the area's main sources of income and employment. From the main street, you can see Arenal Volcano in the distance, looking too small to do the damage it did during its last big eruption in 1968.

The town feels to me like a Tico version of a Norman Rockwell painting. On weekends you'll see people working in their neat gardens or washing their cars out in front of well-maintained homes. Kids playing hopscotch on the sidewalk smile as you walk by; the older folk sit in rocking chairs on bougainvillea-draped tiled front porches.

There's an alternate route from San José to Tilarán that spares you the slow and winding Lake Arenal road. From San José you drive toward the Pacific coast, and then go north for an hour or so on the much-improved Pan-American Highway. At Cañas you bear east on Highway 142, which winds through very pleasant rolling hills reminiscent of the Sierra Nevada foothills in Northern California except for the big volcanic boulders strewn among the grazing cattle. Golden grasses wave in the wind, stately trees spread their shade, and creeks run in the clefts of the hills.

Getting to Tilarán is even easier from the international airport in Liberia; it's about an hour on Highway 142 from that airport to Tilarán. From Tilarán to the northern Nicoya beaches (like Playa Hermosa, Playas del Coco, or Tamarindo) takes less than two hours.

Monteverde

In 1951 a small group of Quakers left Fairhope, Alabama, to settle on 1,200 fertile hectares (3,000 acres) high in Costa Rica's Cordillera de Tilarán. Of the fewer than 50 emigrants, 5 had just been released from prison for refusing to register for the draft. The judge had told them that they should obey the law of the land or leave the country, and after their release, the latter is exactly what they did. They chose Costa Rica because it had recently abolished its army and had done away with the death penalty years earlier. Besides draft resisters, the group also included farmers, teachers, and a retired rural mail carrier.

It's hard to imagine that in the 1950s there was still an opportunity to be a pioneer, but at that time many parts of Costa Rica were still inaccessible or very sparsely settled (some parts still are today). The Quakers needed horses and oxcarts to convey their belongings to their new home; the roads were so bad that not even Jeeps could make the journey.

The land they purchased was at 1,400 meters (4,600 feet) elevation and straddled both the Guacimal River and the Continental Divide. Plant life was riotous and varied, a mix of tropical, subtropical, and, with the mist drifting in from the Atlantic side of the mountain, cloud forest as well. Wilford Guindon, one of the original settlers, spoke of the land's "drippy tropical tangle." That tangle supported (and still supports) a great variety of wildlife. The more than 400 species of birds include 30 species of hummingbirds and the resplendent quetzal, a little-seen bird that draws naturalists to Monteverde.

Upon arrival, the settlers cleared land for crops and dairy cows, built houses and barns and roads, and founded a creamery that nowadays produces some of the best cheese in the country. Half a century after their arrival, the area is also one of the best-known tourist destinations in Costa Rica, in large part because of the private Monteverde Cloud Forest Reserve, one of the best wildlife reserves in the New World tropics.

Monteverde and nearby Santa Elena are still influenced by Los Cuaqueros (the Quakers), but the settlers have intermarried with local Costa Rican families, and now the two communities have formed a hybrid, with many a bilingual household and customs that include traditional Tico fiestas, Quaker meetings, and the weekly Scrabble games instituted by some of the original settlers.

Over the years, many non-Quaker expats have joined the community, and modern-day Monteverde is an appealing mix of scientists, artists, retired folk, and dairy farmers. Wendy Rockwell, granddaughter of one of the original settlers, was born in Monteverde but went back to the United States to go to high school and college. She brought her California-born husband back to her birthplace, where they now run Chunches (a Costa Rican word for "stuff"), a kind of enlightened minimart, launderette, and bookstore in the heart of Santa Elena. At Chunches you'll find everything from books on midwifery to a decent cappuccino, which you can sip as you wait for your clothes to dry.

Speaking of dry, Monteverde isn't. Like the area around Arenal, Monteverde (which means Green Mountain) is perpetually green. How does it stay so green? Rain, more rain, and then a little more rain. Locals learn not to wait for the skies to clear before getting on with their business. A little rain never hurt anyone, and a lot of rain—well, you'll probably live through that too. If you like perpetually clear skies and dry heat, by all means

visit Monteverde but don't plan to stick around.

It seems to me that settling here would appeal to a very special type of person— someone who is moved by the unusual history of the place and willing to participate in its multifaceted present. Residents here are aware and involved, especially in regard to environmental issues. There are two well-regarded bilingual private schools. Echoing Quaker practice, community decisions are made by consensus. One expat who lives elsewhere in Costa Rica called it a mini Berkeley, after the city in California known for its progressive politics. But you won't find half as many butterflies in Berkeley, nor will you be able to walk through old-growth forest, marveling at how one tree can support so much life, from sinuous vines to blossoming bromeliads. Monteverde is like that tree: A surprising variety of species have found a home here.

SOUTHERN INLAND VALLEYS
San Isidro de El General

Besides being the only stretch of the Pan-American Highway not called Highway 1, Highway 2 south of San José will put even the most confident driver to the test. One hundred kilometers (62 miles) from the capital, the road reaches the 3,500-meter (11,483-foot) peak at Cerro de la Muerte (Hill of Death), and then plunges dizzyingly down. Landslides often block the way, potholes proliferate with each heavy rain, and dense fog adds spice to the brew. Big trucks and diesel-spewing buses often hold up long lines of cars, with drivers waiting their turn to hazard passing on the winding road. But it's a stunning drive, especially when the mist clears to reveal jaw-dropping views.

What you'll see below, if the weather cooperates, is the Valle de El General, a 100-kilometer-long (62-mile-long) depression between the Talamanca range and the Fila Costeña. At about 700 meters (2,300 feet) in elevation, the valley is balmier than the Central Valley but not as hot as either coast. At the north end lies San Isidro de El General, the regional capital and a natural stopping-off point for those looking to hike up nearby Cerro Chirripó, at 3,819 meters (12,530 feet) the highest peak in Central America south of Guatemala; raft the Ríos Chirripó and General; or continue on to Dominical and other Pacific beaches. It's also a bustling agricultural market town of around 45,000 people, the center of a fertile zone where pineapples are the major crop.

After the drama of the journey, the town itself may underwhelm, though it's a pleasant enough place. Laid out in a grid, the town is centered on the plaza at Calle Central and Avenida 0, with a concrete church at one end and an astonishing number of taxis lined up on three sides of the square. San Isidro de El General is a young town—founded in 1897, but built mostly after World War II—and there's a palpable sense of commerce rather than history here. The town is growing fast and wide, spreading out into the valley around it.

The non-Ticos you'll see around town—those who aren't on their way to climb a mountain, run a river, or surf the beach break at Dominical—most likely don't live in the town proper but have made their stand near the beach or in the hills around San Isidro. They come to town to do their shopping, wait in line at the bank, or make use of the hospital, the biggest one for miles. Expats who live in or near the beach town of Dominical, for instance, regularly make the 40-minute drive up Highway 243 for San Isidro's better variety and lower prices, whether they're stocking up on food or shopping for building materials.

Guidebooks often describe San Isidro (also called Pérez Zeledón, after the name of the district) as without interest or charm, but those who come here often find themselves developing an affection for this very Tico town. There's an excellent *polideportivo* (sports complex) at the edge of town, with a gym, a running track, and lush grounds for hiking or picnicking. And there's a good variety of restaurants, bars, and cafés. You'll almost certainly run into other expats—from North America, Europe, and South

near Cerro Chirripó

America—taking a break from their errand-running.

Although the coast is a definite expat magnet, there are those who have settled along the waterfall-rich stretch of road (Highway 243) from Dominical to San Isidro in little mist-shrouded towns like Platanillo and Tinamastes. Some settle in the hills around San Isidro itself, like Ed Bernhardt, founder of the New Dawn Center (www.thenewdawncenter.info), an organic farm and education center 15 kilometers (9 miles) northwest of San Isidro. In the 1980s, Ed left the United States and settled here, choosing the area because it was far from what he saw as the Los Angelization of Costa Rica's Central Valley. The land was cheap, the people friendly, and, as a child of the turbulent 1960s in the United States, Ed wanted to settle in a country dedicated to peace. "The Ticos don't have the scars we carry," says Ed, "growing up with war."

Ed married a Tica, and the couple's two sons, now adults, were born on the farm. "They were like nymphs, running around naked. Then they got socialized, and now they're Ticos." One of his sons attended "the first environmental high school in Costa Rica," founded by former neighbor Alexander Skutch (who died in 2004 at age 99), coauthor of the classic *Birds of Costa Rica*. Ed himself contributed a weekly gardening column to the *Tico Times* and is the author of the highly detailed and useful *Costa Rican Organic Home Gardening Guide*.

San Vito

Heading south from San Isidro, Highway 2 leaves the Valle de El General and enters the Valle de Coto Brus. This is coffee country, with glossy-leaved bushes marching up steep mountains and blanketing gentle slopes. Views of the valley below are spectacular.

Until the 1950s the area was all but inaccessible, and indigenous peoples (the Guaymi and Boruca, among other groups) made up more than half of the area's population. The Pan-American Highway finally cut through to nearby Buenos Aires in 1961, and by then nonindigenous Costa Ricans had begun to outnumber the original inhabitants.

Non-Ticos also had a hand in changing the face of the area. In 1949 an Italian named Vito Sansonetti visited the remote valley and was so drawn to the fertile and heavily forested frontier that he set in motion what was essentially an Italian colonization of the area. Scores of war-stricken families, most from the south of Italy, saw in the plan the opportunity for a fresh start. The Costa Rican government helped to finance a proposal in which 250 families, 20 percent of them Ticos, would settle in what became San Vito. The plan became reality in the early 1950s, and in San Vito today, though most of the Italian settlers have married into Tico families or returned to Italy, there are still traces of their influence, from blue and green eyes to the excellent pasta at places like Liliana's Restaurant, just uphill from the tiny central park.

Early townspeople made good use of the area's temperate climate, planting the bushes that would make the valley the country's largest coffee-producing region.

One of the town's draws is its climate—warm days and nights cool enough for a real blanket. Stands of pine alternate with tall tropical hardwoods draped with vines and orchids. The abundance of budget hotels in town might lead you to believe that this is a tourist center, but don't be fooled—these rooms fill up with Ticos, most of them traveling on business. Besides the Italian colony, other foreign residents have also made their way here.

Life is significantly easier for these newcomers than it was for people like

Dance of the Little Devils

Every year, the Boruca people in south-central Costa Rica enact a centuries-old ritual representing the clash between their indigenous ancestors and the invading Spaniards.

The *diablitos* (little devils) are dressed in elaborate hand-carved and painted balsa wood masks that often have extensions of jute and banana leaves that cover the reveler's body. The devils do mock battle with the *toro* (bull), which represents the invading conquistadors.

The festival begins the night of December 30, with village church bells ringing out the old year. Drummers and flautists accompany the dancers, and the action heats up as participants and onlookers imbibe more and more *chicha* (fermented corn liquor).

The days-long dance traces the evolving interaction between the bull and the *diablitos*. First the *diablitos* taunt the bull, but the bull gains ground and eventually "kills" the little devils. But the devils rise from the dead and throw the bull (represented by his costume) into a roaring fire. The fiesta culminates as the devils leap across the flames in celebration of their enemy's demise.

This is one of the rare examples of living indigenous heritage in Costa Rica, though visitors to the festival give mixed reports: some say it was the highlight of their trip; others feel the community is not particularly welcoming. If you go, be respectful, and ask before you take photos.

The small town where this all happens is called Rey Curre, near a town called Boruca. It's on the Inter-American Highway about 20 kilometers (12 miles) south of Buenos Aires and about 90 kilometers (55 miles) south of San Isidro de El General.

Darryl Cole-Christensen, who came with his family from the United States in the 1950s to carve a farm and a life out of what was nearly impenetrable rainforest. In his book *A Place in the Rain Forest: Settling the Costa Rican Frontier,* he tells of how the roads, when they existed, were too much for Jeeps and, during the rainiest parts of the year, impassable even to horses. He also takes a thoughtful look at the frontier mentality that allowed settlers to "tame" the land but which resulted in the destruction of vast tracts of tropical forest.

"The frontier was generally seen at this time in two ways," writes

Cole-Christensen. "There was the land, and there was the forest. On the land, homes could be raised, communities would rise," and crops could be planted. The forest, on the other hand, "was the great obstacle and antagonist to overcome." Settlers were hardworking and resourceful folk. They saw a fertile land and believed the abundance would shine forth even after they'd cut down the forest and planted crops. What they eventually realized, explains Cole-Christensen, is that the fertility of the rainforest lies in its canopy rather than in the soil. But the farmers prevailed, using their newfound knowledge to raise crops and a community on the land. Cole-Christensen still lives in the area, and his farm, Finca Loma Linda, has been given over to research of tropical sustainable farming methods.

The rich flora of the area also drew Robert and Catherine Wilson, who first came in 1959 and shortly thereafter bought a ridge-top farm that had been denuded by years of cattle grazing. The couple had run a tropical plant nursery in Florida, and they wanted to see what marvels they might be able to raise and sell in the lush environment just above San Vito. When they realized that their location was too remote to be the base for a successful tropical plant business, they allied themselves with the Organization for Tropical Studies (OTS), a worldwide consortium of about 60 universities and research stations, six of them in Costa Rica. The Wilson Botanical Garden was born. Now part of the Las Cruces Biological Station, today the garden welcomes mostly students and scientists, though bird-watching and plant-loving tourists have begun to discover this 280-hectare (700-acre) gem, which boasts 5,100 species of plants, 330 species of birds, and dozens of mammal species, including 37 kinds of bats.

Catherine Wilson died in 1984, and Robert in 1989. The Wilsons loved their adopted land so passionately that they wanted to be buried here on the reserve itself. Friends who tried to honor their wishes ran into problems, however. By Costa Rican law, bodies can only be buried in a cemetery. After much bureaucratic wrangling, a solution was found: A tiny piece of the reserve was declared a cemetery. "A very selective cemetery," says resident biologist Rodolfo Quiros. "Just two people are buried there"—the two expats who dedicated more than half their lives to turning a cattle pasture into a remarkable garden and reserve.

GUANACASTE AND THE NICOYA PENINSULA

In its early years, Guanacaste was independent from the rest of Costa Rica, and to this day the area retains its own flavor distinct from the rest of the country. First its own province, then a part of Nicaragua, Guanacaste didn't officially became part of Costa Rica until 1858. Home of the *sabanero* (cowboy), this area is the country's Wild West—where a maverick spirit combines with the interdependence necessary in a frontier society—and also its Gold Coast, with the lion's share of the nation's beach resort infrastructure.

Local residents consider themselves Guanacastecos first and Ticos second. In fact, the Guanacasteco heritage is so strong that it has seeped into the national character, with the spreading guanacaste tree being the Costa Rican national tree and the local *punto guanacasteco* celebrated as the national dance.

Even the weather here is at odds with the rest of the country, much to a visitor's delight. They say the sun shines brighter here, and it most definitely shines longer. From mid-November through April, the area receives almost no rain, a boon to those from northern climes used to seemingly endless rain, sleet, and snow during the North American winter

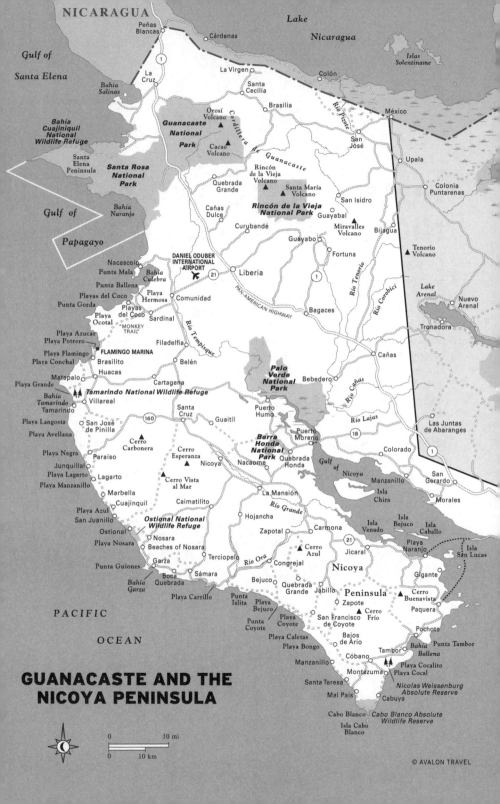

(which is Costa Rica's summer, or dry season). Newcomers can't believe their luck, but even so, by May everyone is ready for the rain that transforms the yellow-and-brown landscape back into a riot of green.

The Lay of the Land

The second-largest province at about 10,000 square kilometers (3,900 square miles), Guanacaste has the fewest inhabitants (around 360,000) of all seven provinces. The heart of Guanacaste is a sparsely populated plain that extends northward to Nicaragua. To the east rise two mountain ranges, the Cordillera de Guanacaste and the Cordillera de Tilarán, and to the north loom several volcanoes, many of which are protected in national parks. The largest towns are small by North American standards: Liberia, the provincial capital and the largest town in the area, has all of 57,000 residents. Every time I visit, there seems to be a new mall or fast-food joint, though it's still the kind of place where you can take your horse through the McDonald's drive-through.

The Liberia airport began to receive commercial flights in 2002, and more and more flights are added each year. This development is transforming not only Liberia (some locals predict it will be the next San José), but the nearby Guanacaste beaches as well, some of which, like Playas del Coco, are only 30-40 minutes from Liberia by car. Another change in accessibility came in 2003 with the long-awaited completion of the Taiwan Friendship Bridge across the Tempisque River, which separates the 130-kilometer-long (81-mile-long) Nicoya Peninsula from the mainland. Previously there was a slow ferry that could carry only 40 cars at a time, and waits were up to two hours. Now you can whiz across the bridge, cutting hours off the trip from San José to mid-peninsula beach towns such as Nosara and Sámara.

On the Nicoya Peninsula, the most bustling towns are inland, strung out along Highway 21, which runs from Liberia through Filadelfia, Santa Cruz, and Nicoya, Costa Rica's oldest colonial city and the place beach dwellers go to do their shopping if they're not up for the trip to the capital. From the inland cities, a web of roads—some paved, most not—extends to remote beaches and coastal towns so laid-back that each day seems to last a week. These are the kinds of places where the local grocery store lets everyone run a tab, and where you run into the same people seven times a day.

Most expat newcomers to Guanacaste choose to live on or near the beach, where ocean breezes alleviate the dry-season heat. The Nicoya Peninsula—most of which lies within the province of Guanacaste—is where you'll find most of the coveted beachfront property, with more ground cleared every day for new development. Many hotels, restaurants, and real estate agencies are owned by foreigners, among them Germans, Americans, Canadians, Italians, Swiss, and French. There are also growing numbers of immigrants from other Latin American countries, such as Argentina, Colombia, Peru, and Nicaragua, drawn to Costa Rica's peaceful and stable environment and looking to escape their home country's economic, political, or military strife. "It used to be," a Peruvian told me about his home of Lima, the capital city, "they'd kill you on your way to work. Now they kill you on your way to *look* for work. Here it's

Palo Verde: Storks, Spoonbills, and Macaws

Centered on the Tempisque River in lowland Guanacaste, the 18,600-hectare (46,000-acre) Palo Verde National Park is known for the density and variety of its birdlife, including the roseate spoonbill, the white ibis, and the endangered jabiru stork. Additionally, this is one of the few places in Costa Rica outside the Osa Peninsula where you're likely to see scarlet macaws.

Off the main tourist track and an hour from any town on unpaved roads, the park contains 15 different topographical zones, from evergreen forests to mangrove swamps. The best time for bird-watching is January-March, when you'll be able to see most of the area's hundreds of migrating and resident species. Dry season is also a good time to spot the park's mammalian life: monkeys, agoutis, peccaries, armadillos, jaguarundis, coatis, and deer.

Nearby hotels and tour companies can arrange day trips here; the intrepid can also camp or stay in the rustic Organization of Tropical Studies field station, where you'll eat family-style with researchers and other nature-loving visitors.

The park is located one hour southwest of Bagaces on an unpaved 28-kilometer (17-mile) road that demands that you take it slow. Once you arrive at Bagaces, go west on the unpaved road opposite the gas station. At several forks in the road, follow signs to Refugio de Fauna Silvestre, which is the more heavily used road.

tranquilo, and you can find a job without much problem."

Every year, a local tells me, the number of foreigners who come to live (rather than just visit) increases. It takes some of them years to build their houses—they go back to the States to work, then come down and build another room. But there are also those with more resources and more time who build fantasy houses overlooking the Pacific or who invest in already-built homes or condos, many in gated communities with golf courses, stables, and their own supply of water and electricity. Some of the country's biggest developments are located in northern Guanacaste, like the Club Med-style Playa Melía Conchal (just north of Tamarindo). In 2003, a large and luxurious resort complex opened along the Gulf of Papagayo, anchored by a Four Seasons hotel and offering up lots and pricey housing options for those who want to own a piece of that coast. Many of the more recent developments stalled out, half built, due to the worldwide economic downturn that hit this country in 2008.

The recovery has been slow. Some have resumed construction; others still languish, often nothing more than an impressive gate and a series of scrubby lots.

It's an odd combination of rapid development and underdevelopment, with rutted dirt roads leading to million-dollar spreads. Infrastructure can be a problem, with overextended municipalities unable to fix the roads or improve electrical, water, and waste-removal systems. Often developers or homeowners shoulder what in other countries would be the state's burden, paying for new roads, stringing electrical wires, and arranging for secure water supplies and waste removal. During the dry season, water can become a real problem, especially with elaborately landscaped grounds and sprawling golf courses sucking up so much of the precious fluid.

In terms of prices, real estate agents and contractors say that building costs here are higher because so much of the material must be trucked in, often via some truly atrocious roads. In Playa Negra, south of Tamarindo, I watched as a truck sent to repair some enormous potholes (which the rains had turned into muddy lagoons) became stuck in one of the very holes it had been deployed to fix. A tractor had to come and pull it out.

From the Gulf of Papagayo down to funky Montezuma at the southern tip of the peninsula, Guanacaste and the Nicoya Peninsula feature stunning beaches and beach towns that range from party central to places so remote they verge on inaccessible.

PRICES

Guanacaste's Gold Coast, which runs from above Playa Potrero to just south of Tamarindo, is one of the priciest areas in the country. New construction is mostly aimed at foreigners with comfortable incomes; condos and new homes start at US$200,000 and climb to over US$1 million. Aside from the dizzying prices at places like the Four Seasons resort complex north of Coco, Tamarindo has the dubious distinction of being the highest-priced town on this high-priced stretch of coast.

Farther south, on stretches of coast that are harder to get to and so remain sparsely settled, you can still find better prices for lots and houses. If you're willing to live inland, you can find much better deals.

How much better? It depends on luck, timing, and (most of all) persistence. As I say elsewhere, there's no substitute for on-the-ground research. The more you know, the better deal you'll get.

MEDICAL CARE

The respected CIMA Hospital, located in the San José suburb of Escazú, opened a small satellite branch in Guanacaste. Near the Do-It Center (kind of like a Home Depot), on the road from Liberia to the beach towns of Playas del Coco and Tamarindo, CIMA Guanacaste will be the area's first full-service private hospital. Though not as full-service as the bigger hospitals of its kind in and near San José.

Where to Live

PLAYAS DEL COCO TO TAMARINDO

The concave sweep of coastline south of Santa Elena and north of the Nicoya Peninsula is dominated by the Golfo de Papagayo, an enormous gulf that holds within its waters smaller and more protected bays and coves, including the nearly enclosed Bahía Culebra (Snake Bay).

More than half of the gulf's stunning coastline and nearly all of the scrubby interior of the Santa Elena peninsula is protected in Santa Rosa National Park, home to oft-deserted Playa Naranjo and a dramatic outcropping just offshore called Witch's Rock, mythic in surfing circles. The route to this remote wave-riders' mecca is either by boat or overland on a time-consuming road that is often in disrepair.

The formation of the park had a few high-profile twists and turns. Several decades ago, Anastasio Somoza, former ruler of Nicaragua, owned the Hacienda Murciélago (Bat Ranch) on the Santa Elena peninsula. In 1979 the Costa Rican government decided it didn't want to host an ousted dictator, and furthermore that the flora and fauna of this remote area needed protection from encroaching development. Hacienda Murciélago was seized and became part of Santa Rosa National Park. Another addition to

Playa Ocotal

the park came in the form of the once-secret Santa Elena airstrip, used by Oliver North and his Contra buddies in their fight to undermine Nicaragua's Sandinista government in the 1980s. Óscar Arias, in his first presidency, and in the role of Central American peacemaker, shut down the strip in 1986. Surfers still refer to a nearby landmark as Ollie's Point, after Oliver North.

More accessible (and ownable) land begins around Nacascolo, at the northern headland of Snake Bay, but even that area is fairly remote. Most people choose to live in the Playas del Coco area, which includes (from north to south) Playas Panama, Hermosa, Coco, and Ocotal. A perfect semicircle of gray sand, Playa Panama is so protected that there are hardly any waves breaking on its quiet shores.

Playa Hermosa is one of the nicer beaches in this area, and the number of visitors it receives reflects that. Condos, hotels, and Airbnb homes line the beach and climb the hill north of town. Boogie boards and kayaks lie in multicolored stacks on the beach, ready to be rented. Roving vendors sell coconuts (for the refreshing milk) and souvenirs; you don't see that on the other beaches in the region, except maybe Coco during high season. The water is cool enough to be refreshing on a hot day but warm enough to stay in for hours without feeling chilled. Waves break close to shore; out beyond the breakers you can still stand. Swells lift you off your feet and deposit you gently back down on the white-sand bottom.

Although there's just one beach, Playas del Coco is always expressed in the plural. The name also applies to the lively strip of a town that runs a few kilometers from the beach inland, where you'll find not only good seafood restaurants and fun dive bars, but also real-life services like banks, hardware stores, and several well-stocked supermarkets; expats from as far away as Tilaran make the drive for the wide selection of products. On the hills above Playa Ocotal, just south of Playas del Coco, million-dollar vacation homes and more modest condos overlook the

Tamarindo is a surfing hotspot with lots of new development.

TAMARINDO TO OSTIONAL

"Tamarindo has surrendered its old identity," a long-time resident told me. "But it hasn't yet achieved the identity to which it aspires."

This beach town's old identity was as a fishing village and surfer haven. Its new identity seems to be up for grabs, as it struggles with its own popularity, including the unsavory characters drawn to any tourist hot spot and wheeler-dealer developers intent on making a killing off this town's painfully loud and fast boom.

The former fishing village has good bones—great weather, a lovely span of white-sand beach, and an international cast of characters.

But as in many towns that develop too fast, the infrastructure, such as it is, can't keep pace with the influx of new residents and the increasing number of visitors. Imagine sushi restaurants, surf shops, and art galleries with First World prices strung along a couple of decidedly Third World roads, dusty in dry season and a stew of mud when it rains. Drivers slow to a crawl as they try to get around the huge trucks bearing building materials for the next condo project.

The town has come a long way, fast, from its origins as a funky little community, where a few in-the-know surfers carved their names on empty waves. The development in this town is staggering, and the prices are some of the highest in the country.

One thing the town has going for it is that it has been dealing with these growing pains for a while now, and may be farther along than other beach towns in solving some of the problems. Many of the local hotels and restaurants are owned and run by Italian, German, Dutch, Swiss, Canadian, and American expats, to name just a few of the nationalities represented in this multicultural burg. Some of

secluded gray-sand beach. Many of the properties available here lie within gated communities, a security plus for owners who only make it down for a month or two every year.

Playas Flamingo, Brasilito, and Potrero are just north of Tamarindo, with Playa Flamingo serving as the central community and boasting one of the prettiest beaches. Some say nearby Playa Brasilito has been compromised by the Melía Conchal Resort, which bulldozed a lot of the funkiness out of the place. Still, a sizable community of expats has settled here and in nearby Playa Potrero. A growing number of bilingual private schools, including the Costa Rica International Academy (which used to be a branch of Country Day School in Escazú), are making the area more attractive to expats with school-age children.

Revival of a Pre-Columbian Past

Jesús Villareal with the book that helps him revive ancient Chorotega pottery designs

Perched on a wooden stool in his open-air studio, Jesús Villareal slips moistened fingers around the rim of a bowl revolving on a potter's wheel. To his right is what looks like an enormous wooden mortar and pestle, in which Jesús's wife, Susan Chavaria, pounds earth to the fine powder required for the best clay. The earth comes from the low hills above town, where locals have been digging for thousands of years. And just as their Chorotega ancestors did, Jesús and Susan will polish the pottery with jade-like stones said to come from nearby archaeological sites. Although Jesús and Susan are part of a long tradition of indigenous pottery making, that tradition had all but died out until recently, when it began to be revived.

Jesús puts aside the still-wet bowl and turns to a row of kiln-fired vases. He dips brushes into little jars of glaze arrayed on the table before him. Earlier Jesús and Susan had carefully ground powders made of earth or dried plants, adding water to create the earth-toned colorings that make their pieces come alive. Behind Jesús is the beehive-shaped kiln in which the family fires the pieces that line the shelves of the gift store at the other end of the studio.

Jesús and Susan also consult a heavily illustrated academic reference work, *Costa Rica Precolumbina*, by Luis Ferrero. The book is as treasured and battered as an old family bible. It has been in the family for about 20 years, Jesús says; he often models his own work after the ancient examples pictured in the book. Such are the ironies of ancient traditions lost and found.

Jesús, Susan, and their family are among a handful of clans that make up the village of Guatíl, the epicenter of a renaissance in Chorotega ceramics that draws tourists and locals interested in the area's pre-Columbian past and its indigenous present. Often presided over by matriarchs who have been working with clay since they were girls and who learned their craft from mothers and grandmothers, the families of Guatíl hope that reviving the work will prove not only spiritually satisfying but also economically viable. Pottery is the only "industry" in this tiny town on the Nicoya Peninsula, 12 kilometers (7.5 miles) east of Santa Cruz.

Roll into town and you won't have to ask where the pottery is – pottery is all there is here. Unless your visit coincides with the arrival of a small tourist van, you may be the only visitor. Take time to talk with some of the artists and to look at their different takes on Chorotega themes. Some figures are half-animal, half-human; others have exaggerated genitalia in celebration of fertility. Plates, bowls, and vases are enlivened with traditional geometric or botanical patterns in black, ocher, and red. Also head down the road to San Vicente, another small town known for its pottery.

Costa Rica doesn't have the majestic ruins of pre-Columbian empires like the Aztec, the Maya, or the Inca. Its modern-day indigenous population is small in comparison to Mexico's or Guatemala's. But pre-Columbian Costa Rica was a crossroad of sorts. Objects and traditions from as far north as Mexico and as far south as Ecuador and Peru found their way here. From these and other cultures came traditions and pottery styles being reborn in towns like Guatíl today.

those business owners and other residents joined forces in 2014 in the Asociación de Desarrollo Integral de Tamarindo (ADIT; Tamarindo Community Development Association; www.playatamarindo.org), an outgrowth of the older Asociación Pro-Mejoras de Tamarindo (Association for the Betterment of Tamarindo). The organization has taken on town issues such as cleanliness, security, and the need for lifeguards.

South of Tamarindo is one of the older developments in the area, a sprawling gated community called Hacienda Pinilla. Billing itself as an exclusive resort community, the development spreads across more than 1,800 hectares (4,500 acres) of a former cattle ranch and stretches along 5.5 kilometers (3.5 miles) of coastline. Pat Pattillo of Pattillo Construction, an Atlanta-based developer, bought the land in the early 1980s and in the last decade transformed it into an upscale complex geared to wealthy North Americans who want to relocate or buy vacation homes.

Pattillo had to start from scratch, building roads; putting in phone, electrical, and sewage systems; and planting tens of thousands of trees in an effort to bring back to life vast tracts of land denuded by cattle grazing.

Farther south, Playa Junquillal, Playa Avellana, and Playa Negra, which used to draw only surfers willing to rough it, are having their own building boomlets as Tamarindo pushes its own envelope. But it's still true that the expats you meet on this stretch of coast are likely to be fiercely independent men (and more rarely, women).

South of the Playa Negra area you'll find small fishing villages, such as San Juanillo, and slightly bigger Tico towns like Ostional, whose beach is known for its *arrivadas*, seasonal arrivals of egg-laying ridley turtles.

Between Ostional and Nosara runs the Río Montaña, often impassable during the rainy season. I had to hire a big tractor (called a *chapulín*, or grasshopper) to pull me across. It was either that or backtrack all the way to Playa Negra, and then head inland for the better roads. The trip back would have added three or four hours to my journey; the *chapulín* cost me about US$5.

NOSARA, SÁMARA, AND PLAYA CARRILLO

Nosara is a quiet place that grows on you. Guidebooks say there's not much to do here, and in terms of sights, they're right. What people do is stick around and soak up the good vibes. The Nosara Yoga Institute up on the hill casts a benevolent eye over the community, and the town attracts residents whose idea of heaven is to perfect their headstand, amble along one of the three absolutely pristine beaches, or paddle out to surf when the waves are big. In the morning, locals meet at Café de Paris for good coffee and even better blueberry muffins.

The town has two main parts: Bocas de Nosara, five kilometers (three miles) inland, which is a typical Tico small town, clustered around the soccer field; and Beaches of Nosara, closer to the beach and home to a large foreign community, made up mostly of American and Canadian expats who live in houses tucked among lush trees and flowers.

Nosara is blessed with stunning natural beauty, and the area has avoided some of the worst pitfalls of seaside tourist towns. Residents are active in keeping their town low-key, and the Nosara Civic Association leads the way. The association began back in 1962, when Allan Hutchison bought 120 hectares (300 acres) in Nosara, built roads, put in electrical wires, and drilled wells to create one of the only private water systems in the country. He sold off parcels within this area and charged

Playa Carrillo

residents a monthly fee for the water and services.

"Water is the key," said Linda Cox, former manager of the association. "If you have good water, everything else is gravy." But Costa Rica is known for its potable water, and the association is about more than a steady supply of water. It also works to improve trash pickup, sends out crews to maintain the roads when the municipality can't afford to, and perhaps most important, works doggedly to see that development doesn't spin out of control.

The association influences development within and outside its boundaries. The fact that few structures in Beaches of Nosara are over two stories high is no accident. Builders aren't following municipal zoning laws but rather are adhering to guidelines set by the association, which will fight in the courts any development it considers antithetical to the understated ambience of the area. One of its biggest fights was against Marbella Corporation, which wanted to build a high-rise hotel on the beach. That battle raged for 18 years, and the association won. "But there

will be more," predicts Linda Cox. "It's a never-ending battle."

About 15 kilometers (9 miles) south of Garza, the next town of any size is Sámara, as unlike Nosara as *guaro* (the locally distilled alcoholic drink) is different from chardonnay. Fans of Nosara are likely to turn up their noses at Sámara's party atmosphere and beachfront development, but both places have their charms. Years ago, the powerful National Tourism Board (Instituto Costarricense de Turismo) developed a plan that set aside certain areas for high-density tourism—large hotels and beachfront development—and designated other areas as low-density. Perhaps building on how things were already shaping up, Nosara was designated low-density and Sámara high-density. This means that developers in Sámara face fewer hurdles than those wanting to build in Nosara, and that the already large difference in character of these two beachside communities is likely to be accentuated in years to come.

an island cemetery near Montezuma

A few miles south of Sámara is Playa Carrillo, a gorgeous pink-sand beach protected by an offshore coral reef. Yachts anchor at the south end of the bay, and hotels and residential communities are being built along this quiet stretch of coast, which boasts its own airstrip.

South of Carrillo, the road gets pretty bad and is often impassable during the wet season. A string of stunning beaches goes all the way down to Cabo Blanco, the southernmost tip of the Nicoya Peninsula. The area is sparsely populated and requires some gumption to visit; you need even more to live there.

MONTEZUMA

The approach to Montezuma is dramatic—you wind down a steep road, catching glimpses of nothing but blue, blue ocean, all the while wondering if there's really a town down there. Turn a sharp corner and there it is—a charming little place tucked into the folds of overgrown hills. Low buildings line the narrow main street, with hibiscus, palm, and acacia crowding in and making the way even narrower. Tourists arrive in rented four-wheel drives, and a few times a day the bus from the Paquera ferry squeezes through and deposits its load of surfers, backpackers, and people like Lauren, a middle-aged pipe fitter from Alberta who comes down a few months every year to swim, read, and relax.

This is a very good place to relax. The influx of mostly young North Americans and Europeans has made Montezuma a cool little "alternative" spot, with excellent vegetarian food, organic ice cream, and a couple of bars that pump out dance music deep into the tropical night.

On one visit I watched as a film crew trailed the finalists for Tica Linda, a national beauty contest, through the streets and down to the beach. The entire town, always slow-paced, ground to an absolute

But before you start to picture Sámara as some sort of evil anti-Nosara, picture this: a beautiful half-moon of a protected bay, with palm trees and vines acting as a green fringe to the gray-sand beach. It's a great place for learning to surf, as the waves never get too big and you can stand in chest-deep water waiting for the perfect one to come your way. There are hotels and restaurants built right on the beach, it's true, but so far they're low-rise and casual open-air bars with sand floors or small *cabinas* partially hidden by beachside vegetation. Consider also that the center of the community is *puro Tico,* the usual town built around a soccer field; the town hasn't yet bifurcated into separate areas for Ticos and expats. The place is very popular with Tico tourists, which suggests that Sámara is the Costa Rican idea of what a beach resort should be. Ticos like the feel of Sámara, and after all, it's their country.

Sea Turtles: Relics of Prehistory

Of the seven species of sea turtles in the world, five can be seen in Costa Rica. Seeing turtles in their own element gliding gracefully through the water, their heavy shells rendered weightless, is an unforgettable experience. But unless you're underwater more often than on land, the place to see these relics of prehistory is on the beach, when they come ashore to nest.

It's an awe-inspiring sight. Female turtles, sometimes singly and sometimes in great synchronized *arribadas* (arrivals), ride in on the high tide, galumph up the beach a little farther, then dig with their flippers like a dog set on burying a bone. Into that hole go up to 100 flexible-skinned, golf ball-size eggs. The turtle whirls its flippers like propellers to bury the eggs, then heads back to sea, her work done. The nesting happens mostly at night. Many weeks later the hatchlings dig their way out and make a mad rush for the ocean, hoping they won't be picked off by dogs, raccoons, gulls, vultures, or human poachers who believe the eggs are aphrodisiacs.

TURTLES IN TROUBLE

Leatherback turtles have been around for 65 million years, but their numbers are now in decline. According to the Leatherback Trust, in 1980 there were over 115,000 adult females, but there are now fewer than 25,000 worldwide. Many things threaten sea turtle survival. Development and its attendant lights can disorient the creatures and cause them either not to come to the beach to lay their eggs or to return to the water without having laid them. Drift net fishing involves a lot of unintended catch, including turtles. Another culprit is climate change. Turtles can die in the hotter, more acidic seas caused by global warming, eggs on beaches are washed away by higher tides from more violent storms before they can hatch. When turtles lay eggs, the gender is not yet determined. Warmer temperatures produce more female eggs; warmer sand can cause more females than males to be born, upsetting the gender balance of the population.

TURTLE VIEWING

Just north of **Tamarindo** on the Nicoya Peninsula, **Las Baulas Marine National Park**

halt as young beauties tottered along in high heels, draped in strategically placed strands of jute. Local surfers were recruited to stand in as atmospheric background. No doubt the town was chosen as much for its funky vibe as for its natural beauty, but the point is, the place has cachet.

The coastline here is convoluted, jutting out into the sea and doubling back on itself. Walk a few hundred meters and you're out of town; walk 10 minutes and you'll find beaches where you'll have the place to yourself except for the occasional pelican, iguana, or troop of monkeys. The jungle rushes right up to the edge of the beach, where brown sand alternates with volcanic rock and pulverized pink and white shells. Rivers and streams cascade over boulders and empty out into deserted coves.

The alternative feel of the area has roots that go back at least to the 1950s, with the arrival of two Europeans who would transform the landscape—or, more accurately, work hard to make sure that the land they loved so passionately would still be there for future generations to enjoy. Olaf Wessberg of Sweden and Karen Morgenson of Denmark had a dream of escaping the Scandinavian winters and of growing organic fruit in tropical America. They tried California, Guatemala, and Mexico, and visited many parts of Costa

attracts the largest nesting colony of leatherback sea turtles *(baulas)* on the Pacific Coast of Costa Rica, with hundreds of female turtles flippering ashore each year.

Nesting season is approximately October-April, which roughly corresponds to Costa Rica's dry summer season. Bilingual rangers lead small viewing groups, lighting the way with their flashlights masked (to avoid disorienting the turtles). For minimum impact, a limited number of visitors are allowed each evening. The ranger station at Playa Grande is open daily 8am-4pm during turtle season; call during other months to confirm hours. There's also an excellent turtle museum at the station.

The park protects 379 terrestrial hectares (936 acres) and 22,000 marine hectares (54,000 acres). In Tamarindo massive condo developments sit cheek by jowl with funky surfer hangouts. A recent moratorium forbids certain kinds of high-rise building, but some projects seem exempt from the new rules, and enough got in under the wire that development is now encroaching on turtle territory.

Just north of **Nosara,** also on the Nicoya Peninsula, **Ostional National Wildlife Refuge** protects 73 hectares (180 acres) of one of the world's most important nesting beaches for the olive ridley sea turtle *(lora* in Spanish). Their mass nesting rituals happen year-round, once or twice a month, often during the last quarter of the moon cycle. During the rainy season (May-November), more turtles come ashore with each *arribada.* The largest *arribada* ever documented was in November 1995, with an estimated 500,000 turtles.

Unlike the enormous leatherback turtles, which are easily disturbed by noise and light, the olive ridleys seem oblivious to just about everything, including their own kind. They crawl all over each other with clawed flippers, bumping shells, intent on only one thing: depositing their eggs in the sand. So many turtles arrive so quickly that most of the first nests are destroyed by later turtles. Because of this, local people are allowed to collect and sell some of the eggs from the first three days of each *arribada.* This practice is designed to prevent poaching and to help the local community. The ranger station at Playa Ostional is open daily 8am-4pm. Guided tours are available with bilingual park employees.

Rica before they found their niche in Montezuma, where they moved in 1955. They spent their time raising 30 varieties of fruits and getting to know and love the diverse flora and fauna of their adopted home. Journalist Bill Weinberg knew the couple and described them as strict vegetarians who "had a reverence for nature that bordered on the mystical, taking great joy in the company of monkeys and coatimundis."

In the late 1950s, the couple watched in horror as more and more squatters moved into the area, clearing land for crops and then selling out to lumber companies and cattle ranches. Afraid that soon the land would be beyond repair, Wessberg wrote an appeal for donations so that he might buy up property around Montezuma and thus protect it from destruction. His call was heeded, with contributions coming from the British World League against Vivisection, the Sierra Club, and the Philadelphia Conservation League, among many other organizations and individuals. Wessberg and Morgenson bought a big parcel of land to the south, on the headland between Cabuya and Mal País, which in 1965 became Cabo Blanco, Costa Rica's first nature reserve. The reserve protects one of the last large tracts of mixed evergreen and deciduous moist tropical forest in the area and is home to rare and threatened species such as curassow, crested guan, brocket deer, and jaguarundi.

If you want to eat, drink, lounge, get a tattoo, or buy handmade jewelry, Montezuma is the place. If you need anything halfway practical, you go to Cóbano, 20 minutes inland (and up and over a steep hill). If you don't have a car and the bus isn't coming for hours, well, you can try to find a taxi, or you can start walking, hoping someone will take pity on you and give you a ride.

To the north of Montezuma is Playa Tambor, a gray-sand stretch of beach chosen by Spain's Barceló company as the site of a massive oceanfront development. This all-inclusive resort, which was the first of its kind in Costa Rica, has everything from a golf course to a 350-seat theater to a helicopter landing pad. Barceló is said to have destroyed wildlife habitats and drained wetlands to build the sprawling complex. Nevertheless, the Costa Rican government not only gave it the green light but also agreed to pave the road to the hotel, to add a new ferry to bring visitors from Puntarenas on the mainland, and to house construction workers who would later be employed by the resort. If the choice is between protecting the environment (enforcing already existing laws) and promoting tourism, Costa Rica often seems to choose the latter.

MAL PAÍS AREA

Southwest of Montezuma, on the Pacific ocean side of the Nicoya Peninsula, Mal País and Santa Teresa are more remote than Montezuma but still draw their share of expats, especially those who appreciate the great surfing on both beaches. From the inland town of Cóbano the road leads southwest to Carmen. Go left at the crossroads and you'll find Mal País; go right and you'll hit Santa Teresa. Keep heading north (the road gets progressively worse) and you'll come to Manzanillo; those in search of remote living and real estate deals head to this Tico town and venture even farther north. Keep going up the coast, and if the road is passable, you'll eventually reach Bongo, Caletas, and Punta Coyote, tiny towns more often accessed from the north or from inland.

The coastline here is beautiful and dramatic, rock outcroppings alternating with long stretches of white sand, and dense foliage covering the hills sloping down to the shore. Carmen and Santa Teresa especially are expanding rapidly and consist of hotels, restaurants, and new homes strung along the two-lane main road, which runs parallel to the beach. Rutted lanes veer off the main road and head for the beach, where due to the pounding waves you'll find more surfers than swimmers.

There's a building boomlet going on in this area, so you'll see big trucks, lots of rebar and cement, and crowds of Nicaraguan workers here to do the heavy lifting.

Despite the changes, and the influx of drug culture, the area still has a laid-back feel. During low season (May-November), you can walk the seemingly endless beach and see just a few people.

THE CENTRAL AND SOUTHERN PACIFIC COAST

The farther south you go along Costa Rica's Pacific coast, the less developed the area and the more tropical the climate. For the purposes of this book, the central Pacific coast is from Jacó to Palmar Norte, and the southern Pacific coast starts where the Osa Peninsula pushes out from the mainland and ends at the Panamanian border.

The central Pacific wins the accessibility contest without even breaking a sweat. From the Central Valley, where the majority of expats and Costa Ricans make their home, central Pacific beach towns like Jacó and Quepos are the most convenient vacation spots in the country. And it goes both ways, of course—residents of these areas can easily shoot up to San José for a shopping excursion or a visit to a well-regarded specialist, or to meet a friend's incoming flight. Roads in the area are relatively well maintained, so travel time from San José to Jacó is under two hours, with Quepos another 40 minutes

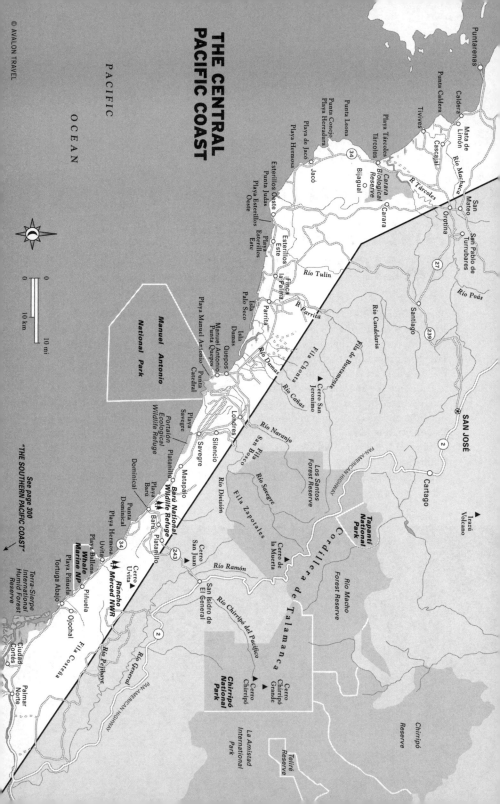

treehouse in the Southern Zone

down the road. After Quepos, the Coast Highway (also called the Costanera) has been improving, though some sections and most side roads still warrant caution.

The Lay of the Land

Geographically, the central Pacific consists of a narrow coastal strip backed by steep and heavily wooded mountains. This juxtaposition makes for some very dramatic beaches, where the jungle pushes right up to the sand and where monkeys and sloths join your afternoon tanning session. The climate offers up two fairly distinct seasons—wet (or green) being May-November, and dry running December-April. Those who consider Guanacaste (in the north) too dry and the Southern Zone too humid feel that the central Pacific coast is, like something out of a fairy tale, just right. Towns like Quepos and Jacó, along with national parks such as Manuel Antonio and Carera, are blessed with a happy medium of rainfall and sunshine. While the summer sees considerably less rain than the winter here, even in dry season you will see a riot of green cascading down the hills to the sea.

The southern Pacific coast's seasons correspond roughly to those of the central Pacific coast, but the dry season here isn't all that dry. Locals are prepared for rain at any time of year, as the area receives 400-800 centimeters (157-315 inches) per year. But the wet season definitely lives up to its name, and May through November is when legendary surf spots like Pavones (with its kilometer-long left-breaking wave) really take off. Thunderstorms are not uncommon late in the year; Caño Island, off the Osa Peninsula, has the dubious distinction of being struck by lightning more often than any other place in Central America.

In stark contrast to the central

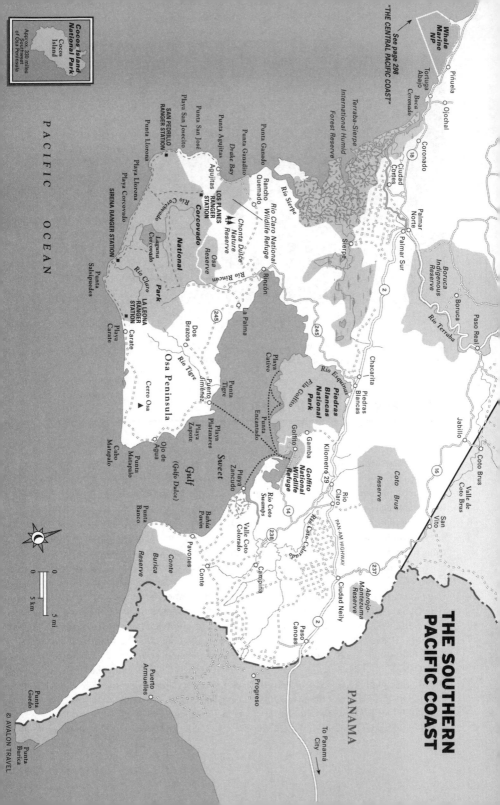

Pacific's straight and narrow coast, the southern coast is positively convulsive, disrupted by swamps and estuaries near the Valle de Diquís, thrust out into the ocean at the Osa Peninsula, and deeply indented at the Golfo Dulce. As the crow flies, the central and southern coasts are roughly equivalent in length, but tracing the shoreline convolutions of the Southern Zone would probably take two to three times longer, if there were roads that allowed you to do so.

But even with all the time in the world and a hardy four-wheel drive, you couldn't drive the whole of the coastline. A road traces the eastern perimeter of the heavily wooded Osa Peninsula, but it stops at Carate. On most maps there's a dotted line running along the Osa's west coast; map keys call it a track, passable in the dry season. It may be passable, but you'll be passing on foot, because this "track" is most often a path, wide enough for one person when it isn't petering out into the bush. On the narrow Burica Peninsula, which Costa Rica shares with Panama, the road ends almost before the land begins its jut into the Pacific.

The lack of roads means that the towns you *can* get to may feel like outposts, islands of civilization amid vast tracts of wilderness. Darryl Cole-Christensen, in his book *A Place in the Rain Forest,* writes of pioneering in the Coto Brus Valley in the late 1950s. The forest was their adversary, he says. Gloomy and dangerous, home to venomous snakes, jaguars, and wild pigs, it was something that had to be fought and cleared as settlers carved out a place for themselves, their livestock, and their crops. Nowadays there has been as much clear-cutting of trees and destruction of animal habitat (even on so-called protected land) here as elsewhere in the country. But the Southern Zone still feels wild, a place that even now provokes primordial fear and wonder.

The area has an interesting pre-Columbian history—the indigenous people here were influenced by cultures from South America, while indigenous peoples elsewhere in Costa Rica had ties to more northerly civilizations. Like the Inca of Peru, the people in southern Costa Rica created gold ornaments using the lost-wax technique; many are in the shapes of local animals such as crocodiles and jaguars. They also created perfectly round stone spheres, some weighing up to 16 tons. These mysterious spheres have generated many theories as to their origin—Erich von Däniken, in his *Chariots of the Gods,* claimed that they were projectiles shot from starships. Others suggest that the spheres were shaped by hydraulic pressure, tumbled with other rocks at the base of thunderous waterfalls. A third explanation, favored by many experts, is that the spheres were created by a process of heating and cooling the stone, causing it to slough off in layers. The spheres were further refined by careful chipping and then were polished through abrasion.

Recent history is just as colorful. Gold fever hit in the 1970s, concentrated in what was to become Corcovado National Park. Puerto Jiménez was a rowdy boomtown, with *oreros* (gold miners) trading nuggets for booze and prostitutes. Longtime locals tell of wild times, with everyone packing a gun and fortunes being made and lost every day. Even a young José Figueres (president from 1994 to 1998) succumbed to the fever and tried his hand at panning for gold. The miners' destructive methods—chopping down the rainforest, dynamiting riverbeds—prompted outrage and led, finally, to the creation of Corcovado National Park in the mid-1980s.

ACCESS

If you're looking to relocate or buy a vacation home along the Pacific coast, geography and climate may be less important

Cocos Island: Hammerheads and Buried Treasure

A 23-square-kilometer (9-square-mile) un-inhabited island surrounded by deep ocean currents lies 532 kilometers (330 miles) off the Pacific Coast of Costa Rica. This wild and remote region is home to 300 species of fish, including large populations of giant manta rays, sailfish, scalloped hammer-head sharks, and whale sharks, the largest of all fish.

Marine mammals—from humpback whales to bottlenose dolphins—also fre-quent the area, as do hawksbill, green, leatherback, and olive ridley turtles.

The sea life is so varied and abundant, in fact, that the waters around the island were named one of the 10 best scuba div-ing spots in the world by the Professional Association of Diving Instructors (PADI). In 1994 Jacques Cousteau called it "the most beautiful island in the world." In 1997 it was designated a World Heritage Site by UNESCO.

All this comes at a price: besides the sticker shock for a chartered dive trip, it can take up to 30 hours by boat from the Pacific Coast port of Puntarenas to reach Cocos Island, 5 degrees north of the Equa-tor, a few hundred kilometers north of the Galapagos Islands.

Cocos Island has been a national park since 1978, but in 2011 the greatly ex-panded protected area was dubbed the Seamounts Marine Management Area. It's an area five times larger than the original national park and includes a fully protected no-fishing zone along with limited-catch zones.

TREASURE ISLAND

The island is also at the center of a swirl of history and legend. Rumors of buried treasure abound. In the centuries prior to Costa Rica claiming the island in 1869, it was a pit stop for all manner of ships, where crews took on fresh water, firewood, and coconuts (cocos in Spanish). The sto-ries go that pirates especially valued Cocos as a hiding place for looted artifacts and gold, hiding the treasure in natural caves or burying it deep in the cloud forest.

In 1818 Captain Bennett Graham, a Brit-ish naval officer turned pirate, supposedly buried 350 tons of gold bullion stolen from Spanish galleons on Cocos Island. He and his crew were caught and most were ex-ecuted, but a woman who'd been part of the crew was sent to a penal colony in Tas-mania for her part in the lootings. Released 20 years later, she returned to Cocos with a treasure map she said Graham had given her for safekeeping. But the island had changed so much in the intervening years that many landmarks on the map, including a huge cedar tree near which she had once camped for six months, had disappeared. The expedition found no buried treasure.

That failure would be echoed in years to come. The best known of the treasure legends is that of the Treasure of Lima (Peru). In 1820, with the army of José de San Martín approaching Lima, Viceroy José de la Serna is supposed to have en-trusted treasure from the city's churches to British trader Captain William Thompson for safekeeping until the Spaniards could secure the country.

The ecclesiastical riches included a solid-gold, gem-encrusted, life-size image of the Virgin Mary. The plan was to have Thompson sail around for several months with the treasure stowed aboard his mer-chant ship, the Mary Dear, until the political situation improved. But the gold and pre-cious artifacts—valued at US$12-60 mil-lion—prompted Thompson and his men to cut the throats of the viceroy's appointed guards. The bodies were tossed over-board, and the Mary Dear—carrying the jewel-encrusted Virgin Mary, among other treasures—sailed to Cocos, where the crew buried the treasure.

Despite these and other stories, no major treasure trove has ever been uncov-ered at Cocos Island, unless you count the island's undersea riches: the whales and sharks and rays and dolphins that lure those who value natural riches as much as those of the artificial variety.

than accessibility. As elsewhere in Costa Rica, the question here is not "Is it beautiful?" but rather "Can you get there?" Yes, the roads have improved, and the days are gone when you needed a horse and several days to reach what are now decent-size towns. But you still need to consider how hard it will be for you to get around. Chances are the more remote the area you live in, the more likely you'll need to go—often—somewhere else. Whether you need a stack of plywood, a big bag of rice, or emergency medical care, what are the roads like that will get you there? Most North Americans can't imagine planning their day (or life) according to the state of nearby roads, but that's the reality in the more remote areas of Costa Rica. And the "wild south" most surely qualifies as remote.

PRICES

The places to look for real estate deals are the towns you've never heard of: little villages not far from bigger name-brand destinations, or bends in the road that catch your eye with their leafy rural charm. Start in a bigger town in an area that appeals to you, and then see what you find within a short drive.

The most expensive areas to buy property on this stretch of coast are condo-heavy Jacó, an hour and a half from the international airport outside San José, and the region around Manuel Antonio National Park, about an hour south of Jacó. Prices in these areas rival those of Guanacaste's Gold Coast, with luxury beachside homes going for over US$1 million and more modest properties starting at around US$250,000.

Some of the heat of those markets has seeped southward; Dominical, for example, is now quite popular.

Forego a water view or beach access, and head a little inland, and you'll find much lower prices.

You will find lower prices as you go farther south, although some remote areas (like the span of coast between Puerto Jiménez and Cabo Matapalo on the Osa Peninsula) have become hot spots of a different sort. They aren't being developed in the ways that more northerly stretches of coast are, but wealthy individuals (like actor Woody Harrelson) have bought up large tracts of land, keeping them relatively pristine but also making it less likely that you'll stumble upon your own little piece of affordable paradise there.

Getting a good price is about doing your homework and being persistent. Great deals don't generally fall into people's laps; you have to go looking for them.

Where to Live

CENTRAL PACIFIC COAST TOWNS
Jacó

Jacó is a beach town turned boomtown. Ease of access is the town's main charm. You can land at the international airport near San José and be at the beach in less than two hours.

As in many beach towns, the layout is basically one long strip, parallel to a long stretch of *playa* that often hosts surf competitions. There are the usual open-air bars and restaurants, souvenir shops, budget *cabinas,* and some larger chain hotels (like Best Western) outside the town proper.

And everywhere you look, there are new buildings—both residential and commercial. Some might even qualify as *rascacielos* (skyscrapers), 14 or more floors

Jacó is a beach town turned boomtown.

of glass and steel rising up from what was recently a low-rise town.

There are also the businesses that make a place not just visitable but livable: banks, medical clinics, hardware stores, and car repair shops. Other beach towns force you to go elsewhere if your needs go beyond food, alcohol, or a new bikini.

Javier Barquero, former manager of Best Western Jacó, describes how the town has changed in the last few years. "Now there's more construction, more investment, more opportunity. Better services. Lots of nice places to go out for a drink or have dinner. But there's also been an increase in drugs and prostitution." Javier, himself from San José, sees Jacó as a town of people who've come from elsewhere. "There are lots of Canadians here," he says. "Some Americans, some Italians."

Among the better-known beaches close to Jacó, Playa Herradura, 7 kilometers (4.3 miles) north, is the site of Los Sueños (www.lossuenosresort.com), a Marriott megaresort and residential complex with hundreds of condos and its own marina. There are also tennis courts and a championship golf course. If you want to see what Playa Herradura looks like without the bother of traveling, rent the movie *1492,* starring Gérard Depardieu as Christopher Columbus—the beach is featured in many scenes. Local indigenous people were recruited to play the indigenous people Columbus encountered; they were paid US$15 a day, with women who bared their chests getting three times that rate. It's said that the 10 weeks of filming contributed US$8 million to the local economy. Ten kilometers (six miles) north of Playa Herradura is Punta Leona, where vacationers from the Central Valley and abroad own condos in a gated community.

Just south of Jacó is Playa Hermosa, a 10-kilometer (6-mile) stretch of gray-brown sand battered by the kind of waves surfers love. It has become a favorite among those who want something more laid-back than Jacó, and many of the businesses serving tourists are owned and operated by expats.

The bartender at a local club told me he came here in 2000 to surf and now has a Tica wife and a young daughter. "It's easier to be a good father down here," he says. "The people are so nice, and the society is less materialistic. There's free medical care, and then you've got an extended family that helps out. Sometimes it's too much," he admits. "Seems like there's a baby shower or birthday party every other day. But there's much less stress down here." He loves Playa Hermosa, but he and his family live in Jacó because there are more services there—health clinics, supermarkets, and the like. "Jacó has some problems, for sure," he says. "But if you don't run in those circles, they don't much affect you."

Quepos and Manuel Antonio

Quepos sits sandwiched between a tranquil harbor dotted with fishing boats and the steep, wooded slope southeast of town. Incoming and outgoing traffic take turns across the narrow bridge into town. Locals walk by with fishing poles over their shoulders or pedal along on bicycles, often with a cell phone scrunched between shoulder and ear. Quepos, with its grid of streets lined with low buildings, was once a banana town. The United Fruit Company built a compound south of town in the 1930s and drew workers from other parts of the country. In the 1950s disease blighted the banana trees, and they were replaced by oil-producing African palms.

Nowadays, Quepos does triple duty as a major sportfishing destination, a working Tico town where you can buy a stove or some new shoes, and the gateway to one of the most-visited tourist sites in the country, Manuel Antonio National Park. Budget travelers often opt to stay in Quepos, but more upscale tourist facilities are strung along the seven-kilometer (four-mile) road that winds through jungle-draped hills from Quepos to the park entrance. There is also a small cluster of hotels, bars, and restaurants at the Manuel Antonio end of the road, all within walking distance of the park.

A 22-hectare (55-acre) marina (www.marinapezvela.com) in Quepos harbor was recently built to replace the dilapidated old pier, originally built by the United Fruit Company. The project may eventually contain hundreds of condos and a mall, but at this phase the marina has just a few high-priced condos for rent, plus wet slips for rent by the day, month, or year for boats ranging from 9 to 60 meters (30-200 feet).

Fans of the area feel like they have it all: swimmable white-sand beaches, a gem of a national park where monkey and sloth sightings are all but guaranteed, lush tropical foliage, and enough tourist infrastructure to ensure good roads and services.

Many real estate offices in town will be glad to help you look for the place of your dreams. It's important to have the inside scoop on the area, and a good agent can provide just that. A local told me about a squatters' town on the road from Quepos to Manuel Antonio (which is lined with luxury hotels and pricey restaurants; not the kind of place you'd imagine a shantytown). Apparently, one of the biggest properties in the area was owned by a drug dealer who didn't come around much. This absentee ownership attracted squatters, who built small houses and planted crops, thereby laying claim to the land. Eventually, some of squatters sold "their" land to other locals, who then sold to foreigners. "Buying property here," the local told me, "you really need someone who knows the area and its history to make sure you know what you're getting yourself into." Just because land was once squatted on doesn't necessarily mean that there would be a problem if you bought it—the property could very well have a clear title, and everything would be ducky. But then again, the property might exist in some legal no-man's-land that would allow you to buy it (or at least pay for it) without actually owning it. (This is true for the country as a whole.)

Many of the hotels, bars, and restaurants in the Manuel Antonio area are owned by Americans, Canadians, Argentines, Italians, and other non-natives, and there is a strong gay male presence, with many establishments gay owned or at least gay friendly. "We are an open-minded place," boasts a sign in English that hangs in the doorway of an open-air bar right off Manuel Antonio beach. Businesses cater primarily to tourists, and as such there are many non-Tico items on offer, like the excellent iced lattes and toasted bagels with cream cheese at the two branches of Café Milagro.

Getting work (as opposed to running your own business) is not easy. A hotel owner told me, "Very wealthy people do come here to hang out, but 80 percent of the people who move here seem to be looking for work. They usually don't find it, because businesses can't legally hire foreigners."

I talked with two Canadian sisters who had managed to land waitressing jobs but quit after a few months. "They hardly gave us any shifts, and the wage was less than two dollars an hour. People here don't tip, and the tourists pick up that custom when they see how much of their bill is tax and 'service.' Somehow we didn't see much of that service charge. It was like charity work, except the customers were really demanding."

Dominical

About 45 kilometers (28 miles) south of Quepos, or an hour from the inland city of San Isidro de El General, lies Dominical. The town is a funky grid of rutted roads framed by the Barú River to the north, the Tinamaste Mountains to the east, and a 4-kilometer (2.5-mile) gray-sand beach to the west. The beach's booming waves are heaven for surfers but not always so great for swimmers. Each year many people succumb to the punishing waves and dangerous riptides; the town has organized a force of lifeguards at the residents' own expense.

The coastline around Dominical is gorgeous, and the forest that comes down to the sea is riddled with rivers and spectacular waterfalls.

Most resident *extranjeros* (foreigners) live outside of Dominical proper; the foreigners you'll see in town are mostly young backpackers and surfers. They stay in beachside *cabinas,* check their email at Internet cafés, take yoga classes at Bamboo Yoga Play, and eat pizza at San Clemente Bar & Grill, where the ceiling is paneled with broken surfboards. Dominical is known as a board-breaking beach; one wit wrote on the remaining half of his board: "This wave was at least two feet tall!"

The town still looks like a bit of an outpost, but it has a lot more services than it used to—even a bank, complete with an ATM, across the coast highway from the entrance to town. The road from Quepos to Dominical has been widened and paved, making coastal access to Dominical a lot easier. But the new road, which encourages high speeds, also makes it easy to sail right by the small and poorly marked entrance to Dominical.

I asked Susan Atkinson, long-time expat and owner of Pacific Edge Cabins, whether the vastly improved road was good news for hoteliers. "Yes and no," she said. "More people will probably come, but the road might bring the type of people we don't want: the Marriott crew, who wants a five-star hotel and expect a bellhop to carry their luggage." Dominical is definitely not Marriott territory—not yet, anyway.

For medical care, there's a clinic in Platanillo, 13 kilometers (8 miles) east

Playa Ventanas, near Ojochal

of Dominical, a doctor and dentist in Uvita, 16 kilometers (10 miles) south of Dominical, and a hospital in San Isidro de El General, an hour's drive over the hill on Highway 243. Those living south of Dominical often head south to Palmar Norte or Ciudad Cortéz for the public hospitals there.

A few kilometers south of Dominical is Punta Dominical, a beautiful high rock outcropping with views down the cliffs to crashing surf below. Some lucky few (almost all foreigners) have built houses to take advantage of this setting. Not far from the rocky point is Playa Dominicalito, reef-protected and providing good mooring and decent swimming. From the mouth of nearby Higuerón (also called Morete) River to Point Piñuela to the south, Ballena (Whale) Marine National Park protects 45 terrestrial hectares (110 acres) and 2,175 marine hectares (5,375 acres), including the largest coral reef on the Pacific coast of Central America. This part of the coast is often called the Coast Ballena after the park.

Uvita and Ojochal

Uvita is a small community 16 kilometers (10 miles) south of Dominical. Once little more than a bump in the road, the town has grown rapidly and now has several banks, a few supermarkets, dental and health clinics, a bakery, a gas station, an Internet café, and several furniture stores and construction companies. It also has a *feria* (farmers market) every Saturday morning.

Ojochal, 20 kilometers (12 miles) south of Uvita, is a tiny town offering unexpectedly good food, in large part due to the resident community of French Canadians, some of whom saw ads in their hometown papers and bought lots sight-unseen with the guarantee of their money back if they didn't like the place. They liked it, they told their friends, and now there's a little piece of Quebec here on Costa Rica's Pacific coast. The French aren't bad cooks, something even Canada couldn't change. The talent seems to have also survived Costa Rica (not known for its cuisine), and one of the joys of being in the area is deciding whether to stop for filet mignon at Exotica or sample the foie gras at Citron, also highly touted by foodies and run by a former cook from Exotica.

Strung along the highway from Dominical to past Ojochal are a number of nice hotels frequented by Europeans and North Americans who've heard about the area's international community and low-key vibe. Though there's a lot to do here—bird-watching, snorkeling, kayaking in the ocean, or hiking to waterfalls—it takes some effort to find out where to go and what to do. This is true in spite of the fact that the area is one of the most well signed I've seen in this country. Uniform signs—blue with icons for food and lodging reminiscent of those on U.S. highways—suggest a community-wide effort aimed at attracting tourists, though Ojochal still seems more geared to residents than tourists. Speaking of residents, they aren't all French Canadians. There are also French from France (one of whom opined that French Canadians were "so American"), Belgians, Dutch, Italians, British, non-French Canadians, people from the United States, and, of course, Ticos.

SOUTHERN PACIFIC COAST TOWNS
The Osa Peninsula

National Geographic magazine called the Osa Peninsula "the most biologically intense place on Earth." This is Costa Rica's Amazon, a tropical rainforest, where tall trees drip vines and lianas, macaws screech, and most of the country's remaining jaguars prowl.

The numbers are staggering: 42,000 hectares (104,000 acres) of land (a good part of the peninsula) are protected in Corcovado National Park, which supports 13 distinct habitats and on which 600 centimeters (236 inches) of rain falls annually. Five hundred kinds of trees

thrive here, as do hundreds of species of birds, mammals, and reptiles. Crocodiles lurk in marshy areas, sea turtles lay eggs on deserted beaches, and tapirs pick their way shyly through the trees.

The peninsula juts 50 kilometers (30 miles) out into the Pacific, sheltering the Golfo Dulce to the south, whose warm, calm waters draw humpback whales, three kinds of dolphins, and all manner of sport fish. On the northern side of the peninsula, beautiful and isolated Drake Bay is usually reached by boat from the riverside settlement of Sierpe; there's hardly a town to be seen on the 90-minute trip, and the river is lined with huge stands of stilt-rooted mangroves.

Though the Osa has had its share of environmental problems, including invasive gold mining, slash-and-burn farming, and the poaching of endangered wildlife, the area's relative inaccessibility has saved it from large-scale exploitation. Visitors need to make an investment of time and effort to sample the peninsula's delights, and prospective residents should have that extra measure of patience and resourcefulness that makes living in the outback an adventure rather than a hardship.

That said, it's getting easier to get to the Osa, at least during dry season. Small planes fly from San José to Puerto Jiménez every day, and charters land at Carate and other makeshift airstrips on demand. You can take a boat from Golfito to Puerto Jiménez, and even the trip by road is getting easier with recent road and bridge repairs. The bus ride from San José to Puerto Jiménez is an 8- to 10-hour trip: driving your own car (four-wheel drive recommended) will make the trip quicker (about six hours) and more comfortable.

Michael Cranford, tree house architect and fine arts painter, has lived on the peninsula since 1998. "The people coming here aren't the pioneers anymore," he says. "The new ones ask where they can park their Jet Ski. They want turnkey condos and SUVs." But the Osa still is not for the faint of heart. "They drop a quarter of a million dollars on a house and business," Michael continues. "Then within a year the Osa spits them out like a watermelon seed."

Puerto Jiménez

With a population of several thousand, Puerto Jiménez is the largest town on the Osa Peninsula. Visitors to Corcovado National Park most often come through Jiménez, and there is an assortment of hotels, restaurants, and bars to serve them. There's also a bank, a post office, a well-stocked supermarket and lots of little markets, a health clinic, a library (supported by donations), and even a mini-mall, complete with elevator and movie theater. The town's pleasant waterfront promenade gives pedestrians amazing views of the dolphin-rich Golfo Dulce. The town's small airstrip rises up out of bird- and crocodile-rich wetlands.

Flying into town is easier than driving, and you're as likely to hear the drone of a light plane as the revving of a car engine. It wasn't long ago that the road into the area was even worse than the potholed tracks drivers now endure; until recently boats were the main method of transport. Still crucial to the area, vessels both big and small find excellent moorage in the deep and calm Golfo Dulce. For tourists, this town is a popular jumping-off point to visit Corcovado National Park.

The town's history is a colorful one, with tales centering on the gold rush of the 1980s, when Puerto Jiménez (to hear locals tell it) was a modern-day Wild West, with blood feuds, horses tied up outside saloons in which gunfights raged, and prostitutes with hearts of gold (or at least pockets full of gold nuggets).

Things are quieter these days, and many of the area's foreign residents like it

that way. Those wanting even more peace than town life can offer settle deep in the jungle or along the spectacular coastline between Puerto Jiménez and Carate, where the road ends and you must walk into Corcovado. Beaches are tucked away between rock outcroppings, and at Cabo Matapalo, on the southeast tip of the peninsula, waves get big enough to draw surfers. Matapalo also draws foreign residents: some operate luxury hotels, and many spearhead environmental and social justice efforts in the area.

Golfito

Golfito is located on a small gulf within the larger Golfo Dulce, and this double dose of protection from the ocean swell means that waves breaking on the town's shore never get more than knee-high. Would that Golfito had similar protection from economic storms. The town started life as a banana port when in 1938 the Boston-based United Fruit Company (now called Chiquita) moved its operations from the Caribbean to the Pacific, fleeing banana blight and labor strikes. During the 1950s, 90 percent of Costa Rica's banana exports were shipped from Golfito, and the banana company was the major employer in the area. But just as it abandoned the Caribbean side of the country, United Fruit pulled out of Golfito in 1985, leaving the land around town pumped full of pesticides that made it hard to grow anything else here.

Since the departure of United Fruit, the Costa Rican government has tried to promote other businesses to shore up the area's depressed economy. The major effort is the Deposito Libre, a duty-free shopping compound opened in 1990 that looks like a prison but draws Ticos from all over the country, especially at Christmastime. They're looking to avoid the high import tariffs on everything from refrigerators to perfume, and Golfito's lodgings are

Expat Experiences: At Home in the Trees

What is it about Costa Rica's Zona Sur that inspires expats to go arboreal? Within an 80-kilometer (50-mile) radius of the heart of the Osa Peninsula, there are at least three examples of foreign residents who've made tree houses central to their lives. These folks definitely get the prize for adapting to their environment, even if it's 20 meters (70 feet) up and peopled by monkeys and macaws.

EVERY SURFACE IS A CANVAS
Humberto deSilva from France and Lisa Brouillard from Quebec have lived in Costa Rica for about 25 years. Their home used to be a bed-and-breakfast, Casa Arbol, and the place is still a work of art—Humberto made the intricately carved cupboards and bed stands as well as the

treehouse at Finca Bella Vista

bathhouse that evokes ancient Rome. He also created a small tree house—like something out of an eco-friendly fairytale—that guests can stay in if they like. He never knows how a project will turn out when he begins. He kept showing me carvings and rooms and tile work and saying, in Spanish heavy with French, "When I finished, I finally saw what it was." Perhaps a swan, a frog, a mandala, or a meditation on humanity.

A TREE HOUSE COMMUNITY IN THE JUNGLE
In 2005, Erica and Matt Hogan were camped in the mud by the Bella Vista River, on a spread of lovely but undeveloped land that they'd just sunk their life savings into. They weren't sure what was going to get them out of the mud, but they dreamed of building a kind of Ewok village, where they'd live in the trees and get to their neighbors' houses via zip line.

Most people would have let that rather whimsical dream sputter and die, but Erica, originally from Oklahoma, and Matt, formerly of Maryland and Washington DC, kept it alive, creating Finca Bella Vista, a sustainable tree house community with lots available

mostly geared to the tourists who, along with other potential shoppers, must stay overnight in or near town before being allowed to shop in the duty-free zone.

Golfito has a full-service marina and sportfishing center in Banana Bay Marina. December-May is sailfish season, June-September is good for marlin, and May-September you're likely to find snook.

Golfito isn't much of a tourist attraction in and of itself, though it's interesting to hang out at the town's dock, watching

rough-and-tumble locals unload headless marlin, or notice that in the old section of town (the *pueblo civil*), rickety houses hang out over the water, and every other business seems to be a bar.

Two kilometers (1.2 miles) south is another part of town that looks like it's in a different country. The Zona Americana was built by United Fruit to house its higher-ups. Generously proportioned wooden homes were built on stilts to combat the damp and catch the breeze. Spacious lawns and gardens give the area

for people who want to live off the grid and in the trees as well as opportunities to stay and study there. There are dozens of zip lines strung on the property, both for squeal-inducing high-wire fun and for the transport of people and tools—workmen whiz above the trees loaded down with building materials and tools.

Their idea of a tree house (there are many schools of thought) stipulates almost no contact with the ground. So they brought in experts from Pete Nelson's Tree house Workshop in Washington State to rig their structures, using a special drilled-in support called the Garnier limb, named after tree house expert Michael Garnier, who has a tree house bed-and-breakfast in southern Oregon.

From the tree houses, some 15 meters (50 feet) up, you can hear the roar of a nearby waterfall, visible from the top floor, and take an outdoor shower while birds chatter, wondering what you're doing in their territory.

AT HOME IN THE TREES

Michael Cranford of Colorado and Rebecca Amelia (aka Blondie) of Massachusetts were drinking margaritas in Boquete, Panama, talking about how as kids they'd retreat to the trees when they needed to get away. A few hours and numerous drinks later, they were sketching tree house designs on napkins.

A few years later, the scrawled blueprints became reality when they hauled a few platforms built on the ground up into an enormous Guanacaste tree on their land on the Osa Peninsula. "We listened to what the tree was telling us," says Michael. They didn't want to drill into the tree, so they used four wooden supports that go from the ground to the platforms that make up their home.

The tree house is a true home, with a spacious, fully equipped kitchen, guest bedrooms, an office for each of them, and a master bedroom. Eighty percent of the wood used for the tree house is downed hardwood from the rainforest that is their backyard. They have Internet and cable, flush toilets, and plenty of hot water in the shower. They've seen a sloth right outside the kitchen, monkeys come through regularly, and scarlet macaws hang out in nearby branches. They rent the place out to vacationers, or enjoy it themselves.

Michael, who's also a painter, an organizer of local music festivals, and a "jungle architect," says, "I learned more about myself working with this tree than I have through any other life experience."

a luxuriant feel that has endured even as many of the buildings fall into ruin.

Golfito is a quick flight from San José (it takes seven or eight hours on the bus, five hours in your own car). There's a fast boat from Golfito to Puerto Jiménez, and you can hire water taxis to Playa Zancudo or Pavones. It's a one- to two-hour drive from Golfito to Pavones or Playa Zancudo.

Playa Zancudo

Playa Zancudo isn't far from Golfito, at least as the crow flies or the water taxi skims. If you drive, however, you'll negotiate a 45-kilometer (28-mile) unpaved route that includes crossing the Río Coto on a two-car ferry.

This seriously laid-back town is strung out along a sandy spit of land between the Río Coto Estuary and the waters of the Golfo Dulce. It's a lovely place, where you can buckle down to the serious task of doing very little. In fact, if you need a lot of stimulation, Playa Zancudo is probably not for you. It has that end-of-the-road

San Lucas Island: Costa Rica's Alcatraz

"If you don't have anything to do," says the graffiti scratched into the cell block wall, "don't come here to do it."

That would have been excellent advice from 1883 to 1989, when the penitentiary on San Lucas Island was synonymous with cruelty and isolation. Inmates labored in the tropical sun, breaking rocks and harvesting salt from the sea, dragging their leg irons and dreaming of escape.

For all those years it was a place of anguish, a place where men became less than human, crammed into dank underground cells, scratching their pain into the prison walls. You can still see the graffiti; one sketch, a woman in a crimson bikini, is said to have been drawn in blood.

The place shut down in 1989, and in 2005 San Lucas Island became a national park. Tourists can now visit the ruins of the prison, spot monkeys and agoutis in the forest, and walk the quiet beaches.

graffiti in the ruins of the old prison

Despite San Lucas's painful past, it is still a relatively unspoiled tropical island, one of a dozen in the Gulf of Nicoya, which separates Costa Rica's mainland from the Nicoya Peninsula. From the deck of the ferry connecting the two, travelers catch a glimpse of overgrown San Lucas with its lovely and deserted beaches.

For 10 years after the prison closed, the island's fate hung in the balance. The local government wanted to raze the remaining prison buildings and erect a mega-resort with hotels, a marina, a golf course, and an airstrip. Costa Rica's Environment Ministry (MINAE) wanted to preserve the prison ruins, study the island's seven pre-Columbian archaeological sites, and declare the 472-hectare (1,166-acre) island a wildlife reserve. Costa Rica's Supreme Court had to make the call, and to the relief of many, it decided on the latter option.

THE ISLAND OF LONELY MEN

Opened in 1873, San Lucas was modeled on the British penal system of that era, which

feel that can either charm the pants off you or drive you nuts. If you end up staying, no doubt you'll have days when it does both.

Some of the town's foreign residents run hotels or restaurants, and that keeps them busy, at least during high season (December-April). Snatches of conversation at local haunts reveal expat concerns: the need to drive eight-plus hours to San José to buy some things for the house or to pick up a friend from the airport; the need to get away, especially in the very

rainy months of September and October; the frustrations of having the power go out or the phone lines on the blink. But there's a general good cheer as well, and a celebration of being in a beautiful spot, pretty much left to one's own devices. The beach here is the focus of many a lazy day. It stretches six lovely kilometers (four miles), is bordered by tall coconut palms, and offers good swimming at the southern end and decent surfing farther north. Anglers will be in heaven, as some of the best fishing in the area can be had close

favored the natural isolation of island penitentiaries. The best-known example of this approach was Australia, to which the British sent criminals whose offenses were "very grave." Before San Lucas became a prison island, Costa Rica set up a penitentiary on Isla de Coco, at that time 36 hours by boat off the mainland and now a destination for scuba divers who go for the schooling hammerhead sharks. Predictably, Coco proved too remote to effectively oversee, and they shut that prison down and built the prison on San Lucas, a short boat trip from Puntarenas.

The most famous of the island's former inhabitants has to be prisoner number 1713, otherwise known as José León Sánchez. In 1950 he went to San Lucas an illiterate felon. Paroled in 1969, he emerged a writer who would receive international acclaim and who in 1999 would finally be absolved of the crime he always maintained he never committed.

The best known of León's 27 books is a novel based on his experiences on San Lucas, *La Isla de los Hombres Solos* (The Island of Lonely Men). The English version, *God Was Looking the Other Way,* is out of print.

León's supposed crime was one of the most highly publicized of its time. One account says that at the age of 19, after consulting with the Toroc (the wise man or shaman) of his town, he was compelled to reclaim the gold and jewels from the country's most opulent church, the Cartago basilica, as the rightful property of the indigenous people of Costa Rica. Other accounts deny he had anything to do with the foiled robbery, during which a church guard was killed. One thing is certain: León was accused of stealing the jewels of La Negrita, the beloved patron saint of Costa Rica. If any crime was designed to outrage the entire country, this insult to its patron saint was it.

After two days of torture, León confessed to the crime. The press dubbed him the Monster of the Basilica, he was excommunicated from the Catholic Church, and he was forced to argue his own case because no lawyer would represent him.

At San Lucas, prisoner 1713 logged 19 years of confinement, two escapes (he was recaptured on the mainland), and 17 attempted escapes. He also learned to read and write in jail, and he self-published his first books there, putting together a primitive press from instructions in an old *Popular Mechanics.*

He was paroled in 1969, and 30 years later, Costa Rica's Supreme Court declared León "absolved of all responsibility" for the crime for which he served 19 years and which made him a pariah in his own country. León, who lives in Heredia, continues to write and is a tireless advocate of prison reform.

by. In fact, there's a well-known annual sportfishing competition, based at Roy's Zancudo Lodge.

The fact that Zancudo is hemmed in by an estuary on one side and the sea on the other has sparked some questions about property ownership in the area. Maritime zone law stipulates that no one can own land until 200 meters (219 yards) up from high tide line, and lately the municipality has been questioning the right of foreigners to lease property in this zone. If you're looking to buy here, be sure to get the up-to-the-minute news by talking to as many foreign residents as possible.

Pavones

At least as small as Playa Zancudo, Pavones has more of a center, even if that center consists of a scruffy soccer field around which the town's few businesses are clustered. There's the open-air cantina, a few humble *pulperías* and casual restaurants, a variety of low-budget *cabinas,* and, in the emotional if not geographic center of town, a surf shop.

Make no mistake, Pavones is a surf town. The famous left-breaking wave is the reason people come, it's the reason a select few stay, and it's the reason non-surfers whine, "There's nothing to do here." It's why most of the town's visitors are young and male with biceps hard from paddling and skin an international brown, making it hard to say whether the guy on the board is Israeli, French, Argentine, Floridian, or Tico. These fellows are also why Pavones has a different tourist season than most other towns in Costa Rica. The usual high season is dry season, December-April, but surfers know that the rainy months (May-October) are when the waves in Pavones really go off.

Even the nightlife, such as it is, revolves around surfing. Guys gather at the cantina to hoist a Pilsen or seven, going into the kind of excruciating detail about the day's waves that only fellow fanatics can appreciate.

Did I mention that Pavones and its environs are absolutely gorgeous? Sometimes the surf vibe is so strong you forget that even civilians can appreciate how the rain-forested hills slide down to meet sandy beaches or how the rocky tide pools burst with life. In contrast to surf spots like Tamarindo and Puerto Viejo, Pavones is harder to get to, which means that only the dedicated make it here, and the town has not yet mushroomed into a more general tourist destination, with the attendant bars and Internet cafés.

Electricity didn't arrive in Pavones until the mid-1990s, and landlines are still hard to come by. Cell phones are ubiquitous; you'll see people scurrying around to find the best spot to catch a signal, yelling into their headsets, "Can you hear me now?"

Property ownership issues are complicated by the area's recent history. After United Fruit pulled out in 1985, foreigners bought up big stretches of coastline. Even financial fugitive Robert Vesco owned land here for a while, as did many others whose sources of income would not bear much scrutiny. In 1988, Danny Fowlie, who'd bought up a fair amount of land around Pavones, was convicted of drug trafficking and put in jail in the United States. His enterprising lawyer sold Fowlie's land to other gringos, and bought some of it for himself, but the Costa Rican government wanted the land (by law it can expropriate the land of convicted felons). Squatters also tried, with some success, to claim the property.

In 1992 a showdown between squatters and those who had bought pieces of Fowlie's land ended in the death of one man (a Tico guard hired to protect gringo-owned land). In 1997 a 79-year-old U.S cattle breeder got into an altercation with a squatter, and they shot each other. Or, to hear the gossip, the squatter's boss shot the old man, then shot the squatter and put the gun in his hand. Whatever the truth of the matter, prospective buyers should be careful, making sure that land being offered them has a clean title and legally belongs to the supposed seller. Locals insist that Pavones now welcomes foreign investors and residents, but there's still a feeling of caution here.

Foreign residents joke that they haven't had to shoot anyone for a few years, and that Pavones is perhaps the most dysfunctional town in the country. Then again there are many towns in Costa Rica that could vie for that honor; perhaps the jokes are meant to keep out all but the intrepid.

THE CARIBBEAN COAST

As the toucan flies, the Caribbean coast is closer to the capital city of San José than fabled Pacific coast beaches like Tamarindo and Montezuma. Puerto Viejo, the east coast version of those offbeat surfer havens, is an easy four-hour bus ride from San José. Puerto Limón, a bustling port and the only real city in the area, can be reached in half that time. The entire coastline, from Nicaragua to Panama, is only 160 kilometers (100 miles) long, while the more convoluted west coast measures 480 kilometers (300 miles). Still, Limón—the province that encompasses the entire east coast of Costa Rica and the mountains that back it up—seems more remote and exotic than the west coast.

The differences are apparent even to the casual observer. The Zona Caribe is more racially mixed than the rest of Costa Rica, with Afro-Caribbean and Chinese people descended from the men who came to build the railroad, and indigenous people whose ancestors were here when Columbus arrived. The area also looks and feels more like the Caribbean islands, with picture-postcard beaches and more evident poverty than elsewhere in the country.

North Americans who move here are often drawn to the natural beauty of the place and also to its slightly rough edge. There are still very few condo projects or mega-malls on the coast, and the people who love it here hope it stays that way.

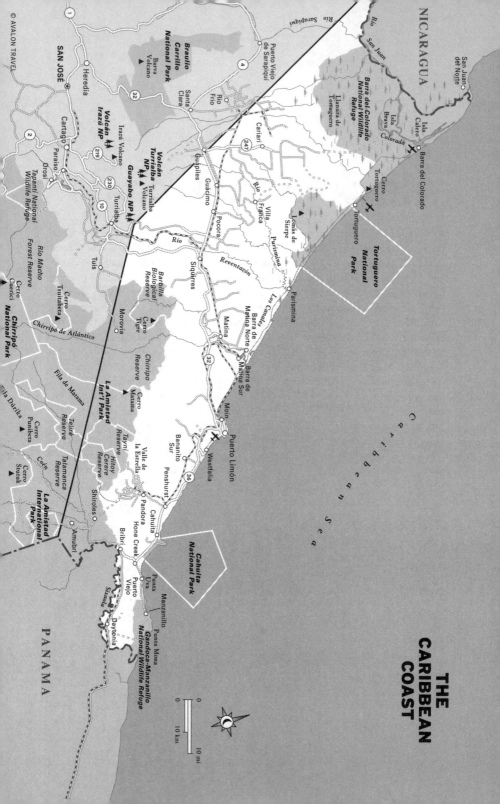

The Lay of the Land

Remoteness and cultural diversity have deep roots in the Zona Caribe. Columbus landed here in 1502, on his fourth and final journey to the New World, but he didn't stay long. Cortéz came and went 22 years later. The conquistadors hoped they'd find gold, but for the most part they were disappointed—there were no gleaming, gold-encrusted cities in Costa Rica, like those found up north in Mexico or down south in Peru. There was no real reason for the Spaniards to stick around; the coast was left to its own devices and became a refuge for rum-runners, gun traders, and mostly British pirates, who between raids would retreat to the swampy interior or hide out along stretches of wild coastline. They traded and sometimes intermarried with indigenous people who farmed and fished the sea and rivers. Among the indigenous groups were the Votos, who had female chiefs; most of the groups here were, and are, matrilineal, meaning membership comes through one's mother.

To this day, the Caribbean coast retains its reputation as a smuggler's haven; nowadays the area is, unfortunately, an important transshipment point for drugs on their way from South America to North America. Florentino Grenald, a guide who specializes in hikes through the Gandoca-Manzanillo Wildlife Refuge, showed me a pristine and deserted white-sand beach that he called Cocaine Beach. A few years back, hundreds of kilos were dumped here when smugglers had boat trouble; locals soon discovered the cache, generously giving the watertight bricks better hiding places in their own homes.

The area's historical isolation meant that the Zona Caribe was pretty much left to its own devices. Often ignored by the government, Limón Province was the poor stepchild in terms of infrastructure, education, and health services (it still is, to some extent). A third of Limón's population is Afro-Caribbean, and black people in Costa Rica didn't have full citizenship until 1949; there were also restrictions on where they could travel and live within their own country. Indigenous people, like the Bribrí and the Talamanca, also had a hard time of it historically, though nowadays they are a much more organized and vocal minority who have done much work to preserve their culture and lands.

Isolation from the rest of the country and neglect from Costa Rica's centralized government may have benefited the Zona Caribe. The natural world fared a bit better on this coast than on the Pacific; although banana companies razed large tracts of forest and then pumped toxic insecticides into the ecosystem, more of Limón Province is protected than any of the other six provinces in the country. Almost half the Caribbean coastline is sheltered in reserves. The isolation also meant that the culture—already quite different from the rest of Costa Rica—retained its individuality. Substandard health care facilities may have helped to preserve some of the folk healing and herbal remedies that came from indigenous cultures and from Africa via West Indian immigrants. Knowledge and use of medicinal plants is common, and folk healers do a brisk business in their communities, with many expats numbered among their patients. Their specialties are various and they go by many names—midwives, bush doctors, shamans, and *sukias,* to name a few. Many work hand in hand with more Western approaches, referring people to nearby clinics if they believe that type of intervention is in the patient's best interest.

The Caribbean coast has always been sparsely settled and less developed than settlements in the interior of the country and on the Pacific coast. In 1882, the Costa Rican government offered land grants here to encourage migration. Around the same time, the railroad was being built, and workers came from as far away as Italy and China, though most came from the Caribbean islands. Of these, the majority came from Jamaica, and that culture's influence is still strongly felt here, in the English patois spoken, the spicy coconut curries served with jerk chicken, and the oversupply of Bob Marley music—hang out in a few bars and you'll reach your lifetime Marley limit in under a week.

"Don't worry about a thing," could be the area's mantra. Don't worry about the rain—the biggest *aguaceros* (downpours) usually come at night, and overcast days provide welcome relief from the dazzling sun. Don't worry if you don't have money for dinner—just pull some red snapper out of the ocean and pick from a dozen varieties of fruit growing year-round on trees that don't seem to be watched over too closely. And don't worry that if you have serious health problems, you'll need to go to the hospital in Limón or—if it's an emergency—that you'll most likely be airlifted to better facilities in the Central Valley.

Despite the rough spots, things move along at an easy rhythm, with a little syncopation to liven up the proceedings. The Caribbean coast is full of surprises, from lacquer-red poison dart frogs jumping out from under leaves to the prevalence of an English that confounds even more than Spanish, because you think you should understand it but don't. The people here constitute a heady brew of Afro-Caribbean, Chinese, indigenous, mestizo, mulatto, European, and North American. The animal life is even more varied. I almost ended up in the Tortuguero River after my hydro-bike collided with an enormous creature that turned out to be one of the few remaining manatees in the area. Probably as startled as I was, the half-ton beast batted its fleshy tail against the boat's pontoons, then thrashed away upriver.

Such wonders are everyday fare in the Zona Caribe, and life is slow enough here to savor them.

The Bribrí village of Yorkín is about half an hour by boat up the Sixoala River.

WEATHER

The climate is also phenomenal, though whether it will inspire awe or lament depends on your constitution. The coast south of Puerto Limón (often called the Talamanca coast) averages a prodigious 240 centimeters (95 inches) of rain per year, with the wettest months being December, January, July, and August. Drier times may be had in September and October, as well as from the second half of February through April. But those in the know say there's no real dry season, just a few months where it doesn't rain quite as much. Still, it's unusual to go more than a day or two without a glimpse of sun and blue skies. Often it rains at night or for a brief spell in the morning and is clear the rest of the day.

North of Limón, the drier seasons are longer, but when the rain comes down, it really comes down. July, the wettest month, averages almost 100 centimeters (39 inches) of rain in just 31 days.

Temperatures stay the same year-round, with lows around 21-23°C (70-73°F) and highs in the 28-30°C (80-85°F) range. Humidity can be high, but cooling breezes help to alleviate the stickiness. The sun is very strong, especially around midday, when it's best to seek out some shade lest you end up looking like the sunburned tourist tree, red and peeling.

ACCESS

Until the late 1970s, travel to this coast meant taking a slow train from San José to Puerto Limón, and travel around the area itself, especially in the north, was by motorized dugout canoe or via the slow *African Queen*-style boats that still bring mail and supplies to outlying areas.

In 1979, the road from Puerto Limón south (which takes you to Cahuita, Puerto Viejo, and Manzanillo) was improved and became passable most of the time, though heavy rains often washed out bridges and stretches of pavement. The 1991 earthquake destroyed the railroad, but by then the coastal strip south of Puerto Limón was fairly well served by Highway 36, which was paved (sort of) to the town of Puerto Viejo. More recently, the pavement was extended south to Manzanillo, a small village located within the Gandoca-Manzanillo National Wildlife Refuge—a reserve that doesn't get half the visitors of the more popular protected areas, but where you can see lots of wildlife,

Water taxis ply the canals of the northern Caribbean coast.

Expat Experience: Advice for Newcomers

A North American who spent many years on Costa Rica's Caribbean coast offers up a few words of praise and advice.

What do you like best about Costa Rica?

I love Talamanca (the Caribbean coast and nearby mountain ranges are also called Talamanca). It's *tranquilo* (peaceful) and green. With Gandoca-Manzanillo Reserve, the indigenous reserves, and the private reserves, 88 percent of Talamanca is protected. And Talamanca has the most cultural diversity in all of Costa Rica. People here are real. For example, I come back from vacation and they tell me I'm fat, or when I vex the women I work with, they tell me. I love my work here and the people who work so hard together to protect this place.

Any advice for people thinking of moving to Costa Rica?

- Rent first.
- Hire locals and pay fair wages–better than fair, even.
- Support local businesses.
- Examine your intentions for wanting to invest here. If you've got an idealized image, rethink it, or you'll get disappointed.
- Have cultural sensitivity: English is not the national language.
- Learn about the area, the language, customs, history–it shows respect.

including rare tucuxi dolphins and an alarming variety of pit vipers.

It wasn't until 1986 that Puerto Viejo, the most touristed town on the coast, got 24-hour electricity; Manzanillo and Tortuguero had to wait until 1988. Private phone lines arrived in Puerto Viejo in 1996, a decade or so later cell phone towers were erected, and now most businesses in the area have email accounts and websites. Puerto Viejo got its first bank (the Banco de Costa Rica) in early 2005. Before that locals and tourists had to travel to Puerto Limón to do their banking.

Nowadays you can fly by light plane from San José to Tortuguero, in the north, and to Limón, on the central Caribbean coast—most flights last no more than 30 minutes. North of Limón there are still very few roads; canals dug in the 1960s to link up lagoons and meandering rivers now connect remote villages and lead tourists to Tortuguero National Park, where huge numbers of sea turtles arrive to lay their eggs, usually close to the very spot where they themselves hatched.

PRICES

Land and home prices (and rents) on this coast are significantly more reasonable than those you'll find on the Pacific coast or in popular Central Valley locations. Local real estate agents say that the two most popular towns for expats, Cahuita and Puerto Viejo, have plenty of one-family homes for under US$200,000.

Where to Live

TORTUGUERO

A remote hamlet reachable only by boat or light plane, Tortuguero has drawn just a handful of permanent foreign residents. Every year, though, tens of thousands of tourists pour into nearby Tortuguero National Park, hoping to catch a glimpse of the tens of thousands of sea turtles that each year flipper their way up the beach, dig a hole in the sand, and lay their flexible-skinned eggs. The nearby rainforest-lined canals are also a big tourist draw, with birds and monkeys and caimans easily visible from small boats that ply the network of waterways built by lumber companies.

Most visitors bypass the ramshackle town and spend their money in all-inclusive lodges along the river, though more and more independent travelers are choosing to base themselves in Tortuguero.

Perched on a sandy spit of land between the often rough sea and a calm lagoon, the town can be walked end to end in minutes. You'll see wooden houses built on stilts, painted various shades of weather-beaten blue, doors and shutters most often flung open to take advantage of the cooling breezes. In recent years more imposing houses have gone up, complete with second floors and daunting gates and fences. There are narrow paths through the village, but most homes are oriented to the river or lagoon, the way residences elsewhere are oriented to the road. Brightly painted dugout canoes are pulled up onto the muddy bank or bob gently in the water. Herons and egrets lurk at the river's edge, keeping a sharp eye out for fish or the shrimp that congregate around the floating water hyacinth. Iguanas sun themselves on the branches of vine-draped trees.

Many locals are originally from Nicaragua, and there's a sense that the nearby border is rather porous, with fishermen and others who work on the water going back and forth with relative ease.

Foreigners often come to work with nature organizations such as the Caribbean Conservation Corporation, founded by biologist Archie Carr in the 1950s to help preserve and study sea turtles. The few nonnatives who settle here tend to be involved in conservation or work as nature guides. Daryl Loth, a Canadian transplant who now works as an independent guide, arrived in 1994 to manage a biological station run by a Canadian nonprofit institute. He married Luz Denia, a Tica, had two kids, and settled down in a riverside home that is also a well-regarded B&B called Casa Marbella. Daryl points out that Tortuguero has its own time zone. "When it's 9am in New York City," he says, "in Tortuguero it's 1973."

Tortuguero gets my vote as one of the most unusual places in the country. Its remote nature can be a challenge, although in the last decade the town has seen a new health clinic and a new ICE (electricity) office go up, sure signs that the central government sees Tortuguero as worthy of state-funded social services. For years there has been talk of a road that would cut a swath through the swampy jungle and end just across the river from this carless village. Residents are actively trying to attract more tourists, and if they succeed, drowsy, aquatic Tortuguero is bound to morph into a very different kind of beast.

PUERTO LIMÓN

The rest of Costa Rica doesn't have much affection for Puerto Limón, citing crime statistics and calling it Piedropolis

("Crack City"). But there's no denying Limón's vitality. It's the economic engine of the area, especially when you take into account its sister port of Moín, five kilometers (three miles) west, where crude oil is processed and shipped, and boats are piled high with bananas bound for Europe and North America. Limón itself is where the *cruceros* (cruise ships) dock. Of the hundreds of thousands of cruise ship passengers that dock in Costa Rica each year, more than half disembark in Limón. Most spend their day ashore on an organized tour that has them bypassing the city, which is a shame, especially for people interested in Afro-Caribbean history. Jamaican political leader Marcus Garvey, for example, founder of the Back-to-Africa movement, spent time here and even built an office for his Black Star Line (a shipping company) in downtown Limón.

A major earthquake in 1991 mangled the wrought-iron balconies and toppled the open-air arcades that gave the city its ragged tropical charm, though there's been much rebuilding since then. The Limoneses walking the street are of every race, with lots of interesting blends that will have you trying to tease out the ancestry of a particularly arresting face.

But all in all, Limón City is not a place that inspires one to dream about buying a little house and settling down, and you'll want to hang on to your purse when you make a visit. The city's one indisputable claim to fame is that it explodes every October in Carnaval, with fireworks, dancing in the streets, and bands from all over the Caribbean and Latin America. Christopher P. Baker, author of *Moon Costa Rica,* says the raucous festival is like the plague: You either flee or succumb. The same might be said for the city itself.

palm-lined path in Tortuguero town

CAHUITA

About an hour south of Puerto Limón is charming and very low-key Cahuita, with its parade of delectable beaches from black-sand Playa Negra to the 14 kilometers (9 miles) of palm-shaded white sand within Cahuita National Park. Lush jungle flanks these pristine stretches of sand, the tangle of foliage so dense in places that 75 meters (82 yards) in from the beach you can't hear the surf. Offshore coral reefs create protected coves excellent for swimming and snorkeling.

The land around the coast tends to be swampy and prone to flooding. In fact, much of the area in and around town was not so long ago under water; brush aside a few centimeters of topsoil a few hundred meters from the beach and you'll hit coral. Here and there coral outcroppings rise up out of the fertile loam, which supports all manner of flowering plants and trees, including jackfruit, ornamental

Puerto Limón's bus station

ginger, carambola (star fruit), and varieties of citrus and palm.

Cahuita is still a modest village, with a main street leading to the entrance of Cahuita National Park. A jungle trail parallels the beach, where monkeys cavort in the trees and crabs scuttle across your path.

Though the town doesn't have the party vibe of nearby Puerto Viejo, Cahuita is still geared toward tourism, with maybe two dozen places to eat in town—from traditional Afro-Caribbean fare to pizza and pasta—and a surprising variety of lodging options for such a small place.

For residents, there's a public school and a small private school that counts among its students both expat and local kids. Basic health care is available at a small clinic in town and a larger one in nearby Hone Creek; for more serious matters, residents travel to Puerto Limón or San José. Some residents head for the Talamanca Mountains to one of many famed indigenous *curanderos* (curers) or seek out Afro-Caribbean bush doctors versed in herbal and folk remedies. One longtime expat "did the whole deal—made the trip, spent the night being eaten by bugs, then stood in line with the other supplicants." When her turn came, she told the *curandero* she wanted to quit smoking. "He gave me a potion, which I drank. Then I traded my lighter for a cigarette."

More than a dozen nationalities are represented among the area's foreign residents, including Switzerland, the United States, Germany, Canada, and Italy.

PUERTO VIEJO AND VICINITY

A tumbledown village on a melancholy coast, Puerto Viejo is also a surfer's haven and a party town for the eco-set. Not everyone here is tattooed and 22, though sometimes it seems that way. Dreadlocks abound.

You may have heard of the Salsa Brava—a hard, fast, dangerous wave that draws riders from near and far. What you might not know is that it's right in town; you can nurse a beer at a beachside bar and have a front-row seat for all the wipeouts.

There are also banks, supermarkets, hardware stores, and other such necessities that make a place livable.

Driving the town's paved main street, you'll need to slow for bike and foot traffic—people pedaling by on beat-up beach cruisers or ambling from lunch to hammock or from coffee to Internet cafés. Heading south out of town, you'll pass Playa Cocles, Playa Chiquita, and Punta Uva, areas with scatterings of long-term North American and European expats.

"Lots of old hippies out there," a townie told me. "Good people." Nobody would hazard a guess as to how many foreign residents there were in the area, but locals

Expat Experience: a Self-Sustaining Farm

Kimberly B. moved from Cincinnati to rural Costa Rica in 2010, but she says that the seeds for that life change were planted much earlier.

"Planted" turns out to be an apt metaphor. Kim and her then-husband had long been interested in living off the land. When they came to Costa Rica, they bought a 9-hectare (22-acre) farm, fertile land bordered by a river and with a natural spring in their backyard. The farm, which Kim now runs by herself, supports coffee, cacao, bananas, papaya, squash, peppers, and passion fruit, to name just a few of the crops that help Beck realize her dream of being more self-sufficient.

REAL VERSUS MANUFACTURED NEED

How did Kim get from latitude 39 in Cincinnati to latitude 10 in Costa Rica? How'd she go from "selling data pipes" to clearing land in the tropics? It started in, of all places, Tanzania, where Kim was a Peace Corps volunteer in a town so remote the kids there had never seen blacktop and the babies cried when confronted with white people. There was no running water and no electricity.

After Kim finished her Peace Corps stint, reentry into the United States wasn't easy. "Living in the United States, there's so much purposeless advertising telling you that you need things no one really needs," says Kim. "In Africa, they do actually desperately need things. Food. Clean water. Rain for their crops." Kim wanted a middle ground between those two extremes.

AN AD ON THE INTERNET

Ironically, it was an ad that pointed her in the direction of Costa Rica. At this point she was back in the nine-to-five grind. Kim had a banner year at her sales job and banked her US$30,000 bonus check, hoping it would be a down payment for a new life.

"I started looking on LandandFarm. com," says Kim, "but the places that looked good—beautiful land in Oregon and California where the growing seasons are long

and we could grow our own food—were really expensive." Then she saw a little ad for land in Costa Rica. "It was just all green," she says. "It was greener than anything else on that site."

Two research trips later, she and her then-husband bought what would become 10 Degrees Above for US$35,000. They looked all over the country but found that the Caribbean Zone was not only less expensive, but better suited their desire for a working farm as well.

BY THE NUMBERS

Kim says they got a good price because the place had been neglected. There were no roads, no electricity, and though there was a natural spring, there were no pipes to make that water available. The only structure on the land was a dilapidated caretaker's shack that had to be pulled down.

Besides the initial US$35,000 for the acreage, they paid a real estate agent US$4,000 in fees and commissions, another US$4,000 to have roads built, a little less than US$1,000 to bring in electricity, and US$22,000 to build a one-room cottage with a tropical hardwood wraparound deck. That latter figure included clearing the land and all the appliances they needed for the house.

They spent about US$6,000 on another small cabin with a front porch that they rent out (they built it on the cement foundation of the dilapidated caretaker's shack they had to tear down). Later they also built a larger two-story home up the hill, having budgeted US$30,000 for that structure.

THE DREAM EVOLVES

The dream began as a joint project, but when the couple split, Beck kept it going. She still does much of the work herself but also finds volunteers through services like helpx.net. She provides lodging and meals, while volunteers get to learn about (and help with) an organic farm on the Caribbean slope of Costa Rica. "I feel proud to have taken the leap," she says. "It's all about enjoying the little bit of time that we have in this life."

cacao fruit

lament that more and more land seems to end up in foreign hands. One local business owner estimated that 75 percent of the town is now foreign-owned. "They flash a lot of money, and people are people—they take it." I asked him if he too was looking to sell out. His reply: "What're you offering?"

The influx picked up steam in 1991, when a newly paved coastal road made Puerto Viejo easily accessible from San José. Locals began selling off their land to newcomers, in part because many considered their farms worthless, since their principal crop, cacao, had recently been destroyed by the *Monilia* fungus.

Some of the foreigners who've arrived are (ironically) now trying to make a living from cacao, which, it turns out, can be grown in ways to avoid *Monilia* and other destructive fungi. In 1987 Peter Kring bought an abandoned cacao farm and transformed it into Finca la Isla Botanical Garden, which includes a botanical garden, a plant nursery, and a small-scale enterprise making chocolate bars from local cacao mixed with organic vanilla or pre-Columbian spices grown on the farm.

Paul and Jean Johnson, who arrived in 2004, run a café, give tours of their chocolate farm, and produce locally sourced organic chocolate that is "tree-to-bar," all under the banner of Caribeans. "We're interested in seeing a movement begin, here in the Caribbean and ultimately in the rest of Costa Rica, where cacao producers work their way up the value-added chain, so that eventually there's lots of little cacao producers that can make high-quality chocolate," says Paul Johnson. He speaks of the *terroir* associated with a chocolate bar in the same way a vintner would describe how soil and climactic conditions affect the grapes grown and wine made in a particular area.

Kring and the Johnsons are part of a loosely organized push to promote the southern Caribbean as a sort of Napa Valley for chocolate, built not on an exportation model but more as a way to draw well-heeled chocolate lovers—the same kind of people, Johnson hopes,

Saving the World, One Bird at a Time

BRINGING GREAT GREEN MACAWS BACK FROM THE BRINK

A great green macaw in full flight appears to be heading straight for Buffie Biddle's head. These dazzling and highly endangered birds have a wingspan of nearly 1.2 meters (4 feet); if they come close, you duck.

Buffie ducks, but turns toward the rush of air so as not to miss the spectacle. Great greens aren't just a vivid green: with wings spread they also flash red and yellow and bright turquoise. Not for nothing have they been called winged rainbows. "He cracks me up!" she laughs, straightening to her full five feet two inches. "They're all playful, but Sandy really pushes the envelope, being an adolescent." Buffie tells me that Sandy is maybe 3 years old, midway along the bumpy road to sexual maturity. At 5 or 6 he'll mate for life, a long haul, as macaws live up to 80 years.

Buffie herself is a youthful 45, with butterflies tattooed up and down her bare arms. She's on her own road to maturity; in this case, the kind that means she has committed to her passions and to figuring out how to follow them out into a world that needs her help. She's a writer, illustrator, wildlife lover, and serial volunteer. Right now she's volunteering at The Ara Project, a nonprofit dedicated to reintroducing both green and scarlet macaws to their former ranges in Costa Rica. This is her second stint at Ara's great green macaw release station on Costa Rica's Caribbean coast.

She's here at a very auspicious time. Earlier this year, something unprecedented happened in the world of the endangered great green macaw: a chick hatched in the wild, the offspring of birds who had been bred in captivity and then released to their former range.

The fledgling is called Pewe, and his arrival is a huge milestone in the conservation of an endangered species.

A COVETED BIRD

Native to the Americas, great green macaws can still be found in isolated areas from Honduras to Ecuador, but conservationists fear there may be fewer than 1,000 adult individuals remaining in the wild due to habitat destruction and poaching. In fact these gorgeous birds, among the biggest in the parrot family, have been coveted since Spanish and Portuguese explorers took specimens back to Europe in the early 1500s. In 2015, U.S. Fish & Wildlife finally declared it illegal to import or sell green greens in the United States. But Google great green macaw and the search engine will still probably try to finish your sentence with "for sale."

Fifty years ago, the great green macaw population rapidly declined in Costa Rica's Caribbean coastal region, its primary natural range in this country. In 1982, two U.S. expats started The Ara Project's predecessor (Amigos de las Aves) to rescue parrots and macaws, then began breeding the two native macaw species, *Ara Ambiguus* (great green) and *Ara Macao* (scarlet) and releasing them to fly free in their natural habitats to reverse that trend.

"Part of why they're endangered is that macaws take a very long time to reproduce," Buffie tells me. "The eggs hatch after a month, but then the parents spend two years teaching their chick how to be a macaw. If their chick gets poached or killed, they mourn, and it takes them a while to start the process again."

"As far as we're aware," says Ara Project board member Emily Yozell, a U.S.-trained attorney and property owner of the great green release site, "this is the first documented attempt to reintroduce great green macaws who have been born and raised in captivity to a natural habitat where the species was once prevalent."

VOLUNTEERS AND LOCALS WORK HAND IN HAND

The Ara Project relies on international volunteers like Buffie, and also employs locals, some of whom are members of indigenous groups native to the area. Site administrator Duaro Mayorga, for example, is a Bribrí native born and raised in the nearby Kekoldi territory; he knows the area and its wildlife like the back of his hand. Duaro says that from 2011 through late 2016, The Ara Project released 45 green macaws into their natural habitat, of which at least 35 are known to be alive and about 20-26 continue to return to the site each afternoon. Duaro honored his people's heritage when he named the new addition to the flock; Pewe is an important term for the Bribrí people, who revere great greens, as the birds play an important role in the Bribrí cosmovision. In their story of creation, *Iriria Tsochok* (Mother Earth) sends out the first messenger, a parrot, to gather all beings. The parrot does so by calling out "Pewe, Pewe."

Duaro says that direct contact between the birds and humans at the refuge is strictly prohibited, although the birds have been raised by humans and have become somewhat accustomed to the presence of visitors.

Duaro and other local employees work with volunteers like Buffie, who at the time of my visit was the sole live-in worker on-site. Among her many duties was leading visitors—tourists, locals, and groups of school children—to observe the birds flying free and teaching them about macaw and rainforest conservation.

Ms. Yozell says that The Ara Project has had a wide range of collaborators: gap year teens and 20-somethings, people who've had pet parrots and want to help nurture free-flying birds, biology or veterinary students, animal lovers, zoo or aviary keepers, or people who simply want to travel in a more meaningful manner.

Buffie wholeheartedly supports the idea of in-depth travel, and she votes with her feet and her bank account. She's done a fair amount of volunteering, often paying for the privilege to do good work. The Ara Project, for instance, charges US$300 a month, and you pay for your own food. But you get training and a place to stay, in this case her own little house with rare (for wildlife volunteers) luxuries like hot water, screens on the windows, and Internet access, not to mention a front-row seat for macaw shenanigans.

Besides their playfulness, Buffie has seen many examples of how the flock works together as a team. When the macaws spotted a large group of howler monkeys in a nearby tree, for instance, "the birds sounded a short alarm call (one squawk), and then they appeared to form a perimeter around the monkeys in the tree, sort of nonchalantly surveying them. No aggression was observed, and after about 20 minutes the macaws went about their business. It was interesting to watch—the birds seemed to be investigating, running a sort of threat assessment. What I love about working with wildlife nonprofits is that I can contribute to important research and species conservation without having, say, a degree in biology," says Buffie.

This idea of citizen science—non-scientists pitching in and making a difference—is gaining ground lately, and can make a volunteer at a rather remote wildlife project feel connected to larger issues.

"Species are disappearing seemingly right out from under our noses," Mary Ellen Hannibal, author of *Citizen Science*, told *Popular Science* magazine recently. "Upwards of 23,000 species are currently threatened with extinction." She and others on the field are hopeful, however, about the upsurge of involvement in projects that aim to slow and reverse the ravages of climate change and species extinction.

If volunteers are important for The Ara Projects' sustainability, the organization's commitment to working closely with local communities is even more so, says Dr. Sam Williams, The Ara Project's executive director. "We empower local key individuals to grow into leadership roles," he says.

Education is also crucial. "It's absolutely vital," says Ms. Yozell, "that The Ara Project informs, educates, and promotes participation of the local human populations within the potential and expanding range of the macaws now flying free."

"We work to inspire awe and appreciation of these magnificent birds," says Dr. Williams.

Buffie puts it more casually. "Just look at them! They're so smart and curious, you can't help but love them. And when you love something, you want to protect it."

Learn more about The Ara Project at www.thearaproject.org.

who'd travel to learn more about wine or whiskey—to the zone.

Besides the handful of foreign-born chocolate entrepreneurs—who grow, produce, or feature chocolate in informational tours—there are indigenous people like the Bribrí, who've been harvesting cacao for hundreds of years, and who include chocolate-making demonstrations as part of the tours they offer to showcase their traditions. Local spas feature "Chocolate Bliss" skin treatments that involve coarsely ground cacao paste as an exfoliant and moisturizer, and area restaurants offer locally made chocolate treats like truffles or banana-chocolate pancakes.

Positioning the area as a haven for chocolate tourism is just one of many ideas that ambitious locals and expats have dreamed up, which include hosting music festivals, craft brew festivals, and athletic events like mountain bike races or triathlons.

Puerto Viejo and its environs are changing rapidly. The 13 kilometers (8 miles) between Puerto Viejo and Manzanillo and the nearby Gandoca-Manzanillo Reserve used to be bad enough to make people think twice about living out that way. Now it's all paved, and some fear that soon that stretch of highway will be as developed as the road between Quepos and Manuel Antonio National Park on the west coast, with dozens of upscale hotels, restaurants, and residences. On the other hand, points out one expat, "the way roads are paved in this country, it'll be full of potholes again in six months. They lay on such a thin layer of asphalt they might as well just paint the dust black. But maybe that's not such a bad thing. We don't want to be too accessible."

RESOURCES

Embassies and Consulates

For general information, visit the Costa Rican embassy website (www.costarica-embassy.org) or the Costa Rican Ministry of Culture and Foreign Relations website (www.rree.go.cr).

COSTA RICAN EMBASSIES AND CONSULATES IN THE UNITED STATES

COSTA RICAN CONSULATE GENERAL

2112 S St. NW
Washington DC 20008
tel. 202/499-2991
fax 202/265-4795
www.costarica-embassy.org
Jurisdiction: all U.S. states, particularly District of Columbia, Delaware, Illinois, Maryland, South Carolina, Virginia, West Virginia, and Wisconsin

ATLANTA

Consulate General
1870 The Exchange, Suite 100
Atlanta, GA 30339
tel. 770/951-7025
fax 770/797-7700
Jurisdiction: Alabama, Georgia, Kentucky, South Carolina, Tennessee

CHICAGO

Consulate General
30 N. Michigan Ave., Suite 1922
Chicago, IL 60602
tel. 312/470-0282
fax 312/577-4271
Jurisdiction: Illinois, Michigan, Ohio, Missouri, North Dakota, South Dakota, Indiana, Wisconsin

HOUSTON

Consulate General
3000 Wilcrest Dr., Suite 112
Houston, TX 77042
tel. 713/266-0484
fax 713/266-1527
Jurisdiction: Arkansas, Colorado, Kansas, Louisiana, Mississippi, Nebraska, New Mexico, Oklahoma, Texas

LOS ANGELES

Consulate General
1605 W. Olympic Blvd., Suite 400
Los Angeles, CA 90015
tel. 213/380-7915 or 213/380-6031
fax 213/380-5639
Jurisdiction: Alaska, Arizona, California, Hawaii, Idaho, Montana, Nevada, Oregon, Utah, Washington, Wyoming

MIAMI

Consulate General
2730 SW 3rd Ave., Suite 401
Miami, FL 33129
tel. 305/871-7485
fax 305/522-0119
consulate_mia@costarica-embassy.org
Jurisdiction: Florida

NEW YORK

Consulate General
225 W. 34th St.
New York, NY 10122
tel. 212/509-3066 or 212/509-3067
fax 212/509-3068
Jurisdiction: Connecticut, Maine, Massachusetts, New Hampshire, New Jersey, New York, Pennsylvania, Rhode Island, Vermont

PUERTO RICO
Consulate General
Calle Tetuan 206, Edificio San Juan/Edificio
del Banco Popular, Suite 506
Viejo San Juan, San Juan PR 902
tel. 787/722-0066
fax 787/725/7730

ST. PAUL
Honorary Consulate
6 West 5th St.
St. Paul, MN 55102
tel. 651/293-1816
fax 651/665-0015
Jurisdiction: Minnesota

TUCSON
Honorary Consulate
3567 E. Sunrise Dr., Suite 235
Tucson, AZ 85718
tel. 520/529-7068
fax 520/577-6781
Jurisdiction: Arizona

COSTA RICAN EMBASSIES AND CONSULATES IN CANADA
OTTAWA
Embassy
350 Sparks St., Suite 701 (Office Tower)
Ottawa, ON, K1R 7S8
tel. 613/562-2855, 1/866/26782-7422
fax 613/562-2582
visitcostarica.com

TORONTO
Consulate General
60 Bloor Street West, Suite 400
Toronto, ON, M4W 3B8
tel. 416/901-5633
fax 416/901-5833
ihuelat@procomer.com

VANCOUVER
Honorary Consulate
P.O. Box 16076, North Vancouver
Vancouver, BC, V7J 3S9
tel. 604/983-2152

Foreign Embassies in Costa Rica

BRITISH EMBASSY
Paseo Colón, between Calles 38 and 40, in the
Edificio Centro Colón, 11th Fl.
tel. 506/2258-2025
fax 506/2233-9938
http://ukincostarica.fco.gov.uk/en
mailing address:
Apartado 815-1007, Edificio Centro Colón,
Piso 11, San José 1007, Costa Rica

CANADIAN EMBASSY
Officentro Ejecutivo La Sabana, Sabana Sur
Edificio 5, 3rd floor
San José, Costa Rica
tel. 506/2242-4400
fax 506/2242-4410
sjcra@international.gc.ca
www.canadainternational.gc.ca/costa_rica
mailing address:
Apartado Postal 351-1077
Centro Colón
San José, Costa Rica

U.S. EMBASSY

Location: In Front of Centro Comercial del Oeste Pavas, Costa Rica.

Street Address: Calle 98 Vía 104, Pavas, San José, Costa Rica

Local Mailing Address: 920-1200 San José, Costa Rica

U.S. Mailing Address: US Embassy San José, APO AA 34020

tel. 506/2519-2000; from the U.S.: 011/506/2519-2000

fax 506/2519-2305; from the U.S.: 011/506/2519-2305

http://costarica.usembassy.gov

Government Organizations

Although these websites are in Spanish, most internet browsers will give you the option of translating the web pages into English.

ASSOCIATION OF AMERICAN CHAMBERS OF COMMERCE IN LATIN AMERICA

AACCLA
www.aaccla.org

BANCO CENTRAL DE COSTA RICA

Central Bank of Costa Rica
www.bccr.fi.cr

CAJA COSTARRICENSE DE SEGURO SOCIAL

www.ccss.sa.cr

Costa Rica's Social Security ministry, which, among the many services it provides, ensures that most of the country's inhabitants can receive medical care at public hospitals.

CÁMARA DE INDUSTRIAS DE COSTA RICA

Chamber of Industries
www.cicr.com

CÁMARA DE LA CONSTRUCCIÓN

Chamber of Construction
www.construccion.co.cr

CÁMARA NACIONAL DE TURISMO (CANATUR)

(Chamber of Tourism)
www.canatur.org

COMPAÑÍA NACIONAL DE FUERZA Y LUZ, S.A.

National Power Company
www.cnfl.go.cr

DIRECCIÓN GENERAL DE ADUANAS, MINISTERIO DE HACIENDA

Costa Rican Customs Office and Finance Ministry
www.hacienda.go.cr

DIRECCIÓN GENERAL DE MIGRACIÓN Y EXTRANJERÍA

Costa Rica Department of Immigration
www.migracion.go.cr

INSTITUTO COSTARRICENSE DE ELECTRICIDAD (ICE)
National Electricity Institute
www.ice.go.cr
Telecommunications, cell phones, phone lines, electricity.

INSTITUTO NACIONAL DE ESTADISTICA Y CENSOS (INEC)
Census Bureau
www.inec.go.cr

INSTITUTO NACIONAL DE SEGUROS (INS)
National Insurance Institute
www.ins.go.cr

INSTITUTO DE VIVENDA Y URBANISMO
Housing and Urban Development Department
www.invu.go.cr

MINISTERIO DE AGRICULTURA Y GANADERÍA
Ministry of Agriculture
www.mag.go.cr

MINISTERIO DE CIENCIA Y TECNOLOGÍA
Ministry of Science and Technology
www.micit.go.cr

MINISTERIO DE EDUCACIÓN PÚBLICA
Public Education Ministry
www.mep.go.cr

MINISTERIO DEL AMBIENTE Y ENERGÍA Y TELECOMUNICACIONES (MINAET)
Ministry of the Environment and Energy
www.minae.go.cr

RACSA
Radiográfica Costarricense
www.racsa.co.cr
Telecommunications, Internet.

SISTEMA NACIONAL DE AREAS DE CONSERVACIÓN
National Park System
www.sinac.go.cr

Environmental Organizations

CARIBBEAN CONSERVATION CORPORATION
www.cccturtle.org
Sea turtle conservation

CERTIFICATION IN SUSTAINABLE TOURISM (CST)
tel. 506/2299-5800
www.turismo-sostenible.co.cr
The Costa Rican Tourism Institute's program to recognize hotels and tour operators that work toward sustainable development.

GUANACASTE CONSERVATION AREAS
www.acguanacaste.ac.cr

MONTEVERDE CONSERVATION LEAGUE
www.monteverdeinfo.com/monteverde_conservation_league.htm

ORGANIZATION OF TROPICAL STUDIES
www.ots.ac.cr

OSA CONSERVATION
http://osaconservation.org
Protects the Osa Peninsula.

PRETOMA
Programa Restauración de Tortuga Marinas
(Sea Turtle Restoration Program)
www.pretoma.org
Since 1977 this well-respected organization has worked to protect not only sea turtles but all ocean resources.

SISTEMA NACIONAL DE AREAS DE CONSERVACIÓN
National Park System
www.sinac.go.cr

People and Culture

MUSEUMS IN SAN JOSÉ
MUSEO DE ARTE COSTARRICENSE
(Costa Rican Art Museum)
East end of Sabana Park
tel. 506/2256-1281
www.musarco.go.cr

MUSEO DE ARTE Y DISEÑO CONTEMPORÁNEO
(Art and Design Museum)
In the old prison building (Antigua Fanal) on Avenida 3 between Calles 13 and 15
tel. 506/2257-7202
www.madc.cr

MUSEO DE INSECTOS
(Insect Museum)
On the UCR campus (San Pedro), in the Music Building
www.miucr.ucr.ac.cr

MUSEO DEL JADE
(Jade Museum)
West side of the Plaza de la Democracia of Avenida Central, between Calle 13 and Calle 13 bis
tel. 506/2521-6610
www.museodeljadeins.com

MUSEO DE LOS NIÑOS
(Children's Museum)
Avenida Central at Calle 17
tel. 506/2258-4929
www.museocr.org

MUSEO DE ORO
(Gold Museum)
Plaza de la Cultura, Calle 5 at Avenida 2
tel. 506/2243-4202
www.museosdelbancocentral.org

MUSEO NACIONAL
(National Museum)
Calle 17 at Avenida 2
tel. 506/2257-1433
www.museocostarica.go.cr

THEATERS IN SAN JOSÉ
TEATRO MELICO SALAZAR
(Melico Salazar Theater)
On Avenida 2, diagonal from the cathedral
tel. 506/2233-5424
www.teatromelico.go.cr

TEATRO NACIONAL
(National Theater)
Plaza de la Cultura, Calle 5 at Avenida 2
tel. 506/2010-1100
www.teatronacional.go.cr

THE LITTLE THEATRE GROUP
www.littletheatregroup.org
Founded in 1949, the Little Theatre Group is the oldest continuously running English-language theater in Central or South America. The group puts on at least four productions a year; new members are always welcome.

CULTURAL CENTERS IN SAN JOSÉ

ALLIANZA FRANCESA
Avenida 7 at Calle 5, 200 meters (219 yard) west of the INS building
tel. 506/2257-5819
www.afsj.net

CASA ITALIA
200 meters (219 yards) south of KFC in Barrio La California
(Calle 29 at Avenida 8)
tel. 506/2224-6049

JEWISH COMMUNITY INFORMATION
www.centroisraelita.com
This website also has broader information about the Jewish community in San José.

COSTA RICAN/NORTH AMERICAN CULTURAL CENTER
100 meters (109 yards) north of the Automercado Los Yoses, near San Pedro
www.centrocultural.cr
They also have branches in the Sábana neighborhood and in the cities of Alajuela, Cartago, and Heredia. They're known for their English classes and for the Eugene O'Neill Theater, which hosts a yearly jazz festival and other cultural events such as live simulcasts from the Metropolitan Opera House in New York.

GAY CULTURE

THE AGUA BUENA HUMAN RIGHTS ASSOCIATION
tel. 506/2280-3548
www.aguabuena.org
AIDs activism.

GENTE 10
www.gente10.com
A magazine and website for gay men.

MUJER Y MUJER
(Woman and Woman)
www.mujerymujer.com
Dedicated to Costa Rica's lesbian community.

CENTRAL AMERICAN HUMAN RIGHTS CENTER
tel. 506/2280-7821
www.cipacdh.org
The center provides counseling and support groups for gay, lesbian, and transgendered people. It's also involved in the June Gay Pride festivities and World AIDS Day each December 1.

Making the Move

VISAS

VISA AND ENTRY REQUIREMENTS
www.costarica-embassy.org

DIRECCIÓN GENERAL DE MIGRACIÓN Y EXTRANJERÍA
(Costa Rica Department of Immigration)
www.migracion.go.cr

RELOCATION ASSISTANCE AND TOURS

ASSOCIATION OF RESIDENTS OF COSTA RICA (ARCR)
Avenida 14 near Calle (Street) 42
San José
tel. 506/4052-4052
fax 506/2255-0061
www.arcr.net
A membership organization that offers help in relocating to and living in Costa Rica. Their seminars (every last

Thursday and Friday of every month except December) are a good place to get an introduction to many aspects of moving to Costa Rica.

LIVE IN COSTA RICA TOURS
U.S. toll-free tel. 800/365-2342 or 877/884-2502
www.liveincostarica.com
Author Christopher Howard offers relocation and retirement tours.

REAL COSTA RICA TOURS
http://blog.therealcostarica.com/the-real-costa-rica-tour
Tim, who runs the Real Costa Rica (www.therealcostarica.com), also offers one-on-one relocation tours that, he says, do not emphasize buying real estate.

LEGAL HELP
COSTA RICA LAW
www.costaricalaw.com
Great site covering all things legal in Costa Rica—from residency petitions to property rights. Roger Petersen, the creator of the site, was born in Costa Rica of a Tica mother and U.S. father. He went to college and worked in the United States before returning to his beloved home in Costa Rica. His books, such as *The Legal Guide to Costa Rica,* and *Costa Rica Immigration Guide*, are available for sale on his site.

PET TRANSPORT
IPATA
tel. 903/769-2267
fax 903/705-6922
www.ipata.com
A Texas-based international trade association of animal handlers, pet moving providers, kennel operators, and veterinarians.

PET ADOPTION IN COSTA RICA
ASOCIACIÓN HUMANITARIA PARA LA PROTECCIÓN DE ANIMALES (AHPPA)
tel. 506/2267-6374
www.animalsheltercostarica.com
The "humane society of Costa Rica" was founded in 1992 and is based near San Rafael de Heredia. It rescues strays, then vaccinates, deworms, and neuters the animals before putting them up for adoption. The website says that about 80 dogs and 50 cats are adopted out per month.

COSTA RICAN TOURISM OFFICES
www.visitcostarica.com
There are at least 12 Instituto Costarricense de Turismo (ICT) office, including the ones in Peñas Blancas, at the border with Nicaragua; Paso Canoas, at the Panama border; at the Juan Santamaría Airport near San José; and Liberia's Daniel Oduber International Airport. The main office is in downtown San José on Avenida Central between Calles 1 and 3.

Apart from the official tourist offices, many cities and towns bristle with signs advertising "Tourist Information." Mostly these are private agencies trying to sell specific tours, but the people there are usually friendly and will give you information even if you don't want to go on their tour.

Housing Considerations

COSTA RICA GLOBAL ASSOCIATION OF REALTORS (CRGAR)

www.crgar.com

tel. 506/8882-7427

The CRGAR promotes professionalism among real estate agents, and brings buyers and sellers together.

MULTIPLE LISTING SERVICE (MLS)

www.mls-cr.com

Not your home country's MLS, this online resource created by the Costa Rican Real Estate Agents Chamber is still in its early days—and is of limited value. Even real estate agents who belong to the chamber say they have far more listings on their own sites than on this MLS.

REGISTRO NACIONAL

(National Registry)

tel. 506/2202-0800

www.rnpdigital.com

The National Registry (also sometimes called the Public Registry), located in San José, is where all properties in Costa Rica are listed, along with information such as the name of the title holder, boundary lines, tax appraisal, liens, mortgages, recorded easements, and anything else that would affect title.

STEWART TITLE LATIN AMERICA

tel. 506/2505-3000 or 506/2288-0644

fax 506/2288-0933

www.stewartlat.com

Provides title searches and title guarantees.

RESOURCES
GLOSSARY OF REAL ESTATE TERMS

Glossary of Real Estate Terms

Before you dive into the world of Costa Rican real estate transactions, you'll need to learn a whole new vocabulary. Here are some of the terms you're likely to encounter.

activo: asset
agencia inmobiliaria: real estate agency
ajuste: adjustment
alquilar: to rent
amortización: amortization
anticipo: advance payment
apreciación: appreciation
arrendador: landlord
arrendatario: tenant
asignar: to assign, to transfer
avalúo: appraisal
bienes: personal assets
bienes inmuebles: property
bienes raíces: real estate
capital: equity
carta de crédito: letter of credit
cedente: assignor
cesión: assignment, transfer

cesionario: assignee
cierre: closing
comprador: buyer
concesión de crédito: extension of credit
confiscación: forfeiture
construcción en progreso: construction in progress
contraoferta: counteroffer
contrato de arrendamiento: lease
corredor de bienes raíces: real estate broker
desvalorización: depreciation
deuda: debt
embargo fiscal: tax lien
escritura de traspaso: deed of transfer
estatuto: bylaw
garantía: collateral
gastos de cierre: closing costs
gastos de mudanza: moving expenses
gravamen: encumbrance, lien
hectárea: hectare (10,000 square meters, about 2.5 acres)
hipoteca: mortgage
hipoteca colectiva: blanket mortgage

hipoteca con tasa de interés fija: fixed-rate mortgage

hipoteca en primer grado: first mortgage

hipoteca en segundo grado: second mortgage

hipoteca sin límite de importe: open-end mortgage

impuesto: tax

impuestos territoriales: property taxes

incumplimiento de pago: failure to pay

ingresos por arrendamientos: rental income

instalación: fixture

interés compuesto: compound interest

inversión: investment

investigación de título: title search

linea de crédito: line of credit

manzana: 7,000 square meters, about 1.75 acres

oferta en firme: firm offer

opción de compra: option to buy

pago inicial: down payment

patrimonio: owner's equity

pedir prestado: to borrow

peritaje: survey

permiso: permit

plazo fijo: fixed term

precarista: squatter

precio al contado: cash price

precio de lista: list price

precio máximo: maximum price

precio real: actual price

prestamista: lender

préstamo: loan

préstamo bancario: bank loan

préstamo hipotecario: mortgage loan

prestar: to lend

prestatario: borrower

presupuesto: cost estimate/budget

promesa reciproca de compra-venta: reciprocal promise to buy and sell

propietario registrado: owner of record

prórroga: extension (of time)

Registro de la Propiedad: National Registry property section

Registro Nacional: National Registry (or Public Registry)

Registro Público: Public Registry (or National Registry)

residenciales: gated communities

respaldo financiero: financial backing

se alquila: for rent

seguro contra incendio: fire insurance

seguro contra inundaciones: flood insurance

seguro contra riesgo: hazard insurance

seguro contra robo: theft insurance

servicios públicos: public utilities

servidumbre: easement

se vende: for sale

sociedad anónima (S.A.): corporation

tasa básica: base rate

tasa de interés: interest rate

tendencias del mercado: market trends

tenencia conjunta: joint tenancy

terrenos sin mejoras: unimproved land

tipo (or taza) de cambio: exchange rate

tipo de interés preferencial: prime rate of interest

título: deed, title

título de propiedad or libre de gravamenes: clear title

traspaso de propiedad: transfer of title

valoración: appraisal

valor declarado: declared value

valor del avalúo: appraised value

valor de mercado: market value

vendido: sold

zona maritimo: maritime zone

zona pública: public zone

zona restringida: restricted zone

zonificación: zoning

Primary and Secondary Schools

THE CENTRAL VALLEY AND BEYOND
San José Area

AMERICAN INTERNATIONAL SCHOOL OF COSTA RICA
(formerly the Costa Rica Academy)
Ciudad Cariari, Herida
tel. 506/2293-2567
fax 506/2239-0625
www.aiscr.net

Founded in 1970, AIS offers pre-K through grade 12, with a U.S.-style curriculum. The school year comprises two semesters, from mid-August to mid-December and from mid-January to mid-June. Classes are in English, and Advanced Placement (AP) programs are available.

BLUE VALLEY SCHOOL
Escazú
tel. 506/2215-2204
fax 506/2215-2205
www.bluevalley.ed.cr

Founded in 1989, this Montessori-influenced school runs from pre-K through high school. Instruction is in English, and both U.S.-style high school diplomas and the International Baccalaureate (IB) are available.

BRITISH SCHOOL
(Escuela o Colegio Británico)
Pavas
tel. 506/2220-0131
fax 506/2232-7833
www.thebritishschoolofcostarica.com

Grades are K-12; classes are taught mostly in English. The school offers Costa Rican and International Baccalaureate (IB) curricula. It is accredited by the European Council of International Schools (ECIS)

and runs on a Costa Rican school-year schedule.

CALASANZ SCHOOL
(Colegio Calasanz)
San Pedro
tel. 506/2283-4730
fax 506/2283-1890
www.colegiocalasanz.com

Founded in 1961, this Roman Catholic school has instruction in Spanish for grades K-11.

COUNTRY DAY SCHOOL
Escazú
tel. 506/2289-0919
fax 506/2228-2076
www.cds.ed.cr

Founded in 1963 and modeled after prep schools in the United States, CDS is one of the most prestigious schools in Costa Rica. Instruction is offered for pre-K through 12th grade, with classes in English and extras such as a full sports program, band and chorus, Advanced Placement (AP) classes, and campus-wide wireless Internet. There's also a branch in Guanacaste.

EUROPEAN SCHOOL
San Pablo de Heredia
tel. 506/2261-0717
fax 506/2263-5793
www.europeanschool.com

Founded in 1989, the European School goes from pre-K through high school and has several hundred students from more than a dozen countries. Key to the school's philosophy is the concept of integrated teaching, in which "a central theme unifies and interrelates academic work in literature, history, geography, and art." The school offers the International Baccalaureate (IB).

FRENCH SCHOOL

(Liceo Franco-Costarricense or Lycée Franco-Costaricien)
Concepción de Tres Ríos
tel. 506/2273-6373
fax 506/2273-3380
http://fr.franco.ed.cr

Instruction is pre-K through high school, with classes taught in French, English, and Spanish.

HUMBOLDT SCHOOL

(Colegio Humboldt)
Pavas
tel. 506/2232-1455
fax 506/2232-0093
www.humboldt.ed.cr

K-12 classes are taught in German, English, and Spanish.

INTERNATIONAL CHRISTIAN SCHOOL

San Miguel de Domingo, Heredia
tel. 506/2241-1445
http://icscostarica.org/heredia

U.S. missionary William Tabor founded this school to promote "academic excellence and the active lordship of Jesus Christ in all respects of life." The school encompasses pre-K through 12th grade and operates on the U.S. academic calendar; the language of primary instruction is English.

LINCOLN SCHOOL

Santo Domingo de Heredia
tel. 506/2247-6600
fax 506/2247-6700
www.lincoln.ed.cr

Offering classes from pre-K through 12th grade, Lincoln is one of the larger private schools in the San José area. It offers either a U.S.-style college-prep curriculum or the International Baccalaureate (IB).

Lincoln is considered a prestigious place to send your child—it's where "the kids of big Costa Rican politicians go," according to one source.

MARIAN BAKER SCHOOL

San Ramón de Tres Ríos
tel. 506/2273-0024
fax 506/2273-4609
www.mbs.ed.cr

Marian Baker offers pre-K through 12th grade instruction in English and operates on the U.S. academic calendar.

METHODIST COLLEGE

(Colegio Metodista)
San Pedro and Sabanilla
tel. 506/2280-1220
www.metodista.ed.cr

Founded in 1921, this bilingual (Spanish and English) Christian school serves students from pre-K through grade 12.

MONTERREY COLLEGE

(Colegio Monterrey)
San Pedro
tel. 506/2224-0833
www.colegiomonterrey.ed.cr

This Christian school provides bilingual (Spanish and English) education for pre-K through 11th grade.

MOUNT VIEW SCHOOL

Guachipelin de Escazú
tel. 506/2215-1154
www.mountviewcr.com

Pre-K through 11th grade.

PANAMERICAN SCHOOL

(Colegio Panamericana)
San Antonio de Belén
tel. 506/2298-5700
www.panam.ed.cr

Pre-K through 11th grade, with NEASC and CIS accreditation, service learning, and U.S.-style Advanced Placement (AP) classes.

SAINT CECILIA BILINGUAL COLLEGE

San Francisco de Heredia
tel. 506/2562-7373
fax 506/2562-7383
http://santacecilia.ed.cr
info@santacecilia.ed.cr
Pre-K through 11th grade.

SAINT FRANCIS COLLEGE

Moravia
tel. 506/2297-1704 or 506/2240-8277
www.stfrancis.ed.cr
K through 11th grade.

SAINT GREGORY SCHOOL

Tres Ríos
tel. 506/2279-4444
fax 506/2279-9727
info@saintgregory.cr
http://saintgregory.cr
Pre-K through 11th grade; instruction mostly in Spanish.

SAINT MARY'S SCHOOL

Guachipelín de Escazú
tel. 506/2215-2135
fax 506/2215-2132
www.saintmary.ed.cr
Pre-K through sixth grade; instruction in English and Spanish.

SAINT PAUL COLLEGE

(Colegio Saint Paul)
San Rafael de Alajuela
tel. 506/2438-2122 or 506/2438-1661
www.saintpaul.ed.cr
"The idea behind this school is to offer a quality bilingual education to Costa Rican students," says a former teacher here. Saint Paul was founded in 1982 and provides bilingual English-Spanish classes from pre-K through 11th grade; the majority of the students are Costa Rican.

UNITED WORLD COLLEGE (UWC)

Escazú
tel. 506/2282-5609
fax 506/2282-1400
www.uwccostarica.org
A two-year college prep program for 16-18-year-olds who want to earn an International Baccalaureate (IB) degree. Part of a worldwide network of 11 such colleges, UWC Costa Rica is the first bilingual school (English and Spanish) in the group and is the only one affiliated with SOS Children's Villages International.

WEIZMAN INSTITUTE

Mata Redonda
tel. 506/2520-1013
http:// centroisraelita.com/app/cms/www/
index.php?id_menu=22
Founded in 1960 and named after Israel's first president, the institute offers a full academic curriculum, plus courses in Jewish identity and religion as well as Hebrew; pre-K through 11th grade.

Turrialba
ESCUELA INTERAMERICANA CATIE

tel. 506/2556-7942
fax 506/2556-1533
School associated with Centro Agronómico Tropical de Investigación y Enseñanza (CATIE, Center for Tropical Agriculture Investigation and Learning), one of the top tropical research stations in the world. Turrialba is about 65 kilometers (40 miles) from San José.

Monteverde
CLOUDFOREST SCHOOL/CREATIVE EDUCATION CENTER

(Centro de Educación Creativa)
tel. 506/2645-5161
www.cloudforestschool.org
This bilingual school serves students in grades K through 11; it's strong in land stewardship and internship programs. Its

student body is made up of approximately 85 percent local Costa Rican students and 15 percent international students.

MONTEVERDE FRIENDS SCHOOL (MFS)

tel./fax 506/2645-5300 or 506/2645-5302
www.mfschool.org

MFS was founded in 1951 by a group of North American Quakers who settled in the Monteverde region. It has a curriculum that meets both Costa Rican and U.S. college prep standards and serves pre-K through 12th grade.

GUANACASTE AND THE NICOYA PENINSULA

ACADEMIA TEOCALI

Liberia, Guanacaste
tel. 506/2666-8780
www.academiateocali.ed.cr

This well-respected bilingual school was founded in 1982; pre-K through 11th grade.

COSTA RICA INTERNATIONAL ACADEMY

Playa Brasilito, Guanacaste
tel. 506/2654-5042
fax 506/2654-5044
http://criacademy.com

This school began as a branch of Country Day School in Escazú then struck out on its own. It offers classes in English from pre-K through 12th grade, and boarding for students in grades 8-12. There's a nice campus, with a gym, a pool, playing fields, a library, and a computer lab.

DEL MAR ACADEMY

Nosara, Guanacaste
tel. 506/2682-1211
www.delmaracademy.com

Pre-K-6th grade; based on the Montessori approach to education.

ESCUELA FUTURO VERDE

Cóbano, on the southern Nicoya Peninsula
tel. 506/2672-0161
www.futuro-verde.org

A small primary school emphasizing constructive learning: building on a child's natural skills.

INSTITUTO PEDAGÓGICO EUPI

Nicoya, Guanacaste
tel. 506/2686-6561
fax 506/2686-4884
www.eupini.com

This 25-year-old institution in the city of Nicoya serves students from pre-K through high school. Instruction is in Spanish and English.

INTERNATIONAL CHRISTIAN SCHOOL

Liberia
tel. 506/2666-3000
www.icsliberia.org

U.S. missionary William Tabor founded this school to promote "academic excellence and the active lordship of Jesus Christ in all respects of life." The school encompasses pre-K through 12th grade and operates on the U.S. academic calendar; the language of primary instruction is English.

LAKESIDE INTERNATIONAL SCHOOL

Playas del Coco, Guanacaste
tel. 506/4001-7993
www.lakesideschoolcr.com

On the road from Liberia to Playas del Coco, this pre-K through high school institution is on site of a catfish farm. Instruction is bilingual, in English and Spanish, and there's chemistry lab and a computer lab.

LA PAZ SCHOOL

Playa Brasilito, Guanacaste
tel. 506/2654-4532
www.lapazschool.org

Teachers formerly from the Country Day School founded this pre-K-high school institution in an effort to have a more affordable bilingual option for the "culturally diverse youth of Guanacaste." They describe themselves as a place-based, experiential, dual language school.

THE CENTRAL AND SOUTHERN PACIFIC COAST

ESCUELA VERDE COSTA BALLENA

Ballena, Puntarenas (near Uvita)
tel. 506/8703-5396
www.escuelaverdecostaballena.com

Primary school with classes taught in both Spanish and English.

FALCON INTERNATIONAL SCHOOL

Playa Heredura, Central Pacific
tel. 506/2637-7400
www.falconicr.com

Pre-K through grade 12; emphasis on arts and technology.

THE CARIBBEAN COAST

CENTRO EDUCATIVO PLAYA CHIQUITA

Playa Chiquita, Limón Province
tel. 506/2750-0754
www.facebook.com/pages/Centro-Educativo-Playa-Chiquita-Punta-Uva/172807386073930

Bilingual and multicultural school serving grades Pre-K through 6.

COLEGIO BILINGÜE SAN FRANCISCO DE ASÍS

Guápiles, Limón Province
tel. 506/2750-0754
www.facebook.com/CBSFA

Pre-K through high school, with most instruction in Spanish.

ESCUELA COMPLEMENTARIA DE CAHUITA

Cahuita, Limón Province
tel. 506/2755-0057
www.complementariacahuita.es.tl/

Founded in 1994, this school serves students from pre-K through high school. Most of the students are Costa Rican, with a smattering of the international students.

Higher and Continuing Education

PUBLIC UNIVERSITIES

INSTITUTE OF TECHNOLOGY

(Instituto de Tecnología de Costa Rica)
www.tec.ac.cr

Campuses in Cartago, San José, San Carlos, Alajuela, and Limón

THE NATIONAL UNIVERSITY

(Universidad Nacional)
www.una.ac.cr

Based in Heredia, the National University also has regional centers in seven areas, including Liberia and Pérez Zeledón.

THE STATE UNIVERSITY'S DISTANCE LEARNING PROGRAM

(Universidad Estatal a Distancia)
tel. 506/2527-2000
www.uned.ac.cr

The main campus is in San José, with more than 30 regional centers scattered around the country.

UNIVERSITY OF COSTA RICA

(Universidad de Costa Rica)
tel. 506/2511-0000
www.ucr.ac.cr

344

The main campus is in San José; there are branch campuses in Alajuela, Cartago, Turrialba, and Puntarenas.

Private Universities and Other Educational Facilities

CATIE (CENTRO AGRONÓMICO TROPICAL DE INVESTIGACIÓN Y ENSEÑANZA)

Turrialba
tel. 506/2558-2000
www.catie.ac.cr

The Tropical Agricultural Research and Higher Education Center was founded in 1942 by what would become the Organization of American States (OAS). This multifaceted institute offers master's and doctoral degrees in areas such as integrated watershed management and tropical agroforestry.

EARTH (ESCUELA DE AGRICULTURA DE LA REGIÓN TROPICAL HÚMEDA)

Guácimo de Limón
tel. 506/2713-0000
fax 506/2713-0001
www.earth.ac.cr

Since 1990, EARTH University in Costa Rica has been educating students to "shape the direction of environmental protection and development in Latin America and the entire global community as a whole." It offers a *licenciatura* (a degree midway between a bachelor's and a master's) in agricultural sciences, among other degrees and concentrations.

INCAE (INSTITUTO CENTROAMERICANO DE ADMINISTRACIÓN DE EMPRESA)

Alajuela
tel. 506/2437-2200
www.incae.edu

Associated with Harvard Business School, this business school just outside of San José would be a good choice for someone looking to specialize in Latin American markets. It offers master's programs in "areas critical for Latin American development" as well as executive training programs and seminars.

OTS (ORGANIZATION FOR TROPICAL STUDIES)

San Pedro, San José
tel. 506/2524-0607; 919/684-5774 in the US
www.ots.ac.cr

Well-respected OTS, a group of nearly 60 universities, colleges, and research centers around the world, has a strong presence in Costa Rica, offering undergrad and graduate studies for students and scientists.

UNIVERSITY FOR PEACE

tel. 506/2205-9000
www.upeace.org

Near Ciudad Colón, this United Nations-affiliated school serves a small international student body as they work toward master's and doctorate degrees in everything from sustainable development to peace-building.

Spanish-Language Schools

The schools listed here are just a sampling of the many operating in Costa Rica. Rates and schedules changes frequently; check websites for current pricing and programs. These schools aren't listed by region because many schools have branches in different parts of Costa Rica.

ACADAMIA DE ESPAÑOL D'AMORE
Manuel Antonio
tel. 506/2777-1143 or 506/2777-0233
U.S. and Canada toll-free tel. 877/434-7290
www.academiadamore.com
Close to Manual Antonio National Park, this school emphasizes immersion in Spanish. Homestays with local families can be arranged.

ACADEMIA TICA
San Isidro de Coronado (near San José) and Jacó
tel. 506/2229-0013
www.academiatica.com
Associated with Instituto Cervantes, a Spanish organization to promote Spanish language and culture, Academia Tica offers two- to four-week programs. Most meet every weekday morning 8am-noon, with starting dates throughout the year. The academy also has specialized programs that include internships or volunteering, and there's a "parent and child" program. There are locations in San Isidro de Coronado, a town 10 kilometers (6 miles) northeast of San José, and in the beach town of Jacó. The Jacó program can include surfing lessons. Homestays can be arranged at both locations.

CENTRO LINGUÍSTICO CONVERSA
Santa Ana
tel. 506/4001-2497
U.S. toll-free tel. 888/669-1664
www.conversa.com
Founded in 1975, the Centro offers small classes; choose intensive (four hours per day) or super-intensive (5.5 hours per day). It's located on a farm above the town of Santa Ana, not far from San José.

CENTRO PANAMERICANO DE IDIOMAS (CPI)
Heredia, Monteverde, and Playa Flamingo
tel. 506/2265-6306
U.S. toll-free tel. 877/373-3116
www.cpi-edu.com
CPI has three campuses—in Heredia (near San José), in the mountain town of Monteverde, and near the Pacific coast beach of Playa Flamingo. Programs last 1-4 weeks.

COSTA RICAN LANGUAGE ACADEMY
Barrio Dent, San José
tel. 506/2280-5164
U.S. toll-free tel. 866/230-6361
www.spanishandmore.com
Courses are offered year-round, and class schedules are flexible. You can choose to study 3-6 hours a day, in small classes or one-on-one with an instructor.

COSTA RICAN SPANISH INSTITUTE (COSI)
Manuel Antonio
tel. 506/2234-1001
www.cosi.co.cr
COSI offers classes in San José and near Manuel Antonio National Park on the Pacific coast.

FORESTER INSTITUTE

Los Yoses, San José
tel. 506/2225-3155
U.S. and Canada tel. 727/230-0563
www.fores.com

Founded in 1979, this school offers 1-4-week programs, with many extras like dance classes and excursions. The institute has hosted many foreign universities' study-abroad programs. They even have one-on-one instruction via webcam.

ILISA LANGUAGE INSTITUTE

San Pedro neighborhood of San José, and Panama
tel. 506/2280-0700
U.S. toll-free tel. 800/454-7248
www.ilisa.com

Billing itself as a "school for professionals" that "does not cater to backpackers," ILISA offers a variety of programs, including small group classes Monday-Friday 8am-noon. Special programs for professionals—such as nurses and teachers—are also on offer. They also have a branch in Panama.

INSTITUTE FOR CENTRAL AMERICAN DEVELOPMENT STUDIES (ICADS)

Curridabat, San José
tel. 506/2225-0508
www.icads.org

Offering "study programs for progressive minds," ICADS allows you to earn college credit while learning Spanish and interning in the areas of public health, wildlife conservation, and women's issues.

MESOAMERICA INSTITUTE FOR CENTRAL AMERICAN STUDIES

San Pedro, San José
tel. 506/2225-0508
www.mesoamericaonline.net

Offers language study, social justice internships and environmental studies.

INSTITUTO UNIVERSAL DE IDIOMAS

Moravia, San José, and Panama
tel. 506/2257-0441
U.S. tel. 727/230-0563
www.universal-edu.com

Intensive instruction and small classes, along with special programs like business Spanish, medical Spanish, and Spanish for teachers. They also have a school in Panama.

INTENSA: INTENSIVE LEARNING PROGRAMS

Alajuela, Escazú, Heredia, and Barrio Escalante in San José
tel. 506/2281-1818
U.S./Canada toll-free tel. 866/277-1352
www.intensa.com

With four campuses in the Central Valley, INTENSA offers programs that last 1-4 weeks. College credit is also available.

INTERCULTURA

Heredia and Sámara
tel. 506/2260-8480
U.S. toll-free tel. 8448-SPANISH
Europe tel. 44/20-3318-3142
www.interculturacostarica.com

Intercultura has campuses just outside San José (in Heredia) and in the Pacific coast beach town of Sámara. Programs range 1-4 weeks and provide four hours of daily instruction. Volunteer programs and cultural enrichment extras are also available.

IPEE SPANISH LANGUAGE SCHOOL

(Instituto Profesional de Español para Extranjeros)
Curridabat, San José
tel. 506/8665-6393
www.ipee.com

IPEE offers intensive 1-8-week courses. There are specialty programs for Spanish teachers and for learning Spanish medical terminology.

LANGUAGE AND INTERNATIONAL RELATIONS INSTITUTE (ILERI)

Escazú and Panama City
tel. 506/2228-1687
www.ilerispanishschool.com

ILERI is located in Escazú, a suburb of San José (and also has a campus in Panama City). The school can arrange volunteering positions around the country after a student has studied Spanish.

NEW DAWN CENTER

San Isidro de El General
tel. 506/2770-4229
thenewdawncenter@yahoo.com
www.thenewdawncenter.info

Spanish classes are offered at this organic farm near San Isidro de El General, along with seminars on natural health care and tropical medicinal plants. Accommodations and meals are available at the farmhouse. The center was founded by Ed Bernhardt, naturalist and author of classics such as *The Costa Rican Organic Home Gardening Guide.*

REY DE NOSARA

Nosara
tel. 506/2682-0215 or 506/8888-9090
U.S./Canada toll-free tel. 87/REY-DE-NOSARA (877/393-3667)
www.reydenosara.itgo.com

This program offers group and private lessons in Nosara Beach, Guanacaste.

UCR'S SPANISH AS A FOREIGN LANGUAGE PROGRAM

San Pedro, San José
tel. 506/2511-8430
www.spanishclasses.ucr.ac.cr

The University of Costa Rica, the largest and most prestigious university in the country, has a "Spanish as a foreign language" program that also gives participants access to a community of more than 30,000 students. Language students, who need not be enrolled in the larger university, are issued student cards, which allow them to use campus libraries and sports facilities. One-month intensive courses are offered most months of the year—classes meet four hours a day, Monday-Friday, and cost around US$600 for the month. Two-month classes on Latin American literature, advanced Spanish conversation, and advanced Spanish literature are also available. Homestays can be arranged.

WAYRA INSTITUTO DE ESPAÑOL

Playa Tamarindo, Guanacaste
tel. 506/2653-0359
www.spanish-wayra.co.cr

This school in the popular beach town of Tamarindo offers small group classes and private lessons. Class and homestay rates go down the longer you stay.

Health

GENERAL TRAVELERS HEALTH INFORMATION
CENTERS FOR DISEASE CONTROL (CDC)
wwwnc.cdc.gov/travel

This U.S. government institution, based in Atlanta, is an invaluable resource for the health issues you may confront when traveling or living in countries all over the world. Be sure to check out the CDC's "Yellow Book," a comprehensive guide for international travelers that is updated every two years. The guide also has a chapter on medical tourism.

WORLD HEALTH ORGANIZATION (WHO)
www.who.int/ith

A United Nations agency based in Geneva, WHO has a special section devoted to travelers' health on its website.

MEDICAL TOURISM RESOURCES
COUNCIL OF INTERNATIONAL PROMOTION OF COSTA RICA MEDICINE (PROMED)
www.promedcostarica.com

This Costa Rican organization promotes and regulates medical tourism in this country.

INTERNATIONAL SOCIETY FOR QUALITY IN HEALTH CARE INC. (ISQUA)
www.isqua.org

A nonprofit independent organization with members in over 70 countries, ISQua "works to achieve excellence in health care delivery to all people, and to continuously improve the quality and safety of care." It's basically a searchable database

for research projects in the field of health care accreditation.

JOINT COMMISSION INTERNATIONAL (JCI)
http://jointcommissioninternational.org

Check this website to see which hospitals or clinics abroad have been accredited by this international regulatory agency.

EMERGENCY CONTACTS
EMERGENCY
tel. 911

FIRE
tel. 1118

RED CROSS AMBULANCE
tel. 1128

REPORTING CRIME
ORGANIZATION OF JUDICIAL INVESTIGATION (OIJ)
tel. 800/8000-645

Crimes should be reported to the nearest Organization of Judicial Investigation (OIJ) office. The OIJ aren't the uniformed officers you see in the street—those are Fuerza Pública, and they're meant to prevent crimes. The OIJ is responsible for investigating crimes after they happen.

U.S. citizens should also call the U.S. Embassy (tel. 506/2519-2000).

REPORTING TRAFFIC ACCIDENTS
TRÁNSITO
(Transit Police)

tel. 506/2222-9330 or 800/8726-7486

If you have a traffic accident, leave the vehicles where they are and call both the Transit Police and the INS Insurance Investigator (tel. 800/800-8000). Both of these officials will come, eventually, to the accident scene upon notification and file their reports. Only after they do so can you legally move your vehicle.

HOSPITALS AND CLINICS IN COSTA RICA

For a Red Cross ambulance, dial 1128 or 911.

Private Hospitals in San José
HOSPITAL CIMA

Escazú
tel. 506/2208-1144 (emergency number)
tel. 506/2208-1000
cima@hospitalcima.com
www.hospitalcima.com
www.cimamedicalvaluetravel.com (for international patients; has information on CIMA hospitals in other countries as well; U.S. toll-free tel. 855-782-6253)

HOSPITAL CLÍNICA BÍBLICA

On Calle Central, between Avenidas 14 and 16
San José
tel. 506/2522-1030 (emergency number) or 506/2522-1000 (general inquiries)
fax 506/2258-7184
info@clinicabiblica.com
www.clinicabiblica.com

HOSPITAL LA CATÓLICA

San Antonio de Guadalupe (a suburb of San José)
tel. 506/2246-3000
www.hospitallacatolica.com

Public Hospitals in San José

For more information on public hospitals and clinics, see the Caja Costarricense de Seguro Social (Caja) website (www.ccss.sa.cr).

HOSPITAL NACIONAL CALDERÓN GUARDIA

Between Avenidas 17 and 19 and Calles 7 and 9 in Barrio Aranjuez
tel. 506/2212-1000

HOSPITAL NACIONAL DE NIÑOS CARLOS SAENZ HERRERA

(Children's Hospital)
Paseo Colón, between Calles 14 and 20 (it's part of Hospital Nacional San Juan de Dios)
tel. 506/2523-3600

HOSPITAL NACIONAL MÉXICO

On the northeastern outskirts of San José, on the Autopista General Cañas
tel. 506/2242-6700, 506/2232-1285, or 506/2232-5504

HOSPITAL NACIONAL PSIQUIÁTRICO MANUEL ANTONIO CHAPUI

(Psychiatric Hospital)
1.5 kilometers west of the U.S. Embassy in Pavas
tel. 506/2232-2155

HOSPITAL NACIONAL SAN JUAN DE DIOS

Paseo Colón, between Calles 14 and 20
tel. 506/2257-6282

HOSPITAL PSIQUIÁTRICO ROBERTO CHACON

(Psychiatric Hospital)
4 kilometers north of La Unión, Tres Ríos, Cartago
tel. 506/2216-6400

HOSPITAL RAUL BLANCO CERVANTES

(Geriatric Hospital)
Paseo Colón, between Calles 14 and 20 (it's part of Hospital Nacional San Juan de Dios)
tel. 506/2542-2100 or 506/2522-7700

**INSTITUTO MATERNO
INFANTIL CARIT**
(Women's Hospital)
Opposite the MUSOC bus stop, Plaza Víquez,
San José
tel. 506/2523-5900 or 506/2222-8851

Central Valley Area Hospitals
HOSPITAL CARLOS LUIS VALVERDE
500 meters north of the Mercado Municipal
San Ramón
tel. 506/2445-5388

HOSPITAL MAX PERALTA
In Barrio La Uruca, on the road to the Cartago
airport
Cartago
tel. 506/2550-1999 or 506/2550-1993

**HOSPITAL SAN FRANCISCO DE
ASÍS**
400 meters west of the bus terminal
Grecia
tel. 506/2494-6444

HOSPITAL SAN RAFAEL
Across from the International Mall
Alajuela
tel. 506/2436-1001

HOSPITAL SAN VICENTE DE PAUL
250 meters south of the main entrance to
Rosabal Cordero Stadium
Heredia
tel. 506/2261-0091 or 506/2277-2400

HOSPITAL WILLIAM ALLEN TAYLOR
200 meters west of Turrialba's Central Park
Turrialba
tel. 506/2558-1300 or 506/2556-1341

Zona Norte Hospitals
HOSPITAL DE SAN CARLOS
2 kilometers north of Ciudad Quesada's
cathedral
tel. 506/2460-1176 or 506/2401-1200

HOSPITAL DE UPALA
100 meters before the Colegio de Upala
tel. 506/2480-0000 or 506/2470-0058

HOSPITAL LOS CHILES
300 meters south of the command post
tel. 506/2471-2000

MONTE SINAÍ
Ciudad Quesada, Alajuela
tel. 506/2460-1080

Central and Southern Pacific Coast and Zona Sur Hospitals
**HOSPITAL DE OSA TOMÁS CASAS
CASAJÚS**
500 meters north of the Oja de Agua School
Ciudad Cortés
tel. 506/2788-8003 or 506/2788-7065

HOSPITAL CIUDAD NEILY
From the main exit to Ciudad Neily, 2
kilometers on the highway toward Paso
Canoas, next to the gas station
tel. 506/2783-4111, 506/2783-4244, or
506/2785-9600

HOSPITAL DE GOLFITO
400 meters north of the Catholic church
tel. 506/2775-7900

HOSPITAL ESCALANTE PRADILLA
East side of the municipal stadium
Pérez Zeledón (aka San Isidro de El General)
tel. 506/2771-0874 or 506/2785-0700

HOSPITAL MAX TERÁN VALS
200 meters south of the Managua de Quepos
Quepos
tel. 506/2777-0922 or 506/2777-3221

HOSPITAL MONSEÑOR SANABRIA
400 meters east of Cabinas San Isidro in El
Roble
Puntarenas
tel. 506/2663-0354 or 506/2630-8000

HOSPITAL SAN VITO DE COTO BRUS

Barrio Tres Ríos
tel. 506/2773-3103 or 506/2773-4028

Guanacaste Hospitals

HOSPITAL DE LA ANEXIÓN

Main street, across from Palí supermarket
City of Nicoya
tel. 506/2685-8400 or 506/2685-8499

HOSPITAL ENRIQUE BALTODANO

Barrio Moracia, next to the Red Cross
Liberia
tel. 506/2666-0011 or 506/2690-2300

Zona Caribe Hospitals

HOSPITAL DE GUÁPILES

100 meters north of the gas station
Guápiles, Limón Province
tel. 506/2710-6801 or 506/2710-2002

HOSPITAL TONY FACIO CASTRO

Across from the ICE office
City of Limón
tel. 506/2539-0000

NATURAL CHILDBIRTH

MIDWIFERY TODAY

www.midwiferytoday.com/international/
costarica.asp
A list of Costa Rica practitioners and
resources.

ACCESS FOR PEOPLE WITH DISABILITIES

THE ASSOCIATION OF COSTA RICAN SPECIAL TAXIS

tel. 506/2296-6443 or 506/2396-8986
This association has a fleet of 40 vans
equipped for wheelchair users.

THE SOCIETY FOR ACCESSIBLE TRAVEL AND HOSPITALITY (SATH)

U.S. tel. 212/447-7284
U.S. fax 212/725-8253
sathtravel@aol.com
www.sath.org
This New York-based nonprofit tries to
"raise awareness of the needs of all travelers with disabilities, remove physical and
attitudinal barriers to free access, and expand travel opportunities in the United
States and abroad."

HEALTH INSURANCE IN COSTA RICA

The government monopoly on all forms of
insurance has been slowly opening to private providers, but the National Insurance
Institute (INS) is still the main insurance
source. Other organizations that can help
arrange health insurance in Costa Rica
are American Legion Post 10 and the
Association of Residents of Costa Rica
(ARCR, www.arcr.net).

CAJA COSTARRICENSE DE SEGURO SOCIAL

tel. 506/2539-0000
www.ccss.sa.cr
Costa Rica's Social Security ministry,
which, among the many services it provides, ensures that most of the country's
inhabitants can receive medical care at
public hospitals.

INSTITUTO NACIONAL DE SEGUROS (INS)

(National Insurance Institute)
tel. 506/2287-6000
http://portal.ins-cr.com

INTERNATIONAL HEALTH INSURANCE

Most U.S. health insurance companies—
like Blue Cross and Aetna—have international policies available.

RESOURCES
HEALTH

INTERNATIONAL MEDICAL GROUP
www.imglobal.com
U.S. toll-free tel. 800/628-4664

INSURANCE BROKERS
You can buy insurance through these companies; their websites can help you compare prices among insurance providers.

GARRETT AND ASSOCIATES
Apartado 5478-1000, San José
tel. 506/2233-2455
fax 506/2222-0007
www.segurosgarrett.com

GLOBAL INSURANCE NET
www.globalinsurancenet.com

INSURANCE CONSULTANTS INTERNATIONAL
www.globalhealthinsurance.com

ITG WORLDWIDE
http://itgworldwide.com

MEDIBROKER
www.medibroker.com

TRAVEL INSURANCE PROVIDERS IN NORTH AMERICA
Some of these companies also provide longer-term international health insurance.

MULTINATIONAL UNDERWRITERS
U.S. tel. 317/262-2132 or U.S. toll-free tel. 800/605-2282
U.S. fax 317/212-2140
www.mnui.com

TRAVELERS
U.S. tel. 203/277-0111 or U.S. toll-free tel. 800/243-3174
www.travelers.com

TRAVELGUARD INTERNATIONAL
U.S. tel. 715/345-0505 or U.S. toll-free tel. 877/216-4885
www.travelguard.com

WALLACH AND COMPANY
U.S. tel. 703/687-3166 or U.S. toll-free tel. 800/237-6615
www.wallach.com

Employment

ASOCIACIÓN DE EMPRESAS DE ZONAS FRANCA DE COSTA RICA
(Free Zones Association of Costa Rica)
tel. 506/2520-1635
http://azofras.com

CÁMARA DE COMERCIO EXTERIOR DE COSTA RICA Y DE REPRESENTANTES DE CASAS EXTRANJERAS (CRECEX)
(Chamber of Representatives of Foreign Companies)
www.crecex.com
tel. 506/2253-0126

CRECEX is an independent nonprofit association of private companies that promotes free trade and enterprise.

CÁMARA DE EXPORTADORES DE COSTA RICA (CADEXCO)
(Chamber of Exporters of Costa Rica)
www.cadexco.net

CÁMARA DE INDUSTRIAS DE COSTA RICA

(Chamber of Industries)
tel. 506/2202-5600
fax 506/2234-6163
www.cicr.com

CENTRO PARA LA PROMOCIÓN DE EXPORTACIONES E INVERSIONES (PROCOMER)

(Export and Investment Promotion Center)
www.procomer.com

COLEGIO DE ABOGADOS

(Lawyers Guild)
tel. 506/2202-3600
www.abogados.or.cr

COSTA RICAN-AMERICAN CHAMBER OF COMMERCE

(AMCHAM)
tel. 506/2220-2200
fax 506/2220-2300
www.amcham.co.cr

COSTA RICAN INVESTMENT PROMOTION AGENCY (CINDE)

tel. 506/2201-2800
fax 506/2201-2867
In New York: 212/984-0631
U.S. toll-free tel. 877/992-4633
www.cinde.org

CINDE is a private nonprofit organization, founded in 1982, that offers free advice and assistance to foreign investors trying to start businesses in Costa Rica. They also have over a dozen downloadable guides that relate to doing business in Costa Rica.

MINISTERIO DE TRABAJO Y SEGURIDAD SOCIAL

(Ministry of Work and Social Security)
www.mtss.go.cr

Among other resources, this ministry has a detailed list of minimum salaries in Costa Rica, in Spanish and using colones as the currency; look for the latest "Lista de Salarios" on their website.

Volunteer Possibilities

ANAI ASSOCIATION

tel. 506/2224-6090
fax 506/2253-7524
www.anaicr.org

This group works to protect tropical ecosystems.

APREFLOFAS

tel. 506/2574-6816
fax 506/2574-6010
www.preserveplanet.org

This organization works mostly in wildlife protection.

THE ARA PROJECT

tel. 506/8730-0890
www.thearaproject.org

A macaw conservation organization

with a breeding program on the Nicoya Peninsula, and a more remote release station on the Caribbean coast (you can book a tour to meet the birds).

ASVO (ASSOCIATION OF VOLUNTEERS WORKING IN PROTECTED AREAS)

tel. 506/2258-4430
www.asvocr.org

Basic Spanish and a one-month commitment are required for volunteering in national park maintenance and turtle conservation.

CARIBBEAN CONSERVATION CORPORATION

www.cccturtle.org

This group works to protect leatherback and green turtles on the Caribbean coast.

CLOUDBRIDGE NATURE RESERVE
www.cloudbridge.org
This private nature reserve on the slopes of Mount Chirripó needs people with backgrounds in biology, conservation, or the environmental sciences to help monitor the recovery of the cloud forest.

ECOTEACH
U.S. toll-free tel. 800/626-8992
www.ecoteach.com
EcoTeach matches U.S. student volunteers with humanitarian and ecological organizations.

FUNDACIÓN PANIAMOR
tel. 506/2234-2993
www.paniamor.org
You'll need good Spanish to work with this very worthwhile agency dedicated to preventing domestic abuse.

HABITAT FOR HUMANITY
tel. 506/2296-3430
fax 506/2520-1567
www.habitatcostarica.org
The Costa Rican branch of this international organization needs help building simple houses and in its office.

PEACE CORPS
www.peacecorps.gov

PROJECTO ASISI
www.institutoasis.com
Founder Alvaro del Castillo presides over this wild animal rescue, volunteer center, and Spanish language-learning facility rolled into one. Volunteer programs include recycling, reforestation, and community construction projects in the Lake Arenal area.

SARAPIQUÍ CONSERVATION LEARNING CENTER
www.learningcentercostarica.org
Teach English or computer skills to locals in a lush and less-visited area of the country; good Spanish preferred; both short- and long-term options available.

VIDA (ASSOCIATION OF VOLUNTEERS IN RESEARCH AND ENVIRONMENTAL DEVELOPMENT)
tel. 506/2221-8367
fax 506/2223-5485
www.vida.org
VIDA matches volunteers with humanitarian and ecological organizations.

VIDA MARINA FOUNDATION
www.vidamarina.org
This foundation works with marine mammals in the Drake Bay area.

Finance

Check out SUGEF and SUGEVAL for financial information about companies registered in Costa Rica. Both are part of Costa Rica's Central Bank. SUGEF's website has much of its content translated into English; SUGEVAL's website is in Spanish.

SUGEF (SUPERINTENDENCE OF FINANCIAL ENTITIES)
tel. 506/2243-4848
www.sugef.fi.cr

SUGEVAL (SUPERINTENDENCE OF SECURITIES)
tel. 506/2243-4700
www.sugeval.fi.cr

Communications

The area code for all of Costa Rica is 506. There are no city codes, and telephone numbers now have eight digits. If you encounter a seven-digit number (on, say, an out-of-date website), a good rule of thumb is to add a "2" in front of numbers starting with 2, 4, 5, 6 or 7. Add an "8" before numbers starting with 3 or 8 (these are cell phones).

PHONE AND INTERNET SERVICE
RACSA (RADIOGRÁFICA COSTARICENNSE)
Avenida 5 and Calle 1, San José
tel. 506/2287-0087
www.racsa.co.cr

PRIVATE MAIL SERVICES
AEROPOST
tel. 506/2208-4848
www.aeropost.com

JETBOX
tel. 506/2253-5400 (main San José office) or 506/2231-5592 (Pavas)
www.jetbox.com

TRANSEXPRESS
(based in Florida)
www.transexpress.com

CABLE AND SATELLITE TV SERVICE
AMNET
tel. www.tigo.cr

CABLE TICA
www.cabletica.com

SKY TV
(formerly called DirecTV)
www2.sky.com.mx/centro-america

Travel and Transportation

AIRPORTS
DANIEL ODUBER INTERNATIONAL AIRPORT (LIR)
tel. 506/2666-9600
www.liberiacostaricaairport.net
Located in Liberia, Guanacaste, this airport is an hour from the northern Guanacaste beaches.

JUAN SANTAMARÍA INTERNATIONAL AIRPORT (SJO)
tel. 506/2437-2400
www.aeris.cr
SJO has international and domestic terminals just north of San José.

TOBÍAS BOLAÑOS AIRPORT
Located in Pavas, this airport is a bit closer to San José than the larger international airport. It's for smaller domestic and charter flights.

DOMESTIC AIRLINES
AERO BELL
tel. 506/2290-0000
U.S. toll-free tel. 888/FLY-1-FLY
(888/359-1359)
www.aerobell.com

NATURE AIR
tel. 506/2299-6000
U.S./Canada toll-free tel. 800/235-9272
info@natureair.com
www.natureair.com
The preferred domestic carrier for many travelers and expats, Nature Air flies its small planes out of Tobías Bolaños Airport all over Costa Rica and also to Granada, Nicaragua, and Bocas del Toro in Panama. Baggage limit is 14 kilograms (30 pounds); surfboards over two meters (6.6 feet) require you to buy three additional seats.

SANSA AIRLINES
tel. 506/2290-4100
U.S. toll-free tel. 877/767-2672
www.flysansa.com
Costa Rica's domestic airline is part of TACA, the Central American airline. It's a good option for regularly scheduled short hops within the country.

FERRY SERVICE
FERRY FROM PUNTARENAS TO PAQUERA AND NARANJO
www.nicoyapeninsula.com/general/boat.php

BUS COMPANIES
CARIBE SHUTTLE
tel. 506/2750-0626U.S./Canada toll-free tel. 800/274-6191www.caribeshuttlewww.caribeshuttle.com
Regularly scheduled van shuttles to major Costa Rica destinations as well as to Bocas del Toro in Panama and San Juan del Sur in Nicaragua. Book online or by phone.

GRAY LINE TOURS
tel. 506/2220-2126
U.S./Canada toll-free tel. 800/719-3905
www.graylinecostarica.com
Gray Line operates shuttle vans between various cities and towns in Costa Rica; you can book online or by phone.

INTERBUS
tel. 506/2283-5573
www.interbusonline.com
Interbus also offers shuttle vans between various cities and towns in Costa Rica; you can book online or by phone.

TICA BUS
www.ticabus.com
These big Greyhound-style busses travel

major routes within Costa Rica and also have international routes.

TAXI AND CAR SERVICES
AIRPORT TAXIS
tel. 506/2221-6865 or 2222-6865

Orange airport taxis are the only ones authorized to pick up and drop off passengers at Juan Santamaría International Airport outside San José (in theory, anyway; red taxis, see below, drop off at the airport all the time). You can pay for the ride (by zone) inside the airport, then be directed to the next taxi in line, or you can reserve a ride by phone.

OFFICIAL RED TAXIS
Regulated by the government, with set fares and meters. Look for the yellow triangle on the door, with the taxi's license number. Hail them on the street or call one of the large cooperatives such as Coopetico (506/2224-7979). Had a problem with a red taxi? Report it at 800/027-3737.

UBER
www.uber.com/cities/san-jose

Uber arrived in Costa Rica in August 2016. You need to have a local SIM card in your phone and to add that number to your Uber account or you won't be able to talk to your driver to verify the pick-up location or other details.

Prime Living Locations

THE CENTRAL VALLEY AND BEYOND
MONTEVERDE
www.monteverdeinfo.com

NOSARA
www.nosara.com

SOUTHERN NICOYA PENINSULA
www.nicoyapeninsula.com
www.peninsuladenicoya.com

TAMARINDO
www.tamarindo.com
www.tamarindonews.com
www.tamarindobeach.net

THE CENTRAL AND SOUTHERN PACIFIC COAST
DOMINICAL
www.dominical.biz

PUNTARENAS
www.puntarenas.com

QUEPOS AND MANUEL ANTONIO
www.quepolandia.com

THE CARIBBEAN COAST
ATEC–ASOCIACIÓN TALAMANQUEÑA DE ECOTURISMO Y CONSERVACIÓN
(Talamancan Association of Ecotourism and Conservation)
www.ateccr.org

This grassroots community organization in Puerto Viejo works to promote ecological and socially responsible tourism in the Talamanca area. The office is also a kind of community center with Internet access and a small bookstore; you can book a variety of eco-friendly tours there.

Miscellaneous Internet Resources

ENGLISH WEBSITES

A.M. COSTA RICA
www.amcostarica.com
Online news, in English, about Costa Rica.

THE COSTA RICA STAR
http://news.co.cr

LANIC
www1.lanic.utexas.edu/la/ca/cr
Although they stopped updating this page in 2015, it's still a great archive of links to all things Costa Rican, from government agencies to educational travel programs.

LIVING ABROAD IN COSTA RICA
www.livingabroadincostarica.com
The author's website

THE REAL COSTA RICA
www.therealcostarica.com

THE TICO TIMES
www.ticotimes.net
The venerable print edition ceased publication in 2012, bit its online counterpart is still widely read.

SPANISH WEBSITES

LA NACIÓN
www.nacion.com
Web version of the most respected Spanish-language daily in Costa Rica. It also has a weekly roundup of stories in English.

INTERNET RESOURCES FOR LIVING ABROAD

AMERICAN CITIZENS ABROAD
www.aca.ch

CIA WORLD FACTBOOK
www.cia.gov/library/publications/the-world-factbook
Detailed profiles of all countries.

EXPAT EXCHANGE
www.expatexchange.com

EXPATICA
www.expatica.com
Focuses on Europe, but has some good general move-abroad information no matter where you plan to live.

JOURNEYWOMAN
www.journeywoman.com

LIVE ABROAD
www.liveabroad.com

PRACTICAL NOMAD
www.practicalnomad.com
Emphasizes independent and socially responsible travel.

TRANSITIONS ABROAD
www.transitionsabroad.com
Excellent resource for anyone who wants to work, study, or live abroad. It also has an in-depth monthly magazine.

RESOURCES FOR RETIREES

AARP
www.aarp.org

EXPLORITAS
(formerly Elderhostel)
www.exploritas.org
"Adventures in lifelong learning."

TRAVEL WITH A CHALLENGE
www.travelwithachallenge.com
Global travel resource aimed at people over age 50.

Spanish Phrasebook

PRONUNCIATION GUIDE

Spanish pronunciation is much more regular than that of English, but there are still occasional variations.

Consonants

c pronounced like 'c' in "cat" before 'a,' 'o,' or 'u'; like 's' in "same" before 'e' or 'i'

g pronounced like 'ch' in Scottish "loch" before 'e' or 'i'; elsewhere pronounced like 'g' in "get"

h always silent

j pronounced like 'h' in "hotel," but stronger

ll pronounced like 'y' in "yellow"

ñ pronounced like 'ni' in "onion"

r always pronounced as a strong 'r' as in "red"

rr a trilled 'r'

v pronounced similar to 'b' in "boy" (not as an English 'v')

y pronounced similar to an English 'y,' but with a slight 'j' sound. When standing alone, it's pronounced like 'e' in "me."

z pronounced like 's' in "same"

b, d, f, k, l, m, n, p, q, s, t, w, x pronounced as they are as in English

Vowels

a as in "father," but shorter

e as in "hen"

i as in "machine"

o as in "phone"

u usually as in "rule"; when it follows a 'q,' the 'u' is silent; when it follows an 'h' or 'g,' it's pronounced like 'w,' except when it comes between 'g' and 'e' or 'i,' in which case it's also silent (unless it has an umlaut ['ü'], when it's again pronounced as English 'w')

Stress and Accent Marks

Words in Spanish follow a few basic rules as to which syllable is stressed (emphasized).

1. Words ending in a vowel, -n, or -s are stressed on the penultimate (next to the last) syllable, as in *nada* (NA-da), *origen* (o-RI-gen), or *esto* (ES-to).

2. Words ending in any consonant except -n or -s are stressed on the last syllable, as in *doctor* (doc-TOR), *ciudad* (ci-u-DAD), or *comer* (co-MER).

3. When rules 1 and 2 above are not followed, a written accent is used, as in *rápido* (RAP-i-do), *compró* (com-PRO), or *limón* (li-MON).

4. Written accents are also used to differentiate between words that are pronounced the same but have different meanings:

si if
sí yes
el the
él he

5. Remember that emphasizing the wrong syllable of a word can turn it into another word entirely. Consider the word *animo*. With stress on the first syllable, we have the noun *A-ni-mo,* meaning "spirit, intention, or courage." With stress on the second syllable (a-NI-mo), we have the first person present tense form of the verb *animar,* meaning "to encourage." Finally, with stress on the final syllable (a-ni-MO), we have the third person preterit form of the same verb.

NUMBERS

0 *cero*
1 *uno* (masculine) or *una* (feminine)
2 *dos*
3 *tres*
4 *cuatro*
5 *cinco*
6 *seis*
7 *siete*
8 *ocho*
9 *nueve*
10 *diez*

11 *once*
12 *doce*
13 *trece*
14 *catorce*
15 *quince*
16 *dieciseis*
17 *diecisiete*
18 *dieciocho*
19 *diecinueve*
20 *veinte*
21 *veintiuno*
30 *treinta*
40 *cuarenta*
50 *cincuenta*
60 *sesenta*
70 *setenta*
80 *ochenta*
90 *noventa*
100 *cien*
101 *ciento y uno*
200 *doscientos*
1,000 *mil*
10,000 *diez mil*
1,000,000 *un millón*

DAYS OF THE WEEK

Sunday *domingo*
Monday *lunes*
Tuesday *martes*
Wednesday *miércoles*
Thursday *jueves*
Friday *viernes*
Saturday *sábado*

TIME

Latin America mostly uses the 12-hour clock, but in some instances—usually associated with plane or bus schedules—the 24-hour military clock may be used. Under the 24-hour clock, for example, *las nueve de la noche* (9pm) would become *las 21 horas* (2100 hours).

What time is it? *¿Qué hora es?*
It's one o'clock. *Es la una.*
It's two o'clock. *Son las dos.*
At two o'clock. *A las dos.*
It's ten to three. *Son tres menos diez.*
It's ten past three. *Son tres y diez.*
It's three fifteen. *Son las tres y cuarto.*
It's two forty-five. *Son tres menos cuarto.*

It's two thirty. *Son las dos y media,* or *Son las dos y trienta.*
It's 6am *Son las seis de la mañana.*
It's 6pm *Son las seis de la tarde.*
It's 10pm *Son las diez de la noche.*
today *hoy*
tomorrow *mañana*
morning *la mañana*
tomorrow morning *mañana por la mañana*
yesterday *ayer*
last night *anoche*
the next day *el día siguiente*
week *la semana*
month *mes*
year *año*

USEFUL WORDS AND PHRASES

Most Spanish-speaking people consider formalities important. When approaching someone for information or any other reason, do not forget the appropriate salutation: good morning, good evening, etc. Standing alone, the greeting *hola* (hello) may sound brusque.

Hello. *Hola.*
Good morning. *Buenos días.*
Good afternoon. *Buenas tardes.*
Good evening. *Buenas noches.*
How are you? *¿Cómo está?*
Fine. *Muy bien.*
And you? *¿Y usted?*
So-so. *Más o menos.*
Thank you. *Gracias.*
Thank you very much. *Muchas gracias.*
You're very kind. *Muy amable.*
You're welcome *De nada* (literally, "It's nothing.")
yes *sí*
no *no*
I don't know. *No sé.*
It's fine; OK *Está bien.*
good; OK *Bueno.*
please *por favor*
Pleased to meet you. *Mucho gusto.*
Excuse me (physical) *Perdóneme.*
Excuse me (speech) *Discúlpeme.*
I'm sorry. *Lo siento.*
Good-bye *adiós*
See you later. *hasta luego* (literally, "until later")

more *más*
less *menos*
better *mejor*
much; a lot *mucho*
a little *un poco*
large *grande*
small *pequeño; chico*
quick; fast *rápido*
slowly *despacio*
bad *malo*
difficult *difícil*
easy *fácil*
He/She/It is gone; as in, "she left" or "he's gone." *Ya se fue.*
I don't speak Spanish well. *No hablo bien el español.*
I don't understand. *No entiendo.*
How do you say. . . in Spanish? *¿Cómo se dice. . . en español?*
Do you understand English? *¿Entiende el inglés?*
Is English spoken here? (Does anyone here speak English?) *¿Se habla inglés aquí?*

TERMS OF ADDRESS

When in doubt, use the formal *usted* (you) as a form of address. If you wish to dispense with formality and feel that the desire is mutual, you can say, *Me puedes tutear* (you can call me *"tú"*). Also see the special note below on *vos,* an alternative for *tú* that's common in Costa Rica but rarely taught in Western classrooms.

I *yo*
you (formal) *usted*
you (familiar) *tú or vos*
he/him *él*
she/her *ella*
we/us *nosotros*
you (plural) *ustedes*
they/them (all males or mixed gender) *ellos*
they/them (all females) *ellas*
Mr.; sir *señor*
Mrs.; madam *señora*
Miss; young woman *señorita*
wife *esposa*
husband *marido; esposo*
friend *amigo* (male) or *amiga* (female)
sweetheart *novio* (male) or *novia* (female)

son *hijo*
daughter *hija*
brother *hermano*
sister *hermana*
father *padre*
mother *madre*
grandfather *abuelo*
grandmother *abuela*

GETTING AROUND

Where is . . . ? *¿Dónde está . . . ?*
How far is it to . . . ? *¿A cuanto está. . . ?*
from. . . to. . . *de. . . a . . .*
highway *la carretera*
road *el camino*
street *la calle*
block *la cuadra*
kilometer *kilómetro*
north *norte*
south *sur*
west *oeste; poniente*
east *este; oriente*
straight ahead *al derecho; adelante*
to the right *a la derecha*
to the left *a la izquierda*

ACCOMMODATIONS

Is there a room? *¿Hay cuarto?*
May I (we) see it? *¿Puedo (podemos) verlo?*
What is the rate? *¿Cuál es el precio?*
Is that your best rate? *¿Es su mejor precio?*
Is there something cheaper? *¿Hay algo más económico?*
single room *un sencillo*
double room *un doble*
room for a couple *matrimonial*
key *llave*
with private bath *con baño*
with shared bath *con baño general; con baño compartido*
hot water *agua caliente*
cold water *agua fría*
shower *ducha*
towel *toalla*
soap *jabón*
toilet paper *papel higiénico*
air conditioning *aire acondicionado*
fan *abanico; ventilador*
blanket *frazada; manta*
sheets *sábanas*

PUBLIC TRANSPORTATION

bus stop *la parada*
bus terminal *terminal de buses*
airport *el aeropuerto*
launch *lancha; tiburonera*
dock *muelle*
I want a ticket to. . . *Quiero un pasaje a . . .*
I want to get off at. . . *Quiero bajar en . . .*
Here, please. *Aquí, por favor.*
Where is this bus going? *¿Adónde va este autobús?*
round-trip *ida y vuelta*
What do I owe? *¿Cuánto le debo?*

FOOD

menu *la carta; el menú*
glass *taza*
fork *tenedor*
knife *cuchillo*
spoon *cuchara*
napkin *servilleta*
soft drink *refresco*
coffee *café*
cream *crema*
tea *té*
sugar *azúcar*
drinking water *agua pura; agua potable*
bottled water *agua en botella*
beer *cerveza*
wine *vino*
milk *leche*
juice *jugo*
eggs *huevos*
bread *pan*
watermelon *sandía*
banana *banano*
plantain *plátano*
apple *manzana*
orange *naranja*
meat (without) *carne (sin)*
beef *carne de res*
chicken *pollo; gallina*
fish *pescado*
shellfish *mariscos*
shrimp *camarones*
fried *frito*
roasted *asado*
barbecued; grilled *a la parrilla*

breakfast *desayuno*
lunch *almuerzo*
dinner (often eaten in late afternoon) *comida*
dinner; late-night snack *cena*
the check; the bill *la cuenta*

SHOPPING

I need. . . *Necesito . . .*
I want. . . *Deseo . . . or Quiero . . .*
I would like. . . (more polite) *Quisiera . . .*
How much does it cost? *¿Cuánto cuesta?*
What's the exchange rate? *¿Cuál es el tipo de cambio?*
May I see . . . ? *¿Puedo ver . . . ?*
this one *ésta/ésto*
expensive *caro*
cheap *barato*
cheaper *más barato*
too much *demasiado*
sales tax *impuesto de ventas*
loose change *menudo*
general store *pulpería*

HEALTH

Help me, please. *Ayúdeme, por favor.*
I am ill. *Estoy enfermo.*
pain *dolor*
fever *fiebre*
stomachache *dolor de estómago*
vomiting *vomitar*
diarrhea *diarrea*
drugstore *farmacia, botica*
medicine *medicina*
pill; tablet *pastilla*
birth control pills *pastillas anticonceptivas*
condom *condón; preservativo*

SPECIAL NOTE: *VOS*

In Costa Rica, as well as in several other Central and South American countries, the pronoun "*tú*" is not frequently heard. More commonly used, and rarely taught to Westerners in their Spanish classes, is *vos*.

Essentially, *vos* is used in the same instances as *tú,* that is, between two people who have a certain degree of casual familiarity or friendliness, in place of the more formal *usted*. The *vos* form is derived from *vosotros,* the second person plural ("you all") still used in Spain. However, *vosotros* is not used in Latin America, even in places where *vos* is common.

For all tenses other than the present indicative, present subjunctive, and command forms, the *vos* form of the verb is exactly the same as *tú*. Hence: *tú andaste/ vos andaste* (past tense), *tú andabas/vos andabas* (past imperfect), *tú andarás/vos andarás* (future), *tú andarías/vos andarías* (conditional).

In the present indicative, the conjugation is the same as with *tú,* but the last syllable is stressed with an accent. The exception is with -*ir* verbs, in which the final *i* is retained, instead of changing to an *e*. Hence: *tú andas/vos andás tú comes/ vos comés, tú escribes/vos escribís.*

In the present subjunctive, the same construction is followed as with the normal subjunctive, except the *vos* accent *á* is retained. Hence: *tú andes/vos andés, tú comas/vos comás, tú escribas/vos escribás.*

In radical changing verbs like *tener, poder,* or *dormir,* the *vos* form does not change from vowel to dipthong *(tienes, puedes, duermes)* in the present subjunctive form. Hence: *vos tengás, vos podás, vos durmás.*

Vos commands are formed by simply dropping the final *r* on the infinitive and adding an accent over the last vowel. Hence: *vos andá, vos comé, vos escribí.* When using object pronouns with *vos, te* is still used. Hence: *Yo te lo escribí a vos.*

One common irregular *vos* form is *sos,* for *ser* (to be). Also, because the conjugation would be bizarre, the verb *ir* is not used in the *vos* form. Instead, use *andar: vos andás.*

Suggested Reading

There is no shortage of books on Costa Rica these days, from glossy coffee table tomes to nuts-and-bolts travel guides. Here's a small sampling of what's on offer.

GUIDEBOOKS AND NATURAL HISTORY

Allen, William. *Green Phoenix: Restoring the Tropical Forest of Guanacaste, Costa Rica.* New York: Oxford University Press, 2003. Natural history that reads like a novel, this wonderful book details the struggles of U.S. scientists Daniel Janzen and Winnie Hallwachs, along with their Costa Rican colleagues, to create a national park in Guanacaste and to introduce a new model of conservation that seeks not only to protect what remains but also to reverse devastation through reforestation.

Alvarado, Guillermo. *Costa Rica: Land of Volcanoes.* Cartago, Costa Rica: Editorial Tecnología de Costa Rica, 1993. A detailed and fascinating look at the fiery mountains that are still shaping Costa Rica. With maps and color photos.

Benz, Stephen. *Green Dreams: Travels in Central America.* Oakland, California: Lonely Planet, 1998. The section on Costa Rica explores the gap between the country's ecological aspirations and its need for economic development.

Bernhardt, Ed. *The Costa Rican Organic Home Gardening Guide.* Cambria, California: New Dawn Center, 2003. The founder of the New Dawn organic farm and education center (www. newdawncenter.org) gives practical and comprehensive advice about starting an organic garden in Costa Rica.

Carr, Archie. *The Windward Road.* Gainesville, Florida: University of Florida Press, 1955. A book about sea turtles in Central America by the man who not only pioneered the study of the creatures but also founded the Caribbean Conservation Corporation.

Cole-Christenson, Darryl. *A Place in the Rain Forest: Settling the Costa Rican Frontier.* Austin, Texas: University of Texas Press, 1997. A remarkable account of pioneering in the southern region now known as Coto Brus. Stick with it and you'll find out a lot about farming, squatters, and how very remote this area was just 50 years ago.

De Vries, Phillip. *Butterflies of Costa Rica and Their Natural History,* volumes 1 and 2. Princeton, New Jersey: Princeton University Press, 2000. The real deal for butterfly fanatics. Lots of color plates. Unfortunately, both volumes are out of print, though you can still find used copies for sale.

Evans, Sterling. *The Green Republic: A Conservation History of Costa Rica.* Amarillo, Texas: University of Texas Press, 1999. Detailed account of the history of the national park system and the rise of ecological awareness in Costa Rica.

Forsyth, Adrian, and Ken Miyata. *Tropical Nature: Life and Death in the Rainforests of Central and South America.* Clearwater, Florida: Touchstone Books, 1987. Very readable account of the wonders of the rainforest from two tropical biologists.

Garrigues, Richard, and Robert Dean. *The Birds of Costa Rica: A Field Guide.*

San José, Costa Rica: Zona Tropical Books, 2007. Excellent and well-illustrated guide.

Janzen, Daniel. *Costa Rican Natural History.* University of Chicago Press, 1983. An 800-page work of love that one reviewer called "an essential resource for anyone interested in tropical biology."

Kaiser, James. *Costa Rica: The Complete Guide.* Destination Press, 2013. The author spent five years researching this book, and the effort shows. With well-written descriptions and excellent photos, it's a real treat!

Parise, Mike. *The Surfer's Guide to Costa Rica & SW Nicaragua.* Los Angeles: Surfpress Publishing, 2010. Though somewhat out of date, this is still a very useful guide for surfers traveling to Costa Rica. Information on 70 breaks on both coasts and more than 100 hotels nearest the breaks. Tips on what to pack, how to pack surfboards, and how to get to remote places.

Stiles, Gary, and Alexander Skutch. *A Guide to the Birds of Costa Rica.* Ithaca, New York: Cornell University Press, 1989. The birder's bible, with color plates.

Wainwright, Mark. *The Natural History of Costa Rican Mammals.* Miami: Distribuidores Zona Tropical S.A., 2007. Compact enough to be a field guide, this book is nevertheless quite comprehensive, with not only color plates of the animals but also drawings of scat and tracks. Wainwright provides details of dens, range, vocalizations, derivations of common and scientific names, evolutionary history, even local folklore and mythology. The book has

400 illustrations and is written in a very clear and sometimes witty style.

Wallace, David R. *The Quetzal and the Macaw: The Story of Costa Rica's National Parks.* San Francisco: Sierra Club Books, 1992. An excellent and very readable book about the formation of the country's park system.

Young, Allen. *Sarapiquí Chronicle: A Naturalist in Costa Rica.* Washington DC: Smithsonian Institution Press, 1991. An entomologist writes about his 21 years of fieldwork in Costa Rica's rain forests. Much of the text is devoted to his study of the butterfly *Morpho peleides.*

HISTORY, POLITICS, AND CULTURE

Biesanz, Mavis, Richard Biesanz, and Karen Biesanz. *The Ticos: Culture and Social Change in Costa Rica.* Boulder, Colorado: Lynne Rienner Publishers, 1999. An excellent book for those who want to understand Costa Rica and its people. The authors take on everything from history to marital relations and gender roles.

Boyle, Frederick. *A Ride Across a Continent: A Personal Narrative of Wanderings through Nicaragua and Costa Rica.* Ulan Press, 1999. A fascinating travelogue, first published in 1923 and now back in print. You can often get a digital copy for free (try http://books.google.com).

Coates, Anthony G., ed. *Central America: A Natural and Cultural History.* New Haven, Connecticut: Yale University Press, 1999. Chapters by different authors, most authorities in their fields, take on geological origins, differences between the surrounding oceans, the importance of natural corridors, the history of native people and colonizers from pre-Columbian to modern times, and current conservation issues.

Edelman, Marc, and Joanne Kenen, eds. *The Costa Rican Reader.* New York: Grove Weidenfeld, 1989. A collection of articles by diverse authors, covering many aspects of Costa Rican history and politics. Includes the text of President Óscar Arias Sánchez's 1987 peace plan, for which he won the Nobel Peace Prize.

Helmuth, Charlene. *Culture and Customs of Costa Rica.* Westport, Connecticut: Greenwood Press, 2000. A useful and very readable introduction to Tican culture, including chapters on visual arts, performing arts, and literature.

Honey, Martha. *Hostile Acts: U.S. Policy in Costa Rica in the 1980s.* Gainesville, Florida: University of Florida Press, 1994. Account of U.S. influence in the isthmus during the tumultuous 1980s. The author lived in Costa Rica from 1983 to 1991 and brings an insider's view to the subject. Arguing that Costa Rica should be the best example of the type of country the U.S. government says it is trying to foster, Honey shows how U.S. actions actually undermined the country until Costa Rican President Arias stood up to U.S. pressure, providing a regional solution with his Central American Peace Plan.

Lefever, Harry G. *Turtle Bogue: Afro-Caribbean Life in a Costa Rican Village.* Selinsgrove, Pennsylvania: Susquehanna University Press, 1992. A professor records the folk history of the Caribbean coast town of Tortuguero.

Molina, Iván, and Steven Palmer. *The History of Costa Rica.* San José, Costa Rica: Editorial de la Universidad de

Costa Rica, 2002. A short and readable introduction to the country's history.

Paige, Jeffery M. *Coffee and Power: Revolution and the Rise of Democracy in Central America.* Cambridge, Massachusetts: Harvard University Press, 1998. Central American politics and development, as seen through the lens of the all-important coffee business.

Palmer, Paula. *What Happen: A Folk-History of Costa Rica's Talamanca Coast.* San José, Costa Rica: Publications in English S.A., 1993. The author, a North American sociologist, has collected fascinating oral histories from the Afro-Caribbean people who settled the towns of Cahuita, Puerto Viejo, and Manzanillo on Costa Rica's Caribbean coast. Out of print, but not impossible to find.

Palmer, Paula, Juanita Sánchez, and Gloria Mayorga. *Taking Care of Sibö's Gifts.* San José, Costa Rica: Editorama S.A., 1993. One of the few books on indigenous Costa Rican culture by indigenous authors.

FICTION AND MEMOIR

Borner, Tessa. *Potholes to Paradise: Living in Costa Rica—What You Need to Know.* Hillary Borner, Publisher, 2001. The author moved from Toronto to Costa Rica in 1994, and with her husband, built and operated Posada Mimosa B&B. The book, which the *Tico Times* called "part diary, part travelogue, and part advice column," describes the Borners' experiences with builders, lawyers, and real estate agents, along with a visit to and the private Hospital Clínica Bíblica, where her husband received triple bypass surgery in 1993. She also describes trying to get reimbursement from Canada's socialized medicine program for treatment received in Costa Rica.

León Sánchez, José. *God Was Looking the Other Way: Thirty Years on the Devil's Island of Latin America.* Boston: Little, Brown and Company, 1973. The English version of this book is unfortunately out of print but can be found if you look hard. It's worth it for this gripping account of a man condemned to life imprisonment on San Lucas Island, off the coast of Costa Rica and until 1989 a notorious penitentiary. The book is a fictionalized account of the author's time as an inmate there.

Ras, Barbara, ed. *Costa Rica: A Traveler's Literary Companion.* Berkeley, California: Whereabouts Press, 1994. Short stories and novel excerpts by Costa Rican authors, organized by geographical zone.

Theroux, Paul. *The Old Patagonian Express.* Boston: Houghton Mifflin, 1979. In this book about riding the rails from Massachusetts to the tip of South America, only two chapters are set in Costa Rica. But what a pleasure to hear about the now-defunct train from San José to Limón and the still-functioning line from San José to Puntarenas, from the best curmudgeonly travel writer alive today. Don't expect travel-brochure bromides: Theroux elevates crankiness to an art.

Weisbecker, Allan C. *In Search of Captain Zero: A Surfer's Road Trip Beyond the End of the Road.* Los Angeles: JP Tarcher, 2002. Chronicles the author's trip through Mexico and Central America in search of good waves and an old friend who has disappeared. The "end of the road" turns out to be on the Caribbean coast of Costa Rica, and there are some nice descriptions of the famed Salsa Brava, a wave near Puerto Viejo that draws highly skilled and adventurous surfers.

CHILDREN'S BOOKS

Baden, Robert. *And Sunday Makes Seven.* Morton Grove, Illinois: Albert Whitman & Co., 1990. Folk tales for kids ages 4-8.

Forsyth, Adrian. *Journey Through a Tropical Jungle.* Englewood Cliffs, New Jersey: Silver Burdett Press, 1996. A lighthearted romp through a Costa Rican forest.

Henderson, Aileen. *The Monkey Thief.* Minneapolis: Milkweed Editions, 1998. A 12-year-old boy visits his uncle in Costa Rica and learns about monkeys, smugglers, and the rainforest.

Norman, David. *Costa Rica Wildlife* and other titles. World Wildlife Fund (WWF) coloring books with descriptions of the plants and animals pictured.

Van Rheenen, Erin, and Maggie Olson. *The Manatee's Big Day: A Costa Rica Animal Adventure.* San José, Costa Rica: Zona Tropical Publications, 2013. A lavishly illustration tale of a manatee and her pals in Costa Rica's wildlife-rich Tortuguero canals.

DRIVING TO COSTA RICA

Pritchard, Raymond, and Audrey Pritchard. *Driving the Pan-American Highway,* 6th edition. San José, Costa Rica: Costa Rica Books, 1997. An old classic that needs updating, but it offers tips on border crossing and sightseeing.

Wessler, Dawna Rae. *You Can Drive to Costa Rica in 8 Days.* Harmony Gardens Publishing, 1998. Tales and advice from two non-Spanish-speaking surfer gringos who made the trip in their 22-year-old VW van. Out of print but the dedicated will probably be able to locate a copy of this spiral-bound effort.

MISCELLANEOUS

Hasbrouck, Edward. *The Practical Nomad.* Emeryville, California: Avalon Travel Publishing, 2011. A cult classic and deservedly so, this book helps you think about the world and how to best move through it. Great practical information (on airfares, for example) and even better philosophy (just what do we mean when we talk about First, Second, and Third Worlds?).

Kohls, L. Robert. *Survival Kit for Overseas Living,* 4th ed. Yarmouth, Maine: Nicholas Brealey/Intercultural Press, 2001. Offering up a fascinating look at culture shock and cultural bias, this book helps readers take inventory of their own cultural "baggage" before venturing abroad. Short on practical details about individual countries but long on strategies for developing intercultural communication skills, no matter where you plan to go.

Petersen, Roger A. *The Legal Guide to Costa Rica.* San José, Costa Rica: Amerilatin Consultares, 2009. Covers everything from property rights to extradition. You can order a copy at www.costaricalaw.com; the author also has a great deal of useful information available online.

Suggested Films

The First Lady of the Revolution (2016) is the fascinating tale of Henrietta Boggs, a debutant from Birmingham, Alabama, who came to Costa Rica in 1941, at the age of 21. Boggs met and married Jose "Pepe" Figueres, who would lead a revolution and then take power in 1948, ushering in the country's Second Republic, a democratic state with no army. Boggs had a rare insider's view during a crucial point in Costa Rica's history. She relates, for example, that Figueres' decision to abolish guns and the army was not just idealistic; he also didn't want anyone having the means of overthrowing him.

Agua Fria de Mar (*Cold Water of the Sea,* 2010), directed by Costa Rican Paz Fábrega, focuses on a young Costa Rican couple vacationing on the Pacific coast who have a strange encounter with a young girl claiming to be an orphan.

The Blue Butterfly (2004), directed by Lea Pool, stars John Hurt as an entomologist who leads a wheelchair-bound boy dying of cancer into the rainforests of Costa Rica to find a blue morpho butterfly. Their search is an arduous one; I guess they didn't know that blue morphos can be seen all over the place, including in the Butterfly Garden in downtown San José's National Museum. Filmed in Limón and Puerto Viejo.

El Camino (*The Path,* 2008), from filmmaker Ishtar Yasin Gutierrez, is a blend of gritty drama and fairy-tale quest. It's the story of two Nicaraguan children making their way on foot, by bus, and by boat to the border with Costa Rica.

Gutierrez has another film in the works, focused on Frida Kahlo and the Costa Rican nurse that was with her day and night in Frida's later years. Called *The Two Fridhas,* the film is due out in 2017.

Caribe (2004), directed by Esteban Ramírez, was the first Costa Rican film to be submitted to the Academy Awards; competing against more than 50 other movies from around the world, it was not nominated. The story is of a love triangle, with a subplot about a beach town trying to stop an oil company from despoiling its shore. Filmed in and around Puerto Viejo in reportedly only five weeks, *Caribe* gives you a nice long glimpse of the less-visited Caribbean coast of Costa Rica and an introduction to some of the environmental issues there.

Carnival in Costa Rica (1947), directed by Gregory Ratoff and filmed in Costa Rica, stars pencil-mustachioed Cesar Romero in a tale of star-crossed lovers trying to thwart an arranged marriage. An actress known as Vera-Ellen plays the young female love interest; she was a former Rockette, but her take on Latin dance seems to be that flouncing and throwing ones head from side to side is all that's required.

Costa Rica: Paradise Reclaimed (1988) is an inspiring BBC-PBS documentary about U.S. scientist Dan Janzen's struggle to found a national park in Guanacaste and to create a new model of conservation, one that seeks to not only protect what remains but also reverse the devastation that has been wrought on the land. You can probably get the documentary from your public library or watch it online.

Gestación (2010), directed by Esteban Ramírez, tells the tale of a teenage Costa Rican girl struggling with an unwanted pregnancy.

El Regreso (*The Return,* 2011), directed by and starring Costa Rican filmmaker Hernán Jiménez, is an appealingly honest and moving film about a young man who returns to his native Costa Rica after living in New York.

Rosita (2005), a documentary by Barbara Attie and Janet Goldwater, looks at a case in which a nine-year-old Nicaraguan girl became pregnant as the result of a rape. Her parents—illiterate Nicaraguan campesinos working in Costa Rica—seek a legal abortion for their child, which pits them against the governments of Nicaragua and Costa Rica, the medical establishment, and the Catholic Church.

SURFING FILMS

Given Costa Rica's reputation for great surf on both coasts, it's no surprise that many surf films are filmed at least in part in Costa Rica. These include *Step into Liquid* (2003), filmed in part in Mal País; *Costa Rica: Land of Waves* (2001); *Endless Summer 2* (1994); *Endless Summer Revisited* (2000); and *Zen and Zero* (2006), directed by Michael Ginthor, a documentary in which writer, surfer, and former Pavones resident Alan Weisbecker plays himself.

MOVIES FILMED IN COSTA RICA

Many other movies not necessarily about Costa Rica are filmed here, at least in part. Often the country stands in for Peru or Mexico. The bear in *Paddington* (2014) is supposed to be from Peru, but the film's opening rainforest scenes were shot in Costa Rica. *The Celestine Prophecy* (2006), about a search for a sacred manuscript in the Peruvian rainforest, was actually filmed in Costa Rica, Puerto Rico, and Florida. Some of Mel Gibson's *Apocalypto* (2006) was filmed here, and Tico actor Mauricio Amuy plays a Mayan chief in the film. Will Smith and son Jaden were in Costa Rica to shoot right in front of the Arenal Volcano for *After Earth* (2013). In 2005 Costa Rica was the filming location for *Death to the Supermodels* ("they're drop-dead gorgeous" is the movie's tagline), directed by Joel Silverman. Silverman's *Surf School* was also filmed here.

The first *Jurassic Park* (1993) snagged some jungle scenes from Costa Rica, and Costa Rica stood in for Africa in Frank Marshall's 1995 film *Congo*. *Spy Kids 2: The Island of Lost Dreams* (2002) was filmed here, as was *1492: Conquest of Paradise* (1992), directed by Ridley Scott and with Gérard Depardieu as Christopher Columbus. And who can forget *Tropix* (2002), directed by Percy Angress and filmed in Guápiles, Playa Escondido, Parque Este, and San José. The film's tagline: "Come to Costa Rica. See endangered species. Become one. More than Paradise . . . will be LOST!"

Index

INDEX

List of Maps

Photo Credits

Title page photo: © Erin Van Rheenen

Page 4 © Barry Hovland; page 5 © Erin Van Rheenen; page 6 © Erin Van Rheenen; page 7 (top left) © Buffie Biddle, (top right) © David Webster Smith, (bottom left) © Erin Van Rheenen, (bottom right) © Erin Van Rheenen; page 8 (top left) © Desafio Adventure Company, (top right) © Erin Van Rheenen, (bottom) © David Webster Smith; page 9 © Erin Van Rheenen; page 10 © David Webster Smith; page 16 © Erin Van Rheenen; page 18 © Erin Van Rheenen; page 20 © Marco Díaz | Dreamstime.com; page 21 © Andres Madrigal | Costa Rica Traveler; page 23 © David Webster Smith; page 24 © Erin Van Rheenen; page 26 © Dmitry Chulov | Dreamstime.com; page 28 © David Webster Smith; page 30 © Erin Van Rheenen; page 38 © Erin Van Rheenen; page 44 © Erin Van Rheenen; page 45 © Andres Madrigal | Costa Rica Traveler; page 46 © Erin Van Rheenen; page 54 © Erin Van Rheenen; page 59 © David Webster Smith; page 61 © Erin Van Rheenen; page 63 © Erin Van Rheenen; page 67 –81 © Erin Van Rheenen; page 83 © David Webster Smith; page 87–95 © Erin Van Rheenen; page 97 © Erin Van Rheenen; page 98–110 © Erin Van Rheenen; page 111 © Erin Van Rheenen; page 113 © Erin Van Rheenen; page 118 © courtesy of Sandra Shaw Homer; page 122 © Erin Van Rheenen; page 124 © David Webster Smith; page 126–134 © Erin Van Rheenen; page 135 © David Webster Smith; page 139 © Erin Van Rheenen; page 144 © Erin Van Rheenen; page 145 © Erin Van Rheenen; page 146 © David Webster Smith; page 156 © Ian Woolcock | Dreamstime. com; page 161 © Erin Van Rheenen; page 163 © David Webster Smith; page 167– 173 © Erin Van Rheenen; page 180– 194 © Erin Van Rheenen; page 196 © Buffie Biddle; page 199– 206 © Erin Van Rheenen; page 212 © Erin Van Rheenen; page 214 © Erin Van Rheenen; page 216 © David Webster Smith; page 217–221 © Erin Van Rheenen; page 225 © Erin Van Rheenen; page 228 © Erin Van Rheenen; page 229 © David Webster Smith; page 231 © Erin Van Rheenen; page 232 © David Webster Smith; page 239 © Erin Van Rheenen; page 241 © Erin Van Rheenen; page 245 © Erin Van Rheenen; page 246 © Erin Van Rheenen; page 248 © David Webster Smith; page 251 © Erin Van Rheenen; page 253 © Erin Van Rheenen; page 255 © Erin Van Rheenen; page 259– 270 © Erin Van Rheenen; page 273 © Marco Díaz | Dreamstime.com; page 274 © Erin Van Rheenen; page 279 © David Webster Smith; page 281 © Andres Madrigal | Costa Rica Traveler; page 283 © Erin Van Rheenen; page 288– 290 © Erin Van Rheenen; page 292 © David Webster Smith; page 293 © Erin Van Rheenen; page 297 © David Webster Smith; page 299 © Erin Van Rheenen; page 304 © Erin Van Rheenen; page 307 © Vdevolder | Dreamstime.com; page 310 © David Webster Smith; page 312 © Erin Van Rheenen; page 315 © Erin Van Rheenen; page 318 © Erin Van Rheenen; page 319 © David Webster Smith; page 322 © Erin Van Rheenen; page 323 © Erin Van Rheenen; page 325 © Emily Starbuck Crone | Dreamstime.com; page 329 © Erin Van Rheenen.

Acknowledgments

Since I first began researching this guide in 1999, I've been privileged to meet some amazing people, both Costa Ricans and expats, who've told me their stories and shared their expertise. You've all helped deepen my understanding of this wonderful place. *Un abrazote, y mil gracias* (A big hug, and a thousand thanks).

Thanks also to the crew at Avalon Travel, especially editor Kimberly Ehart, graphics coordinator Sarah Wildfang, copy editor Ruth Strother, and map editor Kat Bennett.

A special thanks to photographers David Webster Smith, Andres Madrigal, and Barry Hovland for generously contributing their work to this edition.

Also Available

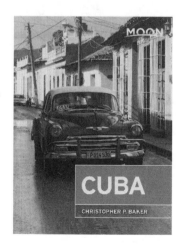

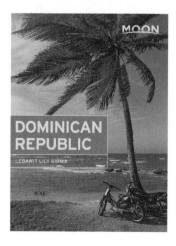

MAP SYMBOLS

▭▭▭	Expressway	★	Highlight	✗	Airfield	⚲	Golf Course
▭▭▭	Primary Road	○	City/Town	✈	Airport	🅿	Parking Area
▭▭▭	Secondary Road	◉	State Capital	▲	Mountain	🔺	Archaeological Site
- - - -	Unpaved Road	⊛	National Capital	✛	Unique Natural Feature	⛪	Church
- - - - -	Trail	★	Point of Interest			⛽	Gas Station
··········	Ferry	•	Accommodation	❧	Waterfall		Glacier
-·-·-·-	Railroad	▼	Restaurant/Bar	▲	Park		Mangrove
▓▓▓	Pedestrian Walkway	▪	Other Location	⊟	Trailhead		Reef
▥▥▥	Stairs	⋀	Campground	⛷	Skiing Area		Swamp

CONVERSION TABLES

$°C = (°F - 32) / 1.8$
$°F = (°C \times 1.8) + 32$
1 inch = 2.54 centimeters (cm)
1 foot = 0.304 meters (m)
1 yard = 0.914 meters
1 mile = 1.6093 kilometers (km)
1 km = 0.6214 miles
1 fathom = 1.8288 m
1 chain = 20.1168 m
1 furlong = 201.168 m
1 acre = 0.4047 hectares
1 sq km = 100 hectares
1 sq mile = 2.59 square km
1 ounce = 28.35 grams
1 pound = 0.4536 kilograms
1 short ton = 0.90718 metric ton
1 short ton = 2,000 pounds
1 long ton = 1.016 metric tons
1 long ton = 2,240 pounds
1 metric ton = 1,000 kilograms
1 quart = 0.94635 liters
1 US gallon = 3.7854 liters
1 Imperial gallon = 4.5459 liters
1 nautical mile = 1.852 km

°FAHRENHEIT / °CELSIUS thermometer — WATER BOILS at 100°C / 212°F; WATER FREEZES at 0°C / 32°F.

24-hour clock face.

INCH ruler 0–4; CM ruler 0–10.

MOON LIVING ABROAD COSTA RICA

Avalon Travel
Hachette Book Group
1700 Fourth Street
Berkeley, CA 94710, USA
www.moon.com

Editor: Kimberly Ehart
Copy Editor: Ruth Strother
Graphics Coordinator: Sarah Wildfang
Production Designer: Sarah Wildfang
Cover Design: Faceout Studios, Charles
Moon Logo: Tim McGrath
Map Editor: Kat Bennett
Cartographer: Kat Bennett
Indexer: Greg Jewett

ISBN-13: 978-1-63121-651-0

Printing History
1st Edition – 2004
5th Edition – September 2017
5 4 3 2 1

Text © 2017 by Erin Van Rheenen.
Maps © 2017 by Avalon Travel.
Some photos and illustrations are used by permission and are the property of the original copyright owners.

Front cover photo: © Robert Harding | Masterfile
Back cover photo: © Pedro Campos | Dreamstime.com

Printed in Canada by Friesens

Avalon Travel is a division of Hachette Book Group, Inc. Moon and the Moon logo are trademarks of Hachette Book Group, Inc. All other marks and logos depicted are the property of the original owners.